Of Meaning And Means

What is the meaning of Vedanta? How does it apply to what we of the West have learned since childhood? By what means can we experience the broadening of understanding and ultimate enlightenment that Vedanta offers?

These are among the questions discussed in sixty-one essays that examine Vedanta from virtually every conceivable angle of vision. The result is perhaps the finest, most comprehensive picture of Vedanta and the most eloquent exposition of its methods ever presented to the Western reader.

"It is a meeting of East and West by way of the minds of intellectuals and mystics from both ends of the world, and this meeting, being honestly and sensibly conducted, is a gathering profitable for any who attend it."

—Thomas Sugrue

Other MENTOR Titles of Related Interest

Vedanta
for Modern Man

Edited and with an Introduction by

Christopher Isherwood

A MENTOR BOOK from
NEW AMERICAN LIBRARY
TIMES MIRROR
New York and Scarborough, Ontario

Published by arrangement with the Vedanta Society of
Southern California.

Those who wish to learn in greater detail about the teachings
contained in this book are advised to communicate with the
Secretary, Vedanta Society of Southern California,
1946 Vedanta Place, Hollywood, California 90068.

MENTOR TRADEMARK REG. U.S. PAT. OFF. AND FOREIGN COUNTRIES
REGISTERED TRADEMARK—MARCA REGISTRADA
HECHO EN CHICAGO, U.S.A.

SIGNET, SIGNET CLASSICS, SIGNETTE, MENTOR AND PLUME BOOKS
are published *in the United States* by
The New American Library, Inc.,
1301 Avenue of the Americas, New York, New York 10019,
in Canada by The New American Library of Canada Limited,
81 Mack Avenue, Scarborough, 704, Ontario

FIRST PRINTING, NOVEMBER, 1972

PRINTED IN THE UNITED STATES OF AMERICA

Contents

Introduction

It is unlikely that many people will read this book straight through, from the first page to the last. Nor is there any particular reason why one should do so. It is not a textbook. Its contents may even sometimes appear to express divergent opinions—though, in fact, they are complementary—and their order of arrangement is designed rather to present small independent groups of essays than to form a single progression of ideas. It resembles a wheel, in that you can touch its circumference at any point you choose and find a direct line leading to the axis, Vedanta philosophy, around which it revolves.

However, I recommend the reader to begin with the first three essays. For they raise a fundamentally important question: "Has Vedanta philosophy a specific contribution to make to the religious thinking of the West?" Or, to put it in another way: "Is there already something that we can describe as Occidental, in contradistinction to Oriental, Vedanta?"

Vedanta (so called because it was first expounded in the Vedas, the earliest Indian scriptures) is a nondualistic philosophy. It teaches that Brahman (the ultimate Reality behind the phenomenal universe) is "one without a second." Brahman is beyond all attributes. Brahman is not conscious; Brahman *is* consciousness. Brahman does not exist; Brahman *is* existence. Brahman is the Atman (the Eternal Nature) of every human being, creature, and object. Vedanta teaches us that Life has no other purpose than this—that we shall learn to know ourselves for what we really are; that we shall reject the superficial ego-personality which claims that "I am Mr. Smith; I am other than Mr. Brown," and know, instead, that "I am the Atman; Mr. Brown is the Atman; the Atman is Brahman; there is nothing anywhere but Brahman; all else is appearance, transience, and unreality."

Nevertheless—since philosophy was made for man, and not vice versa—the exponents of Vedanta have had to recognize that a strict and arduous discipline of intellectual

9

discrimination between Brahman and non-Brahman, Real
and unreal, is not for the average run of humanity. The
unillumined mind is by nature incapable of imagining
Brahman; for it deals in pictures and words, and Brahman eludes all description. Therefore we turn naturally
toward the highest that we can imagine—the God with
attributes which are projections of our own virtues, or the
Godlike Man who has actually lived amongst us upon
earth and can strengthen and purify us by his example.
These we worship and toward these we aspire, hoping,
through our devotion, to become like them. Thus, cults
are born.

Vedanta philosophy does not in any way condemn the
cult. It only reminds the cultist that the cult is not an end
in itself. The God or Godlike Man whom we worship
must not be allowed to come between us and the knowledge that worshiped and worshiper are, essentially, both
projections of the one Brahman. What we adore in a
Christ, a Buddha, in Kali or Jehovah or Kwan-yin, is
our own Atman, our eternal Nature. In these divine personalities, that Nature is revealed; in ourselves it is more
or less obscured. Nevertheless they exist in order that we
may know ourselves. And, in the ultimate light of union
with Brahman, they are merged and vanish.

In India, therefore, Vedanta has endured through the
ages as a nondualistic philosophical structure sustaining
and interrelating many cults of Gods and Divine Incarnations. Misunderstanding of this fact has led some Western
critics to assume that India is polytheistic. She is not. What
is mistaken for polytheism is the recognition that "the
Truth is one, but sages call it by various names," and
that different partial aspects of Truth will appeal to various kinds of religious temperament. The alternative to this
so-called "polytheism" is the cruel and ugly sectarianism
which claims a monopoly of truth for its own particular
cult and is usually ready to persecute in order to enforce
that monopoly. Such monopolistic cultism is emphatically
rejected by Vedanta.

When Swami Vivekananda first visited the United States
(see "About the Ramakrishna Order," page 439) he did
not come as the missionary of a Ramakrishna cult but as
an exponent of Vedanta philosophy. In the majority of
his lectures, he referred to Ramakrishna very seldom or
not at all. Later, back in India, when he talked about this
period, he was accustomed to say: "If I had preached

the personality of Sri Ramakrishna, I might have converted half the world; but that kind of conversion is short-
lived. So instead I preached Ramakrishna's principles. If
people accept the principles they will eventually accept the
personality."

In its work in the Western Hemisphere and in Europe,
the Ramakrishna Order has followed Vivekananda's wise
and farsighted policy. The swamis of the Order, in their
public lectures, stress the Vedantic principles of Ramakrishna rather than his personality; Ramakrishna is presented always as an exemplar (and not the *only* exemplar) of Vedanta; and much is said about the relation of
Vedanta to the teachings of Christ and the Christian
saints.

Naturally, each Vedanta center maintains a cult of Ramakrishna for those who wish to join in worshiping him.
But this is a matter of individual choice, and no student
of Vedanta need necessarily take part in this cult, much
less discard his loyalty to any other divine personality.
Indeed, the Vedantist must do homage to all the divine
personalities, since all are expressions of the one truth of
Brahman.

In the West, the cult of Ramakrishna is still in its infancy, and therefore still surrounded by the external symbols of Hindu religion. There will always be those who are
temperamentally drawn to these externals, who prefer
Sanskrit to English chants, who like to wear saris and perform pujas according to the ancient Indian rituals. Nor is
there anything undesirable in this; the rituals of Hinduism
are very beautiful, and they help one to imagine Ramakrishna within his own cultural setting, to picture him
amidst the actual circumstances of his life on earth.
Nevertheless, such practices are not for everybody; and
Ramakrishna certainly never intended that all his Western
followers should be turned into synthetic Hindus. Just as
Jesus, through the ages, has lost much of his specifically
Jewish character, so the figure of Ramakrishna will gradually become less and less specifically Indian. It cannot and
should not be otherwise.

The cult of Ramakrishna may well grow to world-wide
proportions, but it will never, unless his teaching is utterly
betrayed, become an exclusive cult. Such a cult would be
Ramakrishna without Vedanta; a denial of its founder.
For Ramakrishna's gift to the West is the Vedanta
philosophy which he restated and practically demon-

strated in his own life. And it is Vedanta, rather than the special cult of Ramakrishna, which promises to exert a growing influence upon our Western thought in the immediate future.

At this point it is perhaps advisable to remark that a knowledge of Vedanta did not, of course, enter the Western world for the first time in 1893, with Swami Vivekananda. Schopenhauer, Emerson, Thoreau, and their circle; Max Müller and his fellow orientalists—to name only a few of the Swami's many forerunners—had all studied, discussed, and publicized the philosophy long before that date. What Vivekananda *did* bring to the West was the living example of a man wholly dedicated to the practice of Vedanta—an example infinitely more inspiring and convincing than any book, as Emerson himself would have been the first to admit.

Again, it must be understood that the Ramakrishna Order has never claimed to be the sole authentic source of Vedantic teaching in the West. Such a claim would be absurd. Obviously, there must be many reliable individual teachers to be found in different parts of the Americas and Europe. Such teachers, when met, may be tested very simply. One need only ask them: "What is the aim of your teaching?" If the answer is: "To show you how to know your real Nature; how to become united with Brahman," then the teacher is a true Vedantist. If the answer is: "To show you how to obtain power over others, how to become rich, how to become strong and beautiful and healthy, how to prolong your life, how to read the future, how to summon spirits to do your will," then he is not. This statement may sound ridiculously self-evident, but it is worth making at the present time, when spiritualism, astrology, clairvoyance, mental healing, and the study of occult symbolism preoccupy hundreds of thousands of people. Such studies are often founded upon ancient Hindu lore—the practice of astrology, for example, is still very popular in India—and they tend to be surrounded by an atmosphere of "oriental mystery." But they have nothing whatever to do with the aims of Vedanta.

And now—to return to our main topic—in what manner is the influence of Vedanta most likely to make itself felt?

As far as organized Christianity is concerned, Vedanta would seem to have very little chance of a hearing. The cult of Christ, as preached by the Catholic and Protestant churches, is an exclusive cult. It cannot admit the Vedantist's acceptance of other Divine Incarnations; and it must find his homage to Christ inadequate, since this is not an exclusive homage. And there are other, even more serious grounds for disagreement. For Vedanta also teaches the practice of mysticism; that is to say, it claims that man may directly know and be united with his eternal Nature, the Atman, through meditation and spiritual discipline, without the aid of any church or delegated minister. Organized Christianity has long since condemned this idea as Gnosticism, and has been inclined to question the insights of the mystic, even when he or she has remained an obedient member of the congregation. It cannot be denied that Vedanta does challenge the Church's claim to central importance as the Body of Christ upon earth. It does exalt the validity of the mystic's direct experience far above the authority of creeds, dogmas, and scriptures. And its attitude to the problem of sin is, from the orthodox Christian standpoint, both incorrect and subversive. The reader will find these questions discussed, with great understanding and fairness, in Swami Siddheswarananda's "A Hindu View of Christian Theology."

I can see only one little door through which Vedanta might squeeze into Christendom, and that is the Society of Friends. The Quaker doctrine of the Inward Light is in general agreement with the principles of Vedanta. For the rest, there will be many broad-minded individuals within the churches who will find the study of Vedanta helpful and who will manage to reconcile at least some part of its teaching with their own traditional beliefs. More than this one can hardly hope for, failing a revolutionary reversal of policy by Christian religious leaders.

When, however, we consider the sciences, the prospects of Vedanta are much more encouraging. It is now generally, if rather vaguely, admitted that the trend of scientific thinking is away from materialistic atheism and toward a hypothesis which does not exclude the concept of a transcendent consciousness. If this is granted, we may claim with some assurance that Vedanta philosophy is superior to Christian theology as a potential bridge between science and religion. It is a striking fact—already remarked on by several outstanding scientists—that the world-picture presented by Vedanta is largely in accord with the latest theories of astronomy and atomic physics. (It is not necessary that I should elaborate on this point here. The reader will find references to the Vedanta cosmology in several of our essays, notably one by Swami Gnaneswarananda, and a more formal exposition in an appendix to the translation of the *Bhagavad-Gita* by Swami Prabhavananda and me.) Vedantic influences are also becoming apparent in the field of psychology—as, for instance, in the recent work of Jung. Dr. Hubert Benoit, representing a later generation of psychiatrists, contributes a fascinating essay to this volume. Swami Akhilananda's *Hindu Psychology: Its Meaning for the West* (Routledge & Kegan Paul) deals with the whole subject in detail.

I believe, then, that Vedanta is most likely to influence the West through the medium of scientific thought. In this terrible epoch, when our power to do harm seems at length adequate to the evil of our intentions, we are accustomed to blame science for putting the weapons into our hands. Yet science, like the Hindu goddess Kali, is above good and evil; impartially, she gives us whatever we ask for, and her gifts may prove to be curses or blessings. At our bidding, the men of science have discovered the secret of atomic energy. Can they also discover, before it is too late, a moral sanction which will curb the power of the atom and direct it to peaceful and productive uses? Can science find us a new philosophical synthesis, a restatement of the eternal truths in terms which our modern agnosticism is able to accept?

That is a question which only the future can answer. Meanwhile, an unprecedented exchange of ideas is going on between East and West. We are giving the East our technology and our philosophy of dialectical materialism. What are we getting in return? If it is a greater understanding of what India and ancient China have to teach us, combined with a rediscovery of our own neglected spiritual potentialities—in fact, an Occidental Vedanta—then we certainly have the best of the bargain.

Because I edited our previous anthology, *Vedanta for the Western World*, Swami Prabhavananda wished me to have my name on the title page as editor of this book. Actually, most of the hard work was done by Swami Prabhavananda himself, by Sister Amiya, John Yale, and other members of the Vedanta Society of Southern California.

March 1951

C.I.

Vedanta for Modern Man

Vedanta and Western History

Gerald Heard

I

A NEW RELIGION has come into history—that is Western
Vedanta. For centuries, and perhaps millennia, Vedanta
influenced and molded the East, passing from the richness
of original Brahmanism to the austerity of Theravadin
Buddhism, through the counterrichness of Mahayana and
so again to the counterreformation of Shankara and the
Vedanta we know. But, save for some tentative influences
—such as the missionary effort of Asoka and the small
though steady trickle of Indian ideas through Alexandria
—Vedanta did not really strike the West. Christianity, had
it not been torn from its original rooting spots by Islam
and made to specialize in the Western legalistic form of
Catholicism, would no doubt have exchanged many ideas
with India. As it was, the Christian church did not remain
a live link and the Buddhist missionaries who entered the
Mediterranean world made no distinctive mark. True,
there is a church in Sicily dedicated to St. Barlaam—a
garbled form of Buddha's name made famous and saint-
worthy because of a garbled but very popular story of his
life and renunciation. The width and subtlety of Indian
thought, the range of its cosmology, the depth of its
psychology never, however, succeeded in enlarging that
narrow Hebrew scheme of things that has ever since
cramped and hobbled the religion of the West. That the
Eastern churches of the Levant would have made some
use of this treasury of knowledge there can be little doubt
when we see how many Indian ideas are present in Origen,
how clearly he holds reincarnation, and with what liberal-
ity he wished to draw upon the East for insights, for those

illuminations from "the Christians that were before Christ." The mistake of the Council of Chalcedon of the fourth century in condemning reincarnation was that it removed from Christianity a view of things which till then had been liberally entertained, and with which the cruel finality of everlasting punishment for the mistakes of this one life would not have disgraced the religion of love.

Indeed we may say that the appearance of Vedanta in the West as a living religion, and not as an academic study, is inevitable just because the religious heredity of the West has now outgrown the tight Hebrew pot of cosmology in which it had been growing for two millennia. A faith that taught hell for those who did not get themselves saved in this life was suited enough to put the fear of God into barbarians or into men too busy to do much more than make a dash with their last breath for a deathbed repentance. But for people really interested in the spiritual world, really desirous of growing in spirituality and filled with a real longing to know and love God, such doctrines were, far from being any help, a terrible obstacle. Catholicism has become increasingly dogmatic, Protestantism increasingly secular and humanist. Where were men to find a religion that was intense but not cruelly narrow, wide but not vague, loose but not tepid? Vedanta in the broad range that it is given by the Vedanta activity in America is the answer.

And the very breadth of Vedanta, combined with its force, is bound to embrace and develop much that is now lying latent in our Western thought and spirit. When Christianity went to India it became in form and in much of its spirit Indian. When the reformed Brahmanism that we call Buddhism went into China it took on many of the forms and manners of China—so much so that today when people imagine that warrior spirit Gautama, they think of a rather obese Mongolian dozing. So today when Vedanta comes to the West it will, now that it has been acclimated here, take on and make a distinctive Western Vedanta. What that will be we cannot say. Few historical studies are more interesting than to see what it is that the spirit of an area and province will pick as its peculiar accent and expression of a universal truth. For example, when Tantric Buddhism—a queer enough synthesis in all conscience—entered China by way of Tibet and the shakta-shakti symbol of union was shown to the Chinese, they made no protest as far as can be discovered to this rather startling picture of spirit and expression. They simply dropped that symbol, making gradually their own iconography. So no doubt gradually the West will pick those Asiatic forms and from them make ones of its own which best express for it by symbol that which all agree is in its essence inexpressible.

It is easier to speak of the perennial philosophy, the eternal gospel, the universal religion than actually to define them—or it. We can see that certain general principles run through the great religions that have affected mankind for many centuries. But when we come to consider what are the actual essentials and what are merely matters of time and place, topical and local, then the issue is far more difficult. Probably there is not a religion that is extant that does not in some way and degree meet the deep demands of its worshipers, for relief from the false self, for some vision of a vast meaning in which all may find both loss of their separation and fulfillment of their deepest nature. But certainly religions just as much as individual persons grow old and in their decrepitude they may like ourselves produce ugly features and show evidence of disease. The Congress of World Religions when being summoned in London in the thirties had many sessions of its main committee to decide on how this act of union could be best expressed. The secretary very rightfully wished all religions to be invited. There was, however, a long and inconclusive discussion when a member asked whether all religions would include such tribes as might still wish to practice human sacrifice or even temple prostitution. A great deal of thinking has to be done on Ramakrishna's ecumenical statement that all roads lead to God. It is possible to think of all religions as tending to enlightenment and liberation but only if some of the more decadent and crabbed are considered as those strange and tortuous paths whereby as Blake put it in his gnomic utterance, "Were the fool to continue in his folly he would become wise." You may get to Catalina by sailing straight southwest from Los Angeles. You can also go there via New York, Lisbon, Cairo, Ceylon, and Wake Island and hence come upon it from the seaward side. As the Sanskrit tradition holds that the gods themselves are mortal—only the imageless Brahman is unchanging—so it would seem it is with all religions; they may need to die and transmigrate and their essential nature take form again in another guise in another epoch.

There is, however, another consideration that today arises when we think of the perennial philosophy and especially of Vedanta as its most ancient expression. There may not be progress in history in the way that the nineteenth century thought of historical progress—a process whereby men became better just by going on "and," as Tennyson says, "the thoughts of men are widened with the circling of the suns." But undoubtedly there is an element of irreversibility in history—a process is working itself out. History does not repeat itself—only, as in music a theme given earlier may be repeated and developed further on in the composition. There can be no doubt that no age resembling ours has existed before and that in one respect we have an opportunity denied to earlier ages. Today the world is in touch with every part of itself as never before. We know that in spite of the exclusiveness of certain theologians, religions themselves are strongly inclined, as said above, to borrow from one another. Today there is no doubt we must look forward to, and should anticipate a new syncretism of, the religions of the world.

II

Dr. Heinrich Zimmer concludes his study *Myths and Symbols in Indian Art and Civilization* with a charming fable. He tells of a rabbi who dreamed a number of times that he must leave his own small house in the ghetto of Cracow and travel to Prague, for there on the bridge leading to the castle he would find a treasure. Finally the rabbi agreed to obey his dream. Arriving at Prague and going to the bridge he found it guarded. So he waited for a long while. At last the captain of the bridge, noticing the old man hanging about, spoke to him kindly, asking what he was waiting for. The rabbi, being good to the point of ingenuousness, told him. The captain however remained as friendly, indeed breaking into laughter and becoming confidential. "Why," he told the poor old pilgrim, "I myself had a dream of just the same nonsensical sort, but, as you might say, it was even more upside down! My dream told me to go to the house of an old rabbi in Cracow in the ghetto there—and behind his stove I would find a treasure! You see what nonsense dreams are! There's no treasure on this bridge I can assure you. And you and I know that the last place in the world to find a treasure—this bridge would be better—would be in the dwelling of a starving rabbi in the Cracow ghetto." The rabbi bowed and said nothing more—for he had forgotten to tell his friend where he had come from. He returned back straightway to his home. He dug behind the stove and found a buried bag of gold coins.

Dr. Zimmer used this illustration to point out how much India can help the West and that one of its main services is to send us back to our own branch of the great stream of the knowledge of God that has flowed down all the ages and through every land. True enough our own stream has for the last three hundred years been mainly underground but even then we may (as one may in New Mexico) trace where the water still runs, by the green tree that here and there breaks up and stands fresh among the dry stones of the old surface river bed.

Many people are still inclined to think that spirituality has never been native or natural to the West. That, however, is not true and could only be advanced by one who was not interested in history. Indeed we might say that till three or four centuries ago the West was as deeply interested in spirituality as the East. Sir William Flinders Petrie, the great Egyptologist, once remarked that the East seems asleep to the West because when the East is awake the West is asleep. Perhaps we may try and make the definition more exact and say that when the West is looking outward at the apparent world the East is looking inward.

Certainly, as Dr. Blakney, the latest editor of Eckhart, has pointed out, today the Far East—China—which he has lately been visiting—has become keenly contemptuous of the inner life, despises the Taoist mysticism, and seeks in improving the environment by mechanical means, the only happiness of man. Certainly today we of the West are wearying of our effort to create happiness outside ourselves; and our basic science, physics, is now tending to see the visible world as a projection of our minds or a selection made by them. Increasingly the philosophy of science is returning to epistemology—the study of how our minds apprehend what they take to be objective.

Nor need we think that we are being untrue to our past or taking to a metaphysic for which we have no gift or calling. The West till four centuries ago was not only as religious as the East but also as keenly interested not merely in the path of devotion but in that of spiritual knowledge. The history of the West in regard to pure spirituality is not only interesting but instructive. The great issue of worship of God with form or without form was worked out and disputed in the West and what is more, the spiritual have on the whole tended to be those who have worshiped God without form. The two sources of Western religion are the Hebrew and the Greek. Both of these religious traditions, when they rose to the point that they could become of use to a wide circle of their neighbors, had found it necessary to dispense with forms. To Plato and to Plotinus, to Hillel and to Philo, anthropomorphism was equally unhelpful. It was from this blend of Greek and Hebrew mysticism that there sprang up in Syria the teaching of the Dionysian school, that *via negativa* which by a series of denials, flakes off all incrustation of image and leaves the mind with an essential apprehension.

It is important to remember that though the Western world in the fifth and sixth centuries A.D. was sinking in cultural and mechanic skill, it was this very advanced spiritual teaching that took men's minds. The works of this strange "pseudepigraphist" first passed to Constantinople where they were approved by a church council and thence into France. There they came into the hands of the great Irish scholar, Scotus Erigena, one of the few men of the West who then could translate Greek—in which the works were written. Erigena was such a passionate advaitist that he is said to have been murdered by being stabbed to death with the pencils of his students—a martyr to monism! The violent iconoclastic controversy of the Eastern Church time and again gave the victory to those who would have no images of God and who felt that only in the worship of the imageless could Western man be satisfied. The pure contemplatives of Ireland seem to have followed the same path. Only in India can an intensity of contemplation equal to that of Ireland's be found for this fire of solitary contemplation burned longer in the extreme Western island than it did in the Egyptian desert. And throughout that tradition there is a passion for the formless, a drive toward the jnana contemplation which today we consider as specifically Eastern.

So too with the great Rhineland mystics, though they were probably revived in their interest in pure intellectual love of God by infiltrations from the East. In the monastic system, also, when the solitaries of Ireland (the culdees or lonely anchorites) began to be gathered into small groups, here too the worship of the formless, the jnana approach, is native and cultural to the far West. The first monasteries of western Europe owe nearly everything to these Irish "religious" and the evangelization of central Europe is due largely to their efforts. Columbanus, the great Keltic monk, lies buried at Bobbio in South Italy. It is against this pure and advanced form of religious life and thought that Benedict, the Italian, offers his more formal, organized, liturgical way. Pure mental prayer, contemplation, is to be secondary—and inessential—beside the reciting of the offices, the repetition of the psalter, the performance of the mass. Naturally this is the easier way, and may be a safer, and so it naturally won.

But when the reaction came and these forms were challenged, because they were worshiped formally and not with real devotion, and also because the reality which was claimed for them appeared to be superstitious—then the Church had nothing to oppose to the bleak critical puritanism. The mystic insight and practice, whereby the consciousness may be changed, had been neglected under the excuse of what was called liturgical piety—and the form, perfunctorily performed—an excuse for and not an aid to attention—appeared to be empty of content. Certain it is that all forms do wear out. We can watch in the well-documented and dated history of the West how first in the thirteenth century, motherhood is worshiped. As Henry Adams pointed out, throughout the whole of Chartres cathedral there is in window and in stone only praise of the divine motherhood: the divine man dying on the Tree is lacking. Then a century after, churches of St. Savior are founded everywhere; the sacred body becomes worshiped (Corpus Christi), The Five Wounds, and then the Sacred Heart. Then once more the Virgin begins to absorb devotion, is named as the sole channel of grace, and the cult of the sacred heart, once confined to her divine son, is now extended to her. And we must always remember that, as such shifts of the form of devotion take place, there is always danger—and this of course actually took place during the Protestant revolution—that with the form the spirit will be banished.

The West is little interested in true religion and pure spirituality today because the worship of God with form was challenged, and had exhausted, the attention of devotees. The old forms became empty; no new forms took their place and the worship of God without form had not been inculcated or the method of such worship taught. True enough, for a while Quakerism seemed as though it might be the jnana of the West or at least a devotion to the formless. But the lack of method and of expert knowledge of the mystical approach and an increasing concern with social service drew off the minds of this small communion and the early promise was not fulfilled.

Today, however, we are returning to our original interest in pure spirituality and it must be repeated that that interest (as shown by our pure research in science) tends to be toward jnana more than to devotion of the emotions. Those who wish for worship with forms and images can find it in the West in Roman Catholicism. But those who cannot obtain from the multiformity of Catholicism and its strong tendency to the anthropomorphism, the sense of the presence of the spaceless and timeless being are in need of a free but deep worship such as Vedanta can promise.

III

We have seen that Western man has been in the past as interested in religion as Eastern; that that interest, when keenest, was in the worship of God without form; as the intensity of this devotional interest waned, this formless worship was gradually pushed aside by worship with form; and this worship with form intended toward polytheism.

Further, these forms being rigidly identified with personages asserted in every detail to be specifically historical, when historical critical methods arose and history took on scientific methods of assessing evidence, the forms were regarded as untrue and dismissed. Finally came the vast revolution in Western thought caused by the revolution in the basic science of physics. By 1915 (as Sir Edmund Whittaker points out) classical mechanistic physics, which had been the foundation of materialism, was overturned. Western thought, seeking for a system whereby it might grasp more realistically the nature of the universe, found that it had to abandon mechanomorphism, the assumption that the cosmos is a vast machine. The universe was a nonmaterial power that functioned free of causality as David Hilbert had shown. Hence it was something much more resembling an alive organism. It will be obvious that such a notion certainly ends mechanomorphism. But it does not return us to anthropomorphism. The consequence of the thinking that has led to modern physics is to make a man find as the object of his worship (for worship means worth-ship and worth-ship is our total estimate or esteem of anyone) the timeless and spaceless immanent and transcendent Being.

The first thing then that religion today must provide is a cultus that permits people who have been thus convinced of the fact of deity, to worship Him in spirit and in truth. The future of world faith belongs to whatever religion will give hospitality and welcome to such believers. The religion which will welcome these, teaching them the ways of living (the moral rules) and the mental exercises —the religious methods whereby what is intellectually believed can affect conduct, character, and consciousness— such a religion must win. The future of religion throughout the world could belong to Vedanta if it will guarantee this "holy liberty." We must remember that, whereas a generation ago in the West religion (being still based on anthropomorphism, still supposed to be denied by physics) found its main support among the uninformed, its main challenge among the educated, today this is reversed. The revolution in science (from physics to psychology) has turned the most open-minded thinkers toward theism, while the uninformed and reactionary still cling to a discredited fundamentalist Marxist materialism.

So the new movement toward religion can be adequately met only if a highly spiritual method and worship is offered. We must, however, make a distinction here. There are three worship possibilities to be offered to three types of worshipers. Sometimes people speak as though the choice were either anthropomorphism, the worship of God with physical form, or the pure monistic contemplation of Him who is one without a second. There is, however, a middle term—God without form but with attributes— the Saguna Brahman of Vedanta. This is the outlook of most today who have come by natural theology back to religion. Their need, the terms in which they can conceive of ultimate reality, must then be respected, their mode of worship guaranteed and sanctioned.

On the other hand, it is as necessary to make clear to them and to all other inquirers or critics that those who come to religion through natural theology must learn and extend an equal tolerance to the other forms of worship. Those who come to religion today are many of them scientists—that is to say, men interested in immediate observation of nature. They are not historians. It is only quite lately that scientists have begun to study even the history of science. Most scientists have to learn the historical, the anthropological approach. So they have to learn to respect the method-processes of those who worship God with form. An abacus seems a childish computer to one who reckons in his head. It can be employed with great speed and accuracy by one accustomed to it. To the mathematician his symbols seem incomparably superior to words, yet great poetry can convey things that the neatest formula or equation will miss.

Granted then that the new movement, through natural theology to religion, needs an imageless (though not an attributeless) worship, and that this new movement must learn to sympathize with those whose minds (artistic rather than scientific) worship God with form, we come then to our final question. For those in the West who worship with form, what forms are significantly helpful to them? There are, we know, two basic forms—those of motherhood and of fatherhood. They have, we also know, alternated in the history of man. The primitive matriarchate culture held naturally to the worship of motherhood. When patriarchate culture succeeded, Godhead was conceived as male. With the rise of those cultures in which male and female are seen as complementary, those two aspects have been worshiped. A further extension was given by totemism. Recognition of kinship with all life and of deity as being within all creatures, appeared in the zoanthropomorphic figures (as the Egyptian jackal-headed Anubis). These latter have not lasted in the West and maybe are passing away for good. They do not help in the approach to religion through natural theology. Further, there are the "wrathful" or "power" forms of deity. These are shown by the destructive and by the procreative iconography.

As the European religion developed through the Middle Ages, in thinking of the male concept of deity, Western man abandoned all attempt to render in form the Fatherhood—save for such efforts as shown on the Sistine roof. Iconography concentrated instead on that of the divine young redeemer and his mother. She is a virgin and he an emaciated sacrifice. Hence sex symbolism and erotic devotion are replaced by pathos. This is probably due to chastity being found to be the safe and sane way to illumination, whereas orgiastic erethism was discovered to be extremely dangerous, and to pathos—compassion—being a more safe and more enduring emotion than passionate romantic love. Hence the West, learning the value —and indeed vital importance—of strict continence if complete consciousness (ecstasy) is to be won and held, abandoned not only the shakta-shakti iconography and symbolism, but also that which is its complement, the "wrathful" and destructive aspects of form-rendered deity. It is also worth noting that the completer and finisher of the universe in the Western Trinity is God the Holy Ghost, a hypostasis without form and whose attributes are peace, purity, and inspiration.

To summarize then: Two features seem to emerge from the contact of Vedanta with the twentieth-century West. First, most Westerners are looking for a religion that shall express and render to them an experience of the transcendent-immanent eternal life that physics has now deduced to be the nature of the universe. That Vedanta can give—all is Brahman: thyself art He. Second, those Westerners who, on their way to that experience, need help of forms, are helped by such as are purely compassionate and are specifically psychologically satisfying and which are not involved (as are those of dogmatic Christianity) with statements as to the historicity of the form-features which are found to be psychologically helpful.

Those who are helped by form should not impose their forms on those not so helped, while, conversely, those to whom form is an obstacle should not deny or feel contempt for such helps when used by those who are so assisted to grasp or contact the ultimate reality. The proof of the efficacy of a form or a formless method must in the end be found in the life it produces, in the freedom from greed, emulation, fear, and anxiety that is achieved.

Is Vedanta for the West?

Swami Prabhavananda

Q. I HAVE ONE mental reservation which you can, perhaps, clear up for me: can Westerners, with our quite
different tradition and racial memories, take over methods
and philosophies developed by an Oriental people? Isn't
it essential that we work out our own paths? Our emphasis on externals is no doubt greatly exaggerated, and I
am sure that it leads to conflicts and discontents; yet I
wonder whether we can repudiate this orientation toward
the external world without doing very great violence to
the personalities which belong to us. I am, of course,
speaking in terms of the great masses of the people, and
not in any sense doubting the possibility of individual
Westerners finding, in Vedanta, the path they wish to
follow. But these students are a self-selected group, with a
special affinity for the viewpoints you represent. Whatever
religion our people, en masse, have known about is governed by rigid rules, imposed from without; when individuals in America reject these rules they usually reject all
religion, along with them, throwing out the baby with the
bath water. Can a quite different ideal be held up before
them in a way that is dramatic and appealing enough to
win their emotional support? I do not know.

A. In answer to your question I shall simply state what
Vedanta teaches and stands for. As you come to understand what it is, you will see that Vedanta helps each
man to grow in his own way. Its fundamental principle is
"unity in variety." However, I shall come to that point
later.

One short remark which I wish to make before I go any
further is, that Kipling was talking nonsense when he
wrote the line "East is East and West is West, and never

28

the twain shall meet." I am an Oriental and I have lived
in the West for the past twenty years. I have found no
difference between man and man. Beneath the surface
differences which we find in dress and food and outward
expressions of manners and customs, man is man all the
world over. The same human nature is represented everywhere. All human emotions are felt and expressed in the
same way everywhere.

It is, however, true that India developed her culture
along a certain line which we call spiritual; and the West
evolved a nationalistic and humanistic culture. There is no
question of superiority or inferiority or even comparison
between them. Both are great and both have made mistakes. Now, I believe, the time has come when both must
meet together on the basis of give and take. We of the
Orient must learn from you and you of the West must
learn from us. When there is the exchange of ideas between the two and we each learn from the other, without,
of course, losing our *peculiarities,* there will be, I believe,
a perfect civilization—so far as perfection in a relative
world can be expected.

Now to come to my point! What is Vedanta?

1. It is impersonal. The claim is made that religion is
eternal; it does not owe its origin to any man or personality. There are discoverers, the seers, of the truth that is
eternal. In course of time, various seers and prophets have
been born and various sects have arisen in India. They
each have a certain prophet or seer to whom they owe
allegiance, just as the Christians owe allegiance to Christ.
The Vedanta, which claims to be the eternal religion,
stands as the background of all these various sects and
there is no antagonism between it and other religions in the
world.

2. Vedanta claims that man is divine. To quote the
words of Vivekananda: "Man is like an infinite spring,
coiled up in a small box, and that spring is trying to unfold itself." All struggles, individual or social, are the result of this attempt to unfold. When the struggle becomes
a conscious effort, it is spiritual. As long as the ideal of
life and of life's struggles remains unknown we waste our
effort and go round in a circle; and howsoever we may
attempt to find happiness or freedom in our individual
lives, or to bring the millennium on earth, the result is
failure and disappointment. Through our failures and dis-

appointments, however, we at last wake up to our spiritual heritage.

The West accepts action and achievement in the outer world as the objective of her struggles. Religions (Vedanta, as well as Christian) teach perfection in the full consciousness of God as the goal. Modern Christianity accepts God *as a means* to achieve the physical millennium through actions and emphasis on externals. Vedanta tries to teach the West to go back to the original teachings of Christ and points out that you must never forget that the true happiness and freedom can only be found in the contemplation of God and reaching perfection in Him. That does not mean that the West must necessarily have to give up her emphasis on action and achievements in the external—but make these as means to consciously unfold the divinity. Let your actions and achievements in the outer world be guided by the motive and conscious effort to reach the consciousness of God.

Vedanta has one great peculiarity: it declares that there must be no attempt to force mankind to travel one path; but that we must allow infinite variation in religious thought, knowing that the goal is the same. Let each individual recognize the goal, and let him move towards it in his own peculiar way without doing any violence whatsoever to the "personality which belongs to him." Three hundred years before Christ, when Asoka, the emperor of India, sent missionaries to other lands, he gave them the following instruction: "The basis of all religions is the same, wherever they are; try to help them all you can, teach them all you can, but do not try to injure them."

Rigid rules and disciplines imposed from without do not work in practice and can never help spiritual growth. Why should we follow certain rules of conduct? Because of authority? Because so-and-so tells us to? Any rule imposed from without on the basis of authority, which takes away our freedom of thinking and acting, even though it may be the *right* rule, does not inspire man to carry it into practice. Rigid rules and disciplines of conduct can be followed only if they are self-imposed. Why should we follow certain rules and principles? Because by such following, we shall reach our objective end. That understanding must be the guide to our conduct.

Western Vedanta

T. M. P. Mahadevan

A new thing has come into history—that is Western Vedanta.
—GERALD HEARD

VEDANTA, WHICH IS the philosophy of *total* experience or *limitless* consciousness, knows no distinction of race or color, clime or country. Though it came to be discovered first in India, it was not meant for India alone. Among the qualifications which make one eligible for the study of Vedanta, there is not included any particular locality of birth or genealogy. The *Upanishads,* which are the fountainhead of the Vedanta, address their call to "All ye, children of immortality."

The perennial philosophy which flows from them can slake the thirst of all—the thirst for the eternal. It is true that at any given time in the world only a few may become conscious of this thirst. As a *Upanishad* text puts it, "Hard it is for many even to hear about it (the supreme Spirit); hearing about it many do not comprehend. A marvel is he who can teach it, and able is he who finds it; and a marvel is he who knows it, taught by an able teacher." Those who seek the imperishable Self are as rare as the seeking is difficult. But those rare seekers are not the exclusive products of any particular time or country. One may meet them in the most unexpected places. They may appear in the least expected of times. Space-time conditions do not apply to the Self. It is their wrong application that constitutes maya.

A philosophy which aims to liberate us from the space-time bottleneck cannot, therefore, countenance any false doctrine of territorial rights in spirituality. While the physical dimension of India has its limits, the spiritual common-

wealth of India has no frontier whatsoever. As in the days
of old, so now again, India's gospel of the spirit has its
votaries in all parts of the world. In the West, and especially in America, the sphere of Vedantic influence is
slowly expanding, thanks to the pioneering work of our
swamis there. Some of the best intellectuals of the West
have begun to recognize the excellence of Vedanta and
follow the way disclosed therein. A new chapter is being
added to human history—the chapter of reawakened
Western interest in Vedanta.

The problem of teaching Vedanta to the West is being
solved at the Vedanta centers in the United States. Though
the spirit of Vedanta is the same, its expressions have
varied even in India. Ranging from the unadulterated
absolutism of Shankara to the uncompromising pluralism
of Madhva, there has been a variety of Vedantic doctrines, all claiming their authority from the Vedas. Of the
two main Vedic currents of religio-philosophic thought—
the absolutistic and the theistic—one or the other dominates each of the schools of Vedanta. But there is one
common feature about all these schools, namely, the acceptance of a fundamental reality which the *Upanishads*
call Brahman. The most crucial difference among them is
whether to regard this reality as a personal God or as an
impersonal absolute. Advaita or the Vedantic nondualism
of Shankara adopts the latter view, while the other schools
favor the former. Swami Vivekananda saw clearly that the
form of Vedanta best suited to the Western mind was
advaita. Those who, after him, have been carrying on his
work in the West, have also discovered by experience how
unerring was the Swami's discernment.

There are several reasons as to why advaita-Vedanta is
the best that India has to offer to the West. While for the
nonadvaitic systems of Indian thought there may be found
parallels in the West, for advaita there seems to be none
whatsoever. Even the thought patterns of philosophers like
Fichte and Bradley, to which advaita is sometimes compared, differ from it in essentials. Advaita has, therefore,
a unique place in the thought and experience of mankind;
and if the Western mind has to go out of its climate for a
vantage point wherefrom to look at and comprehend
truth, then, that place must be such that it is not to be
found within that climate. Advaita, I believe, has a distinctive character; it is distinctive, judged not only by the
Western standards of philosophic thought but also by the

Eastern and the Indian, except in so far as these attempt to rise above the relative and the relational. Moreover, advaita is inclusive of, and not opposed to, the theistic approaches to reality. It is idle to argue that God has no place in advaita. Shankara, the great exponent of the nondualism of spirit, which is advaita, has left behind him soul-moving poems of adoration to the myriad forms of the personal deity—poems that constitute a grand testimony to the intense devotion of their author. The worshiper-worshiped relation is a genuine relation; and it is a sublimation of all other relations.

But even this, says advaita, is transcended in the final distinctionless experience. What is more cannot be less. If advaita is more than theism, it cannot be atheism or anti-theism. While the various theistic doctrines may quarrel among themselves, advaita has no quarrel with any. An old teacher of advaita—whom tradition regards as Shankara's grand-teacher—describes advaita as the whole and the original whereof the different religio-philosophic systems are parts and variants.

To the modern Western mind the nondogmatic character of advaita has a great appeal. The European philosophers of an earlier day used to revel in different types of "isms." But now, many a modern thinker is hesitant of embracing an "ism." To the question "To what school of thought do you belong?" many American philosophers, I found out, had no ready answer. The old-time barriers, such as those between idealism and realism, materialism and mentalism, would appear to be vanishing today. And consequently, the Western mind is in an advantageous position to appreciate advaita which is not an "ism." But, then, one may ask: "Is not advaita nondualism?" The reply is: the negation signified by the prefix non- applies not only to duality but also to ism. One of the aims of advaita is to show that the rival views which are called philosophical systems have their limitations, and are serviceable only in so far as they lead to something beyond. It is the total experience that is the goal. The supreme objective of advaita is to urge man not to rest till he has realized that experience.

I referred above to the nondogmatic character of advaita, and mentioned one of the reasons for so characterizing it. There are other reasons also. Let us take for instance the attitude of advaita to logical reason as the instrument of knowledge. The traditional religions do not trust reason, their appeal being to faith. Many of the systems of philosophy in the West and some in the East have no use for any mode of knowledge except the rational. Both these attitudes, it is not difficult to see, are dogmatic. The religions are dogmatic in their belief that there is no place for reason in faith. The philosophies are dogmatic in believing that there is nothing above or beyond reason. While assigning to reason its rightful place in the religio-philosophic quest, advaita points out that the goal of man is not attained with a mere theoretic understanding of the nature of reality. Philosophy is experience and not mere logical knowledge, though logical knowledge is necessary to interpret that experience. While the absolute experience transcends the logic of reason, it is not opposed to it. In his commentary on Gaudapada's four-chaptered work called *Mandukya-karika,* Shankara explains that the principles of advaita which are established in the first chapter on the authority of the Veda, are shown to be intelligible in the next three chapters through logical reasoning. So, reasoning has its use. But at the same time, it should not arrogate to itself omniscience and claim that there is no experience beyond its ken.

The nondogmatic nature of advaita will be evident to those who have taken the care to study its history. There are doctrinal differences in advaita, owing to the fact that the teachers of advaita have found it necessary to adopt different modes of expounding the truth. To questions like "Is the soul one or many?" and "What is the status of the world?" exponents of advaita have given different answers. Even as regards the means to release they have differed among themselves. Is it the path of knowledge that leads to release, or is it the way of devotion to God? While Shankara voted for the former, a late follower of his, Madhusudana by name, while accepting without reservation the advaita metaphysics, argues that devotion is the easier path to the realization of the absolute. Thus, there are alternative modes of approach to advaita. A book which seeks to set forth the doctrinal differences in advaita compares advaita to a mighty river, which, though originating from one source, gets diversified on reaching the plains and serves the interest of diverse people. Seekers are not all of the same mind. To suit their different aptitudes and temperaments, teachers of advaita adopt different methods of setting forth their doctrine. In an age when Buddhism was popular in India, Gaudapada borrowed Buddhist modes of expression to teach advaita. Shankara, in one of his hymns, makes use of the terminology of Kashmir Shaivism. An advaita work called *Paramarthasara* is patterned after the first-known text of the Sankhya system. So, if advaita-Vedanta which has found its way to Western lands has to be expounded in a manner suited to the Western mind, there is nothing to wonder about. It is in perfect consonance with the tradition and genius of advaita.

All lovers of this philosophy, wherever they may be, will be eager to watch the course of its development in the West. Not only India, but the whole world will gain by the induction of Vedanta into Western life—an induction which is quite the antithesis of religious fanaticism and campaigns of conversion.

The Negative Way

Alan W. Watts

To THE WESTERN mind, one of the most disconcerting things about Oriental teachings as found in the Vedanta and Buddhism is their negative language. We receive the impression that they think of God, the ultimate reality, as a void, and of man's final destiny as an absorption in this void with the consequent loss of his unique personality. In the Vedanta, Brahman is almost always described by negations—the nondual, the nonfinite, the formless, the nonparticular. At the same time, the finite world of forms and individual beings is described as the unreal, the *maya,* which must disappear from the awakened consciousness.

In Buddhism, the highest reality is called *sunyata,* the empty, which is neither being nor nonbeing, which is so ineffable that every statement about it must be false. It appears that the way to a realization of the ultimate involves the strict denial of one's own and every other form of existence. Most Western people think that "variety is the spice of life," and therefore do not take at all kindly to a view of the highest good which seems to require the obliteration of all finite experiences. A state of "consciousness" which is neither "conscious nor unconscious," in which all particular things seem to vanish into a luminous haze, does not appeal to them as anything but extremely boring. Furthermore, they cannot see that such ideas of the highest reality have any philosophical cogency. For how can the basis, the ground, of these very solid, concrete, and particular finite experiences be so much of a nothing? How can something so startling, so real-seeming, so simultaneously wonderful and tragic as the everyday world, emerge from so impalpable a void?

The problem here is almost entirely one of language, for

it has never been clear to the Western mind in what *sense* these negations are intended. By contrast, the Christian, Jewish, and Islamic religions appear to be very positive, for their statements about the highest reality are affirmations rather than denials. Instead of speaking coldly about the "nondual infinite" they speak warmly of the Righteous Father, who is a living, personal Being, whose nature is unbounded justice and love. So long as it is imagined that, say, the Vedanta and Christianity are speaking the same kind of language, their ideas must seem to be utterly opposed.

If we do not know the ultimate reality, we stand in somewhat the same relation to it as blind men to color. If I am to describe color to a blind man, I can do it in one of two ways. I can tell him what color is *like,* or I can say what it is *not.* I cannot possibly tell him what it *is.* I can compare it to variations in temperature, speaking of red as "warm" and blue as "cold" though this will perhaps mislead the blind man into thinking that red *is* warm. On the other hand, I can say that color is *not* hard or soft, round or square, liquid or solid. The danger here is that the blind man may easily suppose that I am talking about nothing, for I have denied to color every positive quality which he knows.

To some extent, this is the difference between the religious doctrines of the West and the metaphysical doctrines of Asia. The former wants to say what reality is *like,* and the latter what it is *not,* but the average mind supposes that both are trying to say what it *is.* Hence the confusion.

But the negative mode of approach to the ultimate reality involves rather more than this, and to understand it properly we must try to see exactly what is being negated. Another principle which both the Vedanta and Buddhism hold in common is that, in reality, "all this"—the whole world of experience, including myself and others—is in essence identical with *sunyata* or Brahman. In other words, there is no reality but the absolute, nondual, and ultimate reality. This is taken to be a radical denial of the everyday world, as if distinct people and things had no value or meaning whatsoever.

It is therefore tremendously important to realize that the negative way is not making a negation about reality —about the real "something" which is the basis of everyday experience. The denial applies strictly to the ideas, the concepts, the theories, and the fixed categories of thought whereby we try to understand and grasp what we experience. The metaphysical doctrines of the Orient are saying that you cannot grasp reality in any fixed form of thought or feeling; you cannot nail it down and possess it. We try to do this because almost all of us feel insecure. We have identified our consciousness with a seemingly fixed form—a structure of memories called "I." We discover that this structure is impermanent, and are therefore afraid. We therefore cling all the more tenaciously to life, to "I," and become still more afraid, involving ourselves in a vicious circle of clinging which is called *samsara*—the "round" of existence.

But the real world, which is the basis of everyday experience, cannot be "fixed"—and every attempt to do so results in frustration and vicious circles. Yet this world, this reality which we experience at every moment is Brahman. For example, I point to a tree and say, "This is a tree." Obviously *this* and *tree* are not actually the same thing. *Tree* is a word, a noise. It is not this experienced reality to which I am pointing. To be accurate, I should have said, "This (pointing to the tree) is symbolized by the noise *tree*."

If, then, the real tree is not the word or the idea *tree,* what is it? If I say that it is an impression on my senses, a vegetable structure, or a complex of electrons, I am merely putting new sets of words and symbols in place of the original noise *tree*. I have not said *what* it is at all. I have also raised other questions: "What are my senses?" "What is a structure?" "What are electrons?"

We can never say *what* these things are. We can symbolize them by sundry noises and patterns of thought. We can, in turn, symbolize these noises by other noises—"*Tree* is a *word,*" or "A pattern of thought is an idea"—but this does not really explain anything. We still do not know *what* a tree, a word, a noise, or an idea actually is. And yet we have experienced mysterious "somethings" which we have arbitrarily paired off with each other—the sight of the tree with the noise *tree,* the process of thinking with the noise *idea,* and the noises *tree* and *idea* with the noise *words.*

Human beings are very much bewitched by words and ideas. They forget that they are mere symbols. They tend to confuse them seriously with the real world which they only represent. The reason for this confusion is that the world of words and ideas seems to be relatively fixed and rational, whereas the real world is not fixed at all. Thus the world of words and ideas seems to be so much safer, so much more comprehensible than the real world. The word and idea *tree* has remained fixed currency for many centuries, but real trees have behaved in a very odd way. I can try to describe their behavior by saying that they have appeared and disappeared, that they have been in a constant state of change, and that they flow in and out of their surroundings.

But this does not really say what they have done, because *disappear, change, flow,* and *surroundings* are still noises representing something utterly mysterious.

Our problem, then, is that so long as we try to fit the real world into the "nice little, tight little" world of definitions, ideas, and words (*nama-rupa*), we shall never succeed in doing so, save in the most approximate and impermanent way. On the other hand, to know Brahman, to see God, is to be aware of the real world in its undefined (i.e., infinite) state. This is to know life without trying to capture it in the fixed forms of conventional words and ideas. It is only by convention that the aspect of reality called *man* is separated off from all other aspects —the earth, the air, the sun, moon and stars. It is convenient to do this (which is what "convention" means), but it does not fully correspond to the facts, which are that man is a process continuous with every other process, and that the boundaries between these processes are fixed arbitrarily by the human mind. For example, who is to say whether a man begins and ends with birth and death, or with conception and the final decay of his corpse? Is he limited in space by his skin, or does he extend out to the distance to which he can hear, smell, and see? All these boundaries are as conventional and arbitrary as the length of an inch or the weight of a pound: you can put them anywhere you like, so long as you agree about them with others.

At root, then, to cling to oneself is as absurd as cleaving passionately to an inch. It just cannot be done, and the attempt is pure frustration. To say, then, that reality is not any particular thing, and that individuals are unreal, is in principle exactly the same thing as pointing out that two yards have no existence apart from a real piece of cloth or wood. You cannot make a dress out of two, or two million, abstract yards.

We have to learn, then, to take all conventional distinctions and definitions for what they are—purely arbitrary and unreal conveniences—and to be keenly aware of life *as it is (yatha bhutam)* apart from all definitions, measurements, and arbitrary boundaries. To see the world in this way is to see Brahman, the undefinable. In this sense, every one of us has already an obscure and neglected knowledge of Brahman—but it is not knowledge in the ordinary meaning of the word. Ordinarily, we mean that to know something is to be able to define it. In fact, however, we know a whole world that we cannot define at all, but we do not make friends with it. We are afraid of it, and are always trying to tie it up safely in watertight packages.

When St. Augustine was asked what time was, he replied, "I know, but when you ask me I don't." The same is true of reality. We know it all the time, but when we begin to think about it, it vanishes. Thus it is said in Zen Buddhism, "If you want to see into it, see into it directly. When you begin to think about it, it is altogether missed." For the same reason the *Kena Upanishad* says, "He who thinks that Brahman is not comprehended, by him Brahman is comprehended; but he who thinks that Brahman is comprehended knows It not. Brahman is unknown to those who know It, and is known to those who do not know It at all."

Brahman, then, is the real world as it is in itself, before we begin to describe or define it in any way, before we split it asunder into millions of arbitrary distinctions called feet, inches, stars, trees, men, ounces, pounds, and mountains. A Chinese poem expresses it thus:

> Plucking chrysanthemums along the east fence;
> Gazing in silence at the southern hills;
> The birds flying home in pairs
> Through the soft mountain air of dusk—
> In these things there is a deep meaning,
> But when we are about to express it,
> We suddenly forget the words.

I know, but when you ask me I don't. If you want me to show you God, I will point to the ash can in your back yard. But if you ask, "Then you mean that this ash can is God?"—you will have missed the point altogether.

Study of Indian Philosophy

James Bissett Pratt

THE NUMBER of books that have appeared in the last twenty or thirty years in England and America with the title *History of Philosophy*, and the fact that hardly a single reviewer's voice has been raised in protest against the ignorance therein involved—these are matters worthy of serious consideration. For these "histories of philosophy" begin with the Greeks and end with the Americans, and convey not the least suggestion that anyone outside of the West ever had a philosophical idea. It is, therefore, high time that as much should be done as possible to draw to the attention of American readers the fact that India has a philosophical tradition, and has gone through a philosophical development much longer than our own.

A glance at the curricula of most of our colleges and universities would seem to indicate that the one principle on which they are planned might be phrased: *nothing east of Suez!* To one who has had a taste of the riches which Indian thought and Indian literature can contribute to our intellectual life and our spiritual experience, this deprivation which we Westerners inflict upon ourselves and upon our young people seems pitiful in the extreme. Indian philosophical literature, taking its rise several centuries before the time of Thales, has swept down through the ages, retaining always a characteristic point of view of its own, but developing in a great variety of fresh forms. Indian thought constitutes today the one type of living philosophy independent of our Western tradition. Neither China nor Japan possesses a living philosophical movement of its own. But especially in the last twenty years, Indian philosophy has exhibited, and is exhibiting, a recrudescence of life which must be reckoned with. There are still plenty of the old-style pundits in India continuing the traditional thought of their country; but in addition to them there is a considerable number of independent thinkers, who, while deeply learned in ancient Indian thought, have read widely and intelligently in the classical philosophy of Europe and in the most recent expressions of British and American epistemology and metaphysics. I doubt if there is a single American or British philosopher of our day whose knowledge of Indian thought even distantly approximates the knowledge of European philosophy possessed by any one of a dozen of our Indian contemporaries who could easily be named. The new learning and the fresh point of view which these leaders of Indian thought have acquired is enabling them to initiate a renaissance of Indian philosophy. Their knowledge of Western thinking has not led them to abandon their native tradition, but it has enriched it in their minds, and enabled them to present it, both to India and to the West, in forms more comprehensive and more persuasive than the old. There is every reason to anticipate that in the total human culture of the coming century a large place is reserved for Indian philosophy.

The study of Indian thought of course can never be, for an Occidental, a substitute for the study of the development of our own Western ideologies. But it can do some things for us Westerners which nothing else can do. For one thing, by the very fact of contrast, it can bring home to us more clearly the peculiar genius of our own tradition. It has often been said that no one knows his own language and literature until he has studied also some other; and the idea can truthfully and fruitfully be applied to different types of philosophy. For us of the West there is, moreover, a peculiar sort of mental exercise in the study of Indian thought not to be found elsewhere. For some of the Indian categories, some of their modes of classification, are so remote from all those with which we are familiar, so unexpected and unforeseeable, that the effort to comprehend them, to believe that the author really means what he says, is a uniquely head-splitting experience: and when it is over with, it leaves one with a new appreciation of the fact that our traditional ways of thinking are not the only possible ways, and may not be identical with the ways of the universe.

In still another way the study of Indian thought may bring to us of the West something which we shall highly value. The tendency of nearly all the schools of Western philosophy is more and more steadily setting in the direction of naturalism, and often of a rather crude naturalism. The victories of natural science have hypnotized most of our philosophers. Within the next few decades the "consolation of philosophy" in the West bids fair to become rather cold comfort. From such a world as Western naturalism usually offers, the thoughtful mind which craves something more than a scientific pattern of space-time events may be glad to take refuge in the eternal insights into a spiritual realm spread out before us in the *Upanishads,* the *Gita,* and the Vedanta philosophy.

Religion without Prayers

Christopher Isherwood

IN THE APRIL, 1946, issue of *Commentary*, Professor Irwin Edman has written an article called "Religion without Tears." It asks the question, "Do moderns need an other-worldly faith?" and its answer is, "No, they don't."

This article is worth discussing from a Vedantist point of view, not only because it is moderately and intelligently written, without undue aggressiveness, but because it represents a large body of opinion in the world today.

Professor Edman begins by noting that many people are now turning to religion because they despair of conditions in our society. The nineteenth century believed that scientific progress would automatically increase human happiness; instead, it has brought us to the use of the atomic bomb.

> If anything, of late the dissatisfaction with pure mechanism and pure materialism has grown even more acute. In a society increasingly dominated by things and threatened by them, an account of the universe seems a poor thing which leaves out, or seems to leave out, what human beings chiefly value—the intimations of truth, goodness and beauty in their lives. The saints and the prophets still seem to say more that is relevant to human personality, to its hopes, its aims, its aspirations than do the bleak formulas of the mechanists and the behaviorists. . . .

> If the world of science remains alien to our inmost spiritual needs, where shall we turn? Well, in this age as in previous ones, those who are disillusioned by the formulas and disinherited by the symbols and traditions of the religious past, turn in whatever direction they see a gleam of meaning, hope or consolation. Intellectuals are repeatedly discovering that though they may think they have outgrown theology, they are still in need of religion, of—in the old

yet still pregnant phrase—a faith by which to live. . . . The dilemma is intellectual, and this explains, I think, why solutions are frequently sought by a revolt against intellectualism altogether. . . . The new cults of mysticism at least give surcease from thinking; they provide or seem to provide sesames to protoplasmic peace.

Other escapes are sought in less obviously non-intellectual ways, but anti-rational ones none the less. There is the cult itself, the reassertion of the basic importance of ritual in religion. The sharing of a common ceremonial hallowed by tradition removes one of the curses of the modern world, the sense of belonging nowhere, of having no bonds or attachments, of being a bleak anonymity in a vast megalopolis. Even the retreat to dogma is often an unintellectual or even an anti-intellectual one. It is a flight to authority; it obviates the necessity of coming to one's own even bleak conclusions. . . . There is no doubt that mysticism, ritual and dogma have been assuagements for many persons of a sense of insecurity, of loneliness and emptiness in the modern world. . . .

What does Professor Edman really mean by these remarks? He means, as far as I can understand him, that mysticism *can* degenerate into vague, irresponsible sentimentality, that ritual *may* be practiced as an empty, formal observance, that dogma is *often* only a crutch for weak and lazy minds. Very true. The same thing might be said of one's attitude to a Shakespeare sonnet, a Fourth of July parade, or the Bill of Rights. I have known people who were extremely vague, sentimental, and dogmatic when discussing the theory of democracy or the Marxian dialectic.

Religion, certainly, is what we make of it. Our effort is its reward. Has Professor Edman read Shankara or Vivekananda? I am sure he has. Then how can he possibly write that mysticism offers us "surcease from thinking"? What greater demands could be made upon the human brain than Shankara makes—this merciless, unwearying process of discrimination which he asks us to apply to every moment of our lives? What greater intellectual independence is there than Vivekananda's, who would not even accept the teaching of his own beloved master until he had tested it for himself? Mysticism is empirical, or it is nothing. Ritual is a personal act of recollection and self-dedication, or it is meaningless. Dogmas are hypothetically accepted truths, or they are silly.

Is mysticism other-worldly? Not in Professor Edman's sense. The I.W.W. used to sing:

> You'll get pie
> In the sky
> When you die—
> It's a lie.

And they were right. It is the most pernicious of all lies —the real opium of the people. No great spiritual teacher has ever uttered it. Vedanta, with its doctrine of karma and reincarnation, teaches the exact opposite: every thought, every word, and every action will be paid for, in this life or in lives to come. Believe, if you wish, that death is the end. But do not dare to imagine that you can get away with murder, and be rewarded for it with "pie," into the bargain. If there *is* a personal survival, it follows, surely, that our problems, our karmas, will survive with us, and that these karmas will determine the conditions of our future existence.

However, that is not the point. What has to be emphasized, again and again, is that mystical religion does not lay nearly so much stress on the question of personal survival as its critics seem to imagine. Buddha did not promise his disciples an other-worldly heaven; he promised the "ending of sorrow," here and now. The mystics offer us a way of happiness here in this world; they offer us a way of understanding the true nature of this present life. Certainly, the basis of this happiness and understanding is outside time and circumstance—it is within this world but not *of* it. In that sense, alone, it is otherworldly.

Professor Edman continues:

> The first rehabilitation necessary is a revival of faith in man's own potentialities and in man's own hopes. The lack of confidence in these lies in the fact that by a century-old diffidence men have not trusted their own ideals unless they came from a world beyond this world. But when it is realized, as Lucretius long ago realized, that the most generous and flowering of human values are growths of these same natural energies out of which plants and animals grow, a wonderful resurgence both of human hope and of cosmic piety is possible. . . . The first step needed in the rehabilitation of the human faith in candidly human values is a rediscovery of the reach and scope of human nature itself.

Professor Edman deplores the fact that "there has long been bred in the human imagination a distrust of anything tainted with the material, the fleshly, the earthly." Did the mystics, in fact, feel this distrust? Christ would not condemn the woman taken in adultery; Ramakrishna liked to talk to drunkards and once offered consecrated food to a cat; St. Francis preached to the birds; Vivekananda wrote, "See no difference between ant and angel; every worm is brother to the Nazarene." I suppose Professor Edman would object that Ramakrishna was not worshiping the cat, *as* a cat, but as eternal reality within the creature. He is quite right, but where does this lead him? He says he wants to discover the reach and scope of human nature itself. Doesn't human nature include the mystical experience of eternal reality? Aren't saints human beings? How are we to have faith in some of man's own potentialities while we reject others? I do not want to sound captious, but I simply cannot follow Professor Edman here. "Even theological ideas," he says, "may be transcriptions of facts encountered and truths discovered in actual experience and in the natural world. Filial piety is a familiar human emotion. It becomes sanctified by a commandment, but the commandment simply dignifies what human beings deeply feel." If "actual experience" is our criterion, can we honestly deny the experiences of spiritual religion? They, also, are deeply felt. And the world's scriptures simply dignify them.

But perhaps this is only playing with words. The end of the article, at any rate, is perfectly clear. It raises a very important question.

What is needed is not a counsel of escape into an emptiness called Nirvana or the Absolute. Rather the challenge is to an ordering of personal life through intelligent understanding so that the varied riches of human values may blend and fuse into a rich and vital happiness. And the challenge, too, is the making of a social order in which individuals may come to diversified felicities.

Individual lives cannot be ordered except in an ordered society. There cannot be healthy souls in a sick commonwealth. Thus, the central challenge to a naturalistic philosophy is that of a society harmonized through intelligence. . . . The mystical sense that once declared us all the children of God can now find realization in the awareness of our common humanity. The sadness that comes from the recognition that individual life ends with the grave is mitigated for any generous mind by the continuity of the adventure of mankind, and the participation, even if briefly, in the shape of things to come.

This, of course, is the philosophy of materialistic nationalism. You work for the future, a willing cog in a great machine. You function for a while, wear out, and are discarded. It doesn't matter. The machine goes on.

As Professor Edman tacitly admits, it is a nonrational philosophy—that is to say, it demands faith. You must believe that the spiral of human progress really *is* ascending, that life on this earth will get better and better. It is a faith which is anchored in time, in the future. Only history can prove it right or wrong. Suppose the human species dies out? Suppose we blow ourselves up, or hit a star? Then all our endeavors, *from a historical point of view*, will have been in vain.

Professor Edman would reply that we mustn't look on the dark side of things. We must have courage. Certainly we must—but where is this courage to be found? Only, it seems to me, in the doctrine of nonattached action, of work performed as ritual, which the *Bhagavad-Gita* teaches. Nonattached action, however, is a mystical idea —and so Professor Edman is forced to reject it.

If you reject mystical religion and, at the same time, lose your faith in an earthly utopia—what remains? Nothing but sheer stoicism; the grimmest and most heroic of man's philosophies. It is, indeed, a philosophy for heroes. Ordinary people will always shrink from it. I shrink from it myself. If this is all life offers, why should I stay alive?

My duty to society? What does this actually mean? On the level of "candidly human values," it means my neighbors, Smith, Jones, Robinson, and Brown. I quite like Smith, Jones bores me, Robinson I scarcely know, Brown I detest. If I am to work for them, to dedicate my life to them, I have somehow got to love them all. But how?

I can only love Smith, Jones, Robinson, and Brown— and two billion others—if I can see them *sub specie aeternitatis;* if I can learn to recognize, within each individual, the same eternal reality. In order to do this, I must first find the eternal reality within myself. You can't recognize what you don't know.

The search for reality is a mystical search. It involves prayer and meditation and self-discipline—or, as Profes-

sor Edman would say, "religion with tears." Without it,
I firmly believe, there can be no enduring co-operation
between human beings. Without it, you cannot build the
Just City, on earth or anywhere else. The bricks simply
will not hold together.

And yet I cannot help feeling, as I read this article—
and many similar articles and books—that the humanistic
materialists and the followers of mystical religion are not
nearly so far apart as they imagine. Surely, with good
will and effort on both sides, we can come to understand
each other? Surely we can find a basis of agreement? We
all want the same thing—a faith to live by. The need was
never more urgent. We should study each other's ideas, not
in a spirit of contemptuous criticism, but quietly and
thoughtfully. If words and phrases, too long contaminated
by hypocrisy and careless misuse, are getting between us,
then we must reject them. The alternative is growing
suspicion, the closing of minds, the hardening of hearts—
and, ultimately, perhaps, persecution. And that, as we
ought to have learned by this time, will help nobody.

Reflections on Progress

Aldous Huxley

EVOLUTIONARY CHANGE is regarded as progressive when it is in the direction of increasing independence of, and control over, the environment. Judged by this criterion, the history of life on our planet has not by any means been uniformly progressive. Primitive forms have survived almost unmodified from the dawn of that history down to the present. Man is the contemporary of unicellular organisms which, despite their almost total dependence on the environment, may very likely outlive their more progressive rivals. Moreover, many organisms have undergone progressive changes over a long period of time, only to regress toward a new and specialized kind of dependence upon the environment, as parasites upon more advanced forms. And finally even those species which have changed most progressively are all, at the present time, at the end of evolutionary blind alleys, condemned by their high degree of specialization either to remain what they are, or, if they undergo a series of considerable mutations, to die out through inability to adapt themselves, in their changed forms, to the environment. There is good reason to suppose that all the existing higher animals are living fossils, predestined to survival without much change, or, if change sets in, to extinction. Except for the human species, evolutionary progress would seem to be at an end.

Biological progress, like every other kind of evolutionary change, is brought about by means of mutations, whose consequences are inherited. Human progress might still conceivably be brought about in the same way; but at least within historical times it has not been so brought about. Moreover, since the great majority of mutations

50

are harmful, it seems unlikely that future changes in the germ plasm will do anything to improve the constitution of a species, which is the product of so long an evolutionary development. (Hence the enormous dangers inherent in the use, even for peaceful purposes, of nuclear fission. Mutations can be artificially produced by the kind of radiations associated with nuclear fission—and most mutations, as we have seen, are harmful. It would be a very suitable punishment for man's overweening *hubris* if the final result of his efforts to dominate nature were the production of a race of hare-lipped, six-fingered imbeciles.) If there is to be hereditary progress in the human species, it will be brought about by the same kind of selective breeding as has improved the races of domesticated animals. It would be perfectly possible, within a few centuries, to raise the average level of human intelligence to a point far above the present. Whether such a vast eugenic experiment could be carried out except under the auspices of a world dictatorship, and whether, if carried out, its results would turn out to be socially desirable, are matters about which we can only speculate. Meanwhile it is worth remarking that the hereditary qualities of the more civilized peoples of the world are probably deteriorating. This is due to the fact that persons of poor physique and low intellectual endowments have a better chance of living under modern conditions than their counterparts ever had in the much severer conditions prevailing in the past. Human progress, within historical times, differs from biological progress in being a matter, not of heredity, but of tradition. This tradition, oral and written, has served as the vehicle by means of which the achievements of exceptional individuals have been made available for their contemporaries and successors, and the new discoveries of one generation have been handed on, to become the commonplace of the next.

Many and very various criteria have been used to measure this human progress-by-tradition. Sometimes it is envisaged as a continuation of biological progress—an advance in control and independence. Judged by this standard, the progress achieved in recent centuries by certain sections of the human race has been very great. True, it has not been quite so great as some people like to think. Earthquakes still kill their thousands, epidemics their millions, while famines due to drought, or floods, or insect pests, or the diseases of plants, slowly and painfully destroy their tens of millions. Moreover, many of the "conquests of nature" most loudly acclaimed at one moment have turned out, a few years later, to be a good deal less spectacular than was first imagined—have even taken on the aspect of defeats. Consider, for example, the progress achieved in the most important of all human activities— agriculture. New fields are brought under the plough, produce crops that permit an expansion of the population, and then, almost suddenly, turn into dust bowls and eroded hillsides. New chemicals for the control of insects, viruses, and fungi seem to work almost miraculously, but only until such time as mutation and natural selection produce new and resistant strains of the old enemies. Artificial fertilizers produce bumper harvests; but meanwhile they kill the indispensable earthworm and, in the opinion of a growing number of authorities, tend in the long run to reduce the fertility of the soil and to impair the nutritive qualities of the plants that grow on it. In the name of "efficiency," we disturb the delicate balance of nature; by eliminating one of the factors of the ecological mosaic, or artificially adding to another, we get our increased production, but after a few years outraged nature takes its revenge in the most unexpected and disconcerting way. And the list could be lengthened indefinitely. Human beings are never quite so clever as they think they are.

But the criteria by which biological progress is measured are not adequate when it comes to the measurement of human progress. For biological progress is thought of as applying exclusively to the species as a whole; whereas it is impossible to think realistically about mankind without considering the individual as well as the race to which he belongs. It is easy to imagine a state of things in which the human species should have achieved their progress, at the expense of the component individuals, considered as personalities. Judged by specifically human standards, such biological progress would be a regression toward a lower, subhuman state.

In framing standards by which to measure human progress we must take into account the values which, in the opinion of individual men and women, make life worth living. And this, in effect, has been done by all the theorists of human progress from the later seventeenth century, when the idea first began to seem plausible, down to the present day. During the eighteenth and nineteenth centuries biological progress was reconciled with human progress by means of a doctrine of pre-established harmony. It was assumed as practically self-evident that advances in man's control over his environment would inevitably be accompanied by corresponding advances in individual happiness, in personal and social morality, and in the quantity and quality of creative activity in the spheres of art and science. Those of us who are old enough to have been brought up in the Victorian tradition can recall (with a mixture of amusement and melancholy) the basic and unquestioned assumptions of that consoling *Weltanschauung*. Comte and Spencer and Buckle expressed the matter in respectably abstract language; but the gist of their creed was simply this: that people who wore top hats and traveled in railway trains were incapable of doing the sort of things that the Turks were doing to the Armenians or that our European ancestors had done to one another in the bad old days before steam engines. Today, after two world wars and three major revolutions, we know that there is no necessary correlation between advanced technology and advanced morality. Many primitives, whose control over their environment is rudimentary, contrive nonetheless to be happy, virtuous, and, within limits, creative. Conversely, the members of civilized societies, possessed of the technological resources to exercise considerable control over their environment, are often conspicuously unhappy, maladjusted, and uncreative; and though private morals are tolerably good, collective behavior is savage to the point of fiendishness. In the field of international relations the most conspicuous difference between men of the twentieth century and the ancient Assyrians is that the former have more efficient methods of committing atrocities and are able to destroy, tyrannize, and enslave on a larger scale.

The truth is that all an increase in man's ability to control his environment can do for him is merely to modify the situation in which, by other than technological means, individuals and groups attempt to make specifically human progress in creativeness, morality, and happiness. Thus the city-dwelling factory worker may belong, biologically speaking, to a more progressive group than does the peasant; but it does not follow that he will find it any easier to be happy, good, and creative. The peasant is confronted by one set of obstacles and handicaps; the industrial worker, by another set. Technological progress does not abolish obstacles; it merely changes their nature. And this is true even in cases where technological progress directly affects the lives and persons of individuals. For example, sanitation has greatly reduced the incidence of contagious diseases, has lowered child mortality and lengthened the average expectation of life. At first sight this piece of technological progress would seem to be at the same time a piece a piece of human progress. But when we look at the matter more closely, we discover that, even here, all that has happened is that the conditions for achieving human progress have been changed. Symptomatic of this change is the recent rise of geriatrics as an important branch of medicine, is the granting of pensions to the aged, is the shift of the balance of population, in countries with a low birth rate, toward the higher age groups. Thanks to sanitation, the aged are in process of becoming a socially important minority, and for this important minority the problems of human progress in happiness, goodness, and creativeness are peculiarly difficult. Even in the medical field, technological progress is never the same as human progress. For though we can say without qualification that it would be a good thing if, let us say, malaria could be abolished, yet the mere fact of improving the health of the victims of this disease would not in itself do more than change the conditions in which human progress is attempted. The healthy are not necessarily creative, good, or even happy; they merely have a better chance of being so than do the sick.

Advancing technology increases man's control over his environment, and the increasing control is hereditary in the sense that its methods are handed on by tradition from generation to generation. But, as we have seen, this equivalent of biological progress does not by itself constitute specifically human progress. Within the constantly changing situation created by advancing technology, men must try to achieve specifically human progress by means which are not of a technological nature—namely, politics and education. Politics is concerned with the organization of juridical and economical relationships within a given society, and between that society and other societies. Education, in so far as it is not merely vocational, aims at reconciling the individual with himself, with his fellows, with society as a whole, with the nature of which he and his society are but a part, and with the immanent and transcendent spirit within which nature has its being.

The difference between a good politico-economical arrangement and a bad one is simply this: that the good arrangement reduces the number of dangerous temptations to which the individuals and groups concerned are exposed, while the bad arrangement multiplies such temptations. Thus a dictatorship, however benevolent its intentions, is always bad, because it tempts a minority to indulge in the lust for power, while compelling the majority to act as the irresponsible and servile recipients of orders from above. If we wish to evaluate any existing or still ideal institution, whether political, economic, or ecclesiastical, we must begin by asking the same simple questions: what temptations does it, or is it likely to, create, and from what temptations does it, or is it likely to, deliver us? If it strongly and insistently tempts the individuals and groups concerned to indulge such notoriously deadly passions as pride, covetousness, cruelty, and the lust for power, if it forces hypocrisy and servility and unreasoning obedience upon whole sections of the population, then, on the face of it, the institution in question is undesirable. If, on the contrary, it offers little scope for the abuse of power, if it puts no premium on avarice, if its arrangements are such that cruelty and pride of place are not easily to be indulged, if it invites, not unreasoning obedience, but intelligent and responsible cooperation, then, on the face of it, the verdict should be favorable.

Hitherto most political and economic revolutions have failed to achieve the good results anticipated. They have swept away institutions which had become intolerable because they invited individuals and groups to succumb to dangerous temptations. But the new revolutionary institutions have led other individuals and groups into temptations which were either identical with the old, or, if not identical, no less dangerous. For example, power is as certain to be abused, whether it is exercised by rich men in virtue of their wealth, or by politicians and administrators in virtue of their position in a governmental or ecclesiastical hierarchy.

Large-scale political changes are made primarily in the interest of an individual, party, or class; but a more-or-less sincere desire to achieve specifically human progress often enters in as a secondary motive. How far can such changes produce what is hoped of them? To what extent can a continuing advance in happiness, goodness, and creativeness be achieved by act of parliament? Of creativeness on the higher levels it would be unwise to speak. Why large numbers of men of genius should appear at one period, and why other periods should be without them is a profound mystery. It is different, however, with creativity on its lower levels, creativity as expressed in the arts and crafts of common life. It is obvious that in a society where all the necessary household goods are produced by machines in highly organized factories, the arts and crafts will not flourish. The conveniences of mass production have to be paid for by a diminution in creativeness on the lower, popular levels.

Goodness and happiness are notoriously hard to measure. All that can be said is that, given certain political and economic arrangements, certain temptations to evil and certain reasons for misery may be eliminated. Thus, an efficient police can diminish the temptations to crimes of violence, and equitable arrangements for the distribution of food can diminish the miseries attendant on hunger. Again, a paternal government can, by suitable legislation, diminish the miseries connected with periodical unemployment. Unfortunately economic security in an industrialized society has been achieved, up till now, at the expense of personal liberty. The miseries of anxiety have had to be paid for by the miseries of a dependence, which in some countries has degenerated into servitude. This is a world in which nobody ever gets anything for nothing. Advantages in one field have to be paid for by disadvantages in another field. Destiny only sells; it never gives. All we can do is to drive the best possible bargain. And if we choose to use our intelligence and good will, instead of our low cunning and our lust for power, we can make political arrangements that shall eliminate many dangerous temptations to evil and many causes of misery without, in the process, creating new troubles no less intolerable than those we have escaped.

Meanwhile we must remember that the removal, by political methods, of certain dangerous temptations and certain reasons for misery will not of itself guarantee a general advance in goodness and happiness. Even under the existing political and economic dispensations there is a minority of persons whose lives are prosperous, secure, and untroubled. And yet of these fortunate few how many are profoundly unhappy and how many are actively or passively evil! Within wide limits goodness and happiness are almost independent of external circumstances. True, a starving child cannot be happy; and a child brought up among criminals is unlikely to be good. But these are extreme cases. The great masses of the population live in a middle region, lying between the extremes of sanctity and depravity, wealth and destitution. Provided that they remain within this middle region of experience, individuals can undergo considerable changes of fortune without undergoing corresponding changes in the direction of vice or virtue, misery, or happiness. Private life is very largely independent of public life and even, in some measure, of private circumstances. Certain classes of happiness and even a certain kind of goodness are the fruits of temperament and constitution. There are men and women, of whom it can be said, as it was said, for example, of St. Bonaventura, that they are "born without original sin." There are children who are congenitally unselfish, like that *Pippo buono,* who was to grow up into St. Philip Neri. And to match these inborn and gratuitous virtues, there is such a thing as an unearned joy, an almost causeless beatitude.

> Four ducks on a pond,
> A grass-bank beyond,
> A blue sky in spring,
> White clouds on the wing;
> What a little thing
> To remember with tears—
> To remember for years!

Such is the stuff of which a good part of our happiness is composed; and such stuff is the same at all periods, is available in every conjunction of public or private circumstances. Happiness from this kind of source cannot be increased or diminished by an act of parliament, or even by our own acts and the acts of those with whom we come in contact. It depends on our own innate ability to react to certain unchanging elements in the order of nature.

The ability so to react depends to a certain extent upon age as well as on the constitution of the individual. An adolescent newly discovering the world is happy with a kind of tremulous intensity never to be recaptured during the years of maturity. And this leads us to a very important point, which is that the life of a man is not in its nature progressive, but rises to a peak, continues for a while on a plateau of maturity, then declines through old age into decrepitude and death. The literatures of the world abound in lamentations over life's inevitable regres-

sion from youthful happiness. To an old man who has out-
lived his contemporaries and is declining into second childhood it is absurd to talk of the march either of biological
or of human progress. In his own person he can experience only the opposite of an advance either toward
greater control over the environment, or toward greater
happiness, goodness, and creativeness. And at any given
period, however progressive that period may seem to future historians, a third or thereabouts of all the individuals
then living will be experiencing the biological and human
regress associated with advancing years. Old age under
Pericles or Lorenzo the Magnificent was just as sad, just
as antiprogressive as old age under Abdul-Hamid or
Chilperich. True, the old are in a position to maintain
progress in goodness, if only because in later life many
vices lose their attractiveness; but it is difficult for them to
maintain progress in happiness and creativeness. If such
specifically human progress is ever maintained through a
considerable period, it must be through a succession of
young and mature individuals, whose own lives are still in
a progressive phase.

Historians, when they describe a certain age as progressive, never trouble to tell us who precisely it is that experiences the progress in question, nor how it is experienced.
For example, all modern historians agree that the thirteenth century was a progressive period. And yet the
moralists who actually lived during the thirteenth century
were unanimous in bemoaning the decadence of their
times. And when we read such a document as the
Chronicle of Salimbene, we find ourselves wondering to
what extent conclusions drawn from the sanctity of St.
Francis, the architecture of the Gothic cathedrals, the
philosophy of St. Thomas, and the poetry of Dante are
relevant to the brutish and totally unregenerate lives of the
great masses of the people. If the age was indeed progressive, who experienced the progress? And if most of the
people living at the time failed to experience anything in
the nature of biological or human progress, is it justifiable
to speak of the age as progressive? Or is an age genuinely
progressive simply because future historians, using standards of their own devising, judge it to be so?

In the long history of evolutionary change, biological
progress has been confined to the upper levels of the
vegetable and animal population. Analogously it may be
that specifically human progress is a privilege of the ex-

ceptionally fortunate and the exceptionally gifted. Thus, while the Elizabethan drama was progressing from Kyd to Shakespeare, great numbers of dispossessed peasants were suffering from extreme malnutrition, and the incidence of rickets and scurvy was steadily on the increase. In other words, there was human progress for a few in certain fields, but in other fields and among the destitute many, there was biological and human regress. And yet today, we rank the Elizabethan age as an age of progress.

The experience of technological and even of human progress is seldom continuous and enduring. Human beings have an enormous capacity for taking things for granted. In a few months, even in a few days, the newly invented gadget, the new political or economic privileges, come to be regarded as parts of the existing order of things. When reached, every longed-for ceiling becomes a common floor. We do not spend our time comparing present happiness with past misery; rather we accept it as our right and become bitterly resentful if we are even temporarily deprived of it. Our minds being what they are, we do not experience progress continuously, but only in fits and starts, during the first phases of any new advance.

From politics as a means to human progress we now pass to education. The subject is almost boundless; but, fortunately, in this particular context only one aspect of it is relevant. For, in so far as they are not dependent upon temperament or fortunate accident, happiness, goodness, and creativeness are the products of the individual's philosophy of life. As we believe, so we are. And what we believe depends on what we have been taught—by our parents and schoolmasters, by the books and newspapers we read, by the traditions, clearly formulated or unspoken, of the economic, political, and ecclesiastical organizations to which we belong. If there is to be genuine human progress, happiness, goodness, and creativeness must be maintained by the individuals of successive generations throughout the whole span of lives that are by nature non-progressive and in the teeth of circumstances that must often be unfavorable. Of the basic philosophies of life which can be imposed upon an individual, or which he can choose to make his own, some are favorable to the maintenance of happiness, goodness, and creativeness, others are manifestly inadequate.

Hedonism, for example, is an inadequate philosophy. Our nature and the world are such that, if we make happiness our goal, we shall not achieve happiness. The philosophy implicit in modern advertising (the source from which millions now derive their *Weltanschauung*) is a special form of hedonism. Happiness, the advertisers teach us, is to be pursued as an end in itself; and there is no happiness except that which comes to us from without, as the result of acquiring one of the products of advancing technology. Thus hedonism is linked with the nineteenth-century faith that technological progress is necessarily correlated with human progress. If rayon stockings make you happy, how much happier you must be with nylons, which are the product of a more advanced technology! Unfortunately the human mind does not happen to work this way. Consequently, those who consciously or unconsciously accept the philosophy expounded by the advertisers find it hard to maintain even happiness, let alone goodness or creativeness.

More adequate are those political philosophies, which for millions of our contemporaries have taken the place of the traditional religions. In these political philosophies intense nationalism is combined with a theory of the state and a system of economics. Those who accept these philosophies, either of their own free will or because they have from infancy been subjected to unremitting propaganda, are inspired in many cases to a life of devotion to the national and ideological cause. They thus achieve and maintain a kind of happiness and a kind of goodness. Unfortunately a high personal morality is often associated with the most atrocious public wickedness; for the nation and the party are deities in whose service the worshiper is justified in doing anything, however abominable, that seems to advance the sacred cause. And even the happiness that comes from the service of a cause greater than oneself is apt in these cases to be somewhat precarious. For where bad means are used to achieve a worthy end, the goal actually reached is never the good end originally proposed, but merely the inevitable consequence of using bad means. For this reason the happiness that comes from self-dedication to such political causes must always be tempered by the disappointment arising from the chronic failure to realize the longed-for ideal.

In devotional religions, such as certain forms of Christianity, Hinduism, and Buddhism, the cause to which the worshiper dedicates himself is supernatural and the full realization of his ideal is not "in this world." Consequently their adherents have a better chance of maintaining happiness and, except where rival sects are struggling for power, are less strongly tempted to public immorality than are the devotees of the political religions.

Stoicism antedated the stoics and has survived them. It is the name we give to men's attempt to achieve independence of, and control over, environment by psychological means rather than by mutation and selection or, on the human level, by an ever more efficient technology. Because it depends mainly on the surface will, and because, however powerful and well trained the surface will is, it is not a match for circumstances, the mere stoic has never wholly realized his ideal of happiness in independence and goodness in voluntary detachment.

The aims of stoicism are fully achieved not by stoics, but by those who, by contemplation or devotion, lay themselves open to "grace," to the "Logos," to "Tao," to the "Atman-Brahman," to the "inner light." Specifically human progress in happiness, goodness, and creativity, and the psychological equivalent of biological progress in independence and control, are best achieved by the pursuit of man's final end. It is by aiming at the realization of the eternal that we are able to make the best—and the best is a continuing progress—of our life in time.

Further Reflections on Progress

Aldous Huxley

I SHALL NOW try to throw some light on the idea of progress in its relation to man's final end, the realization that "Thou art That." Seen from the standpoint of the perennial philosophy, biological progress is a heritable advance in the quality and extent of consciousness. In the course of terrestrial evolution life has developed awareness, and in man, the highest product of that evolution, awareness has reached the point where any given individual can (if he so desires, knows how, and is prepared to fulfill certain conditions) open himself up to the unitive knowledge of spiritual reality. Biological evolution does not of itself lead automatically to this unitive knowledge. It leads merely to the possibility of such a knowledge. And it leads to this possibility through the development of free will and self-consciousness. But free will and self-consciousness are the root of specifically human ignorance and wrongdoing. The faculties that make the unitive knowledge of reality possible are the very faculties that tempt human beings to indulge in that literally insane and diabolic conduct of which man, alone of all the animals, is capable. This is a world in which nobody ever gets anything for nothing. The capacity to go higher is purchased at the expense of being able to fall lower. Only an angel of light can become the prince of darkness. On the lower levels of evolutionary development there is no voluntary ignorance or deliberate evil-doing; but, for that very reason, there is also no enlightenment. That is why, in spite of Buchenwald and Hiroshima, we have to give thanks for having achieved a human birth.

Any creature which lives according to instinct lives in a state of what may be called animal grace. It does, not its will, but the will of God-in-nature. Man does not live by instinct; his patterns of behavior are not inborn, but acquired. He is at liberty, within the restraints imposed by society and his own habits of thought, to choose the better or the worse, the moral and intellectual means to the final end or the moral and intellectual means to self-destruction. "Not my will, but Thine, be done." This is the essence of all religion. Free will is given that self-will may be annihilated in the spiritual equivalent of instinct. Biological progress is a straight line; but the spiritual progress which we are at liberty to superimpose on the human end product of biological progress rises in a spiral toward a point corresponding to, but incommensurably far above, the position of the animal that lives according to instinct, or the will of God-in-nature.

Specifically human progress in happiness, virtue, and creativeness is valuable, in the last analysis, as a condition of spiritual advance toward man's final end. Hunger, privation, and misery; covetousness, hatred, anger, and lust; hide-bound stupidity and insensitiveness—all these are obstacles in the way of spiritual advance. At the same time it should not be forgotten that if happiness, morals, and creativeness are treated as ends in themselves instead of means to a further end, they can become obstacles to spiritual advance no less serious, in their way, than wretchedness, vice, and conventionality. Enlightenment is not to be achieved by the person whose aim in life is to "have a good time," to the puritan worshiper of repressive morality for its own sake, or to the aesthete who lives for the creation or appreciation of formal beauty. Idolatry is always fatal; and even the highest human goods cease to be goods if they are worshiped for their own sake and not used, as they are intended to be used, for the achievement of an ultimate good that transcends them.

We now come to progress in relation to the spiritual life—in relation, that is to say, to the conscious pursuit of man's final end. Significant in this context is the Buddha's remark that he who says he is an arhat thereby proclaims that he is not an arhat. In other words, it is fatal to boast of achievement or to take satisfaction in an experience which, if it genuinely partakes of enlightenment, is a product of grace rather than of the personal effort. Progress in spirituality brings contrition as well as joy. The enlightenment is experienced as joy; but this bright bliss illuminates all that, within the self, remains unenlightened, dispelling our normal blind complacency in regard to faults and shortcomings and causing us to regret not merely what we are, but even the very fact of our separate individuality. In total and uninterrupted enlightenment there can be nothing but the love, joy, and peace which are the fruits of the spirit; but on the way to that consummation contrition must alternate with bliss, and progress can be measured by the nature of that which is repented—sins, imperfections, and finally our own individualized existence.

Side by side with genuine progress in spirituality is an illusory progress through experiences which are thought to be apprehensions of the ultimate reality, but which are in fact nothing of the kind. These experiences belong to one or other of two main classes. In the first class we find those emotional intoxications induced by focusing devotion upon a figment of the imagination—for example, the mental image of some divine person. Certain classes of spiritual exercises, such as those devised by St. Ignatius of Loyola, exist solely for the purpose of training the imaginative powers and of arousing intense emotions in relation to the fantasies thus deliberately conjured up. Genuine mystics, such as St. John of the Cross or the author of The Cloud of Unknowing, insist that it is, in the very nature of things, impossible to come to a realization of ultimate reality by the cultivation of the fancy and the feelings; for the fancy and the feelings belong to the separate ego, whereas the immanent and transcendent Godhead can only be realized when the separate ego has been stilled and put aside, when an empty space has been created in the mind so as to make room, as it were, for the Atman-Brahman. The ecstasy of fancy-begotten emotions is entirely different from unitive knowledge of the divine Ground.

The illusory experiences of the second class are those induced by a form of self-hypnosis. Great stress is laid in many of the Mahayana sutras on the necessity of avoiding the false samadhi of the sravakas and the Pratyeka-Buddhas. This is a negative condition, and absence of consciousness rather than its transfiguration. The world is escaped; it is not seen anew sub specie aeternitatis. "If the doors of perception were cleansed," wrote Blake, "the world would appear as it is, infinite and holy." But in this false samadhi there is no cleansing of perception; there is merely a turning away, a temporary abolition of perception. This is a reversion toward the condition of inanimate matter, not a progress toward the final end of unitive knowledge of the divine reality within the soul and in and beyond the world.

What Is Religion?

Swami Prabhavananda

I

THERE ARE MANY theories as to the origin of religion. The Vedantic theory is that it springs from man's desire to transcend the limitations and bondages of life. When, and why, does man seek religion? When he becomes dissatisfied with his present condition of life; when he finds that he cannot overcome its limitations by any other means than by taking recourse to something beyond the knowledge of his senses.

For example, when Buddha saw the three dread woes of mankind—old age, disease, and death—and realized that no man could escape them so long as he lived within the domain of the senses, he renounced everything that life in the world could offer him, and went out in search of that something which would enable him to transcend them utterly.

It may be that religion had its origin in the hearts of the ancient sages and seers; it may be that it reached its highest expression in the experiences of the saints and sons of God. But however much we theorize, we cannot expect to know the real truth of religion until we ourselves find its origin within our own hearts; until we ourselves transcend the limitations and bondages of life. In short, there must originate within our own heart the sense of limitation and the desire to transcend it. You enjoy a drink only when you are thirsty. Your thirst can never be satisfied by another drinking for you.

"Rare indeed is the combination of these three: human birth, longing for liberation, and the association of the holy." Of these again the "longing for liberation" is the key to the door to spiritual life, and when this longing arises man is on the way to attaining fulfillment. This is the truth taught by every illumined soul. "Knock and it shall be opened unto you."

This longing for liberation is the common desire of all mankind. We do not find it in the lower animals. Only in man has self-consciousness evolved, and with it the consciousness of limitation and the desire to transcend it. The beggar is dissatisfied with his lot, and the king is not satisfied. What, then, does this "longing for liberation" mean? It means that "In the finite there is no happiness, in the infinite alone is happiness." We are longing for the infinite, and our thirst can never be quenched in the finite. This great lesson we all must learn, sooner or later: the one motive behind all our struggles and strivings is the desire to reach the infinite.

In the language of the *Upanishads,* Brahman, or God, is Sat-chit-ananda. Sat is eternal being, immortal life. Chit is pure consciousness, infinite wisdom. Ananda is love and abiding happiness. And no matter whether one is an atheist or a believer, a worldly man or a man of dispassion, everyone is seeking immortal life, infinite knowledge, and eternal love. In short, everyone is seeking *God*. What, then, is the difference between the atheist and the believer, the worldly-minded man and the man of dispassion? Just this: the one is seeking the infinite in the finite, while the other, in whom has arisen spiritual discrimination, realizes the futility of such a search and turns his gaze toward the infinite—God—in whom alone he finds fulfillment.

Behind the surface life of man, bounded on each side by birth and death, there is the Atman, the eternal being, the sat. This is the true Self in man, the birthless, the deathless spirit. He who realizes this Atman attains to immortal life, while he who seeks to find immortal life in the fleeting life of the body finds only death.

The thirst for knowledge and power is inherent in every man, but, forgetful of his true being, which is chit, or pure consciousness, the omnipresent Being, he seeks to gather all knowledge from the finite. He forgets to inquire about that knowledge "knowing which, everything else is known." As by knowing a lump of clay we know everything that is made of clay, so, by knowing the Atman —the pure consciousness—we can have infinite knowledge. Only then can our thirst for knowledge and power be satisfied. God shines within us as the pure light of knowledge, and it is the same light which, reflected on the mind and senses, gives them life and consciousness. With the aid of this borrowed light the mind and senses go out to gather knowledge and experience of the outer world. In order to find this pure light of knowledge and infinite wisdom, it is necessary that the mind and senses be turned inward toward God. He alone is the source of all knowledge and all wisdom. "Seek ye first the kingdom of God. . . ." "The Self is ear of the ear, mind of the mind, speech of the speech. He is also breath of the breath, and eye of the eye. Having given up the false identification of the Self with the senses and the mind, and knowing the Self to be Brahman, the wise become immortal."

Man seeks happiness, and in his search he finds himself caught in a current of alternating experiences of happiness and misery. The waves rise and fall, yet always within him there lurks the hope that somewhere, somehow, he will find an abiding and unalloyed happiness. He does not know that the mine of bliss is already within him, that God, the ananda, the blissful Self, dwells within his own heart. "Who could live, who could breathe, if that Blissful Self dwelt not within the lotus of the heart? He it is that gives joy."

All men seek love, and it is possible that they will find it in the world and in their worldly relationships. There may be true, unselfish love between husband and wife, between parents and children, between friends, but always there remains some emptiness in the heart, some lingering desire to taste of a deeper love. For, no matter how unselfish the love may be that one finds in the world, it is but a mere shadow of the real love—which is of God, for God is love. There is no love that can satisfy the heart of man but the love of God. In Him alone is the fulfillment of love—ananda.

The sage Yagnavalkya taught his wife Maitreyi: "It is not for the sake of the husband, my beloved, that the husband is dear, but for the sake of the Self. It is not for the sake of the wife, my beloved, that the wife is dear, but for the sake of the Self. It is not for the sake of the children, my beloved, that the children are dear, but for the sake of the Self. It is not for the sake of wealth, my beloved, that wealth is dear, but for the sake of the Self. It is not for the sake of itself, my beloved, that anything whatever is esteemed, but for the sake of the Self." When we realize that all the love, all the attraction that we hold in our hearts is the love and attraction of God, and when we direct our heart's love toward Him, then it is that we find fulfillment. It is then and then only that we learn to love all beings.

In short, the longing for the infinite God—the Sat-chit-ananda Brahman—is inherent in man, but man, in his ignorance, seeks to find the infinite in the finite, and meets with frustration and disappointment at every turn. The "sinner" becomes a "saint" when he wakes up from his sleep of ignorance and yearns consciously to realize God.

II

"God," it has been said, "is an infinite circle whose center is everywhere and whose circumference is nowhere." The infinite God is centered in every heart, and, in turn, every heart must make God the center of its life and existence, in order that He may be immediately and directly experienced.

The one and only purpose of life is to realize God, to attain union with Him, to know that He is the Self, one with Sat-chit-ananda Brahman. All religions are agreed on this point. Jesus expressed it by declaring: "Be ye perfect even as the Father which is in heaven is perfect," and St. Paul commented upon it by affirming: "Ye are complete in Godhead." This perfection, in the language of the *Upanishads*, is the attainment of immortal life, pure consciousness, and love, or abiding joy—Sat-chit-ananda Brahman.

The attainment of Sat-chit-ananda Brahman, however, is not the acquisition of something new. It is the discovery of the forgotten treasure already within. We *are* that Sat-chit-ananda Brahman, but we have to wake up to that knowledge. Truly has the mystic poet Kabir said:

I laugh when I hear that the fish in the water is thirsty:
You do not see that the Real is in your own home,
And you wander from forest to forest listlessly!
Here is the truth! Go where you will, to Banaras or to Mathura;
If you do not find God in your own soul, the world is meaningless to you.

How true! For indeed the world is meaningless, and life yields no purpose, until we wake up to the realization of the "eternal amongst the non-eternals of life," the "highest abiding joy in the midst of the fleeting pleasures of life."

Yagnavalkya, the well-known seer of the Upanishadic age, taught king Janaka this truth: "Brahman may be realized while yet one dwells in the ephemeral body. To fail to realize Him is to live in ignorance, and therefore to be subject to birth and death. The knowers of Brahman are immortal: others, knowing Him not, continue in the bonds of grief."

Each soul is divine, and perfection is attained by the knowledge and experience of this divinity. The soul is never lost, nor can it ever be lost. Failure to realize God is to remain subject to birth, death, and rebirth. This rebirth, according to Vedanta and Buddhism, is known as reincarnation. A man is born again and again, and remains within the bonds of pleasure and pain, birth and death, until he finally attains union with God. By this process of evolution and reincarnation every being will attain his birthright, which is eternal life. Why, then, do we wait? Why do we continue to go through this repeated round of birth and death, with its bonds of grief and pain, when, already within our hearts, there is that "well of water springing up unto eternal life?"

"As one not knowing that a golden treasure lies buried beneath his feet, may walk over it again and again, yet never find it, so all beings live every moment in the city of Brahman, yet never find Him, because of the veil of illusion by which He is concealed." We need to come out of this gloom of ignorance, to remove this veil of illusion, in order to attain union with Brahman.

Brahman *is*, and *"That Thou art."* This truth is not based merely on the authority of the scriptures, or on the experiences of the saints, seers, prophets, and sons of God. It is based on the fact of one's own experience. You and I and everyone can experience the truth of Brahman. Indeed, we *must* experience it in order to be freed of all bondage. When we are thirsty we have to quench our own thirst.

To experience Brahman is to wake up, as it were, from our long sleep of ignorance. Buddha was once asked: "Who are you? Are you a god?" "No." "Are you an angel?" "No." "Who are you then?" He replied, "I am the Buddha—the awakened one."

Man himself is the measure of all truth, and every man lives in a world of his own. True, there are common and universal experiences known to all, for the same experiences come to all, whether they be of the world and the universe of appearance, or of God and the world of God. What experiences a man will have depends upon the level of consciousness in which he lives; for every level of consciousness exists in all men. According to the mystic philosophy of India there are seven such levels of consciousness. They are: *muladhara,* at the base of the spine; *swadhisthan,* at the root of the genitals; *manipur,* near the navel; *anahata,* in the heart, or, more correctly, near the pit of the stomach; *vishuddha,* near the throat; *ajna,* between the eyebrows, and *sahashrara,* in the brain. Ordinarily, man lives within the three lower centers of consciousness, and his experience is of the world of appearance; his mind dwells on bodily comforts and sense pleasures. Eating, drinking, procreation, and all that goes with them, become the be-all and end-all of his life, while religion or God remains an almost unknown quantity. If, in such a man, the thought of or belief in God arises, it is usually as a means whereby his material well-being may be further enriched.

When, however one begins to experience the consciousness residing in the heart, there comes to him a certain degree of faith in God and in the higher things of the spirit. As this consciousness persists, faith and love increase, and one learns to pray, and delights to dwell in the thought of God. Thus does a man become a spiritual aspirant, and thus he sets about to discipline himself and to practice spiritual exercises. Whenever the mind of such a man descends to the lower levels of consciousness and the hunger of the senses overpowers him, he feels deep remorse, and increases his spiritual self-disciplines. Every struggle brings greater control, until the time comes when the mind begins to dwell constantly in the consciousness of the heart, and the aspirant attains certain mystical experiences. For example, he may see a light within and around himself, and at the same time feel a vivid sense of the presence and reality of God, together with a kind of joy and sweetness which are not of this earth. Or it may be that he will experience ecstasy and become drunk with the joy of the Lord. Yet, even after he has had such experiences as these, it is still possible for his mind to sink occasionally to lower levels and cause him to yield to the grosser passions. Therefore it is expedient that the aspirant live a carefully disciplined life and never expose himself to temptation.

As the aspirant progresses, and his mind rises above the heart to the throat center, he recognizes the shadowy nature of this world-appearance and the futility of life on the plane of the senses. His mind so dwells in God that all worldly talk, all worldly thought, and all selfishness become intolerable to him.

Continuing to rise, the mind next reaches the center between the eyebrows, and the aspirant experiences what is known as savikalpa samadhi. He sees God, talks to Him, and knows His love and grace. Yet, even in this exalted state, there still remains the sense of ego or duality. As Sri Ramakrishna used to say: "In this state one sees the blissful light of God shining through the thin veil of ego which still persists. A great longing then arises in the heart of the aspirant to reach complete union with God. With intensified yearning he struggles to overcome the last traces of the ego which separates him from God, until at last his mind soars to the *sahashrara,* the highest level of consciousness, and he becomes one with God. Then it is that he can truly say: 'I am Brahman!' 'I and my Father are one!' "

Art and Religion

Aldous Huxley

DOES ART hold up the mirror to its period? Or does every period hold up the mirror to its art?

Does the artist follow or lead? Or does he walk alone, heeding only the categorical imperatives of his talent and the inner logic of the tradition within which he works?

Is he the representative of his epoch? Or does he stand for a constituency no wider than that particular class of talented persons—his predecessors, contemporaries, and successors—to which, by the predestination of his heredity, he happens to belong?

All these questions can be correctly answered now in the affirmative, now in the negative, now with a simultaneous yes and no. There are no general rules; there are only particular cases; and most of these cases exist, so far as we are concerned, in a thick night of ignorance.

Here, for example, is the case that presents itself to every tourist who goes to Rome—the fascinatingly enigmatic case of baroque art and seventeenth-century Catholicism. In what way were the two related? What was the nature of the connection between the art forms of the period and the religious experiences of those who lived through it?

Three hundred years after the event all that we know for certain is that the personages represented in baroque religious art are all in a state of chronic emotional excitement. They wave their arms, roll their eyes, press hands to palpitating bosoms, sometimes, in an excess of feeling, swoon away into unconsciousness. We look at them with a mixture of aesthetic admiration and moral distaste, then start to speculate about the men and women who were contemporary with them. Was their religious life as wildly

73

agitated as the life of these creatures of the painters' and sculptors' imagination? And, if so, had the art been modeled on their agitation, or was their agitation due to familiarity with an art that had become agitated for purely aesthetic reasons? Or, finally, was there no agitation in the real world corresponding to that prevailing in the worlds of painting and sculpture? Baroque artists were tired of doing what their predecessors had done and were committed by the inner logic of their tradition to an exploration of the inordinate; therefore the figures above the altars had to gesticulate in a studied frenzy. But the religious life of the people who worshiped at those altars—had that become significantly different from the religious life of the men and women of other periods? Were there not then, as always, a few ardent contemplatives and actives, imperfectly leavening a great lump of the legalistic and the Corybantic, the time-serving and the lukewarm?

I myself incline to the last alternative. Environment is never the sole determinant, and heredity is always at work, producing every variety of physique and temperament at every period of history. All the potentialities of human nature exist at all times, and at all times (in spite of an environment which may be unfavorable to some of them) practically all the potentialities are to some extent actualized. One has only to read Salimbene's *Chronicle* and Law's *Serious Call* in order to realize that there were as many irreligious people in the ages of faith as there were pietists in the ages of reason. The Byzantines who went mad about trinitarian theology were the same Byzantines who went mad about the chariot races. And our own age of atomic physics is also a notable age of astrology and numerology. At every period there exists, not a synthesis, but a mere brute collocation of opposites and incompatibles. And yet at any given epoch there is only one prevailing style of art, in terms of which painters and sculptors treat of a strictly limited number of subjects. Art may be defined, in this context, as a process of selection and transformation, whereby an unmanageable multiplicity is reduced to a semblance, at least, of unity. Consequently we must never expect to find in art a reflection of contemporary reality as it is actually experienced by human beings in all their congenital and acquired variety. Thus, from a study of the restrained and formalized art of the Italian *trecento* who could infer the existence of those wild religious revivals, which were so characteristic a fea-

ture of the period? And, conversely, who from the
frenzies of the baroque could infer the facts of sixteenth-
and seventeenth-century mysticism? Looking at a Carlo
Dolci Magdalen, who could guess what St. John of the
Cross had said about true charity—that it is a matter, not
of feeling, but of the will? Or who, with Bernini's St.
Teresa before his eyes, would ever suspect that Bernini's
contemporary, Charles de Condren, had deplored the
weakness which caused ecstatics to receive God *si ani-
malement?* The truth would seem to be that while the
great masses of the people remained, as ever, indifferent
or fitfully superstitious, and while the masters of the spiritual life preached a worship of the Spirit in spirit, the
artists of the time chose to glorify a Christianity of thrills
and visceral yearnings, now violent, now cloyingly sentimental. And they chose to do so for reasons connected, not
with the problems of life, but with those of art. Their
painting and sculpture did not, and indeed could not, reflect the manifold religious experience of the time, nor did
the religious experience of most of their contemporaries
reflect the prevailing art. Art and religious life went their
separate ways, the artists using religion as their opportunity for developing a baroque expressionism, and the religious using this art as an instrument for achieving the
various kinds of experience for which their temperaments
had fitted them. And precisely the same relations between
religion and art had existed when the "Primitives" were
using a multiform Catholicism as an opportunity for
creating one particular kind of static composition, and
when the religious were using these works as instruments
for the practice now of revivalism, now of contemplation,
now of magic.

From Rome and the baroque let us pass for a moment
to Tuscany and the rococo. A few miles from Siena there
stands among the vineyards a large Carthusian monastery,
called Pontignano, now inhabited by a score of peasant
families. In the old days each of the monks occupied an
apartment of three rooms—a kitchen, a bedroom and a
tiny oratory. The front doors of these apartments give on
to the cloisters and at the back are little walled gardens,
where a man could grow vegetables and dig his own
grave. Every brother lived independently of all the rest, a
solitary in a community of solitaries, a mute among the
silent. Most of the buildings at Pontignano date from the
fourteenth century, but were refurbished by an interior

decorator of the eighteenth. Under his direction the church was adorned with an enormous high altar of wood, painted to look like marble, and the little oratories, in which the monks said their private prayers, were stuccoed over with rococo twiddles, till they looked like the boudoirs of so many provincial Pompadours. To us, with our incorrigible sense of history this conjunction of St. Bruno and Louis XV seems deliriously incongruous. But how did it strike the monks who actually prayed in those oratories? Did they suddenly start to think, feel, and behave like those libertine *abbés*, whom we associate with that kind of decoration? Surely not. "Never reformed, because never deformed," the Carthusian order held on its way regardless of changes in aesthetic fashion. In their newly plastered oratories the brethren meditated on death, just as their predecessors had meditated when the decorations were baroque or Renaissance, Gothic or Romanesque. Styles change, empires rise and fall; but death remains itself, a brute fact, sooner or later, of every individual's experience—a fact that has no history and to which, in consequence, all historical changes, whether political or economic, scientific or artistic, are completely irrelevant. The Pompadourish art in the Pontignano oratories tells us nothing whatever about contemporary Carthusian religion, which was centered, as ever, upon the contemplation of death. All we learn from it is that, when eighteenth-century monks found it necessary to restore ancient buildings, the only restorers available, in an age that was still innocent of pastiche and antiquarian forgery, were men brought up in the current tradition of art.

In our own days the religious are worse off than were the monks of Pontignano. Not living rococo, but the bogus-medieval, or some atrocious piece of mass-produced *bondieuserie* is all that they can find for their purposes. And yet, in spite of the nullity of modern religious art, religion, in all its aspects from the fetishistic to the contemplative, continues to flourish and to produce its good or evil fruits. Man is a whole and so, perhaps, is society; but they are wholes divided, like ships, into watertight compartments. On one side of a bulkhead is art, on the other, religion. There may be good wine in one compartment, bilge water in the other. The connection between the two is not by pipe or osmosis, but only from above, only for the intellect that looks down and can see both simultaneously and recognize them as belonging (by juxtaposition rather than by fusion) to the same individual or social whole.

Spiritual Talks

Swami Turiyananda

On Sannyas

THE LIFE OF renunciation is most difficult; it requires and necessitates living cautiously. One must be very alert and circumspect, never retaliating but graciously enduring. Sow retaliation, and you will reap retaliation. A sannyasin's life is no child's play; it is the great attempt to go beyond all life. And that sannyasin alone will find liberation and freedom whose mind and heart dwell constantly on good, pure, holy thoughts.

On Faith and Grace

One must beware of self-delusion. Those who have absolute trust in God will be at once purified through His grace though they have committed heinous sins before. To a mountain-high heap of cotton, apply a spark of fire. The whole mass will be consumed in an instant. To a room which has been dark for thousands of years, bring a light. Will the darkness leave gradually or immediately? The Lord says in the *Gita*: "Even if a very wicked man worships Me, with devotion to none else, he should be regarded as good, for he has rightly resolved. Soon he becomes righteous, and attains to eternal peace. O son of Kunti, boldly canst thou proclaim that My devotee is never destroyed." Should the greatest villain resign himself entirely to God, he must be welcomed as a devotee. Soon, very soon, he will be transformed into a righteous person. Through God's grace he no longer remains a villain but becomes a pious man. By one who surrenders himself to God, no sin can possibly be committed though many misdeeds may have been committed previously.

On the Relationship with God

When one feels oneself as body, one must consider oneself as the servant of the Lord; when one thinks of oneself as the jiva, the individualized soul, one must consider oneself as a part of Him; and when one feels oneself as the Atman, one is the same as the Lord Himself.

On Happiness

Man tries so strenuously to make himself happy. But there is no success or happiness unless God wills it. Happiness or freedom can be realized in two ways, by identifying oneself with God or by living in eternal self-surrender to Him. Apart from Him there is no freedom of will or happiness.

On Passions

Never let pride delude you into thinking that you have gained control over the passions. For if such becomes your belief, you will soon experience their sharp aliveness. Continually pray, "O Lord, save me from all passions." Passions will last as long as the body lasts, but through His grace they become less and less potent and demanding.

Continence is essential for divine realization. If one can maintain brahmacharya for twenty-eight years, one will realize bhakti, jnana, everything. Lust is called manasya, born in the mind. Only a hero can conquer the senses and go beyond them to the superconscious planes.

On Self-reliance or Self-confidence

Reliance on one's apparent self leads to ruin. To presume to be all-knowing is extremely harmful. Self-reliance or self-confidence means faith in the higher Self. To persist in remaining what one already is or in holding on to one's preconceived opinions at any cost—such self-importance is most unprofitable.

On Worship

One can never be emancipated by adoring a man as man. One must look upon him as God. However much he may have attained in spiritual wisdom and dispassion, however highly endowed with spiritual powers he may be, the worship of him, the man, will not effect liberation. He must be perceived as God Himself. Without such consciousness, worship of him may serve to communicate his spiritual qualities and powers, but nothing more. If one worships a divine incarnation, God-realization is surely granted.

ON HALF-HEARTEDNESS AND SURRENDER

Just see! Most frequently God is nothing more than a matter of words, a verbal expression. A little meditation, a little japam and this is considered sufficient religion. What a life of poverty! The heart must burst with hunger for Him. Nothing but complete self-surrender to Him will satisfy such intense longing. You call Him the inner controller, omniscient and omnipresent, and still you waver and fear to surrender yourself to Him! Thinkest thou that thou wilt realize God the Mother by hypocritical devotion? No, no, this is not a sweet in a child's hand that thou wilt cajole it out of Her. There is no deceiving God. He sees all. If you love anything other than God and do not renounce all for Him, you cannot realize Him. If one considers God to be all in all, how can one find joy in worldly things?

ON RELYING ON GOD

"None else; He alone is my all in all." When one has this attitude, utter dependence, reliance, self-surrender, then one is on the right path. Now you are depending on earthly things, on wealth, man, and learning. Why do we not rely on God instead of our money, our relatives, our friends? "But, O king, know that He is the treasure of those who have nothing. When nothing will intervene between you and Him, then you will realize Him. If, O man, thou wilt cross the ocean of relative existence, thou must give up desires for earthly things."

The Master used to say, "Do whatever you like after making the knowledge of oneness your own." That is to say, know the Lord as the soul of your soul, the life of your life, the eye of your eye, and love Him. Nought else but this is true devotion. Supreme devotion is impossible so long as the smallest desire remains in the mind.

ON THE PLACE AND PRIVILEGE OF BEING MAN

Eating, sleeping, fear, and sexual intercourse—these are the common features of animal and man. The special privilege of man is that he possesses the knowledge of discernment, the gift which allows him to distinguish right from wrong, to make moral judgments. The lower in the scale of evolution a man is, the greater is his pleasure in sense objects. The higher in the evolutionary climb a man is, the greater is his joy in knowledge—a very subtle but intense joy of which those of lower growth remain ignorant and unappreciative. Just observe the multitudes. Their days are spent in sensuous delights, feasting, drinking, playing, hunting, running after women. Are they not even as beasts? If we neglect to refine and elevate our faculties, of what advantage is it to be born a man? Those whose minds have been and are being refined can never stoop to such things.

ON DESIRELESSNESS, WORK, AND TRUE PRAYER

However great a man may be in word and deed, there will be a day when he will have to understand and become desireless. Having attained that state he may again take up work through the will of God. Work will not tighten your bondage if it is work commanded by and executed for a man of realization, who desires for you nothing but good and to whom you have surrendered your all. Such work becomes a key which unlocks bondage. Let your prayer be: "Do not give me such work to do as will make me forget Thee: and wherever Thou keepest me, may I ever remember Thee."

Never utter such a selfish prayer as, "Give me this; do not give me that." Your little selfish ego enters the activity when you do not want to do this thing or that thing. There are many who fear work and actually try to escape and avoid it. In so doing their bondage and selfishness become stronger and greater. Let prayer for bhakti be your prayer. Be always alert and ready to obey His commands. And let the prayer be ever on your lips, "May I keep Thee in mind under all conditions! May I never fall into any company other than Thy devotees!"

ON THE MIND

Is it possible for that state of alertness, awareness, to come automatically? You must indeed practice first. Try consciously again and again to correct yourself; then you will begin to find that your mind has become its own monitor. People want to reach and attain that state immediately. Practice and the skill of self-discipline lead there. The impure is yourself. When you refer to "I" you really mean that impure portion, the selfish "I." The more you think of God, the more He forms and grows within until at last the impure portion vanishes completely and you become He.

It is you who must govern your own mind. None else can do that for you. Again and again the Master has said, "You must try a little. Not until then will the guru reveal the truth." From experience I can tell you that if you advance one step toward God, He advances ten steps toward you. If you do not make the effort no one can be of any help to you. If in your exertion you meet difficulties, we can help you for we also have traveled the same path. Do not let the mental disease of idleness control your mind, for with it the mind refuses to do anything.

It is well to analyze one's mind very carefully. Once the Master requested me to increase infinitely my lust, which caused me to be greatly amazed. He then explained his meaning of lust as being the desire to get, secure, have. Then he said, "Desire to get Him and increase this desire greatly."

ON DEVOTION

Will not the Lord do anything for His devotee? Oh yes, He will, but you must first become a devotee, feeling devotion and loving Him. Bhakti, devotion, is no trifling thing. To obtain it, the surrender and gift of your mind, life, everything is necessary. If that is not possible, then let tears flow for not having attained love for Him. If you feel miserable because you lack Him, know that He is very near you and that the vision of Him and infinite bliss are not far away. Be miserable if you have not realized God, and the more this mood grows the more you will earn His grace. Intensify it still more and yet more.

There are two forms of bhakti. First, the ritualistic or

obligatory devotion entailing the practice of prescribed amounts of japam. Second, there is the loving devotion. At this stage the devotee thinks ardently of God and finds no pleasure in things unrelated to God. For either of these, perseverance is absolutely necessary. To discontinue practice if a little effort does not produce the desired result is folly. Let it be said of you as was said of another, that he practiced so intensely that an anthill grew around him.

ON MEDITATION

Meditation begins with the unification of the meditator, the object of meditation, and the act of meditation. When there is no longer a separation between these three one may be said to be meditating. Japam becomes functional when a portion of the mind continually repeats the sacred name automatically. When this is experienced then it may be said one has advanced a little in japam.

The jnanis meditate in the head, the bhaktis in the heart. Spiritual consciousness expands as a result of heart meditation, and with the expansion of consciousness there no longer remains any fixed location of meditation.

Japam means that one should utter the sacred name at the same time meditating on His form, thinking of Him and loving Him. The mere repetition of God's name while the mind is attached to worldly things will avail nothing. It is essential that we somehow in all ways make Him our own while performing all actions and duties.

ON DIVINE FORMS

The Master possessed and exhibited two moods. Sometimes he did not like divine forms, not even his beloved Kali. At such times his mind was immersed in the absolute. At other times he declared that he could not exist without divine forms, declaring to Divine Mother that he did not desire to see her formless aspect. He who rejects everything and becomes lost in the formless Brahman is as one-sided as the one who realizes only the forms of God and not the formless absolute aspect. There must be a balance sought.

ON YOGA

"The first door of yoga is the control of speech, non-acceptance of gifts, nonexpectation, desirelessness, and

love of solitude." This verse had a profound influence on
me, for I used to indulge in much talk. When I read it, I
thought, "What! I have not entered even the first door of
yoga!" I then resolved to control my speech, I lived by myself, acted as I thought best, and spoke to no one.

ON ATTAINING GOD

Sri Ramakrishna used to say, "A man can be sincere
only by virtue of merits acquired in many past lives."
Swamiji has nicely said, "God is not a commodity like fish
or vegetables to be had for a certain price." The sages
have stated in the scriptures the several paths by which
they attained God. One has stated that one should perform worship in such and such a way. Another says that
one should practice japam. Narada says, "Just as the river
flows intently toward the sea in order to meet it, not
changing its course, even so he who seeks God should
move towards Him and Him alone giving up all other
concerns." It is said in the *Gita,* "Persons who worship
Me alone without being attached to anything else, to them
thus ever zealously engaged, I carry what they lack and
preserve what they already have."

ON PROGRESSING TOWARD GOD

One will surely know within oneself if he is progressing
toward God. Others also know of the progress. All passions, lust, anger, and greed wane; attachment to and for
objects of the senses become less and less, and with detachment peace of heart grows.

The real peace is far off, however. But when you see
that a man's desire for sense enjoyments is growing less
and less and his love is extending over all beings, then you
may know that he is progressing toward God. Simply repeating the holy name will not do. If a hole of attachment
is in the mind the result of all japam runs through it even
as a man irrigating his field the whole day finds that his
field is waterless because of a hole in the wall.

ON STEALING, DEPENDENCE, SLANDER

"He who constantly steals others' property may perform great charities, still he does none. He who always depends on others may live long, yet he lives not. He who

always slanders others may repeat the holy name, yet he does it not." So said Kabir.

What will it avail if one makes charity with money stolen from others? To live long on the charity of others is as good as death. It is useless for a slanderer to repeat the name of God. This is why Jesus said: "Therefore if thou bringest thy gift to the altar, and there rememberest that thy brother hath ought against thee: leave there thy gift before the altar, and go thy way; first be reconciled to thy brother, and then come and offer thy gift."

On Love and Lust

Love and lust are two things very closely allied. Hence Sri Ramakrishna used to say, "Lust is blind, but love is pure and resplendent." It is lust if you have the idea of man, and love if you have the idea of God in your beloved.

On Control of the Senses

All trouble is over if the palate and the sex impulse are conquered. When Sri Chaitanya went to Kesava Bharati for initiation into sannyas, the latter remarked, "You are in the bloom of youth and so surprisingly handsome. Who will be bold enough to initiate you into sannyas?" Sri Chaitanya replied, "Sir, you usually examine an aspirant before conferring sannyas on him. If you find me qualified, you will naturally be inclined to initiate me also. So please examine me and see if I am fit for it." Bharati said to Sri Chaitanya, "Put out your tongue." The guru placed some sugar on the tongue. It remained dry and scattered in the air when blown out. There was no need for further examination.

A man who has controlled all other senses except the palate cannot be considered a master of his senses. When the hankering of the palate is controlled, everything else is controlled.

When the palate is controlled the sex impulse is also controlled. Unless the senses are brought under control there cannot be any spiritual progress. Throughout the *Gita* there is repeated mention of this: "Therefore, O best of the Bharatas, control thou the senses first, and thereby kill this sinful propensity of lust, which destroys one's knowledge and realization."

ON STEADINESS OF THE MIND

One test of the steadiness of the mind is the steadiness detected in demeanor, look, and appearance. As soon as the mind becomes steady the look, outlook, and vision become steady. There no longer remains any restiveness in one's looks and movements.

ON SPIRITUAL POWERS

Powers sometimes come to the spiritual aspirant of themselves, but the moment one places value upon them his spiritual progress is halted. Nor do these powers last. If they are used for selfish ends and purposes their loss is assured. These all belong to the Lord and He makes them pass through you. It is like Sri Ramakrishna's parable: "A spiritual aspirant acquired some supernatural powers which made him proud. But he was a sincere man. So the Lord came to him in the form of a Brahmana and, praising his powers, wanted to have some test. An elephant was passing by. The man, gratified by the request, took some dust and uttering some mantras threw it on the elephant, which immediately fell dead. Then the Brahmana wished to see if he could restore life. This also the aspirant accomplished in a similar manner. After witnessing all these the Brahmana said, 'Well sir, the elephant died and then revived. But of what spiritual gain have these powers been to you?' Saying this He disappeared, and the aspirant was brought to his senses."

ON THE MIND

Sri Ramakrishna used to say that the mind of ordinary men is generally confined to the three lower spiritual centers, while the mind of the spiritual aspirant rises to the center in the heart, whence it ascends higher still to the center in the head, when he attains the state of samadhi. Sri Ramakrishna used to say that gold is gold whether it lies in a ditch or is kept in a room. If power is latent in someone, it will manifest itself wherever you may put him. Have faith in God and pray to Him for devotion.

ON DESTINY

There is nothing preordained. In a way everything depends on our personal exertion. I do not, however, mean to say that destiny is altogether a fiction. Manifest thy manliness by overthrowing destiny through thine own power. To one who is endowed with personal exertion even destiny becomes favorable. God helps those who help themselves. Relying on destiny people often tend toward degradation. Free will also comes under this personal exertion. People make mistakes through their own fault, and then lay the blame on destiny.

We do not know which of the two blades of a pair of scissors is responsible for the cutting. Even so are we unable to ascertain the measure to which destiny and personal exertion are responsible for the accomplishment of an act. And so we conclude that both are equally responsible. It is our present tendency to exert ourselves rather than to wait for destiny to help us out—exertion therefore is within our own control. There is, however, such a thing as resignation to the Lord. It is no weakness to say, "Thy will be done."

ON RENUNCIATION

In the *Upanishads* there is a dialogue between Yagnavalkya and Maitreyi. Yagnavalkya reached the state of sannyas as the natural outcome of knowledge. He said to his two wives, "Now the time has come for my taking up the monastic life. So whatever I have, you both divide between yourselves." Then Maitreyi said, "What shall I do with that which won't give me immortality?" Hearing this Yagnavalkya said, "Maitreyi, I used to love you before, but now I love you all the more." Then he gave her instructions, and she too renounced the world.

But can one give up the householder's life though it is no longer appealing, when there are wife and children? What then will be their fate? It is selfishness, pure and simple. To be in the world and maintain the family, to fulfill one's duties—this also is certainly religion. Nothing will be gained by giving up all of a sudden. One cannot climb to the roof at one bound; one has to ascend step by step. Sri Ramakrishna used to say, "A fruit plucked before maturity rots and gets spoiled. A wound bleeds if you remove the scab before time, but when the wound is healed it drops off of itself." What wonderful illustrations these are! If a man happened to be married, then later regretted the fact and informed Sri Ramakrishna of his intention to embrace the monastic life, he would say, "Wait, do not give up the world. If you are sincere everything will be set right. You have only to pursue faithfully the course laid down in the scriptures. It won't be good for you to leave the world. You have got children; go on doing your duty by them—do it unselfishly." To say that you are renouncing the world with the object of calling upon God would be utterly false. Of course one should devote time to spiritual practices, and this is the time.

Whenever anyone spoke to Sri Ramakrishna about giving up the world, he would say, "If you are sincere you will find the circumstances gradually becoming favorable." He never said, "Leave everything and come away." "If you are sincere," that was what he used to say, because he knew the contents of everyone's mind.

There is no freedom, no respite, until you have done your duties. That which you have given up without performing will be waiting for you—only to appear again. You cannot save yourself by flight. To take up the monastic life is advantageous, while to take up the householder's life is disadvantageous—such considerations as these are futile. You cannot come to the next stage without performing the duties of the previous one.

Aspire after higher things, but never shirk the present duties. The case of those who live a celibate life from their boyhood is different. They have come with such good samskaras that even if they live in the world, they will live there as sannyasins. You are what you are—you cannot jump to a higher stage. Avoidance is not good, nor is it possible. Do your duties in the world but think of God all the while.

ON CONSISTENCY, DETERMINATION, AND OPPORTUNITY

One should be consistent in thought and word. It does not do to allow one's lips to utter that which the mind does not approve. What the mind thinks the lips too should express and vice versa. What comes out from the lips must be carried out at all cost. One who thus practices this internal oneness finds externalities becoming favorable.

Sri Ramakrishna disliked a happy-go-lucky spirit. He used to say of Swamiji, "See what an heroic temperament he has. As soon as he sets his mind on a thing, he applies himself heart and soul to it." Circumstances may or may not be favorable, but who cares? We must strain every nerve to accomplish the thing. If you are determined to do it at any cost, you will find that great obstacles which you thought would overpower you ultimately turn out to help you. But you must struggle sincerely. Does one find circumstances always propitious? Consider what you have got to do as your duty and go on. Are you not undecaying and immortal always? So why should you go about seeking favorable circumstances?

He who wishes to think upon the Lord after all of his engagements have been finished is like the fool who wishes to bathe in the sea after the waves have subsided. Nonsense! Does that moment ever come? Instead of waiting, face the waves, have your bath and come out. The sea always remains the same. So in this world, you must manage to call upon the Lord in the midst of these waves. Surely it is like a wild-goose chase to be always on the lookout for opportunities. Opportunity is now or never. Apply yourself to it, and disadvantages will turn into advantages. Try your best and you will reap an excellent harvest.

ON STEADFASTNESS OF DEVOTION

One must pray from the bottom of one's heart to have a steadfast devotion for God. To make oneself fit, association with holy men and occasional retirement into solitude are necessary. If one is sincere the Lord Himself prepares the way. You have to offer this mind to Him. You have to churn out butter first, then only will it remain unmixed with water. The greatness of a man is in proportion to the amount of self-examination he has made—the degree to which he has an intimate knowledge of his own inner motives impelling his external behavior and is able to control those inner motives rightly. Self-examination is a very difficult task, for it is extremely difficult to detect the tricks which the mind plays.

ON HOLY ASSOCIATION

One is sure to improve in holy company whether one comes as a good or an evil person. It is as one entering a perfume shop; the scent enters the nostrils irrespective of the character of the one entering. Few people are inclined or desire to associate with holy persons, and but few have the capacity to do so. How frequently Sri Ramakrishna would be visited by devotees and their friends. And while engaged in listening to the Master their companions would whisper, "Well, let us go. How long will you be listening?" The devotees, not wishing to leave, the friends would whisper back, "So you remain here, we shall be waiting in the boat."

Holy association is bound to produce good effects, for only life can communicate life. A round body can only give a round shadow. What a tremendous difference there is between reading and hearing a lecture!

On Chastity, Purity, and the Mind

If once bad influences have a hold on the mind it is very difficult to get rid of them. If the youths are convinced of the utility of chastity and the evils of its opposite, they may later marry and become superior citizens. For such as are spiritually bent are free from temptation. Chastity is the very bedrock of spirituality. Unless one is chaste, the mind is never steady. The body is formed of the elements and is swayed by thought. If the mind is disturbed the elements are destroyed. Therefore it should be carefully protected. Only a steady mind can give rise to a bright understanding.

The best element in our body is preserved by chastity. If there is no chastity the mind becomes unsteady. Then the image of the chosen deity is no more clearly reflected in it. Sri Ramakrishna used to say, "If the coating of mercury is all right, then the mirror gives a perfect image, but if there is any break, the image is defective." What is the mind? It is that which gives rise to thought—where the first impression is received. So it is clear that if the very source of thought is agitated, meditation is out of the question. It is difficult to escape if the mind has already received bad impressions. Hence the Lord says in the *Gita:* "Therefore, O Arjuna, first control the organs and kill the wicked lust, which destroys both knowledge and realization."

If the mind, which is outgoing in its activities, is ever so slightly deflected from the ideal, it goes down and down, even as a playball inadvertently dropped at the head of a staircase goes down bumping from one step to another, until it reaches the end of its fall.

ON THE KNOWLEDGE OF BRAHMAN

Does one attain to the knowledge of Brahman by practicing chastity for twelve years?

Undoubtedly. Through the power of ojas the knowledge of Brahman unfolds itself. The knowledge already exists, we have but to unfold it. If you can maintain chastity for twelve years, the mind becomes steady, with the result that the knowledge unfolds itself.

ON ATTACHMENT AND DETACHMENT

Swamiji used to say, "Ready to attach and ready to detach any minute!" We take up a work and get attached to it—we cannot detach ourselves from it. This should not be. We must have power to give up at will—to leave everything behind, for nothing is really ours.

Look at Sri Ramakrishna. Hriday was ordered to depart from Dakshineswar. The durwan came and said to Sri Ramakrishna, "You will have to leave this place." "What do you mean? It is not I, but Hriday who leaves," replied Sri Ramakrishna. The man said, "No, my master has ordered that both of you should go." This decided the question. Sri Ramakrishna put on his slippers and moved toward the gate. Trailokya Babu saw this from the concert room, ran and fell at his feet, saying, "Sir, why are *you* going? I have not asked *you* to leave." Without a word Sri Ramakrishna returned. Just see, there was not the least attachment to his renunciation. What a furor we would have made! Had we been in his place, we would have given the Babu a piece of our mind. Sri Ramakrishna said nothing. He was ready to go or ready to stay.

Sri Ramakrishna used to be shabbily dressed, so much so that one day a man mistook him for a gardener and ordered him to pluck a rose. This he did immediately. Sometime later that man became aware of his error and stammered an apology. Sri Ramakrishna assured him that there was certainly nothing wrong, that by all means one asking for help should be assisted.

ON MEDITATION AND OBSTRUCTION

Meditation can be on divine forms as well as on Om. As one goes on meditating, the mind becomes absorbed in Om. And as one continues repeating Om and reflecting on its meaning the mind becomes steady. Through surrender to God all obstacles to concentration of the mind are destroyed and one realizes oneself.

Patanjali gives a list of distracting influences to yoga:

1. One may become diseased, become mad, or have some serious illness which prevents further progress.

2. Lassitude which is inaction of the mind or torpidity.

3. Doubt which is cogitating whether a thing is this or that.

4. Inadvertence which is not doing that which will lead to samadhi or yoga.

5. Laziness which is the want of proper care or exertion owing to an excess of tamas or dullness.

6. Attachment which is attraction for sense-objects.

7. Delusion which is mistaking one thing for another.

8. Nonattaining of heights, which is not reaching the higher states of samadhi.

9. Inability to stay on in a particular state of samadhi already attained.

These disturb the mind and prevent yoga. All of the obstructions are removed if one meditates on Om. But then, a man may not be disposed to meditate at all.

ON THE NAME OF GOD

The name of God will destroy the very roots of the disease of nescience. Therefore one should practice repeating it even against one's wishes. He who gives it up is lost. The *Gita* says, "The mind, O Arjuna, is controlled by practice and non-attachment." It also says, "One should slowly withdraw one's mind from sense-objects through patient discrimination. Fixing the mind on the Self, one must no longer think of anything else."

ON DECISION, PERSISTENCE, STEADFASTNESS IN PRACTICE

The author of the yoga sutras says, "By carefully persisting in practice, for a long time without intermission, concentration becomes steady." We must attain to a steady concentration. The young plant needs to be hedged around, but when the tree is big, it requires protection no more. We must have steadfastness to the ideal. As soon as we decide that a certain course is right, we must resolve to give up our life for it. We must have decision in our character. "O Arjuna, the decisive judgment here is one, but people of unsettled minds have innumerable varying ideas." We must decide on a particular course and devote our whole life to it.

ON A DISCIPLE

The best disciple is he who acts in anticipation of the master's wish; he who acts after the orders are issued is the mediocre disciple; and the worst disciple is he who gets the order but neglects to carry it out.

ON POWER

Books on yoga say that all power is in us. We must control the mind through proper discipline; then only will its powers be manifested. For the accumulation of spiritual power absolute continence is needed.

ON DISCIPLESHIP

It is very difficult to be a disciple. Have you not heard the story? A man wanted to be a disciple, so he found a guru and said, "Sir, make me a disciple." The guru replied, "Will you be able to be one? A disciple has to draw water, fetch wood, and serve the teacher. Will you be able to do all of this?" And the man replied, "And what has the guru to do?" The teacher made answer, "Not much to speak of. He sits at ease and now and then gives a little instruction. That is all." Then the man said, "If you think it difficult for me to be a disciple, why do you not make me a guru instead?"

How strange it is everyone wants to reap the harvest without sowing the seed. The fit man overcomes his defects bit by bit. If you try to do it all of a sudden, you will not succeed, for they will persist. Therefore one should withdraw the mind slowly.

The Reality of Religion [1]

Rabindra Nath Tagore

IF I HAVE ACCEPTED the honor to address this distinguished gathering, it is only out of respect to the memory of the great saint with whose centenary the present parliament is associated. I venerate Sri Ramakrishna because he, in an arid age of religious nihilism, proved the truth of our spiritual heritage by realizing it, because the largeness of his spirit could comprehend seemingly antagonistic modes of sadhana (spiritual practice), and because the simplicity of his soul shames for all time the pomp and pedantry of pontiffs and pundits.

I have nothing new to tell you, no esoteric truth to propound to you. I am a mere poet, a lover of men and of creation. But since love gives a certain insight, I may perhaps claim to have sometimes caught the hushed voice of humanity and felt its suppressed longing for the infinite. I hope I do not belong to those who, born in a prison house, never have the good luck to know that it is a prison, who are blissfully unaware that the costliness of their furniture and profuseness of the provisions for their comfort act as invisible walls in a castle of vanity that not only rob them of their freedom but even of the desire for it.

The degree of this freedom is measured according to our realization of the infinite, whether in the outer world or in the inner life. In a narrow room we may have as much space as is necessary for living and for the exercise of our muscles; the food may be more than sufficient, it may even be sumptuous; yet our inborn craving for what

[1]Substance of an address given at the Sri Ramakrishna Centenary Parliament of Religions, 1936.

we may call the more, the unattained, if not altogether killed, remains unsatisfied. We are deprived of the infinite, which is freedom of range, both in the outer world as well as in the ceaseless variety of the world of our experience.

But a more profoundly intimate conception of the infinite lies in that intensity of our consciousness, which we can only attain when we realize ultimate value in some ideal of perfection, when in the realization of some fact of our life we become aware of an indefinable truth that immensely transcends it. We, in our human nature, have a hunger for Bhuma (God, the absolute), for immensity, for something a great deal more than what we need immediately for the purposes of life. Men all through their history have been struggling to realize this truth according to the unfolding of their idea of the boundless, and have been gradually changing their methods and plans of existence, constantly meeting failures, but never owning final defeat.

We find that animals have their evolution along the line of the race. They have their individual life which ends with their death. But even in them there is a touch of the infinite which urges them to outlive their own life in the life of the race, accepting sufferings and making sacrifices for its sake. The spirit of sacrifice in the parents is this touch of the infinite—the motive power which makes the race life possible, which helps to develop those faculties in them that will enable their descendants to find better opportunity for food and shelter.

But in human beings has been further evolved a sense of the infinite that goes far beyond the struggle for physical life which merely occupies extended time and extended space. Man has realized that a life of perfection is not merely a life of extension, but one which has its selfless enjoyment of the great and the beautiful.

After we have evolved this sense of the beautiful, of the good, of something that we call truth—which is deeper and larger than any number of facts—we have come into an altogether different atmosphere from that wherein the animals and trees have their existence. But we have come into this higher realm only very lately.

Ages and ages have passed, dominated by the life of what we call the self, which is intent upon seeking food and shelter, and upon the perpetuation of the race. But there is a mysterious region waiting for its full recognition, which does not entirely acknowledge loyalty to physical claims. Its mystery constantly troubles us and we are not yet fully at ease in this region. We call it spiritual. That word is vague, only because we have not yet been able to realize its meaning completely.

We are groping in the dark, not yet clear in our idea of the ultimate meaning at the center of this world. Nevertheless through the dim light which reaches us across the barriers of our physical existence, we seem to have a stronger faith in this spiritual life than in the physical. For even those who do not believe in the truth which we cannot define, but call by the name of spirit—even they are obliged to behave as though they did believe it to be true, or, at any rate, truer than the world which is evident to our senses. And so even they are often willing to accept death—the termination of this physical life—for the sake of the true, the good, and the beautiful. This fact expresses man's deeper urge for freedom, for liberation of itself in the realm of the limitless where he realizes his relationship with the truth which relates him to the universe in a disinterested spirit of love.

When Buddha preached maitri—the relationship of harmony—not only with human beings but with all creation, did he not have this truth in his mind that our treatment of the world is wrong when we solely treat it as a fact which can be known and used for our own personal needs? Did he not feel that the true meaning of creation can be understood only through love because it is an eternal expression of love which waits for its answer from our soul emancipated from the bondage of self? This emancipation cannot be negative in character, for love can never lead to negation. The perfect freedom is in a perfect harmony of relationship and not in a mere severance of bondage. Freedom has no content, and therefore no meaning, where it has nothing but itself. The soul's emancipation is in the fulfillment of its relation to the central truth of everything that there is, which is impossible to define because it comes at the end of all definitions.

The distinctive feature of materialism is the measurability of its outward expression, which is the same thing as the finiteness of its boundaries. And the disputes, civil and criminal, which have raged in the history of man, have mostly been over these same boundaries. To increase one's own bounds one has necessarily to encroach upon

those of others. So, because the pride of power is the
pride of quantity, pride of the mere number of its re-
cruits and victims, the most powerful telescope when
pointed in the direction of power, fails to reveal the shore
of peace across the sea of blood.

Such is the tragedy that so often besets our history
when this love of power, which is really the love of self,
domineers over the religious life of man, for then the only
means by which man could hope to set his spirit free,
itself becomes the worst enemy of that freedom. Of all
fetters those that falsely assume spiritual designations are
the most difficult to break, and of all dungeons the most
terrible are those invisible ones where men's souls are
imprisoned in self-delusion bred by vanity. The self-mag-
nification, with its consequent thwarting of the best in
man, that goes on unashamed when religion deadens into
sectarianism is a perverse form of worldliness under the
mask of religion; it constricts the heart into narrowness
much more effectively than the cult of the world based
upon material interests can ever do.

Let me try to answer the question as to what this spirit
is, for the winning of which all the great religions were
brought into being.

The evening sky is revealed to us in its serene aspect of
beauty though we know that from the fiery whirlpools
which are the stars, chaotic outbursts clash against one
another in a conflict of implacable fury. But over and
through it all there is spread a mysterious spirit of harmony, constantly modulating rebellious elements into
creative unity, evolving ineffable peace and beauty out of
the incoherently battling combatants perpetually struggling to elbow out their neighbors into a turmoil of dissolution.

And this great harmony, this everlasting Yea—this is
truth—that bridges the dark abysms of time and space,
reconciles contradictions, imparts perfect balance to the
unstable. This all-pervading mystery is what we call
spiritual in its essence. It is the human aspect of this
truth which all great personalities have made their own in
their lives and have offered to their fellow beings in the
name of various religions as means of peace and good will
—as vehicles of beauty in behavior, heroism in character,
noble aspiration, and achievement in all great civilizations.

But when these very religions travel far from their

sacred sources, they lose their original dynamic vigor, and degenerate into the arrogance of piety, into an utter emptiness crammed with irrational habits and mechanical practices; then is their spiritual inspiration befogged in the turbidity of sectarianism; then do they become the most obstinate obstruction that darkens our vision of human unity, piling up out of their accretions and refuse dead weights of unreason across our path of progress—till at length civilized life is compelled to free its education from the stifling coils of religious creeds. Such fratricidal aberrations, in the guise of spiritual excellence, have brought upon the name of God whom they profess to glorify uglier discredit than honest and defiant atheism could ever have done.

The reason is, because sectarianism, like some voracious parasite, feeds upon the religion whose color it assumes, exhausting it so that it knows not when its spirit is sucked dry. It utilizes the dead skin for its habitation, as a stronghold for its unholy instinct of fight, its pious vaingloriousness, fiercely contemptuous of its neighbors' articles of faith.

Sectarian votaries of a particular religion, when taken to task for the iniquitous dealings with their brethren which so deeply injure and insult humanity, immediately try to divert attention by glibly quoting noble texts from their own scriptures which preach love, justice, righteousness, and the divinity immanent in man—ludicrously unconscious of the fact that those constitute the most damaging incrimination of their usual attitude of mind. In taking up the guardianship of their religion they allow, on the one hand, physical materialism to invade it by falsely giving eternal value to external practices, often of primitive origin; and moral materialism on the other, by invoking sacred sanction for their forms of worship within the rigid enclosure of special privileges founded upon accident of birth, or conformity, irrespective of moral justification. Such debasement does not belong to any particular religion, but more or less to all religions, the records of whose impious activities are written in brothers' blood, and sealed with the indignities heaped upon them.

All through the course of human history it has become tragically evident that religions, whose mission is liberation of soul, have in some form or other ever been instrumental in shackling freedom of mind and even moral rights. The desecration of truth in unworthy hands—the truth which was meant to raise humanity morally and materially out of the dusky region of animality—is moreover followed by punishment, and thus we find that religious perversity is causing more blindness of reason and deadness of moral sensibility than any other deficiency in our education; just as the truth represented by science, when used for ignoble traffic, threatens us with annihilation. It has been the saddest experience of man to witness such violation of the highest products of civilization, to find the guardians of religion blessing the mailed fist of temporal power in its campaign of wholesale massacre and consolidation of slavery, and science joining hands with the same relentless power in its murderous career of exploitation.

When we come to believe that we are in possession of our God because we belong to some particular sect, it gives us a complete sense of comfort to feel that God is no longer needed, except for breaking with the greater unction the skulls of people whose idea of God, fortunately or unfortunately, differs from our own in theoretical details. Having thus made provision for our God in some shadowland of creed, we feel free to reserve all the space in the world of reality for ourselves—ridding it of the wonder of the infinite, making it as trivial as our own household furniture. Such unmitigated vulgarity only becomes possible when we have no doubt in our minds that we believe in God while our life ignores Him.

Great souls, like Ramakrishna Paramahamsa, have a comprehensive vision of truth; they have the power to grasp the significance of each different form of the reality that is one in all—but the masses of believers are unable to reconcile the conflict of codes and commands. Their timid and shrunken imagination, instead of being liberated by the vision of the infinite in religion, is held captive in bigotry and is tortured and exploited by priests and fanatics for uses hardly anticipated by those who originally received it.

Unfortunately, great teachers most often are surrounded by persons whose minds, lacking transparency of atmosphere, obscure and distort the ideas originating from the higher source. They feel smug satisfaction when the picture of their master which they offer shows features made somewhat in the pattern of their own personality. Consciously and unconsciously they reshape profound messages of wisdom in the mold of their own tortuous

understanding, carefully modifying them into conventional
platitudes in which they themselves find comfort and
which satisfy the habit-ridden mentality of their own community. Lacking the sensitiveness of mind which is necessary for the enjoyment of truth in its unadulterated
purity, they exaggerate it in an attempt at megalomaniac
enlargement according to their own insensate standard,
which is as absurdly needless for its real appraisement as
it is derogatory to the dignity of its original messengers.
The history of great men, because of their very greatness,
ever runs the risk of being projected on to a wrong background of memory where it gets mixed up with elements
that are crudely customary and therefore inertly accepted
by the multitude.

I say to you that if you are really lovers of truth, then
dare to seek it in its fullness in all the infinite beauty of
its majesty, but never be content to treasure up its vain
symbols in miserly seclusion within the stony walls of conventions. Let us revere the great souls in the sublime simplicity of their spiritual altitude which is common to them
all, where they meet in universal aspiration to set the
spirit of man free from the bondage of his own individual
ego, and of the ego of his race and of his creed; but in
that lowland of traditions, where religions challenge and
refute each other's claim and dogmas, there a wise man
must pass them by in doubt and dismay.

I do not mean to advocate a common church for mankind, a universal pattern to which every act of worship and
aspiration must conform. The arrogant spirit of sectarianism which so often uses either active or passive, violent
or subtle, methods of persecution, on the least provocation
or without any, has to be reminded of the fact that religion like poetry, is not a mere idea—it is expression. The
self-expression of God is in the variedness of creation;
and our attitude toward the infinite must in its expression
also have a variedness of individuality, ceaseless and un-
ending. When a religion develops the ambition of imposing
its doctrine on all mankind, it degrades itself into a
tyranny and becomes a form of imperialism. This is why
we find ruthless methods of autocracy in religious matters prevailing in most parts of the world, trampling flat
the expansion of the spirit of man under its insensitive
heels.

The attempts to make the one religion which is their
own, dominate all time and space, comes naturally to men

addicted to sectarianism. This makes it offensive to them to be told that God is generous in His distribution of love, and His means of communication with men have not been restricted to a blind lane stopping at one narrow point of history. If humanity ever happens to be overwhelmed with the universal flood of a bigoted exclusiveness, then God will have to make provision for another Noah's Ark to save His creatures from the catastrophe of spiritual desolation.

What I plead for is a living recognition of the neglected truth that the reality of religion has its basis in the truth of man's nature in its most intense and universal need and so must constantly be tested by it. Where it frustrates that need, and outrages its reason, it repudiates its own justification.

Let me conclude with a few lines from the great mystic poet of medieval India, Kabir, whom I regard as one of the greatest spiritual geniuses of our land:

> The jewel is lost in the mud,
> and all are seeking for it;
> some look for it in the east, and
> some in the west;
> some in the water and some amongst stones.
> But the servant Kabir has appraised
> it at its true value,
>   and has wrapped it with care
> in a corner of the mantle of his own heart.

Work and Worship

Swami Saradananda

ON THE REPETITION OF THE LORD'S NAME

SRI RAMAKRISHNA came to make religion easy, for earnest seekers were being burdened unnecessarily with the weight of so many rules and regulations. He taught that no special times or places are necessary for repeating the Lord's name and the worship of Him in the heart. Regardless of circumstances or surroundings, the name of the Lord can be chanted audibly or within secretly. The Master did not stress or give much importance to external observances. With regard to the means of worship he allowed much freedom. Choose for yourself that which suits you best. If you like to think of God with form, you will reach the goal; if you prefer to think of God without form, that is well also, for you will attain the same goal. Whichever is your choice, be steady, unwavering, persistent. Progress will be yours without fail.

Concerning the changing of clothes, the taking of baths, and other external observances before chanting the name of the Lord and worshiping Him in the heart, do so if possible; if you are unable to practice these traditional observances continue calling on Him unmindful of ought else save Him. The Master once sang a song to me and told me, "Assimilate any one of these ideas and you will reach the goal." The song which he sang went thus:

> O Lord, thou art my everything, the sole support of my life, the quintessence of reality. There is none else beside thee in this world whom I can call as my own.
>
> Thou art happiness, peace, help, wealth, knowledge, intellect, and strength; thou art the dwelling house and the pleasure garden; thou art the friend and relative.

102

Thou art this present life, the sole refuge; thou art the life hereafter and the heaven; thou art the injunction of the scriptures, the guru full of blessings, and the store of infinite bliss.

Thou art the way and the goal; thou art the creator and preserver and the worshiped; thou art the father that punishest thy child, the loving mother, and the storehouse of infinite bliss art thou.

ON DOUBTING THE EXISTENCE OF GOD

If there is doubt in your mind concerning the existence of God, then question Him thus: "I do not know whether thou existeth or not, whether thou art formless or with form. Do thou make known to me thy real nature." You will not remain long in uncertainty.

ON THE WAY OF SELFLESS WORK, OR KARMA YOGA

Through selfless work one's mind becomes purified; then arises knowledge and true devotion. Knowledge is the true nature of the Self which, being covered with ignorance, remains unmanifest. By the performance of selfless work, the covering of ignorance is removed. As the mind becomes increasingly pure, true knowledge begins to unfold; in purity knowledge and the knower become one. There is a story in the *Mahabharata* of a chaste woman who attained knowledge through service to her husband and through performing other household duties. In the *Gita* there is the teaching, "By work alone Janaka and others attained perfection."

ON SPIRITUAL PRACTICES WHICH SOMETIMES SEEM LIFELESS

If one follows the same routine every day it is quite natural that sometimes spiritual practices seem to be automatic. If there seems to be any particular portion of the sadhana on such days which appeals more than another, devote yourself to that specific portion with earnestness. Several days may follow in which certain other practices may be neglected. It matters little, for when the practices are again resumed you will find new delight in their performance.

Before you meditate, think of the Master. In so doing, good results will be assured. Sometimes think that the Lord is in everything and everywhere; that you are, as it were, immersed in Him even as a pot is immersed in the ocean. Let your thoughts be centered on the all-pervading existence whom the sages experience just as a man sees the sky overhead with his eyes wide open.

Benefit and progress can only be known through regular practice; therefore it becomes part of the necessary discipline to have and keep regular periods of time for the practice of spiritual exercises. These practices if performed regularly each day give to the practicer inner strength and inner joy and peace. Practice, and you will begin to feel, to experience for yourself. Why engage in idle talk, speculation, and pointless discussion? It is fruitless and leads to waste. Everyone talks, but no one does anything. Practice japam and meditation. Labor hard and you will know everything in time. Exertion brings its own reward. Why not practice as you have been instructed? See for yourself.

On the Finding of Pleasure in Thinking of the Master's Life

To find pleasure in anything, both the brain and the heart must unite. Through mere intellectualism one does not obtain pleasure. Intellectualism alone leads to lifelessness. If what you have read about the Master appeals to your heart, then alone you will obtain delight by thinking on his life and he in turn will seem to be alive, truly living.

On Outward Circumstances and Adjustment

The scriptures say that one can attain knowledge by practicing spiritual exercises while being engaged in work. It is not necessary to refrain from work. If the mind is drawn toward Him then, where is the need for change of environment? When nothing is possible without His will, then what is the use of planning? Is it not better to depend on Him and do as He wills? Moreover, if one changes one's environment it requires great effort to make adjustments to the new conditions. Therefore let the environment remain as it is and continue calling on the Lord. Overcome all circumstances and environment through

Him. When His will bids circumstances and environment change, then accept the change, not before.

ON WORK

Do the work at hand to the best of your abilities. It is necessary for you to plan and use various means for the fulfillment of your work. Plan well and choose the best means. That work which is assigned or which becomes your share, do it excellently, do it supremely well, not for honor or praise or notice, but because it is your offering to the Lord. It is not good to take up work aggressively, to take on more tasks. One soon finds that one cannot perform any of them well and the result is a disturbed mind clouded by worry and anxiety. This hinders spiritual progress.

ON REALIZING GOD

After one realizes God, the world seems to be a mere appearance like a mirage. One knows well that there is no water in a mirage. Even though there seems to appear a world with names and forms, it is but an illusion, it is maya and remains a nothing. One must first attain knowledge, then one returns to this world of diversity seeing everything as before surely, but no longer being attached or attracted to anything in it. Prior to realizing that a mirage is an illusion, one expects water, but when one has the knowledge of its nature one no longer expects to find water in it. So it is also with one who has attained knowledge. Though the world of diversity is experienced after knowledge, one no longer believes that diversity to be real and therefore ceases to have any attachment to it, seeing only unity and oneness.

Science has reduced our attachment for many things. Take for instance the phenomenon of color. In reality no object has any color of its own. Solar light is composed of seven different colors. Every object absorbs different colors of light and reflects the rest of the spectral colors. The reflected colors become the color of the objects we see. We are attracted by the beauty of colored objects, when in reality the beauty is dependent upon the light of the sun. That which is beautiful to us now may, due to a change of conditions, lose its beauty, even becoming ugly.

To remember these things will aid one to become less attracted to things and objects.

ON MAKING THOUGHT TALLY WITH SPEECH

Be sincere. Your inner life must tally with the outer. We utter the name of the Lord superficially, too superficially so much of the time. We say, "I am thy servant; thou art my master; thou art my Lord; I have renounced all for thee; I call thee, Lord, come unto me." But we harbor withal all sorts of evil thoughts in the mind. This must not be so. As you speak, so you must think. This means that while you take the name of the Lord think of Him alone. Sri Chaitanya used to say, "That is verily That." Which is to say, name is verily God Himself. They are inseparable.

ON WRONGDOING

Sri Ramakrishna used to say, "After making the knowledge of Oneness your own, you can do whatever you like." By this he meant that after attaining supreme knowledge one will be unable to commit any evil deed. How can one who has realized God, attained knowledge through discrimination, renunciation, love, devotion, and purity, do wrong? The purified being cannot desire ill, hurt, or harm another.

ON THE ASKING OF QUESTIONS

As you proceed with your sadhana, you will come to understand more and more for yourself. Keep practicing, you will begin to feel and know. Why engage in idle talk? Continue with japam and meditation faithfully for some time. It is so fruitless to ask abstruse questions. They lead to nothing but wasted time. Why waste time in talking? Get busy and do something. Exert yourself in meditation; its reward will become yours. Follow the instructions you have received and see! Become pure; abandon evil thoughts and work hard. You will gradually come to understand everything by intuitive knowledge. Spiritual practices are not as forced labor, they are a privilege, a wonderful privilege, therefore develop a spirit of eagerness, expectancy, delight. Practice!

Secret of Productive Work

Swami Gnaneswarananda

LIFE HAS BEEN considered by many thoughtful people as a vast field of action. In fact, if anything distinguishes the living from the dead it is activity. No living organism can remain without action even for a single moment. God Himself is working constantly. If He should stop, even for an instant, His whole creation would disintegrate and enter into a state of chaos. It is He who holds the universe together. It is His activity in every atom, the sun, the moon, the stars, the planets; the earth and all it holds are all constantly working. So long as life lasts nothing can be inactive. Then how can we human beings expect to live without working? We cannot. There is something in our nature which is always striving to express itself, always urging us to expand, to attain to the state of absolute perfection. It is this force that drives us forward even in spite of our resistance.

The question is how to convert our activity into productivity, how to attain the highest material success, how to utilize our everyday work for spiritual ends. According to Hindu philosophy, karma, or work, has two aspects—subjective and objective. On the subjective side, man must strive to develop and evolve within himself his spiritual consciousness; on the objective side, he must work in such a way that his inner perfection may be made manifest. No matter what your occupation may be, whether you are a housewife, a street cleaner, a butcher, a banker, or a shoemaker, you can make your work the noblest and best of its kind. You can raise it to the loftiest heights of excellence, beauty, and utility.

Let us consider the objective aspect of karma. To begin with, we must understand that it is through our work that we are going to attain the highest spiritual perfection. We must be convinced that whatever work we do will ultimately lead to self-realization. Do you have a complaint against your occupation? Do you think you are a misfit, that you have been placed in a field of action where you cannot express yourself, where you find a clashing and crossing of ideas and interests? If so, you are wasting your time. Any work done under such conditions and circumstances is impotent, both materially and spiritually. It is vastly important that you love your work and that it suit your temperament.

Herein arises the need for a deeper understanding of the importance of choosing wisely one's field of activity. Many people find that their work is not congenial, that they have made a fundamental mistake in choosing it. They did not take into consideration their *swadharma*— which means one's individual law of development.

According to the Vedantic theory of swadharma, there are several matters to consider in determining one's field of action. First, there is heredity. What have you received from your ancestors? Why is it that you were born of certain parents, inheriting certain tendencies? Hindu philosophy says that you cannot deny your past. You did not spring out of nothing. You had a past in which you acquired certain tendencies and impressions which now exist in your subconscious mind as a highly potent force. In choosing your field of expression you cannot ignore this. We know—quite apart from all questions of a past life— that we were born with certain inclinations and aptitudes. Secondly, there is environment—the social, economic, political, religious, educational, cultural, and climatic conditions under which you were reared. All these conditions have a very definite bearing on your whole life and conduct. Thirdly, there are your instincts, emotions, and impulses, all of which you must analyze in order to determine which way your mind flows, and in order to see what it is that arouses your natural enthusiasm. Fourthly, there are your educational and cultural accomplishments: these too help to determine your swadharma. Nowadays teachers are trying to discover the natural aptitudes of the individual student, especially in the primary schools, and to educate him accordingly. Even so, in later life he is often forced to fit into a monstrous economic and social system wherein his own swadharma finds little space.

If, therefore, you are compelled to work at something

contrary to your own swadharma, you will find it extremely difficult to bring your activity to that degree of material and spiritual productivity that you otherwise could attain. The important thing to remember is not to enter any field of activity for the purpose of acquiring easy money, prestige, reputation, or social standing. That is not the ideal of karma yoga. I emphatically denounce the ideal of "keeping up with the Joneses" as harmful, and unspiritual. That a person should follow any occupation or profession merely because it is profitable to himself, ignoring all other considerations, is both dangerous and degenerating. The primary object in choosing one's vocation should be to find a field in which he is able, because of aptitudes due to heredity, environment, previous attainments, natural tendencies and education, to express himself most perfectly. How many people take these things into consideration when they choose their field of activity? Very few. If everybody's swadharma is to get as much money as possible, there will be more and more conflict and unhappiness in life. A friend of mine expressed this modern tendency very well. He said: "Making a living is too often just making a living. It has no deeper significance." We can, however, spiritualize "making a living." We can harmonize our work with our spiritual idealism and thereby raise ourselves and our work to the height of perfection.

The subjective and the objective aspects of work, material success, and the spiritual state attained by working with a high idealism, are interrelated and react upon each other. If you are not accurate, neat, and pure in your ordinary daily activities, you cannot be so in your inner life. It is possible to judge a person's spirituality simply by watching how he sweeps a room. I remember there was a time when I did not pay very much attention to the practical side of life. I thought that the more careless I was in my daily life the more spiritual I would become. This attitude lasted for a long time. Even after I had dedicated my life to the cause of religion and philosophy I still had this false idea. I felt that, if I wished to develop spiritually, my main occupation should be study and meditation. What business had I in tilling the land, doing hospital work, and sweeping the rooms of the monastery? Whenever I was required to do these things I was always careless, unsystematic, clumsy, and inaccurate. I was interested only in my spiritual disciplines. But later I learned that if one is careless and negligent in one department he is careless and negligent in all departments. If one does not train himself to concentrate on each minute detail, he cannot attain perfection in anything.

At one time, when I was living at the monastery, some of the monks and I were weeding the garden. While we were busily engaged our spiritual teacher came out to see how we were doing. As he watched, he noticed that one of the boys was not pulling out the weeds by the roots. He said: "My boy, you must pull the weeds out by the roots; otherwise you are simply fooling yourself, and wasting your time. If you do not realize the necessity of rooting out the weeds in the garden, how can you understand the meaning of spiritual life? Weed them out, boys!" he exclaimed significantly. "Weed them out, root and all!"

You must be very particular and accurate in every detail of your work. No matter what it is, see that you put yourself heart and soul into it. Throw overboard your hopes of praise and your fear of blame, and work with the sole idea of expressing, through your actions, the perfection which is within you. *Reward is not what you are striving for, but the unfoldment of your own inner nature.*

Now, with this high spiritual motive in mind, wisely study yourself and find out your particular swadharma, your own field of activity. Then it will be a joy to work. Your main occupation will become the dominant note in your life, and you will be able to harmonize with it the various other notes. No longer will your life be a heterogeneous assortment of odd occupations.

Next you must cultivate *shraddha,* or confidence and faith in yourself. Believe that you have the power within you to accomplish any work you undertake. Instead of doubting yourself, feel that you can surmount every obstacle. It is the heroic, the self-confident, the skillful and the faithful who can do great deeds. Cowards never achieve anything great. Yet, even so, faith alone is not enough. One must have control over the means also. Supposing you want to become a great musician, do you think you can succeed simply by faith, or by repeating some mantrams or affirmations? You cannot! Along with shraddha there must go intense study and the application of the methods required to accomplish your end.

For success in any endeavor there are five points which should be appreciated and understood. These points I call the *pentagon of success*. The first to be considered regarding any scheme is the *field of action*. We must examine the field thoroughly from every possible angle before we take up any work. With a clear understanding of the field there will be fewer obstructions and surprises for us to cope with as we go along.

The second is the *fitness of the agent*, which concerns the natural abilities and other qualifications of the agent for a particular work. For example, one should have the proper physical, emotional, and intellectual requirements necessary for a particular occupation. The capacity for the work, the willingness of the agent (neither a slavelike attitude nor an overenthusiastic spirit of competition, but a pure and simple willingness), and also the absence of obstructing conditions, such as family opposition and so forth—these are all factors that must be analyzed and adjusted before entering upon any project.

Next comes the *equipment*. Proper consideration should be given to the necessary implements and instruments for the work undertaken. The agent's ability and skill in handling his instruments and tools should also be considered.

Perfection and economy of effort come next. The energy expended in every action must be regulated and balanced by proper judgment. Three things should be avoided: excessive expenditure of energy, misapplication of energy, and laziness. There are some people who are too extravagant with their energy; in their enthusiasm they are inclined to want to get ahead of others. But after awhile they lose their speed and often fall behind. If you wish your work to attain the highest degree of excellence every detail must be perfect. To do the right thing at the right time to the right person must be your constant endeavor. If you want to live a harmonious and successful life you must be able to adapt yourself to the demands of the time, the place, and the needs of the people whom you contact.

The fifth and also the most important element yet remains. Without it, even though the field may be right, the agent perfect, the equipment excellent, and effort wisely expended, one still cannot be certain of the results. The Sanskrit name for this fifth element is *daiva*, which Emerson translated as the "unscheduled ingredient." Literally it means the intervention of destiny or the influence of an "unseen hand" in our affairs. Some may call it fate or luck, but whatever we call it, it is an element over which we have no control. We have to recognize it and make allowances for it in all our plans. This recognition will help us to keep selfishness and self-importance out of our actions. It will help us to free our mind from attachment to the fruits of action, and create in us calmness and spiritual poise. We learn to surrender our will and all our actions to a higher power, realizing that, in spite of all our efforts, of ourselves we can do nothing. The attainment of so-called success brings vanity and conceit; it creates obstacles to our spiritual growth. But if we understand and recognize that there is an unseen and unknown influence working in our life and guiding our destiny, we shall learn to curb our pride and arrogance, we shall learn to give up all desire for the results of our work. In other words, by making our work a means to an end, by the practice of karma yoga, we shall learn to appreciate the spiritual value of work, and so move steadily forward toward the goal of perfection and Self-realization.

The Meaning of God

Swami Nikhilananda

IN INDIA, THE LAND of Rama, Krishna, Buddha, Shankara, and Ramakrishna, the reality of God is seldom questioned. Throughout its length and breadth are to be seen all-renouncing sannyasins, living symbols of God's reality. Even today, in Banaras, there are thousands of people devoting the final stage of life to the practice of spiritual discipline. Instead of spending time in rest, they cultivate dharma, or righteousness, which a Hindu considers to be his true friend. At the time of death, one must part with everything—children, wife, and material possessions, including one's material body. Dharma alone accompanies a man as a true friend from this life to the next. The Hindu scriptures say that a man should relinquish his ego for the sake of the family, his family for the sake of the country, his country for the sake of the world, and everything for the sake of God.

To a Hindu, the indubitable proof of God's existence is experience. God exists because Christ and Ramakrishna saw God. Saints are the most persuasive testimony of God's existence. In their presence it is not possible for an earnest soul to remain skeptical for any length of time. For instance, a man in Calcutta, when in a doubting mood, could go to Dakshineswar, where Ramakrishna, only the other day, lived and communed with the Divine Mother, and all his doubts would be resolved. Those memories are still vivid and fresh. As one sits in Ramakrishna's room or under the banyan tree where he meditated, one can no longer doubt the validity of superconscious experience. During Sri Ramakrishna's lifetime many agnostics used to visit him. Perhaps they did not understand his spiritual absorption, but they all felt uplifted in his presence. Spiri-

113

tual experience is the proof that a man's lower nature—his greed and lust—can be subdued, and that in this very life he can conquer death. This experience is open to all.

Sometimes the presence of suffering and evil in the world creates doubt about God's reality. Why does a just and compassionate God permit cruelty, injustice, and war? The existentialists say that even if God exists, He is supremely unconcerned about humanity and regards it with a frozen stare. But the presence of evil does not distress a genuine Hindu. He says that the reality of God, who lives from everlasting to everlasting, cannot be judged by what happens to our two minutes' existence on earth. God is not a municipal scavenger whose primary function is to remove poverty, disease, and physical distress. The *Bhagavad-Gita* says that God does not look into good or evil, or into a man's sin or virtue; these arise when he comes under the delusion of maya. When the inner spirit is hidden by the veil of ignorance, selfishness arises and a man feels love and hate. Impelled by these, he performs good or bad action and reaps pain and pleasure. Life on earth is governed by the law of karma. But God like a magnet attracts all. When a man's selfishness is removed by good action and his heart becomes pure through contemplation of God, he feels the force of God's irresistible attraction. A real lover of God is not distressed by physical suffering. Even while experiencing the excruciating pain of cancer, Sri Ramakrishna would often sing: "Let my body suffer from the agony of illness, but may my mind enjoy the bliss of God!" Like individual karma, collective karma is responsible for a nation's prosperity or adversity. National selfishness and greed bring war. But at all times, those who are pure in heart feel God's attraction.

What is God's nature? The Hindu tradition says that God is infinite. A Hindu is not dogmatic. Sri Ramakrishna used to say that it was a mistake to hold that God could only be this and not that. He often compared God to a lake. People go to a lake with vessels of different sizes and fill them with water. Each vessel is filled with the same water, according to its capacity. Out of His infinite aspects, God reveals to a devotee only what he can comprehend and also gives him single-minded devotion to that particular aspect, through which he ultimately attains complete God-consciousness. God is often compared to the mythical stone called Chintamani, which reflects the thought of one who gazes into it; for every thought is reflected in him. God is generally described in Hinduism as existence absolute, knowledge absolute, bliss absolute; as immortality, fearlessness, and the repository of infinite blessed qualities; as our creator and preserver.

The Hindu philosophers speak of two aspects of God: cosmic and acosmic, relative and transcendental. The relative aspect, again, can be viewed as immanent or personal. Now these do not represent independent realities. When viewed from different standpoints, God appears in different ways. For instance, when a man regards himself as a psychophysical being, God is regarded as an extracosmic, personal reality. When he considers himself to be a living soul, he becomes a part of God. In his deepest contemplation, when a man forgets his individuality, his inner spirit becomes one with the divine spirit. Christ asked the common man to pray to the Father in heaven; to the more advanced, he compared God to the vine and living beings to its branches; and to St. John he said that the Father and the Son were identical.

The acosmic or transcendental aspect of God is deepest and highest. Contemplating it, a man sees neither the world nor his own individual self. The relationship of subject and object disappears. The *Upanishads* say that as a man embracing his loving wife does not know either the inner or the outer world, so the soul, absorbed in the Godhead, sees neither itself nor another. One obtains a glimpse of such identity in aesthetic contemplation. The transcendental reality is devoid of attributes. It is unknowable to the mind or the senses. The *Upanishads* designate the acosmic reality by the pronoun "it" and not by "he" or "she." This reality cannot be called the knower because there is no object outside it which it can know. It cannot be called the thinker because it is devoid of mind, which is the organ of thinking. It is free from doubt; therefore it does not reason. It cannot be called the creator because it has no unfulfilled desire. Nor can one describe it as an actor because it is free from any of the motives that generally impel one to activity. The acosmic reality, called Brahman in Vedanta, is not even said to be one, which is used as a correlative of two. Therefore they speak of it as one and without a second, or as "not this, not this." The experience of this acosmic reality is indescribable. Sri Ramakrishna, after the experience of the transcendental Brahman, had to come down three levels, as it were, before he could utter the word Om. Such an all-annihilating experience is not possible as long as the aspirant is conscious of the slightest trace of the ego and of the world. It was revealed, by Christ, to John alone.

The Godhead belongs to a lower level. It permeates the universe. The immanent God is not a person, but it is endowed with such human attributes as love, kindness, and mercy. It is called the world soul, the inmost essence of all things. The *Upanishads* say that it dwells in the earth, but is different from it, and that by remaining within, it controls the earth. We further read in the *Upanishads* that though devoid of feet, it goes everywhere; though devoid of hands, it grasps all things; and though devoid of ears, it hears all. Creation, preservation, and destruction are the spontaneous manifestations of its nature. It sees all things at once and contemplates everything from the standpoint of eternity. That is why it is beyond good and evil. To see things from a partial standpoint is evil. For a man who is conscious of his individuality, what is conducive to self-expression is good; but selfishness is ultimately sin. From the cosmic standpoint, all things happen in the cosmic mind and have a cosmic significance. A man suffers when he separates an event from its cosmic environment and views it from his own standpoint. Individuality is an illusion, which proper investigation removes. If one analyzes oneself, one cannot really discover an individuality separate from the rest of the universe. If you peel off the layers of an onion, one by one, you do not find anything inside. Clinging to individuality gives rise to the notion of pain, evil, and suffering. When we find ourselves to be one with the universe, we do not see evil or suffering—even death becomes insignificant. Men are like berries on a tree: a fruit here and there may drop, but as long as the tree exists there will always be berries. As long as a single creature is alive, I am living also; as long as a single being is happy, I am happy also.

This immanent aspect of Godhead, called the universal form, is described in the eleventh chapter of the *Bhagavad-Gita*. Arjuna was troubled on the battlefield at the thought of the impending death of his friends, relatives, and other near and dear ones. He thought that if he fought he would be the instrument of their destruction. Sri Krishna revealed to Arjuna that creation, preservation, and destruction proceed simultaneously in the cosmic mind. All things first happen there and then are accomplished in the tangible world through the instrumentality of human beings. Arjuna was asked to be God's instrument in the fulfillment of his divine purpose on earth. "Even without you," said Sri Krishna to Arjuna, "all these warriors standing arrayed in the opposing armies shall not live. Therefore stand up and win glory; conquer your enemies and enjoy an opulent kingdom."

It is extremely difficult for an ordinary mortal, identified as he is with body-consciousness, to contemplate God's universal form. To see in one instant all things happening everywhere—birth and death, love and hate, war and peace, creation and destruction—is a staggering experience. A man is often confused even to think of a simple family problem; how infinitely difficult it is for him to see at one glance everything that is happening on earth! And yet the earth is but a fraction of the universe —a little bubble in the infinite ocean of existence. The universal form of the Lord dazed Arjuna. He wanted to see reality as a personal God, his chosen ideal, Vishnu, with diadem, mace, discus, and lotus.

The personal God is another manifestation of reality in its cosmic aspect. To see reality through the personal God is like looking at the bright noonday sun through a colored glass. It is like enjoying strong perfume by sprinkling a drop on a piece of cotton. Man does not create the personal God. God himself assumes a personal form for the welfare of His devotees. There are many forms of the personal God which are projected when the universe evolves from the primordial womb. They are known as the Father in heaven, Jehovah, Allah, Shiva, Kali, Vishnu, and so on, and are as real as the universe. These personal forms offer the foothold by which we can mount to the realization of the impersonal. Christ addressed the personal God as his Father in heaven; and Sri Ramakrishna addressed God as Mother. Our prayer and worship are directed to Him who is communed with through symbols in the form of a cross or a crescent or an ark, or of an image in a temple, or through a sound symbol such as Om. In whatever form a man worships God, God accepts that worship. He should be contemplated with undistracted love; for it is this sort of love that reveals His true nature. He accepts the love-offering of His devotees, be they a simple leaf or a flower or a handful of water. He is the goal, the support, the lord, the witness, the refuge, the friend, the savior, and the redeemer. It is important to remember that a symbol is not God. A Hindu does not worship the image as God, but he worships God through an image. To worship an image as God is idolatry; but to worship God through an image is a valid form of worship. A symbol is like a window or vista opening on the horizon of the infinite. Man can use a finger to point out the moon, but the finger is not the moon. In the end, the personal God merges in the world soul and ultimately in the transcendental reality.

There is still another conception of God. The measure of man's spiritual depth is love. Real adoration demands that he should establish an intense relationship with his spiritual ideal. It is natural for a human being to contemplate God as endowed with human characteristics; therefore Hinduism accepts the divine incarnation—God's taking a human form. If God is the savior of humanity, He must appear in times of human crisis. The *Bhagavad-Gita* says that whenever virtue declines and vice prevails in the world, God incarnates Himself as man for the protection of the righteous and the punishment of the wicked. The divine incarnation is inscrutable to the finite mind. It is hard to understand through reason how God can accept a human body and all the limitations of humanity and at the same time preserve his divine essence. Shankara, in his introduction to the *Bhagavad-Gita,* says that the Lord, by controlling His divine power, *appears* to assume a human birth, to dwell in a human body, move about as a man, and show compassion to humanity. The divine incarnation is a fact of the spiritual world. As a Christian mystic remarked: "God becomes man so that man may become God." But Hinduism does not limit God's incarnation to a particular person or time. Hindu mythology speaks of ten divine incarnations related to the different stages of life's evolution on earth. God is the protector not only of human beings but of all living beings. It is not difficult to concede the appearance of God on earth when life was threatened by danger at different periods of evolution. Thus, it is said that God appeared as a fish when life existed only in the water in the form of fish or other sea creatures. When land emerged in the course of evolution, and living beings dwelt both on land and in the water, God incarnated Himself as a turtle. Before the emergence of human beings, when only animals lived on earth, God incarnated Himself as a boar. Then came His incarnation as half man and half lion. The next incarnation was born in the form of a man—brutish, cruel, and primitive—when human culture had just started to evolve. Then God incarnated Himself as Rama, the ideal husband, son, and ruler; as Krishna, the teacher of the *Bhagavad-Gita;* and as Buddha, the God-man of a highly civilized society. The Hindu tradition speaks of another incarnation to come, called Kalki, who will be born when unrighteousness has almost overpowered the world.

Christ said that one can see the Father only through the Son. Man can best understand the higher spiritual truths through human symbols. It is a Buddha or a Christ or a Ramakrishna that makes God vivid and real.

An incarnation is different from a saint, however profound may be the saint's spiritual experience. The incarnation is born with spiritual knowledge. At the time of his birth, a thin veil covers, as it were, his divinity, but this veil is quickly rent by spiritual disciplines. Even during the period of childhood an incarnation gets a glimpse of his divine nature, as one sees in the Bible in Christ's discussion with the scholars in the temple. But a saint attains to his spiritual vision by tremendous effort; with the incarnation it is almost spontaneous. A saint can help a struggling soul but cannot redeem him. An incarnation can give salvation. A saint may be compared to a small boat that somehow manages to cross the sea, but an incarnation is like a big ship that can take many passengers across the water. A saint is a small flower with one drop of honey; an incarnation is a honeycomb—all sweetness. A saint may be compared to an archaeologist who, while exploring an old city, discovers a fountain covered by dirt. When the dirt is removed, the water, which is already there, gushes forth. An incarnation is like an engineer, who can sink a well even in the desert and bring out water.

As has already been stated, there are many incarnations of God. A devotee can choose any one suited to his taste and temperament, and accept him as his chosen ideal. He should worship Him with single-minded devotion, but give unbounded respect to others. All religions, directly or indirectly, accept the idea of the God-man. Mohammed, Buddha, Moses, and other prophets are regarded with the same devotion, by their respective followers, as an incarnation is regarded by a Hindu or a Christian.

There are other manifestations of God unknown to ordinary human minds. The creation is vast, and God's

forms are infinite. They are revealed to us in the depth of
contemplation. One should not remain satisfied with a
particular manifestation of Godhead, but should go forward until one is completely absorbed in reality.

The Hindu tradition accepts all forms of worship.
Swami Vivekananda has said that man does not proceed
from error to truth, but from truth to truth. The devotee
can commune with the Godhead through concrete rituals
and ceremonies, or unselfish love, or philosophical discrimination, or through selfless action. Religion is a path;
it is not the goal. All religions are valid in the sense that
they are suited to different temperaments and they all lead
to the hilltop of God-consciousness. Ramakrishna practiced Christianity, Islam, and the disciplines of other
religions—all ultimately leading him to the experience of
the same reality. When he followed the Christian disciplines, he left aside the Hindu methods, and thereby he
showed that the Christian can achieve salvation by being
steadfast in his devotion to his own ideal.

Worship and Meditation

Swami Prabhavananda

WORSHIP AND MEDITATION form the inner core of every true religion, for it is through loving worship of God and continuous, unbroken communion with Him, that the inner vision of reality opens. When we experience God, our life becomes transformed, our consciousness illumined.

Religion, to be practical and effective, must transform our life and consciousness. Life as we know it is full of discord, disharmony, and suffering. It seems to have no purpose, no meaning.

True, there is no denying the facts of experience, of happiness, of the possibilities of great successes in our life in the world. But what do they amount to after all? There is no ultimate satisfaction in them. They are always mixed up with pain and suffering, with failure and frustration. Happiness and misery, health and disease, birth and death—these are called the pairs of opposites. They are like the two pages of the same leaf. Take the one and you have the other also.

It is for this reason that Buddha was so emphatic in saying that the spiritual aspirant, who seeks an illumined consciousness, must learn first the noble truth that life is full of suffering. Christ echoed the same truth when he declared: "He who loveth his life shall lose it," or when he said: "In the world ye shall have tribulation; but be of good cheer; I have overcome the world."

We all see suffering in the world. We do not need a Buddha or a Christ to tell us about it. And yet, while we all have the experience of evil and suffering, we do nothing to change our state; even though a Christ or a Buddha

121

shows the way to overcome all misery, and to reach the bliss of liberation in life.

The illumined seers who have attained that supreme goal tell us unequivocally that behind this surface life there is a deeper life which knows no death; behind the play of happiness and misery there is the infinite happiness; beneath the limited, obstructed, and distorted consciousness, there is the pure, infinite consciousness. In short, there is Brahman, God—behind the world-appearance. It is only when we realize God that we overcome evil and suffering, and experience unalloyed bliss; and that we can experience while living in the world.

Know God. Realize Him. That is the one chord running through the varied notes that make up the many religious teachings of the world. That is the one chord which Sri Ramakrishna, in these modern times, touched upon again and again. His central theme has been, see God, realize Him, and thus make your life blessed. At one time some people complained to Sri Ramakrishna that he was leading the young men gathered around him away from the world and their worldly duties, by teaching them the ideals of renunciation and the knowledge of God. To this complaint Sri Ramakrishna replied that he was not asking the young men to neglect their worldly duties, but merely teaching them how to know God, so that, by the light of that knowledge, their hearts would be illumined, and worldliness would not touch them.

In order to know God an inner vision needs to be awakened. The power of inner vision, the transcendental consciousness, is in every one of us. Only it lies dormant. It needs to be awakened. This awakening comes through loving worship of God and an unbroken communion with Him.

God *is.* The proof of this fact lies in that He can be known. This knowledge is neither inferential nor is it derived from sense perception. It is a direct, immediate experience. To clearly distinguish between this God-knowledge, and our ordinary knowledge, let me state that in all our inferential or so-called direct experience, there is always the division of the subject, the knower, and the object of knowledge. In the immediate experience of God, this division does not exist. If God were known in the same way as an object is known or perceived, He would still remain unknown, inasmuch as the true nature of objects, which Kant calls the thing-in-itself, remains unknown. What we know of an object is only an idea, a sensation, interpreted by our own minds, suggested of course by the given object. The Hindu philosophers point out that there is an inherent division between *thought* and *being*. To quote Shankara: "The slightest interval between subject and object is detrimental to truth. In the idea or knowledge of an object there is something given with a touch of foreignness." To know God, the thing-in-itself, God must be realized not as separate from the subject, which *has* the idea, nor as separate from the object, which *suggests* the idea, but as the resolution of both subject and object into absolute unity. This resolution is transcendental consciousness.

The experience of pure, transcendental consciousness, is, however, not communicable through words; but communicable, perhaps, in the sense that a Christ or a Ramakrishna could awaken this consciousness in his disciples through a touch. We learn how all the disciples of Sri Ramakrishna received this immediate knowledge of God by a touch from the Master. The effect of this knowledge is described in the *Upanishads* as follows: "When one knows Him, who is the Supreme, the bondages and the attachments of the heart are loosened, all doubts cease, the effects of evil karmas are burnt up."

God is indefinable and inexpressible. Sri Ramakrishna used to say, "Everything has been defiled through the lips of man. [That is, uttered and expressed by man.] The scriptures have come out through the lips of man, but the truth of God remains unexpressed." The scriptures indicate, they make the attempt to express the inexpressible. To further quote Sri Ramakrishna: "True it is that the Vedas and other scriptures speak of Him. But do you know what their speaking is like? When a man returns from seeing the ocean for the first time and is asked to describe it, he exclaims in amazement, 'Oh, what a vast expanse! What huge waves! What a thundering roar!' Like unto this is the talk about God."

Now the question is, how is it possible to worship God, to meditate on Him "whom words cannot express, and from whom the mind comes away baffled, unable to reach"? No, it is not possible to contemplate or worship the absolute reality. "There, who sees whom? Who worships whom? Who talks to whom? Who hears whom? Where one sees another, where one talks to another, where one hears another, that is little, that is finite. Where none sees none, where none speaks to none, that is the highest, that is the infinite, that is the Brahman."

This is the state to be attained. In this state of attainment there is neither creation, nor created, nor creator; there is neither known, nor knowable, nor knowledge. There is neither *I*, nor *you*, nor *he;* there is neither subject, nor object, nor relation. Those who have attained to this state have reached that absolute, infinite reality which the *Upanishads* describe as *neti, neti,* "not this, not this." But to those who have not reached this state, this ultimate reality, the undifferentiated Brahman, the Ground, appears as nature, soul, and the interpenetrating sustainer of both—God, "from whom all these things are born, by whom all that are born live, into whom they, departing, return."

In the *Srimad Bhagavatam* we read how, when Prahlada was absorbed completely in the consciousness of Brahman, he found neither the universe nor its cause; all was to him one infinite, undifferentiated by name and form. But as soon as he regained the sense of individuality, there was the universe before him, and with it the Lord of the universe—"the repository of an infinite number of blessed qualities." So it was with the shepherdesses of Brindavan. As soon as they lost themselves in their absorbing love for Krishna, they realized their union with him, they became Krishnas, but when they knew they were shepherdesses, they looked upon Krishna as one to be worshiped, and immediately "unto them appeared Krishna with a smile on his lotus face, clad in yellow robes, and adorned with garlands, the embodied God of love." In the life of Sri Ramakrishna we find how, many times during the day he would become absorbed in God, where he would realize the unitary consciousness, and then again, as he would come back to the normal consciousness, he would speak of God, the blissful Mother. In that state, where the universe disappeared, and the sense of ego was lost, there would remain the one undifferentiated Brahman; again as he remembered himself in normal consciousness, he would have the vision of the benign form of the blissful Divine Mother.

The scriptures, as already stated, *indicate* the one truth, the infinite existence, the infinite wisdom, the infinite love. But as the Rig Veda declares: "Truth is one, sages call it by various names." The seers, drunk with the intoxicating bliss of that one existence, express that variously. It is from these seers that we learn of God, as it were, in His various aspects. To quote Sri Ramakrishna:

Infinite is God and infinite are His expressions. He who lives continuously in the consciousness of God, and in this alone, knows Him in His true being. He knows His infinite expressions, His various aspects. He knows Him as impersonal no less than as personal. Kabir used to say, "God the impersonal is my father, and God the personal is my mother." Brahman, absolute existence, knowledge and bliss, may be compared to an infinite ocean, without beginning or end. As through intense cold some portions of the ocean freeze into ice, and the formless water assumes form, so, through intense love of the devotee, the formless, absolute, infinite existence manifests itself before him as having form and personality. But the form melts away again with the rise of the sun of knowledge. Then also is the universe no more. Then is there but one infinite existence.

Then again, there are the avataras, the incarnations of God. In the *Upanishads* it is declared: "A knower of Brahman becomes Brahman." To quote Swami Vivekananda:

God is both the subject and the object, He is the "I" and the "you." How is this? How to know the knower? The knower cannot know himself; I see everything, but cannot see myself. The Atman, the knower, the Lord of all, the real being, is the cause of all the vision that is in the universe, but it is impossible for him to see himself or know himself, excepting through reflection. You cannot see your own face except in a mirror, and so the Atman, the Self, cannot see its own nature until it is reflected, and this whole universe, therefore, is the Self trying to realize itself. This reflection is thrown back first from the protoplasm, then from plants and animals, and so on and on from better reflectors, until the best reflector—the perfect man—is reached. Just as a man who, wanting to see his face, looks first in a little pool of muddy water, and sees just an outline. Then he comes to clear water and sees a better image, and at last to a looking-glass, and sees himself reflected as he is. Therefore the perfect man (the avatara) is the highest reflection of that being who is both subject and object. You now find why *perfect* men are instinctively worshiped as God in every country. They are the most perfect manifestations of the eternal Self. That is why men worship incarnations such as Christ or Buddha.

"Truth is one, sages call it by various names." There are an infinite number of facets, as it were, to the infinite God.

He can be loved and worshiped and meditated upon through any of these facets. Some worship Him as the inner light—the sorrowless light within the shrine of the heart. Others worship Him as a personal being, "the repository of the infinite blessed qualities." Others worship Him as "God the father" or "God the mother." Others again worship Him in His incarnations as Krishna, Christ, Buddha, or Ramakrishna. He is with form and without form; He is personal and impersonal, and beyond; He is absolute existence, absolute knowledge, and absolute bliss; and He is the indefinable, inexpressible reality.

Sri Ramakrishna gave the illustration of the water in the ocean. It is formless. But when vessels of many shapes and sizes are dipped into the water, the water assumes the forms of the vessels. What is contained in them is the formless water. Similarly, though God is indefinable, inexpressible, predicateless, the various ideas of God, are, as it were, the forms and expressions assumed—and they contain nothing but the inexpressible, indefinable truth.

There is a Hindu prayer which says: "They call you by so many names; they divide you, as it were, by different names, yet in each one of these is to be found your omnipotence. You are reached through any of these." Religion becomes narrow, the spiritual aspirant becomes dogmatic and fanatical, when there is an insistence upon one ideal of God, or just one door as the approach of truth. The religion of Vedanta gives freedom to choose any ideal of God, to follow the path of God through any door. To quote Swami Vivekananda:

> The eternal Vedantic religion opens to mankind an infinite number of doors for ingress to the inner shrine of Divinity, and places before humanity an almost inexhaustible array of ideals, there being in each of them a manifestation of the Eternal One. With the kindest solicitude, the Vedanta points out to aspiring men and women the numerous roads, hewn out of the solid rock of the realities of human life, by the glorious sons, or human manifestations of God, in the past and in the present, and stands with outstretched arms to welcome all—to welcome even those that are yet to be—to that Home of Truth, and that Ocean of Bliss, wherein the human soul, liberated from the net of Maya, may transport itself with perfect freedom and with eternal joy.

But this liberalism or universality does not mean that today you worship God in one way and tomorrow in another; it does not mean that you can worship God as Christ one day and as Krishna or Divine Mother or the inner light another day. It is amazing to see how many different subjects the so-called liberal teachers of religion give their students to meditate upon. The tender plant must be hedged around until it has grown into a tree. The tender plant of spirituality will die if exposed too early to a constant change of ideas and ideals. Vedanta, which is founded upon the ideals of liberalism and universality, insists that there must be one chosen ideal, one chosen deity to love, worship, and meditate upon. To quote Sri Ramakrishna:

> You must be like the fabled pearl oyster. It leaves its bed at the bottom of the ocean, and comes up to the surface to catch the rainwater when the star Swati is in the ascendant. It floats about on the surface of the water with its shell wide open, until it has succeeded in catching a drop of the rainwater, and then it dives deep down to the bottom of the ocean, and there rests until it has fashioned a beautiful pearl out of the raindrop.

Have one chosen ideal or chosen aspect of the deity, which in Sanskrit is called *ishtam,* and worship that ideal with single-minded devotion, yet know at the same time that He who is your own ideal is worshiped in all ideals by all sects, under all names, and through all forms. Suppose your ideal is Christ or any avatara; as you worship him, know that it is that same Christ who is worshiped in other names and other forms, and who is also one with the formless, undifferentiated Brahman. That Christ is your own Atman, the Self within, and you must learn to see him as the Atman of all beings.

Now to come to the practice of religion. All religions unanimously declare that the aspirant must have *faith.* The Sanskrit word for faith is *shraddha.* This word has a deeper meaning than is ordinarily understood. In the first place, faith indicates faith in the words of the scriptures and of illumined seers. What do they teach? Simply this: God *is.* Others have attained Him and you also can know Him. Thus faith indicates *self-reliance* and the understanding that it is possible for *me* and for *you,* and *you,* to know God, to realize Him. This faith, again, must be such that it would pleasantly incline our hearts to the realization of this ideal. That is what is meant by living faith. To feel and know that He is our treasure, spiritual discrimination needs to be awakened. We must discriminate between the real and the unreal. We must know that God alone is the abiding reality, and that everything else is *an appearance*. Give your heart to Him and to Him alone, knowing that He is "the end of the path, the witness, the Lord, the sustainer. He is the abode, the friend and the refuge."

However, *faith* alone is not enough; you must also earnestly desire to know Him, and with enthusiasm make the earnest effort to reach Him. Buddha called lethargy the greatest sin. Lethargy, lack of enthusiasm, and want of spiritual fervor arise from the impurities of the mind, the passionate desires for feeding the senses. The Hindu scriptures say: "When the food is pure, the heart becomes purified. In a pure heart meditation becomes unwavering." The word "food," according to Shankara, is "that which is gathered in." Commenting on the above scriptural passage, Shankara says:

> The knowledge of the sensations such as sound, etc., is gathered in for the enjoyment of the enjoyer (ego); the purification of the knowledge which gathers in the perception of the senses is the purifying of the *food*. The phrase "purification of food" means, the acquiring of the knowledge of sensations untouched by the defects of attachment, aversion, and delusion; such is the meaning. Therefore, such knowledge or "food" being purified, the *sattwa* material of the possessor of it—the internal organ—will become purified, and the sattwa being purified, an unbroken memory of the Infinite One who has been known in His real nature from scriptures, will result.

This "unbroken memory of the Infinite One" is meditation. To quote Shankara again:

> Meditation is a constant remembrance of the Infinite One, flowing like an unbroken stream of oil poured from one vessel to another. When this kind of remembrance has been attained, all bondages break. Thus constant recollection is spoken of in the scriptures as a means to liberation. This recollection again is of the same nature as sight: "When he who is far and near is seen, the bonds of the heart are broken, all doubts vanish, and all effects of work disappear." He who is near can be seen, but he who is far can only be remembered. Nevertheless the scripture says that we have to *see* him who is near as well as him who is far, thereby indicating to us that the above kind of *remem-*

bering is as good as *seeing*. This remembrance when exalted assumes the same form as seeing. Worship is constant remembering, as may be seen from the essential texts of scriptures. Knowing, which is the same as repeated worship, has been described as constant remembering. Thus meditation, which has attained to the height of direct perception, is spoken of in the scripture as a means of liberation. "This Atman is not to be reached through various sciences, nor by intellect, nor by much study of the Vedas. Whomsoever this Atman desires, by him is the Atman attained." The extremely beloved is desired; by whomsoever this Atman is extremely beloved, he becomes the most beloved of the Atman. So that this beloved may attain the Atman, the Lord himself helps: "Those who are constantly attached to me and worship me with love—I give that direction to their will by which they come to me." Therefore it is said that to whomsoever this remembering, which is of the same form as direct perception, is very dear, because it is dear to the object of such memory-perception, he is desired by the Atman, by him the Atman is attained.

In order that we may have an unbroken memory of God, we need to practice concentration with regularity, patience, and perseverance. Meditation, that is, an unceasing flow of thought toward God, when we constantly "live, move, and have our being in Him," is a stage in spiritual growth to be attained by the practice of concentration. To practice concentration, we need to sit quietly and properly. This is known in yoga philosophy as *asana* or posture. After assuming the proper posture, shut the doors to your senses. The idea is that you have to concentrate upon God within the temple of the body; you have to learn to worship God within yourself. Whatever may be your chosen ideal or chosen deity, you must learn to see Him as your Atman, dwelling within you. You do not have to pray to God to come to you from afar, but know that He is already dwelling within. Enter within the chamber of your own heart and see the effulgent Lord. The pearl lies at the bottom of the sea; dive deep, and you are sure to find it. God is beneath your outer consciousness, shining within the lotus of your heart. *See* Him. Feel His presence, *seem* to *see* Him. Practice this again and again. My Master used to say: "His grace is upon you. Feel His grace. Pray that you may feel His grace."
heart. Shut the doors and be alone with God. He is, and
    Leave the world with all its distractions at the outer gate, as it were. Enter alone into the chamber of your

you are. Should you pray? Yes, pray, but "pray not for the meat which perisheth"; pray for devotion to the Lord, pray that you may know His grace, and that your heart may be illumined by His knowledge. Yes, pray also for others; pray for all mankind, that He may become manifested in them, and that His grace may be realized by all. Chant the name of the Lord in His presence. If you have been given a *mantram*—the name of God—repeat it before Him. Practice this concentration every day regularly during the early hours of the morning and evening, at noon and at night. Keep up a regularity. That is very important. Form the *habit* of concentration.

That is not enough. At all times during your waking hours form the habit of thinking of God, or practicing His presence. To form such a habit learn to work as a form of worshiping God. As an initial step toward it, try to surrender yourself to God before you undertake any kind of work, and again to surrender yourself and the fruits of your actions when your work is finished. Also, instead of worrying and fretting over your problems, repeat your mantram, chant His name and His praises.

As you continue in your practice of habitual thinking of God, your mind will be purified, joy and sweetness will overflow in your heart. Absorption in Him will follow in due course. You will become drunk with the intoxicating love of God, and your heart will be illumined by His knowledge. "From joy springs this universe, in joy lives this universe, and unto that joy this universe goes back."

Spiritual Unfoldment

Swami Yatiswarananda

I WISH TO PRESENT some material in simple form about a subject which is little understood in the West. It is about the centers of consciousness connected with our own body and mind but of which we know very little. A knowledge of the centers and their workings will certainly help us in living a better life, if we decide to live it. Let me quote from the *Gospel of Sri Ramakrishna*:

> The Lotuses mentioned in the Science of Yoga correspond to the seven mental planes mentioned in the Vedanta. When the mind is immersed in worldliness, it makes its abode in the lowest lotus at the base of the spine. Sexual desires rise when the mind is in the second lotus, the sexual organ. When it is in the third, the navel, the man is taken up with things of the world, eating, drinking, begetting children. In the fourth mental plane, the heart, man is blessed with the Vision of Divine Light and he cries out: "What is all this! What is all this!" In the fifth plane the mind rests in the throat. The devotee talks only on subjects related to God and grows impatient if any other subject comes up in the course of conversation. In the sixth plane the mind is localized between the eyebrows. The devotee comes face to face with God; only a thin glass-like partition, so to speak, keeps him separate from the Divine Person. To him God is like a light within a lantern, or like a photograph behind a glass frame. He tries to touch the Vision, but he cannot. His perception falls short of complete realization, for there is the element of self-consciousness, the sense of "I," kept to a certain extent. In the last or seventh plane it is perfect Samadhi. Then all sense-consciousness ceases and absolute God-consciousness takes its place.
>
> The Bhagavan continued: Some sages, who have reached the seventh or highest plane and have thus attained to God-consciousness, are pleased to come down from that spiritual

131

height for the good of mankind. They keep the ego of knowledge, which is harmless like the rope that is burnt, which
though having the form of the rope cannot bind.

In order to understand the mystery of spiritual unfoldment, it is necessary that we be acquainted with our true
natures and the states of consciousness we pass through
in life.

Our true nature is divine—one with Brahman; such is
the experience of spiritually illumined souls. Ignorance
covers this true nature. Through ignorance we feel we are
separate from God, that we are only finite, mortal beings.
Ignorance is like a strong drink. It makes one forget oneself and it creates fantasies. First it hides our true nature
and then makes us identify ourselves with what we are
not. Through ignorance the true Self becomes identified
with the body, the senses, the mind, and there is created
the fantasy of an ego.

We are caught in these three states of consciousness:
the waking state in which the mind is conscious of the
physical body and is also conscious of the physical world;
the dream state or the subconscious plane in which we live
in a dream world, created by our own mental impressions;
deep sleep or the unconscious state in which we remain in
our causal body in tune with a causal world, out of which
the dream world and the physical world come into
existence.

Men of knowledge tell us that beyond these three states
there is the transcendental consciousness in which one gets
beyond all forms of body; in which one realizes one's pure
spiritual nature. And that is the spiritual unfoldment.

In our conscious state we are identified with the physical
body. We then think we are short or lean, young or old,
light or dark. When we identify ourselves with the mind,
we experience pain or pleasure, misery or happiness.
When identified with the ego, we think, "I am the doer; I
am bound or free."

Patanjali, the teacher of yoga, defines ignorance as regarding "the non-eternal as eternal, the impure as pure, the
painful as pleasant and the non-Self as the Self."

We must get rid of our ignorance and realize our true
spiritual nature. This we cannot do simply by wishing. If
wishes were horses everybody would ride. Let us always
remember the story of the little girl. Her brother had set
a trap to catch birds. She thought it was wrong and cruel.

First she wept. After some time she became cheerful again. The mother asked her the cause. She said: "First I wept; then I prayed for my brother to be a better boy. I also prayed that the trap would not catch any birds. Then I went out and kicked the old trap to pieces."

We must break all old bad habits of thinking, feeling, and acting, form good moral habits, and guide our thoughts, emotions, and actions by the spiritual ideal. We have hypnotized ourselves and must get ourselves de-hypnotized.

As the mind becomes pure as the result of moral disciplines, prayer, repetition of the divine name or holy text, and meditation, we develop the power of introspection. We then discover within ourselves the "secret stairs" of the mystics, a secret elevator with various landing stages connected with different planes of consciousness.

Some of my readers may think I am using a strange language. It certainly needs explanation. Let me put my ideas as clearly as I can. We all know how our thoughts, feelings, and activities change with the change of our moods. These moods have something to do with the centers of consciousness with which we may be connected at particular times.

Schopenhauer says sex becomes the focus of the will as the child grows into the youth. One then lives in a new world of thoughts, emotions, and actions. We feel the stomach when we are very hungry. We feel the heart when we are swayed by deep emotions. We feel the point between the eyebrows when our thoughts are clear and luminous.

It is necessary for us to get a clear conception of the various centers of consciousness and their functions. In describing supersensuous things, sometimes we are forced to use the language of the physical. This is what is done in describing the kundalini, the coiled-up, sometimes called the serpent power, the spiritual power latent in man. It is likened to a coiled-up snake lying asleep at the base of the spine. This is called the "basic" center. The next center is in the region corresponding to the genital organ. The third center is the region corresponding to the navel. The fourth center lies in the region corresponding to the heart. The fifth center and the sixth center correspond to the throat and the point between the eyes respectively. The seventh is the thousand-petaled lotus in the brain.

Each center is a point of contact between the soul and

the cosmic spirit on a particular plane of consciousness. The first three centers, from the bottom up, are connected with the animal life of man; as eating, drinking, sense enjoyment, and sex pleasures. Man's first spiritual awakening comes when his consciousness rises to the center in the heart.

The centers of consciousness are sometimes described in terms of physical plexuses and ganglia with which they are connected. But they must not be identified with them. As Arthur Avalon remarks in *The Serpent Power,* these "lotuses" or centers of consciousness are extremely subtle centers which vitalize and control the gross bodily tracts indicated by the various regions of the vertebral column and the ganglia, plexuses, nerves, arteries, and the organs situated in those respective regions.

Kundalini or the coiled-up power is consciousness in its creative aspect as power. In yogic language it lies asleep, coiled up, at the base of the spine. In the spiritually awakened power flows through the spiritual channel called *sushumna.* This spiritual channel exists side by side with two other channels called *ida* and *pingala.* These are said to exist to the left and right of the spinal column, while the sushumna is in the center. Picture three channels which have their junction at the basic or lowest center. The central one is the spiritual channel, while the other two are connected with man's ordinary physical and psychical life. In the average man the energy that gathers at the junction of the channels flows only through the two side ones but not through the central channel. So all energy is sidetracked and expresses itself in ordinary, worldly thoughts, feelings, and activities.

Now here is something for all spiritual seekers to note. Those who practice spiritual disciplines without physical and mental purity are not only wasting their energy from the spiritual point of view but they are also running the risk of gathering too much energy which, flowing through the worldly channels, might intensify their worldly life, including sex life, and thus harm them greatly. Remember Sri Ramakrishna's parable of the farmer who worked hard to irrigate his field and water his crops but later found that all the water was being lost through rat holes. So worldly desires are the holes through which the energy flows out into the worldly channels in the case of the worldly man.

In all high spiritual paths great stress is laid on the

practice of continence. In the Hindu religious system the student is asked to observe strict continence and never to depart from it consciously. When he enters the householder's life, he does not throw all self-control to the winds. He holds the ideal of a remarkably controlled life before him. Sri Krishna in his last message in the *Bhagavatam* said, "The practice of continence except for the purpose of procreation, the performance of the regular obligations of life, these with purity, contentment, and kindness to animals are among the duties of a householder." The ideal householder is a great hero. He lives the spiritual ideal in a world full of temptations.

While an exception is made in the case of those living the family life, raising children, and serving society thereby, all other spiritual seekers should strive to transmute the energy that expresses itself as sex energy and sexual thought into spiritual power. This greatly helps in the awakening of the latent spiritual consciousness and its flow to higher centers of consciousness, bringing new light and blessings to the aspirant.

An exception is made in the case of householders, for it is not practical to live a life of perfect continence in married life. At the same time, the householder is enjoined to learn complete self-control by a gradual process. As Sri Ramakrishna said: "After the birth of one or two children, the husband and wife must live like brother and sister."

Purity of the body and mind along with sincere spiritual striving ensures spiritual progress. The practice of concentration without sufficient purity is dangerous. If the energy that is increased through concentration cannot move along the spiritual channel, it may express itself outwardly in the form of violent passions in an extrovert, harming oneself as well as others. In the introvert the gathered-up energy may not find an outward expression. In that case it may form an awful whirlpool in the individual, shattering his nerves and mind and making him a complete wreck.

In some cases, as the mind is stirred through meditation, all the good and evil things lying hidden in it may come to the surface with a tremendous vehemence and bring about a physical and mental collapse. Those impure souls who want to play with the "serpent" always come to grief. In some others again the stored-up energy may manifest itself as cheap psychic powers such as clairvoyance, thought-reading, and such powers which make those persons egoistic and spiritually bankrupt. In some cases again there may be a partial awakening of the latent power. The spiritual power may rise to a higher center but fall down with disastrous results, stimulating the worldly desires. But for a sincere soul following the moral disciplines along with the practice of prayer, japam, and meditation there is absolutely nothing to be afraid of. For him the spiritual life is very safe.

Whatever be our spiritual path, Hindu, Buddhist, Christian, or Sufi, the three stages we all have to follow are purification, meditation, and experience of the divine reality or Godhead. Here arises the question, how are we to begin meditation with a view to awakening our spiritual consciousness? One of us once asked our spiritual teacher, Swami Brahmananda, "Sir, how can the kundalini, the latent spiritual consciousness, be awakened?" This is what the Swami replied, "According to some there are special exercises to awaken it but I believe it can best be done through japam and meditation. The practice of japam is specially suited to our present age. There is no other spiritual practice easier than this. But meditation must accompany the repetition of the mantram, the divine name or the holy text."

There are various forms of meditation upon God as father, mother, as effulgent light, and so on. Making the heart the center of your consciousness, think of the divine spirit there in any form you like. Repeat the divine name or holy text, dwelling on the divine aspect it represents. This is a simple form of meditation, but later on it leads to real meditation, which helps in bringing about the union between the individual soul and the supreme Spirit.

The holy word and holy thought have great power. As one repeats the divine name and meditates on the divine Spirit one should feel that the holy vibrations and thoughts are making the body, senses, mind, and ego purer and purer. Breath becomes rhythmic. The vital energy becomes harmonious. Mind becomes pure and calm. The ego tends to become cosmocentric. This leads to spiritual unfoldment stage by stage.

The repetition of the divine name accompanied by meditation produces a divine music which clears the spiritual channel, awakens the sleeping serpent power, and enables it to move along the vitalized higher centers. As consciousness rises higher and higher, it moves along both the horizontal and the perpendicular lines. The soul and the Oversoul are drawn closer together. This is symbolized in the *Upanishads* by the analogy of two birds of beautiful plumage who reside in the same tree. The lower bird looked up and at last realized that they were one. To use yogic phraseology, the lower bird is the individual soul sitting at the base of the spine. The upper bird is the supreme Spirit sitting in the thousand-petaled lotus in the brain. Individual consciousness flowing along the spiritual channel of sushumna reaches the topmost point, realizes its union with the supreme Spirit. This is the ascent of the soul to the highest spiritual point and experience. Most souls do not return from this state to the domain of phenomena again. But as Sri Ramakrishna says: "Some sages are pleased to come down from that spiritual height for the good of mankind." They see the one Spirit shining in all and are full of divine love. It is they who bring us the message of the superconscious. Let us offer our salutations to them. May we follow in their footsteps. May they bless us in attaining spiritual unfoldment, unity, and bliss.

Some Reflections on Time

Aldous Huxley

TIME DESTROYS all that it creates, and the end of every
temporal sequence is, for the entity involved in it, some
form of death. Death is wholly transcended only when
time is transcended; immortality is for the consciousness
that has broken through the temporal into the timeless.
For all other consciousnesses there is at best a survival or
a rebirth; and these entail further temporal sequences and
the periodical recurrence of yet other deaths and dissolu-
tions. In all the traditional philosophies and religions of
the world, time is regarded as the enemy and the deceiver,
the prison and the torture chamber. It is only as an instrument, as the means to something else, that it possesses
a positive value; for time provides the embodied soul with
opportunities for transcending time; every instant of every
temporal sequence is potentially the door through which
we can, if we so desire, break through into the eternal.
All temporal goods are means to an end beyond themselves; they are not to be treated as ends in their own
right. Material goods are to be prized because they support
the body which, in our present existence, is necessary to
the achievement of man's final end. Moral goods have
many and very obvious utilitarian values; but their highest
and ultimate value consists in the fact that they are means
to that selflessness, which is the precondition of the realization of the eternal. The goods of the intellect are truths
and, in the last analysis, these are valuable in so far as
they remove God-eclipsing delusions and prejudices.
Aesthetic goods are precious because they are symbolic
of, and analogous to, the unitive knowledge of timeless
reality. To regard any of these temporal goods as self-

sufficient and final ends is to commit idolatry. And idolatry, which is fundamentally unrealistic and inappropriate to the facts of the universe, results at the best in self-stultification and at the worst in disaster.

Movement in time is irreversibly in one direction. "We live forwards," as Kierkegaard said, "but we can only understand backwards." Moreover, the flux of duration is indefinite and inconclusive, a perpetual lapse possessing in itself no pattern, no possibility of balance of symmetry. Nature, it is true, imposes upon this perpetual perishing a certain appearance of pattern and symmetry. Thus, days alternate with nights, the seasons recur with regularity, plants and animals have their life cycles and are succeeded by offspring like themselves. But all these patternings and symmetries and recurrences are characteristic, not of time as it is in itself, but of space and matter as they are associated with time in our consciousness. Days and nights and seasons exist because certain heavenly bodies move in a certain way. If it took the earth not a year but a century to move round the sun, our sense of the intrinsic formlessness of time, of its irrevocable one-way lapse towards the death of all the entities involved in it, would be much more acute than it is at present; for most of us, in those hypothetical circumstances, would never live to see all the four seasons of the long year and would have no experience of that recurrence and renewal, those cosmic variations on known themes, which, under the present astronomical dispensation, disguise the essential nature of time by endowing it, or seeming to endow it, with some of the qualities of space. Now, space is a symbol of eternity; for in space there is freedom, there is reversibility of movement, and there is nothing in the nature of a space, as there is in that of time, which condemns those involved in it to inevitable death and dissolution. Moreover, when space contains material bodies, the possibility of orderliness, balance, symmetry, and pattern arises—the possibility, in a word, of that Beauty which, along with Goodness and Truth, takes its place in the trinity of manifested Godhead. In this context a highly significant point should be noted. In all the arts whose raw material is of a temporal nature, the primary aim of the artist is to spatialize time. The poet, the dramatist, the novelist, the musician—each takes a fragment of the perpetual perishing, in which we are doomed to undertake our one-way journey toward death, and tries to endow it with some of the qualities of space: namely, symmetry, balance, and orderliness (the beauty-producing characteristics of a space containing material bodies), together with multidimensionality and the quality of permitting free movement in all directions. This spatialization of time is achieved in poetry and music by the employment of recurrent rhythms and cadences, by the confinement of the material within conventional forms, such as that of the sonnet or the sonata, and by the imposition upon the chosen fragment of temporal indefiniteness of a beginning, a middle, and an end. What is called "construction" in the drama and the narrative serves the same spatializing purpose. The aim in all cases is to give a form to the essentially formless, to impose symmetry and order upon what is actually an indefinite flux toward death. The fact that all the arts that deal with temporal sequences have always attempted to spatialize time indicates very clearly the nature of man's natural and spontaneous reaction to time, and throws a light on the significance of space as a symbol of that timeless state, towards which, through all the impediments of ignorance, the human spirit consciously or unconsciously aspires.

There has been an attempt on the part of certain Western philosophers of the last few generations to raise time from the position to which the traditional religions and the normal sentiments of humanity had assigned it. Thus, under the influence of evolutionary theories, time is regarded as the creator of the highest values, so that even God is emergent—the product of the one-way flux of perpetual perishing, not (as in the traditional religions) as the timeless witness of time, transcendent to it and, because of that transcendence, capable of immanence within it. Closely allied to the theory of emergence is the Bergsonian view that "duration" is the primary and ultimate reality and that the "life-force" exists exclusively in the flux. On another line we have the Hegelian and Marxian philosophies of history, which is spelled with a capital H and hypostatized as a temporal providence working for the realization of the kingdom of heaven on earth—this kingdom of heaven on earth being, in Hegel's view, a glorified version of the Prussian state and in the view of Marx, who was exiled by the authorities of that state, of the dictatorship of the proletariat, leading "inevitably" by the process of the dialectic to the classless society. These views of history make the assumption that the divine, or history, or the cosmic process, or *Geist*, or whatever the entity which uses time for its purposes may be called, is concerned with humanity in the mass, not with man and woman as individuals—and not with humanity at any given moment, but with humanity as a succession of generations.

Now, there seems to be absolutely no reason for supposing that this is the case—absolutely no reason for supposing that there is a collective soul of succeeding generations capable of experiencing, comprehending, and acting upon the impulses transmitted by *Geist*, history, lifeforce and all the rest. On the contrary, all the evidence points to the fact that it is the individual soul, incarnated at a particular moment of time, which alone can establish contact with the divine, to say nothing of other souls. The belief (which is based on obvious and self-evident facts) that humanity is represented at any given moment by the persons who constitute the mass, and that all the values of humanity reside in those persons, is regarded as absurdly shallow by these philosophers of history. But the tree is known by its fruits. Those who believe in the primacy of persons and who think that the final end of all persons is to transcend time and realize that which is eternal and timeless, are always, like the Hindus, the Buddhists, the Taoists, the primitive Christians, advocates of nonviolence, gentleness, peace, and tolerance. Those, on the contrary, who like to be "deep" in the manner of Hegel and Marx, who think that "history" deals with humanity-in-the-mass and humanity-as-successive-generations, not with individual men and women here and now, are indifferent to human life and personal values, worship the Molochs which they call the state and society, and are cheerfully prepared to sacrifice successive generations of real, concrete persons for the sake of the entirely hypothetical happiness which, on no grounds whatsoever, they think will be the lot of humanity in the distant future. The politics of those who regard eternity as the ultimate reality are concerned with the present and with the ways and means of organizing the present world in such a way that it will impose the fewest possible obstacles in the way of individual liberation from time and ignorance; those, on the contrary, who regard time as the ultimate reality are concerned primarily with the future and regard the present world and its inhabitants as mere rubble, cannon fodder, and potential slave labor to be exploited, terror-

ized, liquidated, or blown to smithereens, in order that
persons who may never be born, in a future time about
which nothing can be known with the smallest degree of
certainty, may have the kind of a wonderful time which
present-day revolutionaries and warmakers think they
ought to have. If the lunacy were not criminal, one would
be tempted to laugh.

Sri Ramakrishna—As I Understand Him[1]

Jawaharlal Nehru

I AM GRATEFUL to you for your invitation to come to this celebration, and I am happy to have this opportunity to express my homage to the memory of Sri Ramakrishna Paramahamsa. I do not know that I am particularly fitted to speak about the life and teachings of Sri Ramakrishna, because he was a man of God, and I am a man of earth, engaged in earthly activities which consume all my energy. But even a man of earth can admire, and perhaps be influenced by, a man of God. I admire godly men, and even though sometimes I do not altogether understand them, I have been influenced by what has been written about them by their disciples. These extraordinary personalities —Sri Ramakrishna and others like him—have powerfully influenced, not only their own generation, but succeeding generations. Not only so; they have also powerfully influenced great men and have changed the whole tenor of their lives.

Sri Ramakrishna was completely beyond the average run of men. He appears rather to belong to the tradition of the great rishis of India, who have come from time to time to turn our attention to the higher things of life and of the spirit. For, throughout her long history, and in spite of what has gone on elsewhere in the world, India has never ignored the spiritual values of life. She has always laid stress on the search for truth, and has always welcomed the searchers of truth in whatever guise they have come. Not only so; for, while India has built up

[1]Speech delivered by Pandit Jawaharlal Nehru on the occasion of the birthday celebration of Sri Ramakrishna, at New Delhi in 1949. The text here offered is based on an unofficial stenographic record.

this tradition of the search for truth and reality, she has also built up the tradition of the utmost tolerance toward all who strive for truth, no matter what path they may follow. Unfortunately, that tradition of tolerance has recently been shaken; we have at times fallen into evil ways, and have begun to think that we who walk in a certain narrow path alone are right, and others are wrong. This narrow-mindedness has never been the tradition of India. What made India great was her broadmindedness, and her conviction that truth is many-sided and of infinite variety. How can any one man presume to say that he alone has grasped the entire truth? If he is earnest in his search, he may say that he has seen a particular facet of truth, but how can he say that no one else can do so unless he follows a similar path? India has always encouraged the pursuit of truth and of moral values, and this, perhaps, is the most distinctive feature of her culture. Thus, in spite of the many ups and downs of her history, the original impress still remains.

Sri Ramakrishna had a peculiar way of influencing the lives of people who came in contact with him. From a distance men often scoffed at this man of no learning; yet when they came to him they bowed their heads, and, ceasing to scoff, remained to pray. Many of them gave up their vocations in life and business and joined the band of devotees. They were all great men, and one of them, more widely known than the others, both in India and in other parts of the world, was Swami Vivekananda. I do not know how many of the younger generation read the speeches and the writings of Swami Vivekananda, but I can say that many of my generation were powerfully influenced by him, and I think it would be well worth while, and would do a great deal of good to the present generation, if they also were to study his works and teachings. They would learn much from them. They would, perhaps, catch a glimpse, as some of us did, of the fire that raged through Swami Vivekananda's mind and heart, and which ultimately consumed him at an early age. Because of this fire in his heart—the fire of a great personality expressing itself in eloquent and ennobling language—he spoke no idle words. He poured his heart and soul into the words he uttered. He became a great orator, but with none of the orator's flashes and flourishes; he spoke with a deep conviction and earnestness of spirit.

Much has happened since Swami Vivekananda's time,

things which perhaps make some of us forget those who came before and shaped India in those early and difficult days. Curiously enough, if you read Swami Vivekananda's writings you will find that they are not old. They are as fresh today as when they were written, because what he wrote or spoke about dealt with certain fundamental aspects of the problems of the world today. He gave us something which brings us a certain pride in our inheritance. He did not spare us. He spoke of our weaknesses and our failings. He did not try to hide anything, and indeed he should not, because we have to correct those failings. Sometimes he strikes hard at us, while at other times he points out the great things for which India stood, and which, even in the days of her downfall, helped her to maintain—in some measure—her inherent greatness.

What Swamiji has written and said is still of interest and is likely to influence us for a long time to come. He was no politician in the ordinary sense of the word, yet he was, in my opinion, one of the great founders of the modern national movement of India, and a great number of people who took a more or less active part in that movement later on, drew their inspiration from Swami Vivekananda. Directly or indirectly, he has powerfully influenced the India of today, and it is my belief that our younger generation will take advantage of this fountain of wisdom, spirit, and fire that flowed through him.

In India and in the world we are faced with many problems, terribly difficult problems. How are we to deal with them? There are two ways: the way of the politician and the way of the prophet—I am not speaking of the opportunists. To some extent, unfortunately, the politician or statesman has to be an opportunist, in that he has to deal with things as they are, with the material he has. He cannot put across something which the people do not understand or cannot live up to. He has to face that difficulty always, especially in an age which calls itself democratic. Democracy, I believe, is fundamentally good—but democracy means that what you do must ultimately be understood and appreciated and acted upon by a large majority of the people. If this majority of the people do not understand or do not appreciate it, then even the truth that you possess cannot reach them. So it is that, very often, politicians and statesmen have to compromise, even with the truth, because the people's receptivity of truth is not sufficient. I do not know whether this is good or bad. But so it is, and, looking at it from a statesman's or politician's point of view, there appears to be no alternative, for, if he were to do anything else, he would soon be pushed aside, and another, with a clearer perception of the limitations of the people, would replace him. On the other hand, the prophet deals with truth in a different way. He adheres to truth, whatever the consequences; and often, because of this adherence, he is either stoned to death, or shot, or killed in some other way. That is the way of the prophet. That has been and always will be the way of the prophet. But though the prophet is slain, the truth does not die. Truth is greater than the prophet, and the prophet continues to live in that truth even more vividly than if he had not died.

Always there are these two approaches, the approach of the prophet and the approach of the political leader or statesman. Neither approach can be said to be, at least in terms of today, or in terms of a limited period, a wholly effective approach. In long-distance terms one might say perhaps that the prophet's approach is the better one; but one cannot carry on politics or the public affairs of a country in these days in long-distance terms, even though, generations later, the truth would be appreciated; if he attempted such a course, he would cease to have the opportunity to carry on. Though the prophet's way may be theoretically the better way, it does not seem difficult to believe that its effects would be seen or felt during his lifetime. Yet, on the other hand, however well meant, the politician's and statesman's way leads from compromise to compromise. It is a slippery path, and once one enters that path each succeeding compromise will lead him farther away from the truth. What he may wish to do may be ignored in the existing circumstances. Shall we then hold on to the truth as we see it, or shall we think so much about the existing circumstances as to forget the truth itself? That is the problem that humanity and those who are responsible for the ordering of the affairs of the world have continually to face, and it is indeed a difficult problem. All one can say is that insofar as it is possible the statesman should adhere to truth, or, at any rate, he should aim at truth, even though he may indulge in temporary compromises. Once he loses sight of truth, he may go very far astray. It is difficult to deal with day-to-day affairs without paying some heed to men's understanding of the truth and their receptivity to it. It is important to know how far the truth is understood and finds some kind of reception in men's minds. If the words of the politician are not understood, then even the words of the prophet would have no meaning. Therefore one has to interpret the truth, and even limit it to some extent, with reference to men's receptivity to it.

We are living in an age when scientific and technical progress has gone very far indeed, especially in the United States of America. Technically and industrially the Americans are a very advanced people, and have attained a high standard of material and physical life. I have no doubt that culturally also they are advancing in many ways. Nevertheless, it must be said of the whole world that man's mental and moral growth has not kept pace with his technical and scientific advance, and this is a very dangerous thing, because science and technology are weapons of tremendous power. We have these weapons, if you like, in the atomic power. When it is produced in simpler ways, atomic energy can be used for the tremendous benefit of mankind, or it can be used for destruction on a colossal scale. Science and technology in themselves are neither good nor bad; it is the user of them who is either good or bad. Therefore it is of the utmost importance that whoever holds these tremendous weapons should know how to use them properly. He should be sufficiently advanced, spiritually and morally, to know exactly how to use them to the best advantage. He should know exactly what his ultimate aim is. Unfortunately, humanity as a whole has not yet attained this standard despite all its religions, with all their churches, temples, and mosques. And this is the great misfortune of our age. We fight amongst ourselves for our petty dogmas and customs, and call ourselves religious even while we do not yet know how to behave decently toward our neighbors. And, all the while, the world hovers on the brink of repeated catastrophes.

Thus we find two types of forces in the world—the forces of destruction and the forces of construction. If at this time I say that I have faith in the forces of construction, I cannot justify that statement except by saying that it is simply an act of faith on my part; there is no particular logic behind it. It is just that I believe in it, even though I cannot justify it. Nevertheless, whether we believe in it or not, we should make up our minds definitely as to how we are going to strengthen the unifying and constructive forces, and oppose those forces which disrupt and destroy. And these things, I think, can be done only if we have a moral foundation, and certain moral concepts which will hold together our ideals and our life in general. If we have not these, then, I think, the disruptive forces are bound to gain the advantage.

Now to come back to my first point. Men like Sri Ramakrishna Paramahamsa, men like Swami Vivekananda, and men like Mahatma Gandhi are the great unifying forces, the great constructive geniuses of the world, not only in regard to their particular teachings, but also in their approach to the world, and their conscious and unconscious influence on it. This is of the most vital importance to us. You may or you may not accept some particular advice of Mahatmaji on economic or other grounds; but his fundamental approach to life, his constructive, unifying approach to the various problems— this is of vital importance. His approach—quite apart from the particular advice that he gave—was fundamentally the approach of India, of the Indian mind and of the Indian genius. And, if you are not able to accept that, then you really are on the side of destruction and disruption.

Sri Ramakrishna was a man of God, and had nothing to do with politics; it is his fundamental approach that counts. And while I am a man of politics, not dabbling much in, nor saying much about, other matters, spiritual and the like, nevertheless I do feel that our public affairs and our life in general would become much poorer in quality if that spiritual element and that moral standard were lacking.

India, like the rest of the world, faces difficult problems and questions, and all of us, whether as individuals, communities, groups, or nations, are being put to very severe tests. Because I have faith in India, I believe that she will not only survive these tests, but will make good, because there is a fundamental vitality which has enabled her to carry on through all these millennia of years—despite her weaknesses. But faith is not enough. We have to work for her success, and work always with a clear vision before us. And we must remember that while that clear vision may apply to India, it is essentially a larger vision to be applied to the whole world. It is not a narrowing vision, and our nationalism must not be a narrow nationalism. Swami Vivekananda, though a great nationalist, never preached narrowness. His nationalism was of the kind which automatically became a part of internationalism. And it is this broad approach that we must learn from these great men, and, if we learn it and act upon it to the best of our ability, we shall not only honor their memory, but we shall serve our country, and possibly serve humanity.

Sri Ramakrishna and the Religion of Tomorrow

Swami Prabhavananda

EAST IS EAST, and West is West, but the time has now come when Swami Vivekananda's dream of a perfect civilization, by the merging of the East and West, should be realized.

Before we can understand what the nature of such a civilization would be, we must understand what the West has to contribute and what the East has to contribute. Then only can we see how they could meet for the benefit of all mankind.

What are the predominating characteristics of the modern Western civilization? They can be summed up as a scientific spirit, rationalism, and secular humanism; these again can be traced back to classical antiquity.

It was the Greek mind that laid the foundation of natural science, which means that everything must be tested and proved by experiment and reason. That was the foundation of Greek civilization, and that is the basic principle of the modern West.

Also we find that the Greek mind concerned itself with the natural man, the man as he is known to himself, his bodily desires, and his mental powers. True it is that in such ancient Greek thinkers as Pythagoras and Plato, a certain mystic element is found; yet the Greek mind as a whole was never influenced by this mystic element.

In the medieval age we find that the two great religions, Judaism and Christianity, influenced the thought of the West. Their chief contribution was the insistence upon the insufficiency of the intellect and upon the importance of historic revelation. Both Judaism and Christianity took their stand on revelation: God reveals his will to his lawgivers and prophets.

Superficially this may seem very good, but when righteousness is practiced—not for its own sake—but because of authority, there is bound to grow narrowness and fanaticism. Whenever a man bases his life on authority, in the name of religion, his reason is stifled. He becomes a fanatic. That is why we find that when fanaticism became rampant, most irreligious deeds were done. Down through the ages the name of religion has been marred by bloodshed, killing, and by murder.

With the Renaissance came intellectual and scientific advancement bringing new ideas in social living. But, with the growth of these new ideas, traditional religion was thrown aside, and morality went down. The object of all striving and action was to enrich the physical man, gratify his bodily desires, and satisfy his intellect.

But now the present chaos of the world has brought us to a period of reconsideration. In every country thinkers are beginning to look with suspicion upon the past and present way of life. Are we traveling the right path? How can we live in peace and harmony? We have reached the pinnacle of the old civilization—the scientific and rationalistic outlook of life—and we find ourselves standing on the brink of a volcano.

We have reached the point where we see only darkness, destruction, and annihilation; we are at a period when we must reconsider and readjust ourselves. Everywhere there is the cry to go back to religion. We must base our life on spirituality. That is the cry in the hearts of thinking people. That is the cry in the hearts of the masses.

Now let us see what India has contributed and what Sri Ramakrishna, the prophet of modern India, has contributed.

We have already mentioned the form of traditional religion of the West, based on revelation and authority. We have shown that if we give up our scientific and rationalistic attitude, religion becomes narrow fanaticism. Furthermore, it is not possible at this period of our growth of human civilization to give up that spirit of rationalism. When we look to India, we find a reconciliation between revelation and rationalism. We shall come to this point later.

Religion has always been, and is still, the predominating influence on the mass mind of India. True it is that, as India came in touch with the Western civilization, a type of hybrid was developed who considered religion to be the cause of her degeneration, her slavery to a foreign nation, and who wanted to "throw out the baby with the bath water." But he could not succeed, because religion has been the one deep-rooted, predominating influence in the cultural life of India.

In this connection it is interesting to note that there have been great politicians, great statesmen, born in India in the past few years; but India, as a whole, did not respond to their pleadings and preachings. There was one man, Gandhi, who did exert the greatest influence over the people of India. Was it because he was a politician or a statesman, or was it because he was a mahatma—a religious man? Thus you can see, if you study and understand India, that howsoever degraded India may be, she responds only to religion and to a religious teacher.

Now let us see what form of religion India possesses. There, also, we find that religion is based upon revelation —the same as Judaism and Christianity. But instead of this revelation having to be accepted on authority alone, it is based fundamentally on experience. As one of her great teachers, Shankara, pointed out, "In matters relating to Brahman, the scriptures are not the only authority. There must be a personal experience." To state simply on authority of revelation that God *is,* to state simply on authority that we must practice such-and-such as good, and avoid such-and-such as evil, because that is the law— the command of God—is not sufficient; it does not work in the hearts of people. To know and believe that God is, means that there is a possibility of experiencing Him in one's own life. That must be the guiding principle in the life of a spiritual man. Why should I do that which is good and avoid that which is evil? Because by doing good we reach God, and by doing evil we go into greater darkness. Because this has always been the attitude regarding religion in India, there has never been a stifling of the rationalistic spirit.

Religion to the Hindu is the direct experience of God, union with the Godhead. It is not enough to believe that God is; the living presence of God must be felt. Next, faith in that living presence must be transformed into the vision of God; the words of the scriptures must be transformed into vision. You must come directly and immediately into union with God. That is the definition of religion given in the Indian scriptures.

There comes, however, a rise and fall to every civilization. Though religion has been truly defined in the scriptures, at times this truth becomes forgotten. Whenever this forgetfulness comes to India, we find great spiritual giants rising out of her very soil in different ages to revive that spirit. In this present age when India first came into contact with the Western world, as already stated, there was a real degeneration of religion. But fortunately for India, and fortunately for the world, there came one of the greatest prophets, one of the greatest illumined souls the world has ever produced. His name was Ramakrishna.

Ramakrishna lived near the city of Calcutta, a city engulfed by the greatest tide of Western civilization that ever swept over the people of India. At this period in the history of Bengal, there were born many great thinkers, great writers, but all were imbued with the spirit of the West, and along with them there grew youth movements which sought to inculcate the Western civilization. It was the fashion among the young men of Bengal of that time to think that, to be Westernized, meant to drink whisky and to eat beef.

Unknown and unrecognized for a time, Sri Ramakrishna lived in a temple nearby, practicing his spiritual disciplines in the solitude of the temple. His one ideal, his one purpose of life, was to see God, to experience Him. He worshiped God as Mother. Although he did not go to any school or college, and hardly knew how to read and write, he had the scientific temper and rationalistic spirit of a true scientist. He would ask, "Mother, are you real? Are you true? If you really exist, why don't you reveal yourself to me?" Thus he would pray from day to day, and when the temple bells would proclaim the approach of evening, he would cry out, "Mother, another day has passed, and I have not seen you." To him life was empty, life was a vanity, without the realization of God. He determined the value of all things by one standard: "Does it help me to realize God?" He would take a piece of gold in one hand and a lump of dirt in the other, and say to himself: "This is gold and this is dirt. People give their lives to find this piece of gold. Does it give me God? Yes, I can build a house, I can live comfortably with gold, but does it help me to realize God?" Then he would reply, "Gold is dirt, and dirt is gold," and throw both in the river.

Such was the man living in a temple in India at a time when India was madly chasing the Western culture, and this was the man, who, through his yearning, realized God the Mother. He saw Mother and he talked to Her. Following the first experience of God, he wanted to experiment with the other religions of the world. He followed the teachings of the different sects of India; he followed the religions taught by Christ and Mohammed; and by following each one of these religions he came to the realization of the same ultimate reality. Then was it that he proclaimed, with authority, "The many religions are so many paths to God."

Sri Ramakrishna used to say, "When the lotus blooms, bees come to gather the honey." The seekers after God began to gather around him, and to those who came to him with the earnest, sincere longing for God, he gave the vision of God. Their lives were transformed. However, Sri Ramakrishna did not limit the vision of God to his disciples or to the people of India. He said, "I have many children in far-off countries whose language I do not know, and they will all come to me." He had a vision wherein he saw himself in the center and many people from foreign lands gathered around him, and they were all God-intoxicated. In this vision he saw the future of mankind; he saw that many a soul would be born who would drink of the love of God.

But this does not mean that all the people of the world will come to accept the personality of Ramakrishna. Sri Ramakrishna is only a symbol of a truth, an embodiment of certain spiritual principles. Let us see what those principles are.

God is not merely a hypothesis, He is. God can be realized and must be realized in this very life. Religion is eternal. It has no boundary. It is neither of the East nor of the West. It is neither Hinduism nor Christianity, nor Buddhism nor Judaism. The world is not saved and can never be saved by merely believing in creeds which accept a particular faith; it can be saved by wisdom only. It is not that any or all of the existing religions of the world will be wiped out and that there will be one world religion. Sri Ramakrishna experimented with the existing religions and found that they are all true, inasmuch as they are the ways, the paths, to realize the one God. He came to bring harmony; he came to fulfill and not to destroy.

Now, what about humanism, the prevalent religion of the West? The general welfare of the body and the mind cannot be ignored. You cannot ignore the physical and intellectual man. India, during the past few centuries—

not the India of old—has ignored the external aspect of man, while the West has ignored the inner man by her humanistic ethics and secular outlook of life. In the life and teachings of Sri Ramakrishna we find how, instead of ignoring humanism, he elevated it to the level of the spirit. In this connection I will mention one incident. One day Sri Ramakrishna was in a very high spiritual mood, and in that mood he was, as it were, talking to himself. There were many disciples present, and among them was young Narendra (Vivekananda). Sri Ramakrishna quoted a well-known teaching of Sri Chaitanya, repeating over and over again: "Compassion for mankind!" Then he said: "Compassion—compassion—no! no! no! Not compassion—but service!" Naren listened attentively to these words, and as he left the room, he said: "I have learned a great lesson today. If I live I shall some day give this truth to the world." And what did Vivekananda preach? He preached the ideal of service to God in man. When we learn to see God within ourselves, we learn to see Him in all. We learn to see that our own good lies in the good of all mankind. Thus it is that humanism becomes spiritualized. The ignorant way is to strive to enrich our life on earth, and the spiritual way is to try to find out how best we can live on earth in order that we may reach God.

To sum up: the scientific temper and rationalistic spirit are not opposed to religion and revelation, if by religion we mean experimenting with the truth and experiencing the truth of God. Intellect when elevated and expanded becomes revelation. To accept religion and revelation without this spirit of experimenting and experiencing the truth of God, leads man to fanaticism. Intellectual culture and scientific temper, unless expanded into revelation, leads to its own destruction.

Intellect and revelation are to be harmonized, humanism is to be elevated to the spirit, morality or ethical life is to be spiritualized, external decorum is to be guided by the inner check. In this way harmony can be established between the civilizations of the East and the West.

Memories of Swami Vivekananda 157

Memories of Swami Vivekananda

Sister Christine

I

THERE ARE TIMES when life flows on in a steady, deadly
stream of monotony. Eating, sleeping, talking—the same
weary round. Commonplace thoughts, stereotyped ideas,
the eternal treadmill. Tragedy comes. For a moment it
shocks us into stillness. But we cannot keep still. The
merry-go-round stops neither for our sorrow nor for our
happiness. Surely this is not all there is to life. This is not
what we are here for. Restlessness comes. What are we
waiting for?

Then one day it happens, the stupendous thing for which
we have been waiting—that which dispels the deadly monotony, which turns the whole of life into a new channel,
which eventually takes one to a faraway country and sets
one among strange people with different customs and a
different outlook upon life, to a people with whom from
the very first we feel a strange kinship, a wonderful people
who know what they are waiting for, who recognize the
purpose of life. Our restlessness is forever stilled.

After many incarnations, after untold suffering, struggle,
and conquest, comes fruition. But this one does not know
until long, long after. A tiny seed grows into the mighty
banyan. A few feet of elevation on a fairly level plain determine whether a river shall flow north and eventually
reach the icy Arctic Ocean or south, until it finds itself in
the warm waters of the Black or Caspian seas.

Little did I think when I reluctantly set out one cold
February night in 1894 to attend a lecture at the Unitarian
church in Detroit that I was doing something which would
change the whole course of my life and be of such stu-

pendous import that it could not be measured by previous
standards I had known. Attending lectures had been part
of the deadly monotony. How seldom did one hear anything new or uplifting! The lecturers who had come to
Detroit that winter had been unusually dull. So unvarying
had been the disillusions, that one had given up hope and
with it the desire to hear more. So I went very unwillingly
to this particular lecture to hear one "Vivekananda, a
monk from India," and only in response to the pleading of
a friend. Surely never in our countless incarnations had we
taken a step so momentous! For before we had listened
five minutes, we knew that we had found the touchstone
for which we had searched so long. In one breath, we exclaimed: "If we had missed this . . . !"

To those who have heard much of the personal appearance of Swami Vivekananda, it may seem strange that it
was not this which made the first outstanding impression.
The forceful, virile figure which stepped upon the platform
was unlike the emaciated, ascetic type which is generally
associated with spirituality in the West. A sickly saint
everyone understands, but who ever heard of a powerful
saint? The power that emanated from this mysterious
being was so great that one all but shrank from it. It was
overwhelming. It threatened to sweep everything before it.
This one sensed even in those first unforgettable moments.

Later we were to see this power at work. It was the
mind that made the first great appeal, that amazing mind!
What can one say that will give even a faint idea of its
majesty, its glory, its splendor? It was a mind so far
transcending other minds, even of those who rank as
geniuses, that it seemed different in its very nature. Its
ideas were so clear, so powerful, so transcendental that it
seemed incredible that they could have emanated from the
intellect of a limited human being. Yet marvelous as the
ideas were and wonderful as was that intangible something
that flowed out from the mind, it was strangely familiar.
I found myself saying, *"I have known that mind before."*
Vivekananda burst upon us in a blaze of reddish gold,
which seemed to have caught and concentrated the sun's
rays. He was barely thirty, this preacher from faraway
India. Young with an ageless youth and yet withal old
with the wisdom of ancient times. For the first time we
heard the age-old message of India, teaching of the Atman, the true Self.

The audience listened spellbound while he wove a fabric as glowing and full of color as a beautiful Kashmir shawl. Now a thread of humor, now one of tragedy, many of serious thought, many of aspiration, of lofty idealism, of wisdom. Through it all ran the woof of India's most sacred teaching: the divinity of man, his innate and eternal perfection; that this perfection is not a growth nor a gradual attainment, but a present reality. *That thou art.* You are that now. There is nothing to do but realize it. The realization may come now in the twinkling of an eye, or in a million years, but "all will reach the sunlit heights." This message has well been called "the wondrous evangel of the Self." We are not the helpless limited beings which we think ourselves to be, but birthless, deathless, glorious children of immortal bliss.

Like the teachers of old, Vivekananda too spoke in parables. The theme was always the same—man's real nature. Not what we seem to be, but what we *are*. We are like men walking over a gold mine, thinking we are poor. We are like the lion who was born in a sheepfold and thought he was a sheep. When the wolf came he bleated with fear, quite unaware of his true nature. Then one day a lion came, and seeing him bleating among the sheep called out to him, "You are not a sheep. You are a lion. You have no fear." The lion at once became conscious of his nature and let out a mighty roar. Vivekananda stood on the platform of the Unitarian church pouring forth glorious truths in a voice unlike any voice one had ever heard before, a voice full of cadences, expressing every emotion, now with a pathos that stirred hitherto unknown deeps of tragedy, and then just as the pain was becoming unbearable, that same voice would move one to mirth only to check it in mid-course with the thunder of an earnestness so intense that it left one awed, a trumpet call to awake. One felt that one never knew what music was until one heard that marvelous voice.

Which of us who heard Vivekananda then can ever forget what soul memories were stirred within us when we heard the ancient message of India: "Hear ye, children of immortal bliss, even ye who dwell in higher spheres, I have found the Ancient One, knowing whom alone ye shall be saved from death ever again." Was it possible to hear and feel this and ever be the same again? All one's values were changed. The seed of spirituality was planted to grow and grow throughout the years until it inevitably reached fruition. True, this sublime teaching is hoary with age. It may even be true that every Hindu man and woman knows it, many may be able to formulate it clearly, but Vivekananda spoke with authority. To him, it was not speculative philosophy but the *living truth*. All else might be false; this alone was true. He had realized it. After his own great realization, life held but one purpose—to give the message with which he was entrusted, to point out the path and to help others on the road to the same supreme goal. "Arise, awake, and stop not until the goal is reached."

All of this one sensed more or less dimly in that first unforgettable hour while our minds were lifted into his own radiant atmosphere. Later, slowly and sometimes painfully, after much effort and devotion, some of us found that our very minds were transformed. Great is the guru!

Those who came to the first lecture at the Unitarian church came to the second and to the third, bringing others with them. "Come," they said, "hear this wonderful man. He is like no one we have ever heard"; and they came until there was no place to hold them. They filled the room, stood in the aisles, peered in at the windows. Again and again he gave his message, now in this form, now in that, now illustrated with stories from the *Ramayana* and the *Mahabharata*, now from the *Puranas* and folklore. From the *Upanishads* he quoted constantly, first chanting in the original Sanskrit, then giving a free poetic translation. Great as was the impression which his spoken words made, the chanting produced an even greater effect. Unplumbed deeps were stirred and as the rhythm fell upon the ear, the audience sat rapt and breathless. And so began a new life, a life of study, of meditation. The center of interest was shifted.

After the Parliament of Religions, Swami Vivekananda had been induced to place himself under the direction of Pond's Lecture Bureau and make a lecture tour of the United States. As is the custom, the committee at each new place was offered the choice of several lectures, "The Divinity of Man," "Manners and Customs of India," "The Women of India," "Our Heritage." Invariably when the place was a mining town with no intellectual life whatever, the more abstruse subjects were selected. He told us the difficulty of speaking to an audience when he could see no ray of intelligence in response. After some weeks of this, lecturing every evening and traveling all night, the bondage became too irksome to bear any longer. In Detroit he had friends who had known him in Chicago and who loved and admired him. To them he went, and begged, "Make me free! Make me free!" Being influential, they were able to get him released from his contract, though at a financial loss which seemed unfair. He had hoped to begin his work in India with the money earned in this way, but this was not the only reason for engaging in this public work. The impulse which was urging him on and which was never entirely absent from his mind was the mission with which his Master had entrusted him. He had a work to do, a message to give. It was a sacred message. How was he to give it? By the time he reached Detroit, he knew that a lecture tour was not the way, and not an hour longer would he waste his time on what did not lead toward his object. For six weeks he remained in Detroit, his mind intent upon his purpose, and he would give an occasional lecture. We missed no opportunity of hearing him. We knew we had found our teacher. The word *guru* we did not know then. Nor did we meet him personally, but what matter? It would take years to assimilate what we had already learned. And then the master would some-how, somewhere, teach us again!

It happened sooner than we expected; for in a little more than a year, we found ourselves at Thousand Island Park in the very house with him. It must have been the 6th of July, 1895, that we had the temerity to seek him out. We heard he was living with a group of students. The word "disciple" is not used very freely in these days. It implies more than the average person is willing to give. We thought there would be some public teaching which we might attend. We dared not hope for more. Mrs. Funke has told of our quest in her preface to the *Inspired Talks of Swami Vivekananda*.

Of the wonderful weeks that followed, it is difficult to write. Only if one's mind were lifted to that high state of consciousness in which we lived for the time, could one hope to recapture the experience. We were filled with joy. We did not know at that time that we were living in the man's radiance. On the wings of inspiration, he carried us to the height which was his natural abode. He himself, speaking of it later, said that he was at his best at Thousand Islands. Then he felt that he had found the channel through which his message might be spread, the way to fulfill his mission, for the guru had found his own disciples. Swamiji's first overwhelming desire was to show

us the path to *mukti*, to set us free. "Ah," he said with
touching pathos, "if I could only set you free with a
touch!" His second object, not so apparent perhaps, but
always in the undercurrent, was to train this group to
carry on the work in America. "This message must be
preached by Indians in India, and by Americans in America," he said. On his own little veranda, overlooking the
treetops and the beautiful St. Lawrence, he often called
upon us to make speeches. His object was, as he said, to
teach us to think upon our feet. Did he know that if we
could conquer our self-consciousness in his presence, could
speak before him who was considered one of the great
orators of the world, no audience anywhere would dismay us? It was a trying ordeal. Each in turn was called
upon to make an attempt. There was no escape. Perhaps
that was why certain of our group failed to make an
appearance at these intimate evening gatherings, although
they knew that often he soared to the greatest heights
as the night advanced! What if it was two o'clock in the
morning? What if we had watched the moon rise and
set? Time and space had vanished for us.

There was nothing set or formal about these nights on
the upper veranda. He sat in his large chair at the end,
near his door. Sometimes he went into a deep meditation.
At such times we too meditated or sat in profound silence.
Often it lasted for hours and one after the other slipped
away. For we knew that after this he would not feel
inclined to speak. Or again the meditation would be short
and he would encourage us to ask questions afterward,
often calling on one of us to answer. No matter how
far wrong these answers were, he let us flounder about
until we were near the truth and then in a few words, he
would clear up the difficulty. This was his invariable method in teaching. He knew how to stimulate the mind of the
learner and make it do its own thinking. Did we go to
him for confirmation of a new idea or point of view and
begin, "I see it thus and so," his "Yes?" with an upper in-
flection always sent us back for further thought. Again
we would come with a more clarified understanding and
again the "Yes?" stimulated us to further thought. Perhaps after the third time when the capacity for further
thought along that particular line was reached, he would
point out the error—an error usually due to something in
our Western mode of thought.

And so he trained us with such patience, such benignity.

It was like a benediction. Later, after his return to India, he hoped to have a place in the Himalayas for further training of Eastern and Western disciples together.

But it was not all Vedanta and deep, serious thought. Sometimes after the classes were over, it was pure fun, such gaiety as we had never seen elsewhere. We had thought of religious men as grave all the time, but gradually we came to see that the power to throw off the burden of the world at will and live for a time in a state of childlike joy, is a certain sign of detachment and comes only to those who have seen the great reality. For the time being, we were all light-hearted together.

Swamiji had a stock of funny stories, some of which he told again and again. One was about a missionary to the cannibal islands who upon his arrival, asked the people there how they liked his predecessor and received the reply, "He was de-li-cious!" Another was about the Negro preacher, who in telling the story of the creation of Adam, said, "God made Adam and put him up against de fence to dry," when he was interrupted by a voice from the congregation, "Hold on dere, brudder. Who made dat fence?" At this, the Negro preacher leaned over the pulpit and said solemnly, "One more question like dat, and you smashes all teology!" Then Swamiji would tell about the woman who asked, "Swami, are you a Buddhist?" (pronounced like "bud") and he would say wickedly but with a grave face, "No, Madam, I am a florist."

Again, he would tell of the young woman, cooking in the common kitchen of the New York lodging house in which he had lived with the disciple Leon Lansberg. She had frequent disputes with her husband, who was a spiritualistic medium, and gave public seances. Often she would turn to Swamiji for sympathy after one of these differences. "Is it fair for him to treat me like this," she would say, "when I make all the ghosts?"

II

After leaving Detroit, Swamiji had gone to New York, hoping that there, in the cultural metropolis of America, he might find an opening to begin the work he felt destined to do. He was soon taken up by a group of wealthy friends who loved and admired him and were attracted by his personality, but cared nothing for his message. He found himself in danger of becoming a social lion. He was fed, clothed, and housed in luxury. Again there came the cry for freedom: "Not this! Not this! I can never do my work under these conditions."

Then he thought the way might be found by living alone and teaching in classes, open to all. He asked Lansberg to find inexpensive rooms for both of them. The place which was found (54 West 33rd Street) was in a most undesirable locality, and it was hinted that the right sort of people, especially ladies, would not come to such a place, but they came—all sorts and conditions of men and women—to these squalid rooms. They sat on chairs and when chairs were filled, anywhere—on tables, on washstands, on the stairs. Millionaires were glad to sit on the floor, literally at his feet. No charge was made for the teaching and often there was no money to pay the rent. Then Swamiji would give a secular lecture for which he felt he could accept a fee. All that winter, he worked as he could. Often the last penny was spent. It was a precarious way of carrying on the work and sometimes it seemed as if it would come to an end. After this, a few earnest students took the financial responsibility for the work and there was no further difficulty.

All that winter the work went on and when the season came to an end, early in the summer, this devoted group was not willing to have the teaching discontinued. One of them owned a house in Thousand Island Park on the St. Lawrence River, and a proposal was made to the teacher that they all spend the summer there. He consented, much touched by their earnestness. He wrote to one of his friends that he wanted to manufacture a few "yogis" out of the materials of the classes. He felt that his work was now really started and that those who joined him at Thousand Islands were really disciples.

Early in June three or four were gathered at Thousand Island Park with Swamiji and the teaching began without delay. He came on Saturday, July 6, 1895, and had planned to initiate several of those already there on Monday. "I don't know you well enough yet to feel sure that you are ready for initiation," he said on Sunday afternoon. Then he added rather shyly, "I have a power which I seldom use—the power of reading the mind. If you will permit me, I should like to read your mind, as I wish to initiate you with the others tomorrow." We assented joyfully. Evidently he was satisfied with the result of the reading, for the next day, together with several others, he gave us a mantram and made us his disciples. Afterwards, questioned as to what he saw while he was reading our minds he told us a little. He saw that we should be faithful and that we should make progress in our spiritual life. He described something of what he saw, without giving the interpretation of every picture. In one case, scene after scene passed before his mental vision meaning that there would be extensive travel for us apparently in Oriental countries. He described the very houses in which we should live, the people who should surround us, the influences that would affect our lives. We questioned him about this. He told us the power could be acquired by anyone. The method was simple at least in the telling. First, think of space—vast, blue extending everywhere. In time, as one meditates upon this space intently, pictures appear. These pictures must be interpreted. Sometimes one sees the pictures but does not know the interpretation. He saw that one of us would be indissolubly connected with India. Important as well as minor events were foretold for us, nearly all of which have come to pass. In this reading the quality of the personality was revealed: the mettle, the capacity, the character. Having passed this test, there can be no self-depreciation, no lack of faith in oneself. Every momentary doubt is replaced by a serene assurance. Has the personality not received the stamp of approval from the one Being in the world . . . ?

The original plan was that we should live as a community, without servants, each doing a share of the work. Nearly all of us were unaccustomed to housework and found it uncongenial. The result was amusing; as time went on it threatened to become disastrous. Some of us who had just been reading the story of Brook Farm felt that we saw it re-enacted before our eyes. No wonder Emerson refused to join that community of transcendentalists! His serenity was evidently bought at a price. Some could only wash dishes. One whose work was to cut the bread, groaned and all but wept whenever she attempted the task. It is curious how character is tested in these little things. Weaknesses which might have been hidden for a lifetime in ordinary intercourse, were exposed in a day of this community life. It was interesting. With Swamiji the effect was quite different. Although only one among us all was younger than himself, he seemed like a father or rather like a mother in patience and gentleness. When the tension became too great, he would say with the utmost sweetness, "Today I shall cook for you." To this Leon Lansberg would ejaculate in an aside, "Heaven save us!" By way of explanation he said that in New York when Swamiji cooked, he, Lansberg, would tear his hair, because it meant that afterwards every dish in the house required washing. After several unhappy experiences in community housekeeping, an outsider was engaged for help, one or two of the more capable ones undertook certain responsibilities, and we had peace.

But once the necessary work was over and we had gathered in the classroom, the atmosphere was changed. Swamiji once told us the story of the beautiful garden and of one who went to look over the wall and found it so alluring that he jumped over and never returned. And after him another and another. But we had the unique fortune of having for a teacher one who had looked over and found it no less entrancing, but out of his great compassion he returned to tell the story to those left behind and to help them over the wall. So it went on from morning until midnight. When he saw how deep the impression was which he had made, he would say with a smile, "The cobra has bitten you. You cannot escape." Or sometimes, "I have caught you in my net. You can never get out."

Miss Dutcher, our hostess, was a conscientious little woman, a devout Methodist. How she ever came to be associated with such a group as gathered in her house that summer would have been a mystery to anyone who did not know the power of Swami Vivekananda to attract and hold sincere souls. But having once seen and heard him, what could one do but follow? All Miss Dutcher's ideals, her values of life, her concepts of religion were, it seemed to her, destroyed; in reality, they were only modified. Sometimes she did not appear for two or three days. "Don't you see," Swami would explain, "this is not an ordinary illness. It is the reaction of the body against the chaos that is going on in her mind. She cannot bear it." The most violent attack came one day after a timid protest on her part against something he had said in the class. "The idea of duty is the midday sun of misery scorching the very soul," he had said. "Is it not our duty," she began, but got no further. For once that great free soul broke all bounds in his rebellion against the idea that anyone should dare bind with fetters the soul of man. Miss Dutcher was not seen for some days.

And so the process of education went on. It was not difficult if one's devotion to the guru was great enough, for then, like the snake, one dropped the old and put on the new. But where the old prejudices and conventions were stronger than one's faith, it was a terrifying, almost a devastating process.

We all attended our class lectures. To a Hindu the teaching itself might have been familiar, but it was given with a fire, an authority, a realization which made it sound like something entirely new. He too "spake like one having authority." To us of the West to whom it was all new it was as if a being from some radiant sphere had come down with a gospel of hope, of joy, of life. Religion is not a matter of belief but of experience. One may read about a country, but until one has seen it there can be no true idea. All is within. The divinity which we are seeking in heaven, in teachers, in temples is within us. If we see it outside, it is because we have it within. What is the means by which we come to realize this, by which we see God? *Concentration* is the lamp which lights the darkness.

There are different methods for different states of evolution. All paths lead to God. The guru will put you on the path best suited to your development. With what sense of release did we hear that we not only may, but must follow reason. Before that it had seemed that reason and intuition are generally opposed to each other. Now we were told that we must hold to reason until we reached something higher—and this something higher must never contradict reason.

The first morning we learned that there is a state of consciousness higher than the surface consciousness—which is called samadhi. Instead of the two divisions to which we are accustomed, the conscious and the unconscious—it would be more accurate to make the classification: the subconscious, the conscious, and the superconscious. This is where confusion arises in the Western way of thinking, which divides consciousness into the subconscious or unconscious and the conscious. The West cognizes only the normal state of mind, forgetting that there is a state beyond consciousness—a superconscious state, inspiration. How can we know that this is a higher state? To quote Swami literally, "In the one case a man goes in and comes out as a fool. In the other case he goes in a man and comes out a God." And he always said, "Remember, the superconscious never contradicts reason. It transcends it, but contradicts it never. Faith is not belief, it is the grasp on the ultimate, an illumination."

Truth is for all, for the good of all. Not secret but sacred. The steps are: hear, then reason about it, "let the flood of reason flow over it, then meditate upon it." Accumulate power in silence and become a dynamo of spirituality. What can a beggar give? Only a king can give, and he only when he wants nothing himself.

Swamiji told us that God was real, a reality which could be experienced just as tangibly as any other reality; that there were methods by which these experiences could be made which were as exact as laboratory methods of experiment. The mind is the instrument. Sages, yogis, and saints from prehistoric times have made discoveries in this science of the Self. They have left their knowledge as a precious legacy not only to their immediate disciples but to seekers of truth in future times. This knowledge is in the first instance passed on from master to disciple, but in a way very different from the method used by an ordinary teacher. The method of religious teaching to which we of the West have become accustomed is that we are told the results of the experiments, much as if a child were given a problem in arithmetic and were told its answer but given no instruction as to how the result was reached. We have been told the results reached by the greatest spiritual geniuses known to humanity, the Buddha, the Christ, Zoroaster, Lao-tse, and we have been told to accept and believe the result of their great experiments. If we are sufficiently reverent and devotional, and if we have reached that stage of evolution where we know that there must be some reality transcending reason, we may be able to accept and believe blindly, but even then it has but little power to change us. It does not make a god of man. Now we are told that there is a method by which the result may be obtained, a method never lost in India, passed on from guru to disciple.

For the first time we understood why all religions begin with ethics. For without truth, noninjury, continence, nonstealing, cleanliness, austerity, there can be no spirituality. The ideal must be truth in thought, word, and deed. If this can be practiced for twelve years, then every word that is said becomes true. If one perfect in this way says,

"Be thou healed," healing comes instantaneously. Be blessed, he is blessed. Be freed, he is released. Stories were told of those who had this power, and who could not recall the word once spoken. To the father of Sri Ramakrishna this power had come. Would that explain why such a son was born to him? Then there was the life of Sri Ramakrishna himself. "Come again Monday," he once said to a young man. "I cannot come on Monday, I have some work to do; may I come Tuesday?" "No," answered the Master, "these lips have said Monday; they cannot say anything else now."

Noninjury in word, thought, and deed. Before one has attained perfection in noninjury he has lost the power to injure. "From me no danger be to aught that lives" becomes true for him, a living truth, reality. Before such a one the lion and the lamb lie down together. Pity and compassion have fulfilled the law and transcended it.

Continence-chastity. This subject always stirred Swamiji deeply. Walking up and down the room, getting more and more excited, he would stop before someone, as if there were no one else in the room. "Don't you see," he would say eagerly, "there is a reason why chastity is insisted on in all monastic orders? Spiritual giants are produced only where the vow of chastity is observed. Don't you see there must be a reason? The Roman Catholic Church has produced great saints: St. Francis of Assisi, Ignatius Loyola, St. Teresa, the two Catharines, and many others. The Protestant church has produced no one of spiritual rank equal to them. There is a connection between great spirituality and chastity. The explanation is that these men and women have through prayer and meditation transmuted the most powerful force in the body into spiritual energy. In India this is well understood and yogis do it consciously. The force so transmuted is called *ojas* and is stored up in the brain. It has been lifted from the lowest center of the *kundalini* to the highest." To us who listened the words came to our remembrance: "And I, if I be lifted up, will draw all men unto me."

In the same eager way he went on to explain that whenever there was any manifestation of power or genius it was because a little of this power had escaped up the *sushumna*. And did he say it? or did we come to see for ourselves the reason why the avatars and even lesser ones could inspire a love so great that it made the fishermen of Galilee leave their nets and follow the young Carpenter, made the princes of the clan of Sakya give up their robes, their jewels, their princely estates? It was this divine drawing. It was the lure of divinity.

Austerity. Why have the saints in all religions been given to fasting and self-denial, to mortification of the body? True, there have been those who foolishly regarded the body as an enemy which must be conquered and have used these methods to accomplish their end. The real purpose, however, is disciplining the will. No ordinary will power will carry us through the great work before us. We must have nerves of steel and a will of iron, a will which is consciously disciplined and trained. Each act of restraint helps to strengthen the will. It is called *tapas* in India and means literally, to *heat;* the inner or the higher nature gets heated. How is it done? There are various practices of a voluntary nature: a vow of silence is kept for months, fasting for a fixed number of days, or eating only once a day. With children it is often the denial of some favorite article of food. The conditions seem to be that the vow must be taken voluntarily for a specific time. If the vow is not kept it does more harm than good. If it is kept, it becomes a great factor in building up the character so necessary for the higher practices.

Beyond a few directions in meditation there was very little set instruction, yet in the course of these few days our ideas were revolutionized, our outlook enormously enlarged, our values changed. It was a re-education. We learned to think clearly and fearlessly. Our conception of spirituality was not only clarified but transcended. Spirituality brings life, power, joy, fire, glow, enthusiasm—all the beautiful and positive things, never inertia, dullness, weakness. To hear Swami say, "This indecent clinging to life!" drew aside the curtain for us into the region beyond life and death, and planted in our hearts the desire for that glorious freedom. We felt a soul struggling to escape the meshes of maya, one to whom the body was an intolerable bondage, not only a limitation but a degrading humiliation. "*Azad, azad,* the free," he cried, pacing up and down like a caged lion. Yes, like the lion in the cage who found the bars not of iron but of bamboo. "Let us not be caught this time," would be his refrain another day. "So many times maya has caught us, so many times have we exchanged our freedom for sugar dolls which melted when the water touched them. Let us not be caught this time." So in us was planted the great desire for freedom. Two of the three requisites we already had—a human body and a guru, and now he was giving us the third, the desire to be free.

"Don't be deceived. Maya is a great cheat. Get out. Do not let her catch you this time," and so on and so on. "Do not sell your priceless heritage for such delusions. Arise, awake, stop not till the goal is reached." Then he would rush up to one of us with blazing eyes and finger pointing and would exclaim, "Remember, God is the only reality." Like a madman, but he was mad for God. For it was at this time that he wrote the "Song of the Sannyasin." We have not only lost our divinity, we have forgotten that we ever had it. Up and down, over and over again. "Don't let yourself be tempted by dolls. They are dolls of sugar, or dolls of salt and they will melt and become nothing. Be a king and know you own the world. This never comes until you give it up and it ceases to bind. Give up, give up."

The training Swamiji gave was individualistic and unique. Unless the desire for discipleship was definitely expressed, and unless he was convinced that the aspirant was ready for the step, he left the personal life of those around him untouched. To some he gave absolute freedom and in that freedom they were caught. When speaking of some of those whom we did not know, he was careful to explain, "He is not a disciple; he is a *friend*." It was an altogether different relation. Friends might have obvious faults and prejudices. Friends might have a narrow outlook, might be quite conventional, but it was not for him to interfere. It seemed as if even an opinion, where it touched the lives of others, was an unpardonable intrusion upon their privacy.

But once one accepted him as a guru, all that was changed. He felt responsible. He deliberately attacked foibles, prejudices, valuations—in fact everything that went to make up the personal self. Did you in your immature enthusiasm see the world as beautiful and believe in the reality of good and the unreality of evil? He was not long in destroying all your fine illusions. If good is real, so is evil. Both are different aspects of the same thing. Both good and evil are in maya. Do not hide your head in the sand and say, "All is good, there is no evil." Worship the terrible even as now you worship the good. Then get beyond both. Say, "God is the only reality." Shall we have the courage to say that the world is beautiful when disaster comes upon us? Are not others the prey of disaster now? Is not the world full of sorrow? Are not thousands of lives overshadowed by tragedy? Are not disease, old age, and death rampant upon the earth? In the face of all this anyone who lightly says, "The world is beautiful," is either ignorant or indifferent to the sorrows of others—self-centered.

Terrible in its sternness was this teaching. But soon there came glimpses of something beyond, an unchanging reality. Beyond birth and death is immortality; beyond pleasure and pain is that *ananda* which is man's true nature; beyond the vicissitudes of life is the changeless. The Self of man remains serene in its own glory. As these great ideas became part of our consciousness, we "saw a new heaven and a new earth." "For him, to whom the Self has become all things, what sorrow, what pain can there be, once he has beheld that unity?" Without once saying, "Be sincere, be true, be single-minded," he created in us the most intense desire to attain these qualities. How did he do it? Was it his own sincerity, his own truth, his own straightness which one sensed?

"This world is a mud puddle!" was received with shocked protest, doubt, and a tinge of resentment. Years after, driving along the Dum-Dum Road in a suburb of Calcutta one glorious Sunday morning, I saw some buffaloes wallowing in a pool of mire. The first reaction was a feeling of disgust. It seemed that even buffaloes should find delight in something more beautiful than mire. But no, they felt physical pleasure in it. Then suddenly came a memory, "This world is a mud puddle." We are no better than these buffaloes. We wallow in the mire of this mud puddle of the world and we too find pleasure in it. We, who are meant for something better, the heirs of immortal glory.

Swami refused to solve our problems for us. Principles he laid down, but we ourselves must find the application. He encouraged no spineless dependence upon him in any form, no bid for sympathy. "Stand upon your own feet. You have the power within you!" he thundered. His whole purpose was not to make things easy for us but to teach us how to develop our innate strength. "Strength! Strength!" he cried. "I preach nothing but strength. That is why I preach the *Upanishads*." From men he demanded manliness and from women the corresponding quality for which there is no word. Whatever it is, it is the opposite of self-pity, the enemy of weakness and indulgence. This attitude had the effect of a tonic. Something long dormant was aroused and with it came strength and freedom.

His method was different with each disciple. With some, it was an incessant hammering. The severest asceticism was imposed with regard to diet, habits, even clothing and conversation. With others his method was not so easy to understand, for the habit of asceticism was not encouraged. Was it because in this case there was spiritual vanity to be overcome and because good had become a bondage? With one the method was ridicule—loving ridicule—with another it was sternness. We watched the transformation of those who put themselves into line with the discipline. Nor were we ourselves spared. Our pet foibles were gently smiled out of existence. Our conventional ideas underwent a process of education. We were taught to think things through, to reject the false and hold to the true fearlessly, no matter what the cost.

Far from trying to win us by expediency and by fitting into our conceptions of what the attitude of a religious teacher toward his disciples should be, Swamiji seemed bent upon offending our sensibilities and even shocking us. He, in the days when men did not smoke before ladies, would approach, and blow the cigarette smoke deliberately into one's face. Had it been anyone else, I should have turned my back and not spoken to him again. Even so for a moment I recoiled. I caught myself and remembered the reason for coming. I had come to one in whom I had seen such spirituality as I had never even dreamed of. From his lips I had heard truths unthought of before. He knew the way to attainment. He would show me the way. Did I intend to let a little whiff of smoke turn me back? It was all over in less time than it takes to tell it.

Then we found that this man whom we had set up in our minds as an exalted being did not observe the conventions of our code. All fine men reverence womanhood; the higher the type, the greater the reverence. But here was one who gave no heed to the little attentions which ordinary men paid us. We were allowed to climb up and slide down the rocks without an extended arm to help us. When he sensed our feeling he answered, as he so often did, our unspoken thought, "If you were old or weak or helpless, I should help you. But you are quite able to jump across this brook or climb this path without help.

You are as able as I am. Why should I help you? Because you are a woman? That is chivalry, and don't you see that chivalry is only sex? Don't you see what is behind all these attentions from men to women?" Strange as it may seem, with these words came a new idea of what true reverence for womanhood means. And yet, he it was, who, wishing to get the blessing of the one who is called the Holy Mother, the wife and disciple of Sri Ramakrishna, sprinkled Ganges water all the way so that he might be purified when he appeared in her presence. She was the only one to whom he revealed his intention. Without her blessing, he did not wish to go to the West. Never did he approach her without falling prostrate at her feet. Did he not worship God as Mother? Was not every woman to him a manifestation in one form or another of the Divine Mother? Yes, even those who bartered their divinity for gold! Did he not see this divinity in the nautch girl of Kshetri, whereupon she, sensing his realization of her true nature, gave up her profession, lived a life of holiness, and herself came into the great realization. Knowing the criticism that awaited him in India, he still dared in America to initiate into *sannyas* a woman, for he saw in her only the sexless Self.

Sannyasin and beggar though he was, never did Swamiji forget to be regal. He was generous to a fault, but never uncontrolled in his generosity. Needless to say, there was never a trace of display in any act which he did. If he was with those who had abundance of this world's goods, he accepted what was offered gladly and without protest, even with an alacrity which at times approached glee. But from those who had little, he would accept nothing.

Swami Vivekananda's compassion for the poor and downtrodden, the defeated, was a passion. To this day his birthday is celebrated by feeding of the poor. The downtrodden, the outcasts are on this day served by brahmins and kayasthas, young men of the highest castes. To those in the West it is impossible to convey the significance of such service. Caste and outcaste! Who but a Vivekananda could bring about this relationship so unobtrusively? No arguments regarding caste and the depressed classes. Nothing but heart and devotion. So even in small things while he was still in America. Thus, when asked why he was taking French lessons, he said in confusion, "This is the only way M.L. can keep from starving." Thrusting a ten dollar bill into the hand of another he said, "Give this to

S.; do not say it is from me." When one of the group, a weak brother, was accused of juggling the Vedanta Society's money, he said, "I will make good any deficiency." Then the matter was dropped but he said to one of the others, "I do not know where I could have found the money to make up the loss, but I could not let poor N. suffer."

Even after he left America, Swamiji still had great concern for those he left behind, who found life a great struggle. Especially did he feel for "women with men's responsibilities." Asked whether he endorsed a certain woman who was going about the country as a religious teacher and using his name and reputation to get a following, he said, "Poor thing! She has a husband to support and she must get a certain amount every month." "But Swami," someone said, "she claims to be authorized by you to prepare students for your teaching. She says if we go through her two preliminary classes, then we will be ready to be taught by you. It is so absurd and unscrupulous. To the first class she gives a few gymnastic exercises and to the second she dictates some quotations or gems which she has gathered from various books on occultism. Should she be allowed to mislead people, take their money and use your name?" All that he said was, "Poor thing! Poor thing! Shiva! Shiva!" With this "Shiva! Shiva!" he put the matter out of his mind. Someone asked him once what he meant when he said "Shiva! Shiva!" and he answered with a mischievous twinkle in his eyes, "Shiver my timbers. Ho, ho, ho, and a bottle of rum." That was not flippancy. How could he answer a casual question otherwise? We had noticed that when something disturbed him, after allowing himself to be troubled by it for a few minutes, his "Shiva! Shiva!" seemed to end it. We knew that he had reminded himself of his true nature, in which everything of a disquieting nature was dissolved.

In New York once there was a pitiful little group that clung to Swami with pathetic tenacity. In the course of a walk he had gathered up first one and then another. This ragged retinue returned with him to the house on 58th Street which was the home of the Vedanta Society. Walking up the flight of steps leading to the front door the one beside him thought, "Why does he attract such queer abnormal people?" Quick as a flash he turned and answered the unspoken thought, "You see, they are Shiva's demons."

Walking along Fifth Avenue one day, with two elderly

forlorn devoted creatures walking in front, he said, "Don't you see, life has conquered them!" The pity, the compassion for the defeated in his tone! Yes, and something else—for then and there, the one who heard, prayed and vowed that never should life conquer her, not even when age, illness, and poverty should come. And so it has been. His silent blessing was fraught with power.

To My Own Soul [1]

Swami Vivekananda

Hold yet a while, Strong Heart,
Not part a life-long yoke
Though blighted looks the present, future gloom.
An age it seems since you and I began our
March up hill or down. Sailing smooth o'er
Seas that are so rare—
Thou nearer unto me, than oft-times I myself—
Proclaiming mental moves before they were!
Reflector true—Thy pulse so timed to mine,
Thou perfect note of thoughts, however fine—
Shall we now part, Recorder, say?
In thee is friendship, faith,
For thou didst warn when evil thoughts were brewing—
And though, alas, thy warning thrown away,
Went on the same as ever—good and true.

[1] Written by Swami Vivekananda during his stay at Ridgley Manor, New York, in 1899. "To my own soul," he said, as he handed the poem to Josephine MacLeod.

Memories of Swami Shivananda

Swami Apurvananda

I

IT WAS DURING the later years of Swami Shivananda's life that I became his personal attendant. At that time he seldom slept at night. His greatest spiritual moods were most manifest during those hours, and he would spend the greater part of the night lost in ecstasy, completely absorbed in divine joy. So intense was this joy at times, that many of the devotees who visited him during the day were conscious of it. It seemed to emanate from his entire body. Sometimes while talking he would be in such a high spiritual mood that very few could understand and appreciate the full depth of his words. Seeing this, he would say, "To whom can I talk on these matters? How many can understand? You are still babies in the kingdom of the spirit. Ah! had Maharaj (Swami Brahmananda) been living now, he would have rejoiced with me!"

Out of the fullness of his heart he would sometimes hum or sing religious songs, or chant verses from the scriptures, while at other times he would remain very still and silent. One night, after spending many hours in meditation, he broke the long silence by slowly chanting a verse from the *Gita*.

> Water flows continually into the ocean
> But the ocean is never disturbed.
> Desire flows into the mind of the seer
> But he is never disturbed:
> The seer knows peace.
> The man who stirs up his own lusts
> Can never know peace.
> He knows peace who has forgotten desire.

He lives without craving:
Free from ego, free from pride.

Becoming suddenly conscious of my presence he looked at
me and said: "Know for certain that the man who stirs
up his own lusts can never know peace. However, without
the grace of God, cravings are not completely rooted out.
Out of his abundant mercy Sri Ramakrishna has wiped
away every trace of desire and craving from my heart. I
have realized my true being—*shuddha* (pure), *buddha*
(awakened), and *mukta* (free). I have no desire left in
me; while the body continues to exist to serve the Lord
in his mission, I can truly say that most of the time I am
unconscious of its existence. I remain almost constantly
merged in the bliss of God."

As he said this his whole face lighted up; he looked like
a different person as he once again became silent, diving
deep into the ocean of Brahman. After a long time he
murmured to himself: "The Divine Mother has filled my
heart. I have nothing more to ask. Through Her grace I
have attained the all. What else is there to attain? As Sri
Krishna truly says in the *Gita*, 'Now he holds it, he knows
this treasure above all others.' Only Mother knows why
She still keeps me in this body."

Another night the Swami was seated on his bed as
usual, deeply absorbed in meditation. Occasionally he became conscious, opened his eyes for a moment, and then
closed them again. This continued for several hours. Suddenly a cat came into the room and began to mew.
Hearing it, the Swami opened his eyes, and folding his
hands together, saluted it. I could scarcely believe he was
actually saluting the cat! Seeing my amazement he explained: "You see, Sri Ramakrishna has so lifted up my
consciousness that everything I see, I see as formed of
pure consciousness. Brahman, the one, eternal, pure consciousness, I see playing in all beings and all things. Their
difference lies in name only: behind the names and forms
I see the one reality. I try hard to hide this, but I cannot!
Pure consciousness is everywhere! And it is that I see
manifest clearly in this cat. Sri Ramakrishna has filled my
heart with this experience. People come to visit me, and I
have to talk to them; I eat, drink, sit, walk—but all these
actions I perform from sheer habit. The moment I withdraw my mind from them I see again the play of the divine
consciousness. Names and forms—these exist only when

the mind is on a lower plane. Raise the mind, and, ah! everything is pure consciousness. It is impossible to make this experience understandable to others. He only knows, who experiences it."

One night the Swami was in a more talkative mood. He said: "Service to the guru is extremely important. It is through the grace of Sri Ramakrishna that you are serving one of his children, but, my child, you must practice meditation and japam also. If you practice these regularly, and follow the spiritual disciplines, then only will you realize what Sri Ramakrishna is. When the mind becomes pure through the practice of stern disciplines, then only is the true nature of God revealed. Even though we saw Sri Ramakrishna, even though we associated with him and found his grace, still he made us practice strenuous spiritual disciplines. Even we who saw him could not realize in the beginning that he was God Himself, incarnated to give liberation to the world. It was only after much spiritual practice that this understanding became firm and sure. Of course, without his grace this understanding does not come. We have known that he is God, the veritable God of the universe. In his grace he has made his true nature known to us.

"Practice japam and meditation at dead of night; great good will follow—your mind will be filled with joy. Indeed, you will find so much joy in your meditation, that you will be reluctant to stop. You are here to keep watch over me and to serve me. Why not make japam during these long hours? My needs are few, only very occasionally I require your services, so practice japam earnestly; dive deep, don't live on the surface. If you will practice japam with an absorbed mind you will find the joy of it. You have renounced the world and have come here to realize God. That is the whole purpose of life; you must never forget that ideal.

"Work hard now. Practice japam and meditation unceasingly. Let the Lord become firmly established within your heart, then will come great peace and joy. When, through the regular practice of these spiritual disciplines, you realize your chosen ideal, within your heart, then also you will realize that the chosen ideal and the guru are not separate. You will see that the guru also resides within the heart—with the death of the guru's body the guru does not die.

"If those of you who live with me think that you alone

are serving me, you are very much mistaken. All those who are earnestly doing the work of our Lord and worshiping Him within their hearts—even though they may be thousands of miles away—they are also serving their guru; they too are very dear to us. They please the Lord by serving Him, and so please us also. If the Lord is pleased, the whole world is pleased.

"When, as young monks, we were living at the Baranagore monastery with Swamiji, I had a very strange experience. Our beds were poor makeshifts, and we all slept together inside the one large mosquito net. One night I was sleeping beside Swamiji, and at about midnight I suddenly awoke and found the whole room illuminated. I turned to look at Swamiji, but, to my amazement, instead of seeing him lying there as I expected, I saw several beautiful young boys, about seven or eight years old in his place. The thought crossed my mind as I saw them lying there, that they looked just like so many Shivas, and I saw that it was the light of their bodies that lighted the room. I rubbed my eyes, thinking they perhaps were deceiving me, but the vision persisted. Dumbfounded as I was, I could not go to sleep again. I passed the rest of the night in meditation. Early in the morning when I looked again I saw that the figures had gone and Swamiji was lying there sound asleep. When he awoke and I told him of my vision he laughed at me. However, a few days later when I was reading the different prayers to Shiva I actually found in one prayer a description of Shiva exactly resembling my vision; this convinced me that I had not been mistaken, my vision was true. You see, Swamiji was born of the spirit of Shiva."

As time passed the Swami became quite seriously ill. He could not walk much, so that each day a disciple came to give him a report of the activities of the monastery. One day when the disciple came as usual to give his report, he noticed that the Swami was sitting quietly. His face was grave and his eyes were half closed, and he appeared not to notice the disciple standing before him. Some time passed before he finally became conscious of the presence of the disciple, and then, as he opened his eyes he said slowly: "You see, this world has no longer any reality for me; Brahman alone exists."

II

By this time the Swami's health had completely broken, so that he could no longer go downstairs to take his accustomed walk. Once in a while he would stroll up and down on the upstairs veranda, leaning on the arm of an attendant.

Referring to his semi-invalid condition he one day remarked: "With the lessening of the outward activity, there is an increase in the inner activity. The mine of supreme bliss is within, and it is the will of Sri Ramakrishna that I remain active with that." Sometimes he would sing softly to himself: "The road death travels is obliterated. All doubts of the mind are gone. . . ." His voice as he sang was very sweet.

There were times when the Swami would talk to us about his spiritual experiences. One evening at dusk, while he was sitting on his bed facing the temple, he suddenly turned and said: "Make haste! Bring me sacramental ash of the Lord Shiva, and spread the silken cover over my bed. The Lord has come! Ah! Sri Ramakrishna is here! The Lord Shiva is here!" With that he fell into a deep silence which lasted most of the night.

On another occasion he said, addressing those present: "Couldn't you see Swamiji and Maharaj when they were here a while ago? They stood right here in front of me and talked to me!"

The Swami's diet was usually very simple. For many years he had avoided all rich foods, eating only rice, boiled vegetables, and soup. Indeed, the soup he took was so plain and unsavory that one of his brother disciples would, in fun, call any tasteless soup "Shivananda soup." But now, during these last few years of his life, he would sometimes surprise us by asking for some special rich dish. One morning, rousing himself from a long silence, he said: "Sri Ramakrishna used to speak of *pankal* fish. He would say, 'Pankal fish lives in the mud, yet no trace of mud ever clings to it. In the same way, a man who has attained God may live in the world yet remain unstained by worldliness.' Remembering this, I would like to see a pankal fish—I would like to taste it also!" So, after much searching, with the help of a fisherwoman, we managed to find a few of these fishes, and when the Swami saw them he was as delighted as a schoolboy. However, when they were cooked and he took a bite or two, he smiled and said: "My desire to eat pankal is quite satisfied!"

At another time he wanted to eat a mango, but his doctor advised against it, because of the Swami's severe asthma at the time. When he was told what the doctor had said, he said quite seriously, "But I must eat mango!" It was impossible to refuse him, so he was given a little of the juice. After taking a sip he said: "I wanted to taste mango again, and now I am satisfied. You see, my children, it is difficult for me to explain why I want to eat these different delicacies. It is not through greed!" Then after a pause he continued: "No! I have not even the least clinging to life left in me, to say nothing of the desire for food!" And in the silence that followed it seemed to us that his mind soared to another world far beyond our vision.

One day a woman disciple came to the Swami and pleaded with him to bless her son who was gravely ill, and restore him to health. The Swami remained silent, and when the woman repeated her request he said: "If it is the will of Sri Ramakrishna your son will get well." The mother went away, only to return a few days later, stricken with grief. Her son had died. Weeping bitterly she said: "You said my son would live, Father! Then why did he die? Why did he die?" The Swami waited a little while for her sobbing to subside, then said: "I knew, my daughter, that your son would not live, but how could I tell you, his mother? That is why I said that he would live if it was the will of Sri Ramakrishna. Do not grieve, my child. I bless you that Sri Ramakrishna may wipe away all sorrow from your heart. Learn to love him as your son. Through his grace there shall be no emptiness in your life; your heart shall be filled with a sweet tranquility." Thus blessed, the devotee went away, and the words of the Swami were fulfilled. Her life was completely transformed.

One afternoon when the Swami was sitting in his room, some strangers from Calcutta came to visit him. They all appeared to be distraught with grief, especially one of the women, whose hair was disheveled, and whose face was distorted with weeping. After introducing themselves to the Swami, one of the men explained why they had come. Pointing to the half-crazed woman beside him, he told him that, a few days ago, their only son had died accidentally, and since that time the mother had been utterly inconsolable; she could neither eat nor sleep, and no words of comfort could bring her peace. Then, folding his hands in supplication, he continued, "So, hearing of you, we have come to you for your blessings. Please bless my wife that she may find peace. My own grief I can bear, but if my wife continues in this way, I think she will die. I beg you, please help her." All the time the man was talking, the poor distraught mother continued to moan: "Oh, my son, why is it that I cannot see you any more?"

The Swami listened with great sympathy, and then, as if to himself, he spoke: "Ah! how can I console them! Their minds have become like hot iron in their sorrow. But you, O Lord, see and know everything. In your mercy, soothe their hearts with your peace." Then, turning to the bereaved father he said: "I do not know how I can console you in your grief. The Lord alone can ease your sorrow. God is kind; why He causes such suffering and misery He alone knows. . . ." Before he could finish speaking, the woman clutched at his feet, crying, "Oh Father, shall I never see my son again? If I could see him just once more, if I could know where he is and what he is doing, I would grieve no more!"

Tenderly the Swami spoke: "My child, how is that possible? None can see the dead. Pray to the Lord, He alone can assuage your grief. I tell you, my child, through His grace your heart will find peace." But the woman would not be comforted. She still continued to plead for one last glimpse of her son, while all the time she still clung to the Swami's feet. Then it seemed that, all at once, a change came over the Swami. His face glowed, and looking at the picture of Sri Ramakrishna, he spoke like one in a trance: "Will you really be satisfied if you see your son just once more? Very well then, I tell you that, through the will of Sri Ramakrishna, you shall see him!" As he spoke, his voice seemed to come from a great way off, and a deep silence fell upon the room. The mother stopped her pleading, and peace was upon them all as they silently left the room.

Although we knew in our heart of hearts that the words of an illumined soul are always fulfilled, still some of us who were present doubted. Why had the Swami spoken so? Could the dead really be seen? Why had he spoken with such assurance? Three days later we knew. In the afternoon the parents came again to see the Swami. They seemed like entirely different people. The face of the grief-demented woman of a few days ago was bright and smiling, and as she prostrated at the feet of the Swami, she said: "Father, my grief has left me. Through your grace I have seen my son, and he is happy. I saw him playing with Sri Krishna. Not only have I seen my son, I have seen my Lord also!" In an ecstatic mood the Swami replied: "I am nobody, my daughter!" Then, pointing to the picture of Sri Ramakrishna, he continued: "He is everything. He is our innermost soul. Everything is his will. Blessed be his name!"

Because of the misdemeanors of one of the novitiates, Swami D. complained to the Swami, and suggested that he call the boy to him and try to correct him. After listening attentively, he said: "Sri Ramakrishna taught us to see an ocean of goodness in a drop of good. He not only taught us this, but he himself practiced it. How else could we have found refuge in him? He did not see our evil traits; he drew us unto himself by his great love. That is how we found shelter in him. Who is there completely free from evil tendencies? None who come here are already perfect; all come to attain perfection, and through the grace of Sri Ramakrishna the bad traits in all will gradually be corrected. Let all live patiently, taking refuge in him. His grace will bring perfection to all."

Still the Swami persisted, until Swami Shivananda became very grave and said sternly: "Do you think your insight is greater than mine? Through Sri Ramakrishna's grace we are able to see a person inside and outside. I cannot tell you in how many different ways Sri Ramakrishna taught us. We can know what kind of a person a man is and what his spiritual tendencies are, even at a glance. You cannot correct a person by scoldings or by lip teachings merely. If you can, try to transform the minds of people by your own inner spiritual power." With folded hands Swami D. prostrated, saying: "Revered sir, I have been mistaken; I am guilty of seeing the faults of others. Please forgive me!" To this the Swami replied affectionately: "If you really wish to correct another and help him, pray earnestly to Sri Ramakrishna for his welfare. Talk to him! If he so wishes he can transform the lives of people by a mere glance!" After a few minutes' silence he continued: "Those who have taken refuge in Sri Ramakrishna are blessed indeed. Each one is great, whether he be a senior or junior in the Order. In each one there has come a divine awakening. Through the good deeds of many past lives, one finds refuge in the holy Order of Sri Ramakrishna."

Swami Shivananda loved everybody equally, and prayed earnestly for the good of all. His blessings were upon all. At one time while he was President of the Order some malicious people tried to belittle the Ramakrishna Mission and the swamis of the Order, by publishing articles of criticism in a newspaper they controlled. When the Swami learned of this, he merely prayed that the critics might find a truer understanding and be freed of their desire to harm the Order.

One of the descriptions given in the scriptures of an illumined soul is that of a little child. Swami Shivananda was no exception. Sometimes he would be sitting on his bed with the *Gospel of Sri Ramakrishna*, the *Gita*, and other scriptures on one side of him, and children's story books and picture books on the other. He even had a little drum. With these toys he would delight himself, tapping on the drum with boyish glee. Explaining the state of his mind at such times he said: "You see, this mind has now a natural inclination to become absorbed in the consciousness of the absolute, and in this way I try to keep it down to the normal plane of consciousness. Just as a mother engages her children with toys, so do I try to engage my mind with these innocent playthings!"

One day, in the course of conversation the Swami said: "You have made Sri Ramakrishna your ideal, and he represents the highest ideal of renunciation. You must never forget that you have taken refuge in him, and that it is your blessed good fortune to belong to his holy Order. In this, you have undertaken a great responsibility. We, his direct disciples, have not long to live in the flesh, and it is by your examples that the people of the future will be guided. Always remember that renunciation is the most precious adornment a monk can wear. The greater your renunciation and dispassion, the nearer you are to God. Indeed, it is not easy to become a true monk. The ideal monk is he who can renounce all cravings in thought, word, and deed. Ceremonial vows and the wearing of the *gerrua* cloth do not make a monk. Learn to be dispassionate and detached; ask for nothing. Surrender yourself wholeheartedly to the Divine Mother. She will supply all that is needed in your own life and all that is needed for Her work."

Early one morning the Swami was to initiate a disciple.

After making the necessary preparations I was about to leave the room when the Swami said: "Why do you go away? There is nothing secret about the mantram. All the mantrams are in the scriptures, but you should know that when the mantram is given to the disciple by an illumined teacher, it becomes a living seed. The teacher, by his spiritual power, gives life to the word, and at the same time awakens the spiritual power latent in the disciple. That is the only secret of initiation."

One day a young attendant of the Swami humbly approached him and said: "Revered sir, often, while serving you, I make mistakes which displease you. You have attained union with God, so that now, whatever you say comes true. This thought worries me, because, if in your displeasure you speak harshly to me, your words may do me harm! Please tell me if I am wrong in thinking so!" Silently the Swami looked at the young brahmachari, and his eyes were filled with deep compassion and love. "My son, Sri Ramakrishna was born for the good of mankind. We are his associates, and have no other wish than the welfare of all men. We cannot think of doing even the least harm to anyone—consciously or unconsciously. He will not let us. You are living here in my company, and serving me wholeheartedly. Sri Ramakrishna brought you here and placed you in my care. Once in a while I may speak harshly to you, but it is always for your good. It is necessary that you be corrected and made perfect. My harshness is superficial; in my heart I have only love and affection, and a deep compassion. Know that for certain. In order that your mistakes may be corrected, in order that all your struggles and strivings, in short, in order that the very current of your life may be directed toward the one goal, union with God, I may sometimes take recourse to strong methods. Your welfare is ever in my heart; if you could know how earnestly I pray for your good, such doubts would never arise in your mind. No, my child, behind my words there is no anger, even though the scriptures say that 'the anger of an illumined soul is also a blessing to a disciple'!"

III

One afternoon when the Swami was seated in his room a spiritual aspirant approached him and, after introducing himself, said: "Revered sir, three years ago I had the great good fortune to meet Maharaj. He was extremely kind to me, so that, after my first meeting with him, I used to come whenever I could find the opportunity, and sit at his blessed feet and practice the spiritual instruction he gave me. In my heart I accepted him as my master, and one day I asked him to initiate me. He was very kind, and said: 'Yes, you shall have initiation, but wait a little while. Do not be in a hurry. The mind must first be made ready; then everything will be easier for you. For the present continue to follow my instructions.' I continued to come as often as I could, but now, alas, he is gone! He passed away before he could give me the initiation he promised. Now I have come to you, because I feel in my heart of hearts that you are not only Maharaj's apostolic successor, but also that his spiritual power is working through you. Please be gracious unto me that I may not again be disappointed."

Looking into the earnest face of the man before him, the Swami replied: "How blessed you are! Already you have received Maharaj's grace. He has instructed you; know for certain that his words are living words, and have great power behind them. Follow the instructions he gave you and you are bound to realize your desired goal. I do not think you need initiation, but if you call upon him with a longing and a yearning heart you will surely see him, and, if need be, he himself will initiate you. His grace is mighty. You should realize that Swami Brahmananda is not just an ordinary illumined soul. He is an associate of God—his eternal companion. By just one look of his a man may be freed from all worldly bondages and attain illumination—if Maharaj so wills. Remember this, when God appears as man for the good of the world He brings with Him such great souls as Maharaj that His message may be spread and His divine purpose fulfilled. Otherwise, as a general rule such rare beings do not come to this world. Furthermore, is Maharaj *dead*? Can such a soul *die*? It is only the encumbering body that drops away when its mission is fulfilled. No, my friend, in his spiritual body Maharaj still lives and continues to bestow his blessings upon the Lord's devotees. You will see him again, I do assure you."

"Yes, I know that what you say is quite true," replied the devotee. "My own experience has recently proved it. After the passing away of Maharaj I felt deeply grieved because he had not initiated me. My mind became extremely restless and I prayed earnestly to the Lord to show me the way. He heard my prayer, for, just three nights ago, Maharaj himself appeared to me in a dream-vision and initiated me with a sacred mantram. But, such is my strange misfortune, on waking I forgot part of it, and, try as I may, I cannot recall the missing syllables. Consequently, my grief is such that I have come to you. Unless you can help me I shall go mad. Please, I pray you, do help me. I know it is within your power to do so. Indeed, I am firmly convinced that, through you, Maharaj will fulfill my longing."

Swami Shivananda listened attentively to the outpourings of the distraught man, and, impressed by his sincerity, remarked: "You have nothing to fear. You have the grace of Maharaj, and through his grace your desire will be granted. Do not be disheartened because you have forgotten the mantram. In his own good time Maharaj will again instruct you. Call upon him with yearning and he will shower his blessings upon you."

But the devotee would not be comforted. Repeatedly and insistently he urged the Swami's intercession until, moved by his earnest importunities, he got up, and, asking the devotee to wait outside, went into Swami Brahmananda's room which adjoined his own. There he remained for about half an hour, then, opening the door, he beckoned to the waiting man to join him. Together they re-entered the room; after a while, the Swami came out alone, his face beaming with spiritual joy.

Later, when the devotee came out he prostrated himself low before the smiling Swami and said: "My joy is full, for this day Maharaj has again given me, through you, the mantram he gave me in my dream. As soon as you uttered the words I recognized them. Most holy sir, you have made me very happy. Now, I pray you, bless me that I may have the vision of my chosen ideal in this very life."

"Blessed indeed you are!" replied the Swami. "It is because of the good karmas of many past lives that you have received such rare blessings in this one. Now dive deep! Dive deep in your meditations, so that, with the help of the treasure you have received this day, you may realize the goal. A true devotee surrenders himself utterly to the Lord and depends entirely upon His grace and guidance. The Lord shows His grace in many ways; therefore, take refuge in Him, pray earnestly to Him for love and devotion, faith and knowledge, and in the ripeness of time He will reveal Himself, and you will find fullness of heart."

The devotee: "I am a householder. I live in the world and have many responsibilities and entanglements. Please, bless me that I may be freed from all these, and that I may pray to the Lord with all my heart and soul."

The Swami: "Even though you do have our blessings, still you must practice your disciplines. Regularly practice japam of the mantram you have been given, and at the same time pray earnestly to the Lord: 'O Lord, help me, I beseech you, that I may properly meditate upon you and that my mind may lose itself at your blessed feet.' Pray thus, knowing that He will hear and answer. He alone is the guru in every heart. He is the inner guide, the father, the mother, friend—man's all-in-all. The Lord alone is man's very own—his constant companion. With one-pointed devotion practice repetition of your mantram. This practice will bring you to meditation, and gradually there will come a feeling of great joy. This feeling of joy again is another form of meditation in that it brings the thought of His presence. The forms and ways of meditation are indeed many. First hold the living, luminous, divine form of your chosen ideal within the lotus of your heart, then try to think that it is the light of His radiance which illuminates the cave of your heart. Thus meditating, your heart will be filled with an ineffable joy. Gradually the divine form will melt in the vision of a conscious, blissful light, and in that vision you will experience ecstasy.

"The first thing needed is an earnest desire to know God, and this is attained through purity of heart. As you call upon God with a yearning heart the impurities of the mind will be washed away, and the heart will become purified. When the heart is completely cleansed of all its impurities it will itself act as the guru. From within your own self will come the knowledge of how to proceed and what to do to find Him. Sri Ramakrishna used to say, 'The breeze of grace is always blowing, but you must set your sails to catch the breeze.' Through repeated practice of your spiritual disciplines you will come to feel the breeze of God's grace."

Devotee: "At times it is extremely difficult to know what is the proper attitude to take in one's dealings with the world and one's duties. It is very hard to please everybody."

The Swami: "You may already have read the *Gospel of Sri Ramakrishna*. Read it again carefully. In the Master's simple teachings are contained all the answers to all your problems. Always remember this: the world belongs neither to you nor to me. It belongs to its Creator. Live in the world with the attitude that all whom you call your own, wife, children, friends, relatives—all belong to God. They are not yours. When you serve them think that you are serving God in so many different forms. By adopting this attitude you will gradually lose all attachment to the world. At the same time practice spiritual discrimination, for through its practice dispassion will arise.

"When the rest of the world lies sleeping, wake up and meditate. That is the best time for meditation. One needs to struggle harder in the beginning of spiritual life. But by and by, through struggle and practice, you will become inebriated with the joy of God. After all, is there any enjoyment in worldly pleasures? Let a man but once experience even a fraction of the joy of God, and worldly pleasures will become tasteless and insipid."

Devotee: "Is it necessary to keep count while making japam?"

The Swami: "Japam can be performed in three ways—verbal, semiverbal, and mental. Mental repetition is the highest form of japam. By cultivating this mental habit it becomes possible to perform japam at any time, whether while walking, sitting, working, or even sleeping. For, as the habit becomes established the mantram will continue even unconsciously in sleep, and with it a continuous current of joy will flow in the mind. But, for the beginner, it is better to keep the count. Try to sit for meditation at least twice a day regularly, and each time make it a point to repeat the mantram never less than a thousand times. The more times the better.

"Sri Ramakrishna used to tell us that word and God are identical. While practicing japam try to keep the mind fixed in the shining form of the chosen ideal. That is, make japam and meditate at the same time. The Lord sees the heart of His devotee, not the number of times he repeats His name or how long he sits in one position. One single repetition of God's name, if made with complete and whole-souled devotion, is far better than the thousand vain repetitions of a distracted mind. Intensity of feeling, intense yearning, and intense earnestness—these are the important virtues. God reveals Himself to the yearning heart. But it must be remembered, this intense yearning for God does not come in a day. Practice is needed. Through intense practice of spiritual disciplines all divine virtues will arise in the heart. Whenever possible seek the company of holy men. Association with the holy inspires devotion to God.

"Doubts arise only so long as the mind is outgoing. As the mind becomes more and more indrawn, as it becomes more and more concentrated at the lotus feet of the Lord, and as it dives deeper and deeper into the realm of the spirit, doubts fade. There remains only pure joy. The heart overflows with pure love for Him.

"But of course doubts will entirely cease to exist only after the vision of God. 'The knot of the heart, which is ignorance, becomes loosened, all doubts are dissolved, all evil effects of deeds are destroyed when He who is both personal and impersonal is realized.'"

William Law [1]

Aldous Huxley

THE WORLD IN ITS concrete reality is complex and multitudinous almost to infinity. In order to understand it, we are compelled to abstract and generalize—in other words, to omit what we choose at the moment to regard as irrelevant and to reduce such diversity as still remains to some form of homogeneity. What we understand is never concrete reality as it is in itself, or even as it appears to be to our immediate experience of it; what we understand is our own arbitrary simplification of that reality. Thus, the worker in natural science abstracts from the concrete reality of actual experience only those aspects which are measurable, uniform, and average; in this way he is able (at the price of neglecting qualities, values, and the unique individual case) to achieve a limited but, for certain purposes, extremely useful understanding of the world. In the same way the historian achieves his much more limited and questionable understanding of man's past and present by selecting, more or less arbitrarily, from the chaotic mass of recorded facts, precisely those which exhibit the kind of homogeneity that happens to appeal to a man of his particular time, temperament, and upbringing. This homogeneity is then generalized as a principle, or even hypostatized as *Zeitgeist;* and these in turn are used to explain events and elucidate their meanings. Such facts as do not suffer themselves to be explained in this way are either explained away as exceptional, anomalous, and irrelevant, or else completely ignored. I may perhaps be permitted, in this context, to quote a passage from an

[1] Published later as an introduction in *Selected Mystical Writings of William Law,* edited by Stephen Hobhouse (New York: Harper & Brothers, 1948).

essay, which I wrote some years ago on Mr. Christopher Dawson's historical study, *The Making of Europe*.

Occasionally, it is true, Mr. Dawson makes a generalization with which I find myself (with all the diffidence of the unlearned dilettante) disagreeing. For example, "The modern European," he says, "is accustomed to look on society as essentially concerned with the present life, and with material needs, and on religion as an influence on the moral life of the individual. But to the Byzantine and indeed to medieval man in general, the primary society was the religious one, and economic and secular affairs were a secondary consideration." In confirmation of this, Mr. Dawson quotes, among other documents, a passage from the writings of St. Gregory Nazianzen on the interest displayed by his fourth-century contemporaries in theology. "The money-changers will talk about the Begotten and the Unbegotten, instead of giving you your money; and if you want a bath, the bath-keeper assures you that the Son surely proceeds from nothing." What Mr. Dawson does not mention is that this same Gregory reproaches the people of Constantinople with an excessive interest in chariot racing, an interest which, in the time of Justinian, a century and a half later, had become so maniacally passionate that Greens and Blues were murdering one another by hundreds and even thousands. Again we must apply the behaviorist test. If men behave as though they took a passionate interest in something—and it is difficult to prove your devotion to a cause more effectively than by killing and being killed for it—then we must presume that the interest is genuine, a primary rather than a secondary consideration. The actual facts seem to demonstrate that some Byzantines were passionately interested in religion, others (or perhaps they were the same) were no less passionately interested in sport. At any rate, they behaved about both in the same way and were as ready to undergo martyrdom for their favorite jockey as for their favorite article in the Athanasian Creed. The trouble with such generalizations as that of Mr. Dawson is that they ignore the fact that society is never homogeneous and that human beings belong to many different mental species. This seems to be true even of primitive societies displaying the maximum of "co-consciousness" on the part of their members. Thus the anthropologist, Paul Radin, well known for his work among the Red Indians, has come to the conclusion that monotheistic beliefs are correlated with a specific temperament and so may be expected to crop up with a certain specific frequency irrespective of culture. If this is true, what becomes of a generalization like Mr. Dawson's? Obviously, it falls to the ground. You can no more indict an age than you can a nation.

We see then, that there is no reason to believe in the homogeneity of the Dark Ages or the Middle Ages. Still less is there any reason for believing in the homogeneity of more recent periods, such as the eighteenth-century "Age of Enlightenment." And, in effect, we find that the age of Gibbon is also the age of Cagliostro and the Comte de Saint-Germain; that the age of Bentham and Goodwin is also the age of Blake and Mozart; that the age of Hume and Voltaire is also the age of Swedenborg and the Wesleys and John Sebastian Bach. And this same Age of Enlightenment produced even stranger sons than these visionaries and magicians, these indefatigable revivalists, these lyrical poets and musicians. It produced the first systematic historian of mysticism, Gottfried Arnold; it produced one of the greatest writers of spiritual letters for the guidance of practicing mystics, J. P. de Caussade. It produced, in Louis Grou, the author of a book of mystical devotion, worthy to take its place among the classics of the spiritual life. And finally, in William Law, it produced a great philosopher and theologian of mysticism.

The notion that any given historical period is homogeneous and uniform is based upon the tacit assumption that nurture is everything and nature nothing at all. By nature, as the most casual observation suffices to convince us, human beings are not all of the same kind; physically, intellectually, emotionally, they vary in the most astonishing manner. Historical generalizations can be valid only if the unifying force of social heredity is always much stronger than the diversifying force of individual heredity. But there is no reason to suppose that it always is much stronger. On the contrary, it is manifest that, whatever the nature of the social and cultural environment, individual physique and temperament remain what the chromosomes made them. Nurture and social heredity cannot change the psychophysical facts of the individual heredity. They merely condition the overt expression of physique and temperament and provide the individual with the philosophy in terms of which he may rationalize his actions. Thus, in an age of faith, the findings of the born empirics and skeptics must be in accord with what is locally regarded as divine revelation and religious authority; for only in this way can they be made to seem intellectually plausible and morally respectable. In a positivistic age the findings of those who are naturally religious must be shown to be in accord with the latest scientific hypothesis; for only on this condition will they have a chance of being taken seriously by those who are not congenitally devout. Individuals, whose native bent is in a direction opposed to that prescribed by the prevailing social patterns and cultural traditions, have to make one of four possible choices —to force themselves into a reluctant but (consciously, at any rate) sincere conformity; to pretend to conform hypocritically, with an eye to the main chance; to dissent, while rationalizing and justifying their noncomformity in terms of the currently orthodox philosophy, which they reinterpret to suit their own purposes; to adopt an attitude of open and unqualified rebellion, rejecting the orthodox rationalizations no less completely than the orthodox behavior patterns. Any kind of individual can be born into any kind of social heredity. It follows that, at any given period, the prevailing social heredity will be unfavorable to the full development of certain kinds of individuals. But some of these nonconforming individuals will succeed, nonetheless, in breaking through the restrictions imposed upon them by the time-spirit—in being, let us say, romantics in an age of classicism, or mystics in defiance of a social heredity that favors born positivists and natural materialists.

In the days when men still did their thinking along theological rather than scientific lines, when they sought to find the primary rather than the secondary causes of events, the facts of individual heredity were explained by a theory of predestination. For our ancestors, Augustinism provided a plausible and intellectually satisfying explanation of human diversity; to us, Augustinism seems a thoroughly inadequate explanation and it is through Mendelism that we seek to understand the observable facts. The earlier hypothesis attributed the phenomena to the good pleasure of God; the latter leaves God out of account and concentrates on the mechanism whereby differences are brought about, preserved, and modified. They agree, however, in regarding individual differences in physique and temperament as things foreordained and, to a considerable extent, unmodifiable by environment.

All the evidence points to the fact that there are born mystics and that these born mystics can pursue their vocation in the teeth of an antimystical environment. Shall we then conclude that the practice of mystical contemplation is reserved exclusively for those whose psychophysical make-up in some sort predestines them for the mystical life? The general consensus of those best qualified to preach on this subject is that this is not the case. The mystical life is possible for all—for the congenitally active and devotional no less than for the congenitally contemplative. Self-transcendence can be achieved by any-one, whatever his or her hereditary constitution and whatever the nature of the cultural environment; and in all cases self-transcendence ends in the unitive knowledge of God. That self-transcendence is harder for certain individuals in certain surroundings is, of course, obvious. But though for many the road to the unitive knowledge of God may be horribly difficult, it seems impious to believe with Calvin and his predecessors and followers that the divine good pleasure has predestined the greater number of men and women to inevitable and irremediable failure. If few are chosen it is because, consciously or unconsciously, few choose to be chosen. "Thy kingdom come, Thy will be done" is the one will and the one hunger that feeds the soul with the life-giving bread of Heaven. "This will," Law continues, "is always fulfilled; it cannot possibly be sent away empty; for God's kingdom must manifest itself with all its riches in that soul which wills nothing else; it never was nor can be lost but by the will that seeks something else. Hence you may know with the utmost certainty that, if you have no inward peace, if religious comfort is still wanting, it is because you have more wills than one. For the multiplicity of wills is the very essence of fallen nature, and all its evil, misery, and separation from God lies in it; and as soon as you return to and allow only this one will, you are returned to God and must find the blessedness of His kingdom within you."

To the practicing mystic *Tat Twam asi* is an axiom, as self-evident in Europe as in India, as much a matter of immediate experience to an Eckhart, a Ruysbroeck, or a Law as it was to a Shankara or a Ramakrishna. What follows is Law's commentary on the precept to "love God with all your heart and soul and strength."

To what purpose could this precept of such a love be given to man, unless he essentially partook of the divine nature? For to be in heart, and soul, and spirit all love of God and yet have nothing of the nature of God within you, is surely too absurd for anyone to believe. So sure, therefore, as this precept came from the Truth itself, so sure is it that every man (however loath to hear of anything but pleasure and enjoyment in this vain shadow of a life) has yet a divine nature concealed within him, which, when suffered to hear the calls of God, will hear the voice of its heavenly Father and long to do His will on earth as it is done in Heaven. Again, to see the divinity of man's original, you need only read these words: "Be ye perfect as your Father which is in Heaven is perfect." For what could man have to do with the perfection of God as the rule of his life, unless the truth and reality of the divine nature was in him? Could there be any reasonableness in the precept or any fitness to call us to be good as God is good, unless there was that in us which is in God? Lastly, "Thou shalt love thy neighbour as thyself" is another full proof that God is in us of a truth, and that the Holy Spirit hath as certainly an essential birth within us as the spirit of this world hath. For this precept might as well be given to a fox as to a man, if man had not something quite supernatural in him. For mere nature and natural creature is nothing but mere self and can work nothing but to and for itself. And this not through any corruption or depravity of nature, but because it is nature's best state, and it can be nothing else either in man or beast.

For the mystic, I repeat, *Tat Twam asi* is an axiom; but for those who have not had the immediate experience that "Thou art That," he tries to find arguments in support of this (to him) self-evident truth—arguments based upon other immediate experiences more widely shared than the mystical realization that Atman and Brahman are one. Law's arguments in the preceding passage are based in part upon the words of Christ, accepted as revelation, in part upon the observable fact of disinterested love for God and for men for God's sake. Another line of argument is to be found in the final chapter of *What Is Life?*, the book in which an eminent mathematical physicist, Professor Erwin Schrödinger examines the problems of heredity in terms of quantum mechanics. Dr. Schrödinger writes:

Immediate experiences in themselves, however various and disparate they be, are logically incapable of contradicting each other. So let us see whether we cannot draw the correct, non-contradictory conclusion from the following two premises:

>(1) My body functions as a pure mechanism according to the Laws of Nature.

>(2) Yet I know, by incontrovertible direct experience, that I am directing its motions, of which I foresee the effects, that may be fateful and all-important, in which case I feel and take full responsibility for them.

The only possible inference from these two facts is, I think, that I—I in the widest meaning of the word, that is to say, every conscious mind that has ever said or felt "I" —am the person, if any, who controls the "motion of the atoms," according to the laws of nature. In itself the insight is not new. From the early great *Upanishads* the cognition *Atman-Brahman* was, in Indian thought, far from being blasphemous, to represent the quintessence of deepest thought into the happenings of the world. The striving of all the scholars of Vedanta was, after having learned to pronounce with their lips, really to assimilate in their minds the grandest of all thoughts.

Space does not permit me to cite Dr. Schrödinger's interesting comments on the fact that "consciousness is never expressed in the plural, only in the singular" and his hypothesis that the "pluralization of consciousness" is the consequence of its connection with "a plurality of similar bodies." Enough, however, has been quoted to make it clear that, while it is impossible that the fact of any immediate experience should be proved by argument, it is nonetheless possible to argue from the premises of other immediate experiences in such a way as to make the existence of the first experience a plausible and probable matter—so plausible and probable that it becomes worth while to fulfill the conditions upon which, and upon which alone, that experience can enter one's life as a fact of consciousness.

In the Society of the Holy

Swami Omkareswarananda

I

IT WAS THE afternoon of a beautiful spring day in March, 1916, when a young Indian girl came to the monastery to see Swami Brahmananda, the president of the Ramakrishna Mission. Forced into marriage by her parents, she had run away from her husband to the monastery, and as soon as she was brought into the presence of Swami Brahmananda she fell at his feet, saying: "O Father, I have no desire to live a worldly life. I wish only to spend my days here at the monastery under your guidance. My one desire is to worship God and realize Him. To Him alone I would surrender myself, body, mind, and soul."

Deeply touched by her evident earnestness and guilelessness of character, the Swami replied: "My child, this is a monastery! How can you stay here? Go back to your parents; they are worried about you. Stay with them; study the scriptures and read the teachings of Sri Ramakrishna and Swami Vivekananda. Pray to Sri Ramakrishna. He knows the yearnings of your heart and will answer your prayers. Later on you may go to the Nivedita School for girls or to the Ashrama of Gouri-Ma. You have the true understanding. Vain indeed is this human birth unless one has love for God!" But the young girl refused to return to her parents' home, so the Swami blessed her and sent her to the Ashrama.

After she had left, the Swami walked slowly into the library where he found Swami Premananda writing a letter. He sat down beside him, and almost immediately went into a highly ecstatic mood. Those who watched him could catch only a glimpse of the joy which shone

199

through his radiant face. His expression and behavior were indescribable. Swami Premananda watched him for a while, then, turning to the young monk who was also present, said "Watch Maharaj! That mood which you see in him is known as the paramahamsa state!"

In a little while Maharaj returned to normal consciousness and said to Swami Premananda, "Who can understand the divine play of Sri Ramakrishna? Swami Vivekananda wanted to see a convent established for young women, and now I see that some day soon his desire will be fulfilled. Young women are becoming imbued with the ideal of renunciation as taught by our Master. That girl who came today was like a goddess in her beauty, her purity, her earnestness, and her guilelessness!"

Later in the day Swami Premananda was seated in meditation under a tree in front of Swamiji's temple. With him were several young monks also meditating. At the close of the meditation period a young monk broke the silence by asking: "Revered sir, why is it that the earnestness and enthusiasm which we feel at the beginning of spiritual life is not sustained? Why does it not continue always the same?" And the Swami answered, "Three things are necessary to strengthen our enthusiasm: association with the holy, devotion to the chosen ideal, and purity of conduct." "But, sir," replied the boy, "here at the monastery we have the holy association of the direct disciples of Sri Ramakrishna!"

"Sri Ramakrishna used to say," replied the Swami, " 'a water vessel made of bitter pumpkin skin may travel to every holy place in the company of a holy man, but it still remains bitter.' What do you understand by holy association? You have to watch their lives, see their purity, their devotion, love and compassion, and imitate these in your own life." Then, turning to the young monk who had witnessed the ecstatic mood of Swami Brahmananda, he continued: "Did you carefully study and observe the blissful state of Maharaj? This is the paramahamsa state. Sri Ramakrishna experienced that quite frequently. With your whole body and mind serve the holy. Question them, and follow their teachings with faith and reverence. Only thus may you be cleansed of the impurities and worldliness accumulated from many lives. By imitating the holy, devotion increases and the heart becomes purified. The association of the holy is the only remedy for worldliness; for a holy man is the living manifestation of God.

"When the heart is purified and the mind becomes one-pointed, subtle, and pure, one attains the vision of God. Retire into solitude occasionally; practice discrimination and self-analysis, and try to discover the subtle obstacles that obstruct your path to spiritual progress. You will find that there are many subtle impressions, habits of thought and action lying dormant and hidden in the subconscious regions of the mind. Analyze yourself in solitude, find out the obstacles and then struggle without compromise to remove them.

"Craving for sense objects is like the sedge that obscures the clear water of a pond, and association of the holy is like the stick used to remove it, that the water may shine through. However, cravings are never entirely uprooted until the Atman is realized. It is written in the *Gita:* 'When a man enters Reality, he leaves his desires behind him.' It is also true that unless the desires are left behind you cannot have the vision of God. Desirelessness and the vision of God are like the opposite sides of the same leaf.

"Sometimes dispassion arises suddenly in a man, due to frustration. Sense objects become like bitter poison to him. But such dispassion is like the fire kindled in a heap of straw. It soon burns itself out. In order to become stabilized in renunciation and dispassion one must try to become absorbed while repeating with single-minded devotion the name of God. Sri Chaitanya used to pass the whole night practicing japam. Practice! Struggle! Struggle hard! Nothing is ever achieved without a struggle."

"But, sir," protested one of the boys, "I don't like practicing japam for a long period at a time. It becomes tiresome. It seems to force me out of my seat!" The Swami smiled. "It is the restlessness of your mind that forces you out of your seat," he answered. "Sri Ramakrishna used to say 'The thread cannot pass through the eye of the needle as long as there is one fibre out of place.' Worldly desires, past habits, are like that. They are the distractions. If you cannot practice japam long, study the scriptures, chant, pray, and engage yourself in unselfish works. Through the faithful practice of discrimination and spiritual disciplines the mind gradually comes under control. Yet to try to force the mind under control all at once may prove disastrous. It must be done gradually, and with patience. The angler has to sit patiently and wait. Cling to the pillar of patience whenever the mind is drawn toward the whirlpool of delusion. Even when a large fish swallows the bait and is caught on the hook, the angler still plays a while before drawing his catch to the bank. To land it forcibly might break the cord. Sri Krishna says: 'The mind is restless, no doubt, and hard to subdue. But it can be brought under control by constant practice, and by the exercise of dispassion.' Little by little, and with untiring patience a man must free himself from all mental distractions. This can be done with the aid of the intelligent will.

"Love one another. Watch yourselves and see that your love for one another never lessens. Remember, the Ramakrishna Mission has been founded on the rock of love.

"Never think that this Mission has been established to create a new sect. There must never be sectarianism; that would be its downfall. This again, does not mean indifference! Indifference is a lack of one-pointed devotion to the chosen ideal. Never be indifferent. Be broad-minded and liberal, and at the same time hold fast to your own chosen ideal. My arms are ever open to embrace all who come here, be they Hindus, Mohammedans or Christians.

"Because you have become monks is no reason why you should scorn householders. Never make a *sect* of monks. Whoever loves God and prays to Him, whoever has made Sri Ramakrishna his own, him I regard as my very own, whether he is a monk or a householder. Vain is this world to one who has not learned to love God.

"The ceremony of renunciation and the wearing of the gerrua robe are not enough. Sri Ramakrishna was the soul of purity and renunciation. Hold fast to him as your ideal, and to make your mind pure. Let not the thoughts of lust, hatred, jealousy, selfishness ever enter the doors of your mind. Whenever such thoughts try to creep in, pray, pray earnestly, and remember the ideal set before you by Sri Ramakrishna and Swamiji, and struggle unremittingly to free your mind of all impurities. Repeat occasionally this prayer of purity:

> May my skin and my bones be purified;
> May my flesh and my blood be purified;
> May the marrow of my bones be purified;
> May all my body be purified.
> May I be free from attachments.
> May I be free from impurities!
>
> May my organs of sense be purified;
> May my organs of action be purified;

May all my actions be purified;
May I be free from attachments.
May I be free from impurities!

May my mind be purified;
May my vital energy be purified;
May the earth and the air be purified;
May fire, ether, and water be purified.
May I be free from attachments.
May I be free from impurities!
May I be pure! May I be pure!
I am verily the Atman!
I am pure! I am free! I am blissful!"

As the Swami finished the prayer, deep silence fell upon the group. No one spoke for some time, for the words of the Swami were full of power and the minds of all those present were elevated to a higher consciousness. After a while the Swami himself broke the silence. "May you all be purified! Brush aside all hatred, jealousy, selfishness, and egotism. Let discrimination guard the doors of your mind, and let not any evil thought enter therein.

"With the fire of dispassion burn away all the impurities of the unregenerate mind. Then only will you realize God and feel His grace. Then only will you see the one, infinite, omnipresent, blissful God dwelling within your own hearts and within the hearts of all beings.

"Ah! I see Him! The blissful one! Alas, the vision of the unregenerate man is upon the vanities of lust and gold! He cannot see the blissful one—so blind is he!

"If you wish to become holy, you must sacrifice all ego. Sri Ramakrishna used to say 'When the ego dies, all troubles cease.' The holy man is a teacher of mankind. To preach religion one must be pure in heart. Mere lecturing is not enough. If a man preaches religion who has not first purified his own heart, he merely feeds his own ego. There are many such, but they can never touch the heart of man.

"Preach by the example of your own life! Let your life, your actions, show that you are indeed children of Sri Ramakrishna. That is what I want to see. Worldly name and fame! What are they? Consider them as things that have been spat out. Whether people speak well of you, or ill, what does it matter? Let the Lord be ever seated within your heart, and silently work as an instrument in His hands."

II

It was the evening of March 14, 1916, the day following the public celebration of Sri Ramakrishna's birthday. Swami Premananda and Swami Akhandananda, disciples of the Master, were seated on a bench on the eastern veranda of the Belur Monastery, overlooking the Ganges. Several other swamis and young brahmacharis (novices) were seated on a bench near by. Presently Swami Achalananda, who was one of the group, addressed Swami Premananda: "Revered sir, please tell us something about Sri Ramakrishna. To hear of him directly from you is far more inspiring and uplifting than to read of him and his teachings in the *Gospel*."

"Very little of the Master's teaching is recorded in the *Gospel*," replied the Swami. "There is too much repetition. M. used to visit the Master occasionally and would note down his teachings as he heard them. But Sri Ramakrishna taught his disciples differently, according to their different temperaments and their capacity of understanding. His teachings to the monastic disciples were given in private. As soon as the householder disciples would leave the room he would get up and lock the door and then speak to us living words of renunciation. He would try to impress upon our young minds the emptiness and vanity of worldly enjoyments. In his great mercy he would point out to us how dry and hot the world is—like a desert, and how, like a mirage, it burns the heart but never slakes the thirst. He taught us how to discriminate and analyze the body, made up as it is of flesh, blood, bones, etc., so that our minds would not run after the enjoyments of the flesh. He would tell us of the great power of the all-bewitching maya, and how man, forgetting his divine heritage, fell ever and again into her clutches. Deep down within his heart man knows full well that there is no lasting happiness to be found in the mad pursuit of worldly enjoyments, and yet, like the camel who chews thorny bushes even while his mouth bleeds, man still stirs up his lust for enjoyment even while he suffers. To satisfy his lust man needs gold. Lust and gold! These are the chains that drag a man down to the pit of worldliness. He alone soars high who shakes himself free of these chains. He who renounces sexual appetites—not only outwardly, but also the cravings of the mind—he it is who has renounced all worldly pleasures. He alone is a man of true renunciation. Renunciation is not in the garb of a monk, nor is it in the renunciation of fish and meat.

"Spiritual aspirants of many different sects would come to visit Sri Ramakrishna at Dakshineswar, and all of them found great satisfaction in talking to him. To each he was able to show the way to further progress along his own particular path, so that each thought that the Master was a perfected soul of his own particular sect. They could not know that Sri Ramakrishna was as broad as the sky and as deep as the ocean, and thoroughly acquainted with all the different sects and paths. For he had followed them each in turn, and by each path he had reached the one and the same goal.

"Never forget that the ideal of life is to realize God, to gain His vision. You have renounced the world to reach that goal. Struggle hard to grow in love and devotion to Him and attain Him. He is the very life of our life, the soul of our soul. He is the Lord of our heart, He is our very own. Yearn for Him with a longing heart. How blessed you are that you have the privilege of serving and associating with such ever-free souls as Swami Brahmananda and others who were the associates of God incarnate! Do not neglect this opportunity. You are men! Be gods! Teach others by the examples of your own lives."

Swami Premananda remained silent for a while, then continued: "I see very clearly that, after we are gone, multitudes will come to learn from you young men."

A young Swami: "But, revered sir, how can that be? If multitudes are to come, they should come while you are still living."

Swami Premananda replied: "Do not think that you are any less great than we! You have received the grace of the Holy Mother. Do you think we have become great just because people have come to take the dust of our feet? No! We first saw Sri Ramakrishna and then renounced the world; you are great indeed because you have renounced the world without seeing him!"

Young Swami: "But revered sir, Sri Ramakrishna made you great."

Swami Premananda: "No! Sri Ramakrishna did not make us great; he made us 'nobodies.' You also have to become 'nobodies.' Wipe out all vanity and all ego sense. 'Not I, not I, but Thou, O Lord.' Look at the life of Nag Mahashay! There was not the least trace of ego in him.

G. C. Ghosh used to say, 'Maya tried to bind Nag
Mahashay and Vivekananda in her net, but Nag Mahashay became smaller than the smallest, so that maya's net
could not hold him, and Vivekananda grew bigger and
bigger; he became one with the infinite, and the net was
too small to bind him.'

"Do you know of what this net of maya is composed?
Sense objects, lust, gold, name, fame, ego, vanity, selfishness, and so on. With all these maya binds the mind of
man. Come out of this net, and the mind will run straight
to God. All bondage is in the mind. All freedom is in the
mind.

"The worldly man is drunk with the objects of sense,
with name, with fame, with lust, with gold. Be you also
drunk, but be drunk with selfless works, with love of God,
with ecstasy, with samadhi!"

Swami Brahmananda now came and sat silently beside
Swami Premananda. Swami Shivananda followed and sat
on a bench facing them. Many young swamis and brahmacharis—about sixty altogether—came and sat around
the swamis. In the presence of Swami Brahmananda, the
spiritual son and most beloved disciple of Sri Ramakrishna, the minds of all were filled with joy; they became
lost in contemplation. Stillness reigned within their hearts;
all nature seemed to stand still, while the Ganges flowed
silently by.

Some time passed in that great silence, until, after a
while, it was broken by a remark about the well-known
Shankara monastery at Puri and the abbots connected
with it. Then, as the conversation drifted from one subject
to another, Swami Brahmananda said: "Once, when I was
at Puri, I met a holy man whose name was Ranga Swami.
He was about ninety-five years old, and a man of great renunciation. He was always drunk with the love of God.
He would eat only that which had first been offered in the
temple. At one time he was very ill, and I wanted to give
him some medicine, but he refused to take it. Knowing
his habit I arranged with the priest of the temple to offer
some milk to the Deity, and with that I mixed the medicine which the Swami took as sacramental food."

Swami Shivananda broke in: "I also knew that man! He
went to Puri when he was fifteen years old, and lived continually in the temple for eighty years!"

In the course of conversation a well-known writer and
preacher was mentioned.

Swami Shivananda: "But what can he know about religion? He is steeped in worldliness. He who does not live the life of renunciation cannot be a teacher. Dispassion is the first principle of spiritual life. A man of learning may write books or give lectures, but if he has no dispassion in his heart, and if he does not practice what he teaches, his words cannot be effective, for they have no power behind them. They merely create a momentary sensation.

"The other day I learned that a certain preacher of the Brahmo Samaj was complaining that more people were coming to the Belur Math and fewer to the Brahmo Samaj, and that someone had suggested that they introduce a girls' choir to attract the people. When the revered Shivanath Shastri heard this he remarked that if the Brahmos would incorporate into their lives more of the dispassion and renunciation of the monks of the Belur Math, they too would attract people."

Swami Brahmananda: "Shivanath Shastri is a sincere soul and has a great regard for truth. He is earnest in his desire to realize God. He is living now at Bhubaneswar and is practicing spiritual disciplines. He already has some inner awakening. After all, he had the blessed good fortune to associate with our Master. Bijoy Goswami was another great spiritual leader in the Brahmo Samaj, and it was a great loss to the Brahmos when he left it."

Swami Shivananda: "One day Swamiji, Swami Akhandananda, and I were traveling on the river Ganges. Swamiji was speaking very highly of Maharshi Devendra Nath Tagore, when all at once we noticed the Maharshi's yacht at some distance from us. We approached nearer to pay our respects to the Maharshi, who, when he learned that we were disciples of Sri Ramakrishna, seemed very happy to meet us, and repeatedly remarked: 'Ah! how great is the love of Sri Ramakrishna! How great is his devotion!' The Maharshi then asked Swamiji to recite some passages from the *Upanishads*, which he did. After listening for some time he said, 'I understand and appreciate the devotional passages in the *Upanishads;* I do not care for the nondualistic ideas.' "

After listening to the discussions for some time, Swami Premananda remarked: "When Shivanath Shastri or some other of the learned members of the Brahmo Samaj would visit Sri Ramakrishna, he would sometimes become just like a little child and ask them: 'Is my condition really like that of one who is mad? Tell me, have I gone crazy, thinking of God?' And indeed, there were some who really did think that our Master was a madman!"

Swami Brahmananda: "Only a jeweler can know the value of a jewel. There was once a poor man who found a diamond. He had no idea of its value, so he took it to the vegetable market to have it appraised. The vegetable man looked at it, and then offered him five cents worth of vegetables for it, but the poor man thought it was worth twenty cents worth of vegetables. Upon being refused, he took it to a rice merchant who offered him one bag of rice, but he wanted four bags. Next he went to a goldsmith, and he was offered one hundred rupees. This offer aroused the greed in the poor man, and he began to realize that the diamond was really valuable, so he took it to a jeweler who offered him twenty thousand rupees. Even this did not satisfy him, so he took it to the finest jeweler in the city. As soon as the jeweler saw it he realized its real worth and immediately offered him a million rupees. And that is how it goes. A holy man is judged according to the worth and capacity of the appraiser. By some Sri Ramakrishna was regarded as a holy man, by others as a perfected soul or as a great devotee of God. Some regarded him as a madman, while still others as an incarnation of God."

The Sixth Patriarch

Aldous Huxley

In Dwight Goddard's extremely valuable compilation, *A Buddhist Bible,* there is one document of which I am specially fond—"The Sutra Spoken by the Sixth Patriarch." That blending of Mahayana Buddhism with Taoism, which the Chinese called Ch'an and the Japanese of a later period called Zen, achieves its earliest formulation in this account of Hui-neng and his teaching. And whereas most of the other Mahayana sutras are written in a somewhat forbidding philosophical style, these recorded reminiscences and sayings of the Sixth Patriarch exhibit a freshness and liveliness which make them quite delightful.

Hui-neng's first "conversion" took place while he was still a youth. "One day, while I was selling firewood in the market, I heard a man reading a Sutra. No sooner had I heard the text of the Sutra than my mind became all of a sudden enlightened." Traveling to the Tung-tsen monastery, he was received by the Fifth Patriarch who asked "whence I came and what I expected to get from him. I replied that I was a commoner from Sun-chow, and then said, 'I ask for nothing but Buddhahood.'"

The boy was then sent to the granary of the monastery, where for many months he worked as a laborer, hulling rice.

One day the Patriarch assembled his monks and, after reminding them of the uselessness of merit in comparison with liberation, told them to go and "seek the transcendental wisdom within your minds and write me a stanza about it. He who gets the clearest idea of what Mind-Essence is, will receive the insignia and become the Sixth Patriarch."

Shin-shau, the most learned of the monks and the man

209

who was by all expected to become the Sixth Patriarch, was the only one to do as the Abbot had commanded.

> Our body may be compared to a Bodhi tree,
> While our mind is a mirror bright.
> Carefully we cleanse and watch them hour by hour,
> And suffer no dust to collect upon them.

So he wrote; but the Fifth Patriarch told him to go back to his cell and try again. Two days later Hui-neng heard someone recite the stanza, knew immediately that its author had not achieved enlightenment and himself dictated, to someone who knew how to write, the following lines:

> By no means is Bodhi a kind of tree,
> Nor is the bright reflecting mind a case of mirrors,
> Since mind is Emptiness,
> Where can the dust collect?

That night the Fifth Patriarch summoned the youth to his cell and secretly invested him with the insignia.

Not unnaturally Hui-neng's fellow monks were jealous, and many years elapsed before he was generally recognized as the Sixth Patriarch. Here are a few examples of his utterances, as recorded by his disciples.

"Since the object of your coming is for the Dharma, please refrain from having opinions about anything, but try to keep your mind perfectly pure and receptive. I will then teach you. When he had done this for a considerable time I said, 'At the particular moment when you are thinking of neither good nor evil, what is your real self-nature?' As soon as he heard this, he became enlightened.

"People living under illusion expect to expiate their sins by the accumulation of merit. They do not understand that the felicities to be gained thereby in future lives have nothing to do with the expiation of sin. If we get rid of the principle of sin within our own minds, then and only then is it a case of true repentance.

"People under delusion are stubborn in holding to their own way of interpreting samadhi, which they define as 'sitting quietly and continuously without letting any idea arise in the mind.' Such an interpretation would class us with inanimate beings. It is not thinking which blocks the Path; it is attachment to any particular thought or opinion. If we free our minds from attachment on the one

hand and from the practice of repressing ideas on the
other, the Path will be clear and open before us. Otherwise
we shall be in bondage.

"It has been the tradition of our school to take 'non-ob-
jectivity' as our basis, 'idea-lessness' as our object and
'non-attachment' as our fundamental principle. 'Non-ob-
jectivity' means not to be absorbed in objects when in contact with objects. 'Idea-lessness' means not to be carried
away by any idea which may arise in the process of exercising our mental faculties. 'Non-attachment' means not
to cherish craving or aversion in relation to any particular
thing or word or idea. Non-attachment is the characteristic
of Mind-essence or Suchness.

"Where thinking is concerned, let the past be dead. If
we allow our thoughts, past, present and future, to become
linked up into a series, we put ourselves under bondage.

"Our true Nature is intrinsically pure, and if we get rid
of discriminative thinking, nothing but this intrinsic purity
will remain. Nevertheless in our system of Dhyana, or
spiritual exercises, we do not dwell upon purity. For if we
concentrate our mind upon purity, we are merely creating
another obstacle in the way of the realization of Suchness,
namely the delusive imagination of purity.

"The Sutra says, Our Essence of Mind is intrinsically
pure. Let us each realize this for himself from one momentary sensation to another."

The account of the Patriarch's last days is unfortunately
too long to quote in full. About a month before his death
Hui-neng informed his disciples of his impending departure and gave them some final words of advice, among
which the following are notable. "You are especially
warned not to let the exercise for concentration of mind
fall into mere quietism or into an effort to keep the mind
in a blank state." And again, "Do your best, each of you.
Go wherever circumstances lead you. Listen to this stanza:

With those who are sympathetic
You may have discussion about Buddhism.
As to those whose point of view differs from ours,
Treat them courteously and try to make them happy.
Do not dispute with them, for disputes are alien to our
    school,
They are incompatible with its spirit.
To be bigoted, to argue with others in disregard of this rule

Is to subject one's Mind-essence to the bitternes of this
mundane existence."

On his last day the Patriarch assembled his disciples and
told them that they were not to weep or mourn for him
after his death. "He who does so is not my disciple. What
you should do is to know your own mind and realize your
own Buddha-nature, which neither rests nor moves,
neither becomes nor ceases to be, neither comes nor
goes, neither affirms nor denies, neither remains nor de-
parts. If you carry out my instructions after my death,
then my going away will make no difference to you. On
the other hand, if you go against my teachings, even were
I to remain with you, no benefit would be yours."

After this he sat reverently until the third watch of the
night, then he said abruptly, "I am going now," and in a
moment passed away. At that time a peculiar fragrance
pervaded the room and a lunar rainbow appeared to link
the earth and heaven; the trees in the grove turned pale
and the birds and animals cried mournfully.

Days with Swami Turiyananda

Swami Atulananda

I

ALTHOUGH THE SOLAR eclipse of 1907 was still a few days off, Kurukshetra was already crowded with fifty thousand pilgrims from all over India, when Swami Turiyananda alighted from a packed train that halted at the little railway station. It was evening of the first day of the great religious festival. The rest houses and temporary shelters and tents were filled with men, women, and children, all huddled together like sheep in their folds. We went from place to place but could find no shelter and there remained nothing to do but spread our blankets with other pilgrims under the protecting branches of a magnificent banyan tree. So using our little bundles as pillows we sat down and rested.

Presently a woman approached us and, with palms folded against her breast, asked whether we had had supper. When the Swami answered that we had not yet eaten she hastily retreated, and, from her own camp, brought us milk, wheat cakes, and a vegetable curry. Simple as the meal was, we both enjoyed it heartily. Then we rolled ourselves in our blankets and lay down to sleep.

I was watching the brilliant stars through the branches of the tree when, after a while, I saw the Swami sit up.

"What is the matter, Swami?" I asked.

"Gurudasa," he answered, "now you are a true sannyasin."

"That is what I want to be, Swami," I responded, and I quoted from Swamiji's "The Song of the Sannyasin":

Have thou no home. What home can hold thee, friend?
The sky thy roof, the grass thy bed; and food

213

What chance may bring; well cooked or ill, judge not.
No food or drink can taint that noble Self
Which knows itself. The rolling river free
Thou ever be, Sannayasin bold. Say *"Aum tat sat, aum!"*

"That is it! That is it!" the Swami exclaimed. "We are
Mother's children; we have nothing to fear. She gives
and She takes. Blessed be Her name." Then followed one
of his familiar eulogies of Swamiji. "He was the true
sannyasin. In luxury and poverty he was the same. He
knew that he was the Atman, the witness, ever free. Weal
or woe meant nothing to him. The world was his stage.
And how well he played his part! He lived for the good of
others. There was no selfishness in him. He had no ax to
grind. He lived and preached the Master's message. Our
Master used to say: 'He can do anything he pleases. Nothing can spoil him!' "

Then, after a little pause, "But we have to be careful.
Maya is so powerful. We are so easily caught and deluded."

"But," I interposed, "Mother can protect us."

"You are right, Gurudasa; never forget that. Always
trust in Her. What is life without Her? It is all sham. She
alone is real."

Another pause, and then: "Now try to sleep a little.
Tomorrow we may find a better place."

I tried to sleep but could not. The experience was so
novel and thoughts came rushing into my mind. The
Swami was lying down again but I don't think he slept any
more than I did. It must have been long after midnight
when I saw him get up.

"Gurudasa, it is raining," he said. "We must get shelter
somewhere!" I had not noticed the sudden change in the
sky, but as I listened I heard raindrops falling on the
leaves of the tree. We got up and with our blankets over
our heads went in search of shelter. But, as before, we
found every place filled. The Swami, however, was determined to get in somewhere. And so against the loud pro-
tests of the pilgrims, we pushed our way into one of the
open sheds. There was a great hubbub, loud voices and
sleepy voices, abuse and discussion of which I understood
very little. I thought they would throw us out bodily. But
suddenly the noise quieted down and a little room was
made for us. We laid down wedged in between other pilgrims like sardines in a box. We were out of the rain any-

how, and presently I fell asleep. When I awoke in the morning I found that a child was using my legs for a pillow. I was sore all over, for I had been lying on a hard earthen floor.

As I said before, we were in an open shed, that is, it had only three walls. And now the sun was shining through the open space. Many of the pilgrims had already gone out to wash themselves at the well nearby. We followed their example, and when we returned we found the shed half empty, for many of the pilgrims had gone in search of better lodgings.

I asked the Swami how he had succeeded in getting inside the shed when the opposition was so strong. He laughed and said, "You don't know us yet. We make a big noise but there is nothing back of it. You, in the West, take everything so seriously. Here you will see two men talking and gesticulating as if they were going to murder each other. But five minutes later they sit and smoke together and talk as if they were old friends. That is our way. These people are not educated but they have good hearts. When they saw that we were really in trouble they made room for us even though it inconvenienced them. I told them that you were a stranger in a strange land, and a sannyasin. At once they became curious and wanted to know all about you. Then they said, 'Come, brothers, we will make room for you.' You will always find it so. Sannyasins are respected all over India, especially by the poor. They are simple and kindhearted; not sophisticated like some of our educated people. Swamiji loved the poor. His heart bled for them. 'They are my gods!' he used to say. That is why our Mission works so much among the poor. All over India we have centers for them. We educate them and give them free medical treatment. We serve God in the poor."

After a while he said, "We are on the battlefield of Kurukshetra where Sri Krishna preached the *Gita*." Then he began to chant from memory the second chapter. A few pilgrims came and listened. He chanted in a loud voice with much feeling.

Just as the Swami finished chanting, a man approached us. He scowled and said, "What are you doing in my shed?" Swami replied, "We are sannyasins, we are taking shelter here." "Who is the sahib?" he asked. (We learned later that he suspected me of being an English spy in disguise.) Swami told him who I was and that I had come to

see the religious festival and bathe in the holy waters of
Kurukshetra. At this he became quite amiable and said,
"You may both stay here as my guests. I will supply you
with food." He called a servant and told him to place some
straw under our blankets. Then, saluting us very humbly,
he went away.

When he had gone, Swami said to me, "See how Mother
plays! Now we can be at peace. Do you think you can
stand it?"

"Yes, Swami," I replied. "I am sure I can."

A little later a servant brought us food—unleavened
wheat cakes and molasses. He brought this every morning. And every evening, for nine days, we had wheat
cakes and lentil soup. Sometimes our host would come
and ask how we were getting along. There were other pilgrims in the shed but we had sufficient room to spread our
blankets. These pilgrims cooked their simple meals on
little earthen stoves built against the inner wall. As there
was no outlet for the smoke the air often became suffocating, and it made my eyes smart. But we did not complain since it could not be remedied. We got along very
well except that I suffered from fever now and then. I
was, however, able to move about. On the days when I
had fever, I could not eat the coarse food, and Swami,
full of tender solicitude for my health, would buy me a
cup of milk.

In the evening many would come to converse with the
Swami and to receive spiritual advice from him. He
would talk for hours till late in the night, never tiring. He
was always ready to speak on religion. After our morning
bath and meal we would go about among the pilgrims,
visit other sannyasins and holy places. We were shown the
exact spot where Sri Krishna delivered the *Gita* to Arjuna;
the place where Bhishma expired at his own will, his body
resting on a bed of arrows, and many other places sanctified by tradition. Most interesting of all was the great con-
course of different monks of different sects. There were
naked monks and those who wore only clouts, the rest of
their bodies besmeared with ashes from the sacred fire.
Others wore salmon-colored robes and turbans. Some had
long shaggy hair bleached by the sun and hanging down
their shoulders or coiled like a little tower on top of their
heads. Then there were shaven monks, and brahmacharis
in white tunics. It was the most motley crowd I had ever
seen.

Erudite pandits and sannyasins held discussions or read and chanted from the Vedas, while sitting cross-legged under the trees or in front of their little tents or straw huts. One monk had taken the vow of perpetual silence; another took food only when it was offered to him. One monk in a red robe had taken the vow to remain standing in one place for nine days, his arms resting on a trapeze attached to the limb of a tree. There was something to interest us wherever we went.

Then came the day of the eclipse, when everyone must bathe during the auspicious hour when twilight enfolded us. The crowds were so vast and the rush so great that though the reservoirs were of enormous dimensions it was difficult to enter the water. But we succeeded in dipping three times when the eclipse was full. It was a grand spectacle, this bathing in the sacred waters by thousands of enthusiastic devotees.

Afterwards we discussed the merit of bathing and other religious performances. Swami said: "It all depends on our mental attitude, on our faith and belief. Where there is true devotion the result is good. It purifies the mind. We must try to see Mother in everything. That will make us spiritual." Then he quoted from the Chandi, "To that Divine Mother who dwells in all living beings in the form of Consciousness, we bow down again and again."

"She is in everything and She is everything. She is the river, She is the mountain, She is all." "That is a grand vision. Our Master had that. He did not see the Ganges, he saw only Brahman."

When the festival was over we separated. The Swami remained at Kurukshetra for a few days as the guest of a man who took him to his home at Anup Sahar, and I left for Delhi and other places on my way to the Belur Math.

II

Three years had passed since I left Swami Turiyananda at Kurukshetra where we had been together during the great religious festival of 1907. And now, on the 7th of April, 1910, I met him again at Kankhal where Swami Premananda and I arrived by the early train from Banaras.

On my arrival at the Shevashrama I went at once to his room where he was expecting me. When I entered I found him seated on his bed. He had a peaceful expression in his face and eyes. His voice was low but steady; and behind his physical weakness I detected great inward strength. Every movement, even his voice indicated this.

After a few words of mutual greeting, the Swami inquired after my health. "You look weak and much reduced," he said. "Why did you not consult a good physician in Calcutta? It is the food. Our food does not agree with you. We don't know how to take proper care of our health; that is why we suffer so much. Be strong; don't be weak. But never mind the body. I have been near death for the last six months, but I did not care. I had no fear. I was ready to go. But Mother did not allow it yet. I realize more and more that She does everything. We are only machines. We cannot do anything unless She allows it. May we never forget it."

"But why does She make us weak?" I asked.

"She knows," the Swami answered. "There may be good in weakness also. Nothing is absolutely bad. But we are not able to judge."

In the afternoon I told Swami that I had received a book dealing with symbolism.

"Why do you trouble yourself with symbolism?" he asked. "Our Master's teaching is so simple and easy. It is the straight path. Once a learned pandit came to him and for two hours spoke on Vedanta philosophy. Then the Master said, 'Sir, what you say may be very beautiful, but I don't understand all these things. I know only my Divine Mother and that I am Her son.' This opened the pandit's eyes. 'Blessed you are, sir!' he exclaimed. The Master's simplicity so touched him that he wept."

In the evening we talked about America and the students and friends there. "Mother was so kind to take me there," the Swami said. "They are all near and dear to me. Often I feel their presence. I sometimes close my eyes and call up one of them. Of course they do not know it; it is only my imagination! But it satisfies me."

Speaking about the attitude of different people toward me, he said, "Everything is our own projection. Good and bad are in our own mind; we should try to see good everywhere. When Mother is near, all is well. In Her absence difficulties arise."

The following morning a young man arrived from Holy Mother's village. Holy Mother had initiated him into the order of sannyasins and had given him a letter addressed to Swami Turiyananda asking him to perform the necessary rites. He had stopped at many places on his way to Kankhal and had found that the food outside Bengal did not agree with him. Hearing this, the Swami said, "I wonder sometimes how we could live as we did in our youth. Now I find it difficult, but through strength of mind I can still do it, even though the food is still poor. In those early days we did not care. Food, health, body were of no consideration. We had an ideal and for that we lived. We used to meditate much. We would get food only once a day—a few pieces of bread collected from many houses, and a little buttermilk. Anything satisfied us. And I got stout and strong. Perhaps in old age we require better food. But that is also mental. We think the food worthless and we don't get nourishment from it. Those are happy days when we don't think of our bodies."

A brahmachari asked, "Maharaj, what is a good subject for meditation?" "Any subject that appeals to you," the Swami replied. "All lead to the same goal. That will adjust itself."

Speaking about the relationship between guru and disciple, the Swami said, "The guru should hold the disciple through love. He should not bind him, but give him full freedom. He who binds will be bound himself. He should rule from the heart, not from the head. His aim should be to dispel delusion, to clear the vision."

Then came the question of obedience. "The disciple should obey through love, not through fear. That would be slavery. Those who want power exact obedience. They want to rule. That is littleness."

The following day the Swami spoke about Swamiji. "He had wonderful powers; he influenced many. But few acknowledge it. Many give his teachings as their own. He was fearless." And he quoted, "The wise knowing the Brahman become fearless."

"Do they become fearless of rebirth also?" I asked.

"For them there is no rebirth. Or if there is, you cannot call it birth, for even then they are free. Shiva, Shiva, Om tat sat! They are fearless because they are not attached. When Mother is known, attachment goes. The world then becomes so small, so insignificant—a little mud puddle." A faraway look came into his eyes and he became silent. His face seemed to shine with a peculiar light.

The following day he spoke about his American experience and his travels with Swamiji. "It is all Mother's grace," he said. "Shiva, Shiva! Without Her all is misery.

Her grace comes when we implore Her; when our heart continually goes out to Her."

A few days later when Swami was able to walk about a little, he came to my room. Seeing Sri Ramakrishna's photograph on my table, he said, "He stands alone; there is none like him. One day Keshab took him to a photographer and asked him to stand quietly for a moment. He obeyed like a child, and that is how his picture was taken."

In the afternoon I went to his room and found Swami Premananda there. He was eating some grain. "Wait, Swami," I said, "I will bring you a little salt." When I came back, Swami Turiyananda, quoting from the Bible, said, " 'Ye are the salt of the earth: but if the salt hath lost its savour, wherewith shall it be salted?' How powerful are the words of Jesus. 'Foxes have holes, and birds of the air have nests; but the son of man hath nowhere to lay his head.' He was a true sannyasin."

"Living in India," I said, "gives one a better understanding of the Bible. The Biblical stories are enacted here every day. I can picture Jesus' life much better since I have seen how the sannyasins live. To be here is a wonderful experience."

"Yes," Swami replied, "and especially when you see it with the eyes of a monk."

Then I spoke about Lady Minto's visit to the Belur Math. She had asked the monks there what Sri Ramakrishna taught. One had answered, "He taught from the Hindu scripture." When the Swami heard this, he said, "His words were scripture. He taught even more than the scriptures. But he himself used to say that everything he taught could be found in our scriptures."

"Did not his teachings differ somewhat from Shankara's maya theory?" I asked.

"Yes," he replied. "Shankara taught only one phase, how to get freedom, nirvana. Our Master first gave freedom and then taught how one should live in the world. His touch would make you free. But those who follow his instructions also get free. His word had such power. Be free first. Then see Mother in all! Be Her playfellow. We don't care for nirvana; we want to serve the Lord. We have touched the grandame and cannot be made thief again." (Sri Ramakrishna used to say: "As in the play of hide-and-seek, the person touching the grandame is free to go wherever he chooses without being pursued and made a thief of, so also in this world's playground there is no fear

for him who has touched the feet of the Almighty. He
attains freedom from all worldly cares and anxieties and
nothing can ever bind him again.")

"When life becomes painful we go to Her, and remembering Her, find peace. Because Sri Ramakrishna taught
from the simple things of everyday life, we are constantly
reminded of him. He taught us to see Mother in everything—in trees, in flowers, in insects, in human beings.
Alive or dead, we are always in Mother. First we realize
this and then remember it constantly. Then the world
cannot taint us. How difficult life is without Her. But with
Her, how easy it becomes! We become fearless!"

The doctor now entered the room. After examining the
Swami he said, "He will be well soon, if he is careful. He
is still very weak. It will take a long time."

When the doctor had left, I asked the Swami whether
his physical weakness had affected his mind also. "No," he
replied, "for the mind has something to rest on." "On
Mother," I said. "Exactly," he replied. "Ordinary people
identify themselves with the mind. I have seen my mind
as something separate from me. How then can I identify
myself with mind again? I realized my critical condition,
but I had no fear."

Later on in the day I read to him the notes taken during his *Gita* classes in the Shanti Ashrama in America. He
enjoyed the reading. Then he told me his experiences during his pilgrimage to Kedar Nath. He and two other
swamis had been without food for several days, when
they were caught in a snowstorm. Weary and cold, they
were about to give up their lives in meditation, when they
came to a miserable hut where they spent the night. The
following day they reached a village and got food.

When I came to his room again, he began at once,
"What we know we must put into practice. Through
practice new knowledge comes. Do something; practice!
Bondage and freedom are both in the mind. The Atman is
beyond mind."

"Can one who has had realization do wrong actions?"
I said.

"Some say yes," he replied, "through their past karma.
But for them it is not sin. They are unattached. No new
karma is created in their case. They can do or abstain
from doing at will. They are masters of their mind. Try to
live with those who have mastered the mind. If you cannot
live with them, think of them. Mind controls mind. The

mind can be concentrated in many ways, through meditation, singing, reading, etc. Always watch your mind. Be master of the senses and mind.

> May we hear with our ears what is right and good;
> May we see with our eyes what is holy and beautiful;
> May we keep our body and mind under control.
> Om tat sat."

In the course of our conversation, Latu Maharaj was mentioned. One amongst us said, "He had no education." "But he is a wonderfully spiritual man," I said, "and he knows the scriptures." "He not only knows the scriptures," the Swami interposed, "but he is the scriptures personified. He lived with our Lord."

Toward evening a party of pilgrims came to see the Swami. One of the men remarked that meditation is dangerous without a guru. The Swami did not agree with him. "Pranayama (breathing exercises) is dangerous," he said, "without proper instruction, but not meditation. In the sixth chapter of the *Gita* you will find instructions for meditation."

Speaking about a person who had received ill treatment from others, Swami said, "He bore no ill will. That is wonderful, the true religious spirit. That is Mother's grace. She held him by the hand. Always remember that whatever befalls us is Mother's doing, and for our own good. Mother will keep him always, I am sure. Of course at times he felt hurt, but he realized that it was a weakness. Why should we feel miserable at bad treatment? But everyone is weak at times; and then we suffer. If Mother is near, that which otherwise would be suffering is no longer suffering. We should not judge harshly those who try to harm us. Never lose faith in Mother. Faith keeps us. Everyone feels depressed at times, but all do not show it."

Later he said, "When I get a letter from you, I get a picture of your mental state, and I answer as if by inspiration, without much thought."

The following day I found Swami Premananda, Swami Kalyanananda and others in his room. The talk was on Swamiji's work in the West. He said, "Swamiji was fearless. He taught the highest without compromise. He always gave and asked nothing in return; if others give one drop, they expect a bucketful!"

Swami Premananda said, "We have seen two men, our

Master and Swamiji. No other men can be compared to them." Swami Turiyananda replied, "When I saw Sri Ramakrishna for the first time he was much emaciated, but his face was shining. He came to Calcutta in a carriage. When he left the carriage he walked like one intoxicated. He was in samadhi. I thought, 'Is this Suka Deva come again?' Once he came out of samadhi, he asked, 'Who am I? Where am I?' Then he asked for something to eat. But before he could eat, he was again in samadhi."

Swami Premananda and Turiyananda now sang together in Bengali some of the songs Sri Ramakrishna used to sing. One of the songs was about the black bee tasting the honey of the blue lotus, forgetting all the other flowers. In like manner should the mind rest at the blue feet of Kali, forgetting all the world. Swami Premananda imitated the way in which Sri Ramakrishna sang and also his gestures. "Sri Ramakrishna sang very beautifully," he said, "and he could never bear it when others sang out of tune."

In the afternoon Swami read from *The Master as I Saw Him*. When I entered the room he laid aside the book and said, "Realization means to see Mother in all; to treat all alike. That is the blessed life, to see the Shining One behind the external."

The following morning Swami was not feeling well. He had slight fever and toothache. He said, "Mother is kind to send pain. It is for our good. Only we are so self-loving, we do not realize it. We must depend on Her for Her alone, and nothing else." "But," I asked, "must we depend on Her for our external wants?" "Certainly," he replied. "For everything. Our body, mind, and soul are given to Mother. On whom else should we depend? Let Her give, or let Her take, it is all the same. Why should we care? Blessed is he who can realize this."

Religion and Other-Worldliness

Swami Prabhavananda

> The Self-Existent made the senses turn outward. Man, therefore, looks towards what is outside, and sees not the inward being. Rare is the wise man who, desiring immortality, shuts his eyes to outward things and so beholds the glory of the Atman within.
>
> KATHA UPANISHAD

REACHING GOD we attain immortal bliss. God becomes realized only by shutting our senses to outward things and turning our minds toward the kingdom of heaven within. We must gather the scattered forces of the mind and direct it with a concentrated heart toward God, the abiding reality. The natural inclination of man is to seek and express life in the outside world, to find enjoyments outside. But religion tells us to overcome this natural desire and seek the true abiding happiness in God who is within.

Man as he knows himself is not the real man. The world is not as it appears to be. Behind this surface life, where we experience the play of life and death, there is a deeper life which knows no death; behind our apparent consciousness, which gives us the knowledge of objects and things, and the experiences of pleasure and pain, there is the pure, infinite, blissful consciousness. This truth of God is experienced only by those blessed souls who turn their gaze inwards.

Somehow man got caught in the net of ignorance. It is the nature of ignorance to accept the unreal, the shadow, for the real. But mother nature works in an unrelenting way. We may accept the shadow as the reality; we may seek life, love, happiness in the fleeting objects, persons, and things, accepting them as abiding, as real. But mother nature gradually reveals the truth, "God alone is the unchangeable reality, and in Him only is to be found abiding happiness."

Through experience we learn of spiritual discrimination. Through spiritual discrimination we at last come to the understanding: "Not by wealth, not by progeny, not by much learning can the immortal bliss be attained, but by renunciation alone."

The watchword of religion and spiritual life is this renunciation of the thirst for life in the world.

In season and out of season, we hear a charge against Oriental religions that they teach world- and life-negation. Christianity, on the other hand, they say, is a religion that teaches world- and life-affirmation. We do not see how this claim can be justified for Christianity, when the great one of Galilee, the ideal man of renunciation, declared the bold, naked truth: "He who loveth his life shall lose it; and he that hateth his life in the world shall keep it unto life eternal." The ideal of the West may be world- and life-affirmation, but to justify this ideal as the ideal of Christianity is to preach neo-paganism masquerading as the religion of Jesus.

Neither Jesus nor Buddha nor Ramakrishna nor any seer or prophet would ever make any compromise with the ideal of spiritual life. They all declare with one voice that God and worldliness cannot go together.

Let us not try to cover the sore spot with a rose petal. Let us not try to justify the cravings of the flesh and the senses by scriptural injunctions. On the other hand, let us try to understand what is meant by the ideal of renunciation. Does it mean that we must commit suicide or run away into mountain caves or monastery cells to practice renunciation? Suppose we commit suicide and get rid of this body. But can we get rid of the cravings of our minds? Suppose we hide ourselves in a mountain cave or in a monastery cell, can we hide ourselves from the world that we carry within our own minds?

Where is the root of all cravings? Where is the source of worldliness and thirst for life? The root is ignorance. Ignorance is to accept the unreal for the real. The first-begotten child of ignorance is the sense of ego. All cravings and thirst for life and worldliness are centered round this ego. This ego is a false self, not the real I. It is the outcome of false identification of the Atman (the spirit within) with the body, mind, senses, etc. This sense of ego can be said to be a figment of our ignorant mind. It has no real existence. Peel off one layer after another of an onion, and what remains? Nothing. What is this ego? Are you the body, the mind, the senses, the intellect? Are you any of these, or a combination of these? Is any of them permanent? As you analyze to find what your ego is, you reach a point where you realize that it is only a shadow. Yet we build our whole world round this shadow of an ego.

Behind this ego is the real man, the Atman, God. To renounce this ego is the meaning of renunciation. Otherworldliness, which is taught by religions, is shunning the shadow of life for the real life which is in God. By losing yourself you find God and with Him the whole universe. Suppose you have money in the bank. You can get and use that money only if you sign a check. The ego is to be signed off to its source before you can find the fullness of life which is in the Atman, and which is your very birthright. The ego has no meaning, it is only a shadow, and it never finds any fulfillment anywhere until it is returned to its source.

Man *is* spirit and *has* a body and mind. Through ignorance he forgets that he is the spirit and identifies himself with the body, mind, senses, etc., and thus there arises the sense of ego. Religion teaches us to overcome this ignorance and realize that our real life, love, happiness can be found only in spirit, in God. "Nature is for the soul and not the soul for nature." Man, as spirit, is the witness, the experiencer of body, mind, and this whole world. We have this world before us, and we are given the body, mind, intellect, etc., in order that through their aids we can unfold and realize the spirit within. If we seek enjoyments of the body, or pleasures of the mind, if we seek life, love, happiness in the ego, we shall be using the spirit, our real Self, or God, as a means for some other end, and thus "loving life shall lose it."

Whether we wish it or not, and though we accept this surface life as real, this apparent world as real, nature in her unrelenting manner forces us to lose all these appearances. Still we may go on chasing the shadows and never finding any fulfillment.

Religion tells us to wake up from this sleep of ignorance, stop chasing the shadows; gather all the forces of the mind, intellect, senses and direct them to the realization of the one end—which is God, the abiding reality, the Atman within.

Live your life in the world not as an end in itself, but as a means to live in God. Use your body and mind as means to unfold the divinity within. That is what is meant by renunciation and other-worldliness. The mind that is outgoing is to be turned toward the kingdom of heaven within to behold the glory of God.

Does this mean that we shall cease all outward activities and live in silent contemplation of God? No, on the contrary, we must be active in order that through actions we may attain purity of heart. Without purity of heart, contemplation of God is impossible. We must work, but work in such a way that instead of causing feverish restlessness in us, instead of feeding and enriching the ego, our work will be an aid to free ourselves of ego and to live a life in God. Here is the secret of work taught in the *Gita:*

> He puts aside desire,
> Offering the act to Brahman.
> To the follower of the yoga of action,
> The body and the mind,
> The sense-organs and the intellect
> Are instruments only:
> He knows himself other than the instrument
> And thus his heart grows pure.
> United with Brahman,
> Cut free from the fruit of the act,
> A man finds peace
> In the work of the Spirit.

In simple words, spiritual life is life in God. It is to fix our mind's gaze upon the Supreme Lord. If only we learn to turn our thoughts to God, we shall know the fun and joy of life. My Master used to say, "People talk of enjoying life, but they do not know how really to enjoy it." How can they find life and its joy in the shadows? Dive deep within yourself, think of God, pray to Him, surrender yourself to Him, be united with Him. He is the source of life, happiness, love, knowledge. In Him alone one finds fulfillment.

He is the one Atman dwelling in every creature. By diving deep within yourself, as you unite your heart with His, you reach the center, the heart of all beings. You learn to see God within the shrine of your own heart and you learn to see Him shining in the hearts of all. You can never limit yourself to your ego and all the selfishness that goes with it. Your self has become the Self in all.

Your life then is lived in the service of God and becomes a dedication to the altar of mankind. You learn to love your neighbor as your very Self.

Religion teaches us that in order that we can enter into the kingdom of God we must have *faith* in the ideal, knowing that there have been illumined seers in the past to whom God became revealed and that it is possible for everyone to have that revelation. Then let your faith incline you pleasantly towards realizing that ideal. "Where your treasure is, there will your heart be also." Learn through spiritual discrimination that God and God alone is your real treasure. Give your heart to Him.

With this burning faith create a taste for living in His contemplation. In the beginning it will seem dry, the mind will not find any joy in prayer and meditation. But practice regularly at intervals to devote yourself to God and His thought. You will begin to taste the sweetness of life in Him. Then will arise enthusiasm to devote yourself more and more to Him.

Next you will find a flow of spiritual current within yourself, and there will arise a constant remembrance of God. Life has two currents running in opposite directions. If you live on the surface current your life flows towards worldly thoughts, thoughts of "me" and "mine." And on this current there are ebbs and tides, happiness and misery, life and death. There is another current of life underneath flowing in an opposite direction. This leads you to immortal bliss. There is constant joy, for you touch the living presence of God as you touch that current.

Mysticism and Reincarnation in Greece

Swami Vividishananda

THE ANCIENT GREEKS were men of the world, noted for their heroism, love of nature, and appreciation of beauty. Believing in the maxim: "a sane mind in a sane body," they primarily directed their efforts towards the realization of an ideal which consisted in a happy life with perfect health, strength, and symmetry of form. Having keen sensibilities, they enjoyed the life of the senses, although they emphasized the cultivation of reason as an important auxiliary. They were advocates of rationalism and humanism more than of mysticism and showed great interest in civic virtues and mundane affairs. Mystical tendencies seem rather foreign to the Greek temperament. Naturally, the mystery cults and the teachings of Pythagoras and Plato, pre-eminently mystical in tone and character, appear to be a clear departure from the Greek tradition, suggesting foreign influence.

Orpheus, the master musician of legend and poetry, was the founder of the mystery cult that bears his name. He had the gift of enrapturing the souls of men by playing on his lyre and he could also tame wild beasts, making a lion and a lamb play at his feet by his music. He believed in the inherent immortality and divinity of the soul and its gradual evolution through reincarnation. He spoke of the ecstatic experience in which the soul steps out of the body, as it were, and becomes possessed with God. The soul, according to Orpheus, is thus not a feeble double of the individual as Homer and the ancient Egyptians believed, but a fallen god, and must by all means rise to its full divine stature. The goal is to attain this divinity by getting rid of embodiment with passions and appetites which imprison the soul and cause it untold pain and sorrow.

229

According to Orpheus: "Man is required to free himself from the chains of the body in which the soul lies bound like a prisoner in a cell. It has a long way to go before it can find its freedom. The death of the body frees it for a little while, but it passes on to a new body. It continues the journey perpetually, alternating between an unfettered separate existence and an ever-renewed embodiment, traversing the great circle of necessity in which it assumes many bodies. Birth is not the beginning of a new life but admission into a new environment. This wheel of birth goes on until the soul escapes from it by attaining release." The release comes when the soul realizes its divinity through purification. Orpheus and his followers prescribed, as disciplinary measures, meditation, wearing of ordained clothes, avoidance of bloody sacrifices, and ascetic practices like abstinence from flesh and certain kinds of fish.

Pythagoras, who lived and taught in the second half of the sixth century B.C., drew his inspiration from the teachings of Orpheus and regarded him as his chief patron. Keenly interested in the study of music, Pythagoras developed musical talents and founded the science of music. Like Orpheus, he could charm men and beasts by playing on the lyre. He also believed in the healing power of music and had the reputation of healing sickness by music. Music to Pythagoras was a comprehensive harmony or equilibrium of motion and activity which pervades the entire universe. It is the life and soul of the universe, without which the sun, stars, heavenly bodies, and everything would be disjointed and thrown apart, leading to universal disaster and chaos. Experiments in music led Pythagoras to the understanding of numerical ratios and thus was laid the foundation of the mathematical science credited to him. He would look at the starry heavens and admire the orderliness of the universe, likening it to orchestral music. He would often ask his disciples to imitate this orderliness by cultivating poise and serenity.

Pythagoras believed in the immortality of the soul and its reincarnation. His biographers tell us that he had the extraordinary power of remembering his own past lives as well as of divining those of others, and that he would occasionally make demonstrations of this power. Once, moved by the barking of a dog that was being beaten by its master, he pleaded for mercy, saying that he recognized in the dog a departed friend. This power was a gift bestowed upon him as Heraclides by Mercury, in a previous incarnation. Pythagoras would say that when he as Heraclides died, his soul was reborn as Euphorbus, the Trojan who was killed by Menelaus. The shield which he owned and was proud of fell to Menelaus as a trophy and was dedicated to Apollo. After he as Euphorbus died his soul reincarnated as Hermotimus, still retaining his past memory. When people doubted him about this he went to the territory of the Branchidae and entering the temple of Apollo, showed them his shield which Menelaus had dedicated there. When he as Hermotimus died he reincarnated as Pyrrhus, a fisherman of Delos. After the death of Pyrrhus his soul was reborn as Pythagoras.

Regarding the problem of the hereafter Pythagoras held: "After death the rational mind, having been freed from the chains of the body, assumes an ethereal vehicle and passes into the region of the dead where it remains till it is sent back to this world to inhabit some other body, human or animal. After undergoing successive purgations, when it is sufficiently purified, it is received among the gods and returns to the eternal source from which it first proceeded." The cycle of births, with checkered experiences, is a necessity, helping toward the purification and evolution of the soul and the realization of its higher nature, which Pythagoras understood to be in essence divine.

Recognizing the fundamental unity and sanctity of all forms of life, Pythagoras taught noninjury as one of the cardinal principles of his philosophy. Like the mystery cults, he also enjoined upon his followers various ascetic practices for the disciplining of the mind. Above everything else, he emphasized the practice of continence, silence, and *theoria* by which he meant the contemplation of God. Once someone asked him: "What are we here for?" His significant reply was: "To gaze upon the heavens." Nothing can purify the soul more effectively than contemplation. When through contemplation all the impurities are destroyed, the mind becomes transparent like a mirror and reflects God who dwells within.

Pythagoras was well aware of the many limitations—the aches and pains embodiment brings in its train—but he believed that one should make the best of his life here. He would say that men in this world are like foreigners, sojourning in a strange land. Their bodies are the tombs of their souls and yet they must not try to escape by suicide. Being chattels of God, their herdsman, how can they get away from here without His express command? Besides, so-called escape by self-destruction would not bring liberation. So long as there is impurity within, they will be forced to start over again from where they would end, and the wheel of births will continue to revolve. Pythagoras likened this world to a place holding Olympic games, which draws all sorts of crowds with varying interests: first, onlookers whose sole object is to see the spectacles and enjoy the fun; next, shopkeepers who display their wares and look for profit and gain by buying and selling; lastly, players who take part in the game. Similarly, in this world we find many who are motivated by desires for luxury, riches, power, or dominion, others who are ambitious and seek personal glory, and only a blessed few who have a clear idea of the purpose of life. They are the philosophers—the salt of the earth, who strive for release from the fetters of life through contemplation and vision of God, and help others to do the same.

Pythagoras was a philosopher in this sense—a true philosopher, and his followers claimed that he had the exalted vision of God and reached the threshold of divinity. Because of his spiritual greatness he had a tremendous hold over those who accepted his leadership. A contemporary of Buddha, Zoroaster, and Confucius, he spent the greater part of his life in Italy where he settled, although he was by birth a Greek. According to Iamblichus, Pythagoras traveled extensively and visited different parts of the then known world, availing of every opportunity to study and learn wherever he went. During his travels he must have come across the Egyptian, Assyrian, and Indian teachings. Herodotus mentioned that Pythagoras got his ideas about transmigration from Egypt, but it is more likely that he obtained them from India. As we study Pythagoreanism—its doctrines and practices, transmigration included—we note a decided Hindu and Buddhistic stamp, which can be accounted for only if we accept Indian influence. Many scholars hold this view and cite evidences. In *The Legacy of India* H. G. Rawlinson states:

> It is more likely that Pythagoras was influenced by India than by Egypt. Almost all the theories, religious, philosophical and mathematical, taught by Pythagoras, were known in India in the sixth century B.C. and the Pythagoreans, like the Jains and the Buddhists, refrained from the destruction of life and eating meat and regarded certain vegetables such as beans as taboo.

Empedocles (494-434 B.C.) was a poet, philosopher, and mystic of Greece, and believed in reincarnation and immortality. In his poem entitled *The Purifications* he discussed this belief. Recognizing the inherent divinity of the human soul, Empedocles considered embodiment as degeneration and bondage. The soul has to regenerate itself and get back to its pristine state of purity, perfection, blessedness, and freedom. The process is long and tedious, involving experiences of various kinds. The soul has to expiate by going through the bodies of plants, animals, and men, and asceticism combined with contemplation is the means. Men of wisdom who have attained release, according to Empedocles, are like gods on earth, setting examples to others by their righteous living.

Plato, who lived between 427-347 B.C., was the most outstanding philosopher of Europe, an ardent disciple of Socrates and undoubtedly the greatest of his disciples. He was a young man of twenty when he met Socrates and joined the group of enthusiasts and intellectuals who followed the gadfly through the streets of Athens. From the very first, Plato's love and admiration for Socrates was great, and with the passing of days instead of diminishing it increased as is evidenced by the fact that he made Socrates the mouthpiece of his philosopy in the *Dialogues*. Plato followed in the footsteps of Socrates and what had been aphoristically stated by the master was developed and elaborated by the disciple.

It is a matter of history that Socrates had to pay dearly for his ideas, being born ahead of his time. Although acclaimed the wisest man and venerated by many as "the noblest and gentlest and best of all," he had his enemies who accused him of corrupting the youth by teaching a strange philosophy of Self-knowledge in preference to the traditional religion of the gods. His enemies had the upper hand and the innocent man was unjustly condemned to die, but like a true philosopher he took his fate calmly and refused to escape. Knowing very well that there is no death for the soul, he sought happiness not in this world but within—in the realization of his real Self. In the dialogue called the *Phaedo*, Plato dramatically describes the closing chapter of his master's life, which has become one of the masterpieces of mystic literature. To the friends and admirers who came to bid the last farewell, the parting words of Socrates before he drank the fatal cup of hemlock were: "And there [in the other world], my friends, no one is ever put to death for his opinions. . . . So be of good cheer, and do not lament my passing. . . . When you lay me down in my grave, say that you are burying my body only and not my soul."

Socrates had a fairly large devoted following who tried to intercede for him and arrange for his escape. Plato was the foremost and the most influential of them. After the execution of the master, thinking it prudent to leave Athens for the time being, Plato went on a long journey.

> Just what countries he visited we cannot say. It is quite probable, however, that he went to Italy, where he became acquainted with the mystical philosophy of Pythagoras, "the founder of mathematics and the father of music." From there he is said to have traveled to Sicily, to Cyrene, to Egypt, to Judea and even to the banks of the Ganges. If he didn't visit all these countries in person, he certainly visited them in his thoughts. For when he returned to Athens, after a pilgrimage of twelve years, his mind had become a treasure house of all the accumulated wisdom of the world.[1]

The mystic tradition as prevalent in ancient Greece found its full expression in the philosophy of Plato. Like philosophers of the Orphic and Pythagorean schools, Plato also was a believer in the divine origin of the human soul —its reincarnation and immortality. In the dialogues attributed to Plato we find him upholding this belief by his usual dialectic, presenting proofs and answering objections. The doctrine of reminiscence which he advocated is one among many proofs which establish the pre-existence of the soul. By reminiscence he meant recollection of things experienced before—in previous lives. Not only did the soul exist heretofore, it will also exist hereafter. The soul, although an emanation of God, gets mixed up in the world of phenomena and acts strangely, caught under the spell of ignorance. Obsessed by insatiable desires, it is forced to reincarnate again and again in different surroundings and planes, in accordance with its deeds. Even as a sleep-walker aimlessly roams around, chasing phantoms, an embodied soul, not spiritually awake, pursues pleasures which are deceitful and ephemeral, and this goes on from birth to birth. Embodied life is like imprisonment, bringing in its wake pains, limitations, and indignities of many kinds. To

[1] *Living Biographies of Great Philosophers* by Henry Thomas and Dana Lee Thomas, p. 10.

call it life is a misnomer; it is, according to Plato, veritable death, carrying as it does a body which is virtually the tomb of the soul.

The cycle of births and deaths, involving experiences pleasurable and painful, is a necessary evil. It prepares the soul in its onward march, purifying and disciplining it, until it becomes whole again and reaches its destiny—the divinity. In the apologue of Er the Pamphylean with which Plato concludes the *Republic,* we find Lachesis, daughter of necessity, sitting in the judge's chair in the other world and deciding the lot of disembodied souls according to the life they lived on earth—determining what kind of incarnation, what station and what opportunity each soul would have in future. Lachesis is none other than karma personified—the inexorable law of action and reaction, of compensation and retribution, which none can escape with impunity.

The history of the average men living in this world is a tragic story of degeneration in captivity due to ignorance, and Plato illustrates it by his famous simile of the cave, in which one finds an echo of the Hindu doctrine of maya. Think of an enormous cave, dark, uncomfortable, and unhealthy, where some unfortunate souls have been huddled together since their birth. Having their backs to the entrance of the cave, which is just a small aperture, and bound hand and foot, they do not have any freedom of movement, nor do they have any knowledge of the outside world of sunshine, joy, and beauty, except the vague and dim reflection of it as cast upon the wall of the cave in front. The cave here represents the world of phenomena as registered in one's consciousness through the senses and the fetters that bind the souls down are the fetters of the flesh and senses. The purpose of a man's life is to obtain release from these fetters, and then he will have the blessed privilege of basking in the sunshine of the realm of ideas and enjoying its fresh air. The world of phenomena, however real and attractive it appears, is just a shadow or sham—a fool's paradise of make-believe. It does not have any existence apart from or independent of the realm of ideas—the source of joy, beauty, goodness, truth, perfection, and freedom.

According to Plato:

There are two orders of reality: The unperceived, exempt from all change, and the perceived which changes perpetually. The soul is unperceived, simple, indissoluble, immortal; the body is complex, dissoluble, mortal. When the soul is mixed up with the senses it is lost in the world of change; when it withdraws from the senses, it escapes into that other region of pure, eternal, unchanging being.[a]

Plato said in the *Phaedo*:

> And thought is best when the mind is gathered into herself and none of these things trouble her—neither sounds nor sights nor pain nor any pleasure,—when she has as little as possible to do with the body and has no bodily sense or feeling but is aspiring after being.

By thought Plato did not mean discursive thought or intellectualism, but the stillness of contemplation brought on by purification and self-control—a state in which there is no intrusion of the senses and of the crude world of phenomena. Contemplation perfected and deepened culminates in the beatific vision—a blessed state of innocence beyond sense and speech, in which one comes face to face with reality as it is. In his dialogues Plato spoke of the beatific vision. It is an experience vouchsafed to the philosopher-mystic who has attained the clarity of vision by going through the long cycle of births and deaths and learning to reject the world of phenomena.

As a practical supplement to his philosophy, Plato proposed, in the *Republic*, an elaborate scheme of education and training by following which a nation would be able to bring into being an ideal race of mystic philosophers who would be the rulers of men and guide the destinies of men.

The theories of the soul, its nature and destiny, as enunciated by Plato, are decisively Indian in spirit and content. If we read the Platonic dialogues carefully and compare them with the *Upanishads* and the *Bhagavad-Gita*, we find many exact parallels. "The mind of Plato," says Stutfield in his *Mysticism and Catholicism*, "was charged with Orphic mysticism, mainly derived from Asiatic sources. India, always the home of mystical devotion, probably contributed the major share."

---

[a] *Eastern Religions and Western Thought* by S. Radhakrishnan, vol. IV, p. 144.

The Path to Reality

Mimi Frazer

> Be ye transformed by the renewing of your mind.
> ROMANS 12:2
>
> And ye shall know the truth, and the truth shall make you free.
> JOHN 8:32
>
> Be ye therefore perfect, even as your Father which is in heaven is perfect.
> MATTHEW 5:48

So LOFTY ARE these sentiments, so sublime the ideal, yet so diaphanous the way, that often we turn unwittingly for comfort to the more "practical" parts of the Bible. Shall we not be just as Christian as the next person, we ask ourselves, if we continue to lead an ethical life, maintain our present faith in God, and love our neighbors as much as possible except when they're unreasonable? And so the eternal promise hidden behind Christ's teachings lies unexplored, untasted, and forgotten. Yet the truth remains. Shining eternally through dogma and creed, unperturbed by the inevitable "softening" of history, these three commands form the living essence of all the great religions of the world. But it is not enough merely to feel their inspiration; it is not enough even to believe them fervently, for spiritual life begins only as they are *lived*.

But how, exactly, does one begin? What is meant by the "renewal of the mind," and in what manner shall we "be transformed"? What is the nature of this ultimate "freedom"? How practical is it and how desirable?

Whatever our present religious belief may be—or, indeed, if we have none at all—let us broaden our horizon, call in reinforcements, and turn back for a moment to the oldest religion in history—the religion of the Vedas. For if the urge to understand life, the desire for immortality, and the craving for lasting happiness may be taken as

237

universal characteristics of the human soul, then surely no goal could be so infinitely desirable as the goal defined in the Vedas as absolute knowledge, absolute existence, and absolute bliss. Furthermore, this kingdom of heaven is not literally one to be "attained," but, we are told repeatedly, *it exists already within us.* Call it God or what you will, it is that within us which is immortal, changeless, perfect. It is our own reality. Eternally free, embracing yet transcending all, it is none other than the Self. That we do not recognize it—that we neither feel its joy nor live by its truth—is due solely to our own ignorance.

Meanwhile, the reality of the world we see about us is rapidly diminishing in a most bewildering degree. Modern science and classical philosophy now agree completely in finding the universe we live in both "unknown" and "unknowable" except as a concept of the human mind which can, at best, be expressed only in abstract mathematical symbols. For with the acceptance of the theory of relativity, the nature of ultimate reality threatens to elude the scientist's last desperate grasp for all time. The significance of this fact can scarcely be overlooked, for it is the first time in history that science, as a whole, has bowed a humble head before a mystery it cannot solve, and admitted the permanent inability of the human intellect to penetrate its secret. The conclusion is self-evident. Reality, if it exists at all, must be found in another direction, and by another process entirely. Is it now high time, then, that we listen more attentively to the words of those great mystics who not only claim to have found this reality within themselves, but who can explain to us the ignorance which hides it?

Perhaps your religion has taught you that this ignorance is due to the "original sin" of man, which only human repentance and God's grace can remove. That is one way of looking at it, but there are other ways, too. Truth is many-faceted. Let us look at the same problem explained from another angle, by another race, and at a time when the star of Bethlehem was scarcely in its infancy.

The Hindu saint Patanjali defines ignorance as the mistaken identification of the Self with that which is noneternal: a process of self-delusion by which we superimpose upon our real nature the limitations and imperfections of the finite world. Identifying ourselves with the body, we experience its pain, and fear its death as our own. Identifying ourselves with the senses, we spend our lives running after the objects which please them, and avoiding those which do not. Identifying ourselves with the mind, we remain continual victims of its moods, its sorrows, its ignorance, and its ever-shifting desires. Identifying ourselves with all three, we perpetuate the sense of ego and continue to experience indefinitely the illusion of separateness between man and man, and man and God. Yet our limitations are not self-existent: they are merely self-imposed.

How, then, *shall* we identify ourselves with the eternal —immanent within us, so hidden to our everyday awareness? For a little analysis of this problem of ignorance, from the standpoint of science as well as religion, will show that not only is the ordinary human mind an utterly inadequate instrument for the detection of absolute reality, but, as we will see later, it actually obscures that reality by its very nature. On the other hand, the human mind is the only instrument we have available as the quest for truth commences: a dilemma from which religion alone has been able to point a satisfactory solution—to change and perfect the instrument, *and literally to renew the mind.*

Now, such spiritual renewal lies far beyond the confines of psychology as we know it in the West. According to the more comprehensive Hindu psychology, consciousness is the property of the Self alone—the divinity within— not of the mind. The mind itself being material and finite, its seeming intelligence is but a reflection *through* it of the borrowed light of the Self. In other words, consciousness illumines and lends awareness to the mind just as a current of electricity lends light to a lamp, yet the light cannot rightly be called the property of the lamp itself.

What is the nature of this pure consciousness, this supreme intelligence, which activates our every thought and deed—and to which is due the very principle of life itself? We cannot answer. We cannot *know*, so long as our cluttered and impure minds distort it past all recognition. A windowpane of frosted glass may admit the light efficiently, yet its rough and twisted surface will give no inkling of the view which lies beyond. Nor can we detect the One behind the manifold; the image of the sun is broken into fragments on a wind-tossed sea. Awake or dreaming, our restless minds are never quiet for an instant. Even after dreamless sleep, our continuity of memory proves that we have not been released from a fraction of the heterogeneous contents of our minds. These contents, these distorters of reality, are twofold in nature. As the waves or vibrations which we call "thought" pass through the so-called "conscious" mind, they leave latent impressions in the subconscious mind as seeds of future action and future thought. Moreover, when waves of a similar nature arise in the conscious mind repeatedly, the resultant impressions coalesce and deepen into a tempting channel down which future thought will tend: thus are formed the habit-patterns of our characters. We therefore react to the world about us, not as free agents, but bound and conditioned by the contents of our own minds. Clearly, then, merely to control the conscious mind is not enough: we must root out also the subconscious impressions which condition it. Such a process has been successfully demonstrated, to a relatively minor degree, by modern psychoanalysis; but in religion alone has it been carried to its logical and ultimate completion. To renew the mind is to empty it of all these binding contents that pure consciousness may shine through it undistorted, and leave revealed the depths of that still being which is our very Self, and where alone resides the promised kingdom of heaven.

Ethical thought and conduct, are, of course, the first essentials in all religious discipline. Without them the mind cannot hope to attain the smallest measure of the tranquility and peace necessary to carry on spiritual life. Yet religion itself transcends them, for even the highest of ethics still depends upon the distinction between good and evil. Where God alone exists, opposites cannot appear. True compassion and unselfish love spring neither from idealism nor an inward sense of duty, but arise spontaneously within the heart which has directly experienced the Self in all beings, and all beings in the Self. However far beyond our reason or our understanding such an experience may be, the lives of saints throughout the history of the world—in all religions and in all ages—bear witness to this truth.

With ethical living once established, various religious paths are open to the aspirant, any one of which, if followed with perseverance, will lead him to the goal. Yet simultaneous practice of them all will quicken spiritual desire and hasten the way. Those who are emotional by nature are usually inclined to the devotional path, preferring the dualistic approach to God through the worship of one of his aspects or incarnations, rather than the cool austerity of nondualism. For the mind dominated by the love of God seeks not its own pleasure. By constant thought of God it becomes controlled and purified.

Aspirants who are more intellectually inclined may prefer to emphasize the path of knowledge. Reading and study here have their place, but study is usually of a particular kind. It is taken for granted that to one who is ready to begin an intense spiritual life, religion is no longer a controversial subject. He has had enough of arguments, and the acquisition of relative knowledge for its own sake no longer interests him at all. He studies merely to deepen his spiritual convictions, and for this reason confines his reading mainly to scriptural works, and the writings of saints and other illumined teachers. By ceaseless inquiry, and by constant discrimination between the real and the unreal, he seeks to understand his true identity. Intellectually convinced that the Self dwells free of body, senses, mind, or ego—for whom they serve only as instruments— he gradually ceases to identify himself with their joys and sorrows, their pleasure or their pain. He analyzes the problem of desire and witnesses his own bondage—for he sees that each desire, in its seeming fulfillment, sows the seeds of future desires: that is, the impressions left in the subconscious mind will eventually rise to the surface and demand fulfillment again and again. In time he clearly understands, and at last rebels against, his own slavery. Thenceforth regarding his own ego as illusion, standing witness to its claims, his thoughts or actions leave no hold upon his mind, and of such renunciation is freedom born.

Worship and study, however intense, are rarely possible except in combination with work of some kind. Yet, just as the aspirant may incline his heart and mind toward truth, so may he also incline all his activities. As a devotee or dualist, he surrenders the fruits of all his work to God, and works for Him alone. As a nondualist he works for work's sake only, not for the results, regarding the Self alone as the witness of all action.

Through such practices as these, the aspirant gradually remolds his thought and character. But the goal still lies ahead, for complete purification of the mind is possible only with the highest religious experience. Until this point is reached, spiritual practices can only alter, but not eliminate, the action of impressions already acquired. With self-control these may be increased or decreased in intensity, overpowered by opposite impressions, or reduced to a state of dormancy. But their potential action is not yet destroyed. To aid in bringing about their final extinction most effectively, the practice of meditation is required.

The technique of meditation is little known in the Western world and too often has been misrepresented. It is not "making your mind a blank," a tranquil daydream, nor any poetic flight of fancy, however sublime. Far from being a letting-go of the mind, it is an intense ingathering of all mental forces toward a single center—to the exclusion of every other idea, however closely allied. Beginning with simple concentration and ending in complete absorption, meditation is that focused energy of the mind which alone is capable of penetrating the world perceived so shallowly by the senses. A power universally demonstrable, it is neither mysterious nor "occult." For when the mind repeatedly or continuously holds within its grasp a single object or idea, it attracts unto itself the inherent characteristics of that object or idea. As a very simple illustration, concentration on fire will, in time, produce the impression of heat. The qualities of an object thus uncovered by repeated mental association will vary from the obvious to the profound according to the intensity of concentration and the period of time over which it is prolonged.

While the tremendous power of the concentrated mind is of untold value in all branches of learning, in spiritual life it is an absolute necessity. For it is meditation alone which effectively controls the mind, strengthens the will, and integrates the total personality. The deliberate and habitual surrender of the mind to the single thought of God not only unifies the scattered mental waves of the conscious mind, but purifies the subconscious, as well, by impressing it with a single idea so constant and so strong that the force of opposing impressions is greatly mitigated before they rise to the conscious level, or rendered totally inactive.

Psychic experiences and powers often occur naturally as a result of meditation, but while these may encourage perseverance, they have no other value, and are usually regarded as obstacles. A competent teacher alone can interpret the validity of such experiences as do come, warn against the pitfalls which may lie along the path, and guide the student safely toward the goal. It is he alone who knows the path best fitted to the requirements of each individual temperament, and can instruct accordingly.

Concentration becomes meditation when, through prolonged practice, thought flows toward the chosen object "as smoothly as oil poured from one vessel to another." Effort and the sense of time then vanish into nothingness: only subject, object, and meaning remain. The single-pointed mind experiences a peace never before dreamed of, and the subtler secrets of nature gradually become revealed.

Deep meditation is the open door to the transcendental consciousness which the Hindus term samadhi, and the Christians call union with God. Much misunderstanding has arisen concerning this state of illumination—a misunderstanding which will necessarily continue until the finite mind which questions it is itself transcended. Those who have experienced it insist that it is not a state at all— but our natural being to which we awaken as out of a dream when truth at last reveals itself. This truth, this living experience of what we have heretofore merely *believed,* is not the sudden acquisition of knowledge, however sublime. It is the being and becoming of that which we have worshiped. It is the ultimate awakening to our own identity.

Thus religion begins where reason leaves off, and where the intellect cannot penetrate. To clear away the obstacles, to purify the mind of everything that is *not* God, is the whole of spiritual endeavor. What lies ahead we may only faintly glimpse by faith, intuition, and the words of those who themselves have reached the goal. We may be sure of only this: that the ocean of truth will claim its own inevitably, as all rivers return into the sea. We may hasten the process, or delay it by our ignorance—but to surrender ourselves to the deepening current is the ultimate secret of living.

"All the World's a Stage"

Franz Dispeker

"BRAHMAN ALONE IS REAL; the universe is unreal." When we first hear this truth, we think we understand, but the more we consider and analyze it, the more difficult it is for us to grasp its significance. How can this universe, which seems so wonderfully or so terribly real to us, be unreal, and Brahman, who is altogether imaginary and unreal to us, be real?

When we are told that there is no creation, or that creation is only a degeneration, that we mistake the "rope" (God) for the "snake" (universe), we can grasp it intellectually, but cannot, as Sri Ramakrishna says, "assimilate" it. Here we are, a poor, snake-conscious people, living in a snake-universe, vainly trying to know how we ever became so stupid as to see a universe of time, space, and causation, of multiplicity and relativity, when all the time there is but one absolute being: why we experience happiness and misery, when there is just one absolute bliss! In reply to these bewildering questions we are told that we are not ignorant, but omniscient; not unhappy, but ever blissful; not suffering disease and death, but immortal. Why this is so cannot be answered. If a man dreams that he is to be executed for a crime which he has not committed and wonders in his dream why he is to be punished, there will be no answer either. Let him wake up from his dream and the question will not arise. In the same way, this life has been called a "prolonged dream" from which we have to wake up.

We wake up from sleep and find that our dreams are contradicted by our waking experience, that they were unreal. But the process of awaking from this "prolonged dream" may take many lives, and during this time the

244

world will often seem very, very real to us. Therefore it is necessary to find—not a solution, because there is only the one, to "wake up"—but at least some sort of an explanation or working hypothesis other than that the universe is unreal or a dream.

An explanation has been given by the seers and prophets, but surprisingly little emphasis has been laid upon it, except perhaps by Sri Ramakrishna, who, in his teachings, talks very frequently about it. He says: "As long as there is left a sense of ego in us, so long the objects seem real and we cannot very well say that the world is a dream and unreal. To me Brahman is the unchangeable reality. I admit also the reality of the universe as His divine play. He who has realized Brahman knows that He is the absolute reality and also knows that it is He who has become the universe. I see Him with eyes closed and I see Him in the universe with eyes open. He is the indivisible Sat-chit-ananda, absolute existence, absolute knowledge, and absolute bliss. Again it is He who has become the universe and its living beings."

At once the question will arise, why should He the absolute, the indivisible Sat-chit-ananda, become the universe and its living beings? Sri Ramakrishna answers it as follows: "God the Mother has created this world in play. She is the Mahamaya, the power that creates, preserves, and dissolves. It is She who deludes the world with Her delusion and it is She who removes the delusion and gives liberation. Take refuge in Her and obtain Her grace."

This conception of the universe as being the play of God is by no means an exclusively Indian idea. The words "and lead us not into temptation" in the Lord's Prayer, can be explained only if Christ saw God Himself, in one aspect, as the great deluder and tempter.

Christian mystics have expressed the idea very definitely. To quote only two. Says Angelus Silesius:

All this is just God's play; why else should He create?
He made the creature merely for His own pleasure's sake.

And Jacob Boehme, in answer to the question of a disciple as to why God allows so much quarrel and disunity, says: ". . . and thus the Eternal has assumed sensibility and diversity . . . in order that there can be an eternal play in the Infinite Unity, and an eternal cause for joy. And it is the painful which must serve as ground and as cause for this movement. Herein lies the mystery of the hidden wisdom of God."

When we hear for the first time this theory of the universe being God's play or sport, we are horrified! What sort of a God can He be who, "for His own pleasure's sake," creates and destroys, inflicts suffering, disease, and death on living beings? Is He malicious, cruel?

Let us again turn to the teachings of Sri Ramakrishna. To a disciple, who asks why there should be so much suffering in the world he says: "Everything is a play of the Divine Mother. In this play there have to be the pairs of opposites: joy and sorrow, virtue and vice, knowledge and ignorance, good and evil. The play cannot continue if any of the pairs of opposites is eliminated from Her creation. . . ."

Disciple: "But this play of God is death to us!"

Sri Ramakrishna (smiling): "Tell me who you are! God alone is, and it is He who has become this universe, with its beings and the twenty-four cosmic principles. 'As the snake I bite, as the healer I cure.' God is the ignorant man and God is the enlightened man. God as the ignorant man remains deluded. Again He as the guru gives enlightenment to God in the ignorant."

And to the question whether God is partial Ramakrishna answers: "But God Himself has become everything. Is there anyone but Himself? To whom could He show partiality?"

We seem to be moving in a vicious circle. The reader may well ask whether it is any easier for the average human being to see God everywhere and in every being in the universe than to conceive of the world as a dream or as unreal. We know that only after the highest spiritual experience of nirvikalpa samadhi is it possible to see that God Himself has become this world and its living beings or to see this universe as unreal. But what about the nonillumined majority? Is it not easier for them to make the effort to see God's play everywhere in the universe than to try to deny its existence or its reality?

Let us see how it works when we endeavor to apply this theory of God's play to our everyday life. Let us start with the beautiful and pleasant aspect of life.

Naturally, it is not difficult to see God in the beautiful: in a brilliant sunset, in the beauty of flowers, or in a painting. We hear Him in the song of the birds, in the busy hum of the bees, in a symphony. We feel His nearness in a mother's love and we see His light in the eyes of the lover —at least as long as the love lasts. But that is not all. From our plane of relativity we see that this great cosmic power, the Divine Mother, is not merely "all good, all joy, all love." How can She be? How can we know good without its opposite, evil? How can we know pleasure without knowing pain, or health without disease? The pairs of opposites are the very basis of Her play. Sri Ramakrishna worshiped the image of Kali. To us in the West this image may seem barbarian, and yet it represents the truth in a very bold manner. In Her two left hands She holds a man's severed head and a sword, and with Her two right hands She offers boons and benedictions to Her devotees. The two aspects of life are harmonized in Her. She is the compassionate and affectionate Mother of the universe, and again She is the terrible bringer of death and destruction.

We must be able to accept both sides of life, not only the soothing hum of the bee, but also the ominous drone of the B-29! They are the obverse and reverse of the same coin. If we apply this theory of God's play to our every-day life, we shall no longer take ourselves and our various experiences quite so seriously. We shall not be so easily elated by gain, nor overdepressed by loss. We shall come to realize that, after all, nothing is permanent, everything changes, and the play will go on, even without us! We are all actors on the same stage. Perhaps it would be better to say we are merely puppets in the hands of that cosmic power which moves us at will. After all, what does our so-called free will amount to? A man may think that he has achieved great things by his own will, not realizing that he had the good fortune to work—though unconsciously—in accordance with the cosmic will. Without God's will or grace man can achieve nothing. There is a beautiful passage in one of the Hebrew scriptures expressing this truth:

> "Have I not free Will?" saith the fool;
> But the wise know that in all the chains of worlds
>   There is no creature
> That has any will apart from my Own Will. . . .

Therefore, when we make plans we should always bear in mind that, though man proposes, God disposes! This attitude may well be the first step toward that virtue of self-surrender, so difficult to practice.

If we think of ourselves and our fellow beings as actors on the same stage and under the same direction, will the one who plays the part of a king or a rich man look down upon his colleague who plays the part of a street sweeper or a beggar? He will not; especially when he realizes that it is all a play, and that the king of today may be the beggar of tomorrow, all parts being interchangeable and subject to change without notice! Can there be any harmony in an orchestra if the violinist shouts at the cellist, or the flute player rebukes the violinist? Must not each player do his best, according to the direction of the conductor? In the same way, it is up to each one of us to play our part as best we can, and to give credit to our fellow players, believing that they, too, are doing their best. This means we must neither despise nor condemn anybody; neither criticize everything nor anybody; nor see the faults in others, but rather make the effort to see the good in all. We may fail many times, because we are subject to the law of attraction and repulsion. We are not saints yet! So often we meet a person who, upon first acquaintance, is positively repulsive to us, either in appearance or in behavior. (Also, proud in our own conceit as we are, we forget that attraction and repulsion are mostly reciprocal!) Then is the time when we should make the effort to see in him a fellow actor, trying to play his part as a manifestation of the same Being. If we have any complaints or criticisms to make, it is better that we take them to the source rather than direct them toward the individual. Be bold, ask the Divine Mother why She manifests herself in such an unpleasant and disagreeable way.

If we can make a habit of directing our anger or dissatisfaction directly toward God, we are bound to think of Him more frequently. Even though we may perhaps only tell Him our troubles or scold Him and blame Him, at least we shall think of Him, and thus become more intimate with Him. If we find ourselves afraid of a blasphemy, let us pray: "O Lord, You must excuse me, but why have You made me so stupid that I cannot understand You?" But why should we fear a blasphemy? Cannot the infinite ocean of Brahman absorb all troubles, all anger, all blame, and yet remain unaffected? After all, there is only one blasphemy, and that is to forget God.

We may ask ourselves why it is that God has blindfolded us so thoroughly; why He has stricken us with such intense ignorance; why He has hidden Himself so completely that we have to fight the inner and outer nature, even the very elements, in order to find Him. The answer to these questions is intimated in the *Bhagavatam.* In the story of creation we read that Brahma received the command from God to create. "Brahma's first human creations were saints, who, immediately upon being created, fell into deep meditation, finding no interest in the things of the world." Under such conditions it was impossible to get the play started, so, perhaps for this reason it was necessary for the Creator to resort to more drastic means!

But, have we really any right to complain? Is not God said to be the wish-fulfilling tree which grants all our desires? Is not the very fact that we are playing here on this planet the proof that we like the play? If we ask ourselves honestly and sincerely, we shall have to admit that we enjoy it. Perhaps after a particularly heavy blow we may feel disgusted for a time, but does it last? He who is really, sincerely, and earnestly disgusted, will find a way out. The seers, the prophets, and all the illumined souls have stopped their play, at least so far as this world's playground is concerned, and they have shown us this way.

As long as we are caught in the play, we should try never to forget that, with our limited mind and five senses, which deceive us at every turn, we see only an infinitesimal part of the whole. I am reminded of an incident. A friend of mine was in great distress, and I, hoping to console him, started to talk about God and harmony and beauty. Before I got very far, he turned to me, demanding what I meant, and how I could dare to speak of a God and harmony and justice in a world full of disharmony, murder, and injustice. It so happened that my friend was an amateur collector of old paintings, and our conversation took place before a very beautiful Van Dyck. Turning to the picture, I asked him: "Do you consider this Van Dyck to be a painting of perfect beauty and harmony?" "Of course I do!" he replied. Thereupon I marked off a little dark spot which was a part of a cloth on one of the figures, and asked him: "Now, what answer would you give to the same question if all you could see of the picture was just this little dark spot. You would ask me how I could even dare to speak of a beautiful Van Dyck, when all you could see would be just a dirty little patch of black." So with us all. We live on this little speck of dust, called earth, and try to judge the whole of God's creation by what we see with the mortal eye.

Instead, let us have faith in the words of those who have realized the whole and known the truth. Sri Aurobindo Ghose expresses it very beautifully, when he says: "Love is the keynote, Joy is the music, Power is the strain, Knowledge is the Performer, the infinite All is the composer and audience. We know only the preliminary discords which are as fierce as the harmony shall be great: but we shall arrive surely at the fugue of the Divine Beatitudes."

The Way to Liberation

Swami Prabhavananda

KAPILA, THE GREAT PHILOSOPHER of ancient India, defined the goal of liberation as "the complete cessation of miseries," thereby expressing the aspiration of all human beings. Whether a man believes in religion and God or not, he wants to be free of the bondages of suffering and misery. Whatever the means and methods he adopts to this end, they may and may not help him to overcome his immediate miseries, but they can never overcome them all.

This "complete cessation of miseries," this aspiration of all human life, is, say the seers, made possible only by spiritual knowledge.

All the religions of the world, however divergently they may express their goal, are at one in their essence; they define it in a positive way as "perfection in God." The *Upanishads* explain this perfection as the unitive knowledge of Brahman, the realization of our identity with the infinite being, infinite wisdom, and infinite bliss, or the abiding love. This is also what is understood as entering the kingdom of God by being born in spirit. And certainly Christ emphasized very clearly the possibility of the birth in spirit even while living on earth; he never intended that we postpone our attainment of the kingdom of God till after death.

Whatever you are in your present life determines your life after death. According to a Bengali proverb, even though a husking machine may go to heaven, it will still husk there. The *Upanishads* declare explicitly that perfection is to be attained "here and now, not after the fall of the body."

The scriptures of the Hindus describe the characteristics

251

of a man liberated in life. Sri Krishna states them in the teachings of the *Gita*:

> He knows bliss in the Atman
> And wants nothing else.
> Cravings torment the heart:
> He renounces cravings.
> I call him illumined.
> Not shaken by adversity,
> Not hankering after happiness:
> Free from fear, free from anger,
> Free from the things of desire.
> I call him a seer, and illumined.
>
> When he has no lust, no hatred,
> A man walks safely among the things of lust and hatred.
> To obey the Atman
> Is his peaceful joy:
> Sorrow melts
> Into that clear peace:
> His quiet mind
> Is soon established in peace.

This perfection to be achieved is said to be the very nature of our being. Liberation is not something that can be had from another, nor can it be attained from somewhere outside. *It* is your birthright. You are already "pure, perfect, and free." Realize it.

The cause of our bondage is ignorance of our true nature, and it is the knowledge of the Atman, the true Self within, that can make us free. Our sufferings and our limitations are immediate experiences, and it is only the immediate and direct experience of the kingdom of God within that can relieve us of them. The world or humanity is not saved by merely coming to Christ or to Buddha; but by realizing the Christ within through direct experience, or by becoming a Buddha, an awakened soul, is man saved.

Man's awakening comes by stages. The first and foremost stage is the *desire* for liberation. Buddha called it "right aspiration." It is said that human birth is blessed inasmuch as the desire for liberation is awakened only in human life, and this desire for liberation is man's desire to transcend that self-consciousness which is evolved in man only. To reach the infinite wisdom, the sense of *ego* must be transcended. We must lose the little self to win the universal Self.

This desire does not arise in man as long as he is feverishly engrossed in satisfying his animal desires. Therefore he must strive to live an ethical life and learn to discipline his life and conduct by regularly devoting himself to the worship and contemplation of God. Lust and greed are the animal desires; they are like a perpetual fever that eats away man's very vitals. The diseased mind is to be healed by the regular practice of self-surrender to God through devotional worship. It is then only that the mind becomes pure and tranquil and that we thirst for liberation.

The thirst for liberation has been defined as the desire to liberate one's own self and to live in the service of God manifest in all beings. Buddha defines it as the aspiration to live in love with all beings, and Swami Vivekananda tells us to be gods, and help others to become gods.

Next comes spiritual *discrimination*. We must discriminate between the appearance and the reality, between that which is ever changing and eluding our grasp and that which is abiding and eternal. "Labor not for the meat which perisheth, but for that meat which endureth unto everlasting life."

Herein comes the real struggle against our lower nature, our past habits and tendencies. Through discrimination we learn the folly of running after shadows, even while our animal nature again and again tries to assert itself. We fall down from the ideal many times before we fully reach it. But there is no real failure as long as we keep up the struggle. In this fight against our lower nature we should guard the gate with the sword of discrimination, and then enter into the shrine of the Atman. However, it is not so easy unless we keep constant guard and have recourse to the practices of spiritual disciplines such as japam, worship, and prayer.

A young disciple came to Sri Ramakrishna to learn how to overcome lust. The master simply asked him to perform japam regularly. "Chant the name of God," he told him, "and the crows of lust, greed, etc. will all fly away." Yes, it really is as simple as that, if we will but keep awake our discrimination and practice the simple spiritual exercise. We must convince ourselves that God is the only abiding treasure, and learn to place our heart in him through repeated practice, "for where your treasure is, there will your heart be also."

Through spiritual discrimination we arrive at the next

stage in our progress, when our cravings for sense objects become less and less, and the ego becomes less assertive. The less the ego is felt, the more God is revealed. At this stage we begin to feel the presence of the infinite Being within us. This is an actual experience of the living presence. True it is that, as a spiritual discipline, we must learn to feel the presence of God, to contemplate upon Him within the shrine of our hearts. But at this particular stage, when the ego no longer asserts itself, and the craving for objects has become weaker, the divine presence is actually felt. As this feeling increases, one experiences what the mystics call ecstasy, and this ecstasy may be accompanied by a particular vision of the deity, or there may be no vision of form at all.

However, ecstasy does not last; therefore there must be no letdown in our struggles to achieve union with God. We must repeatedly practice the presence of God, for then only will the actual experience of the presence continue in us.

Many a time a spiritual aspirant may be misled by thinking that, because he has experienced a vision or ecstasy, he has reached the goal. Thinking thus, he may relax, and then again the ego will creep in, and with it craving for sense objects will arise, or there may be aroused in him a desire for name and fame. Therefore he must be constantly on guard; he must "hold on to the pillar," as my master used to say.

When, however, through repeated practice—and we may pass through many failures—we become established in the consciousness of the actual living presence within, the craving for sense objects and all its attendant evils is finally overcome. True dispassion arises, for then it is that the unreality of the world appearance is felt.

Next we arrive at the stage when God is not felt merely as a living presence, but we begin to feel our very identity with Brahman. Continuous meditation on this identity of the Atman and Brahman leads to absorption and the transcendental consciousness. If a man reaches this transcendental consciousness but once only, he has attained the goal. Sri Ramakrishna used to say, "When the spring breezes begin to blow you do not need a fan." In the same way, a continuous breeze of grace is felt; the aspirant has become liberated in life. The struggle is ended.

To quote the *Yoga Vasishtha*: "When a man has awakened to the knowledge of Brahman, his impure mind is

dead, his thirst is gone, his ego has disappeared and the
cage of delusion has been shattered to bits. When a man
has attained the peace beyond passion by realizing the
supreme, pure, absolute Reality, nothing, either of this
world or of heaven, can turn him away from enjoying it."

Suffering

John Yale

SOMETHING THAT COMES as a bombshell to the newer aspirant is how painful spiritual life is. Here you have turned to religion because life without it was intolerable. But now that you have made the new start, life still is intolerable. You are suffering just as much as before; perhaps in different ways, but certainly as much, if not more. You wonder why this should be.

Cheery reassurances from other people are of almost no help at all. The admonition that you should be glad to struggle because you would not want to miss the thrill of the strife merely sets your teeth on edge. And having to listen to the even more fanciful suggestion that you would not want things different, on the basis that you would not consider disrupting the play of the Lord, only adds to the pain. If there is any logic in such arguments it is certainly lost on you at the very time when you need a remedy most.

You really have to think the problem of suffering through for yourself and work out your own ideas on the subject. You can do this most efficiently by examining various hypotheses and then forming your own opinion.

One theory is that the lot of the saint, or would-be saint, is actually no more painful than that of the worldly person. He is just more introspective and imagines that it is. The advocates of this solution invite you to stop thinking about yourself. Look instead at the misery of people who never give a moment's consideration to religion. Life is vexatious no matter how you live. Try to remember that you are no worse off than anybody else. It is as easy as that.

But is it? For the evidence seems generally to favor the

other side. The spiritual candidate probably does suffer more, or at least more subtly. As Gerald Heard has observed, where there is no spiritual consciousness at all, "you have pandemonium and homicidal frenzy, persecution-mania, insane suspicion, and insane cruelty." Big, gross agonies. "When the ego has been checked but not resolved, then we find private suspicions, miseries, complaints, and hidden hatreds." But when the ego "has begun to be eliminated, then we find it . . . lurking in the corners of the mind in irrational worry, over-sensitiveness, and mind-body distress."

The failures of the conscientious man are considerably more upsetting than those of the man who does not care. The unguarded word, the involuntary flash of old selfishness, the unmeant wounding of another—these sting the tender heart like nettles.

Anyone familiar with the life stories of the Christian saints knows how agonizing these latter brands of pain can be. Teresa experienced the worst torments imaginable while trying to follow what she sensed to be the will of God in the face of discouragement or disapproval from her ecclesiastical superiors. Ignatius had to wage a running battle with scruples for years after his conversion. Having scruples meant that you kept feeling that without intention you had sinned. Tormenting indeed to a sixteenth-century Spanish monk! The desolations which were experienced by many others are well known, spasms of doubt as to the genuineness of one's faith, of the worthwhileness of the religious struggle, of the very authenticity of God.

Poulain, in his impressive treatise on Catholic mysticism, lists the pain-producing agents as these: tedium, distractions, doubts, alternations of joys and sufferings, and possession of what he calls "the sensitive appetite." This latter may be worded unfamiliarly, but the condition it refers to is instantly recognizable. It is that frustrating state where, in Poulain's old-fashioned language, earthly things are distasteful, but the soul has as yet experienced no sample of heavenly joys.

A second explanation of the enigma of why a good man should suffer rests on the justice theory. According to this, everything has its price; you may buy eventual bliss, but only at the cost of present woe. If your portion during life were less painful than that of the unregenerate man, or even equally so, this would put a utilitarian value on religion. People would be getting something for nothing, and fairness would be insulted. You must foot the bill if you would win the treasure.

But if analyzed carefully, what this explanation claims is that religion does not have the power to deliver you from pain, or it projects that deliverance into some distant afterlife. If not denying liberation, this theory certainly postpones it. But this is at odds with reason, which insists that to be adequate, religion must liberate us here and now. Logic suggests that if you attain sainthood, you should attain it by your own efforts while you are living, not by way of someone else's authorization later, after you are dead. Likewise, if you solve the problem of suffering, you should be able to solve it in this life, not the next one.

The accumulated evidence of the centuries has shown how realistic, how eminently scientific in his observations Buddha was. He saw that as usually played, life represents a poorly written little dramatic effort in which the interest all dissipates after the first act, running on into sheer inanity at the final curtain. A group of social scientists under Professor Robert Havighurst at the University of Chicago has recently confirmed in quantitative terms the accuracy of Buddha's findings and given the lie at last to that ancient cliché that a religion acknowledging life to be painful is unforgivably pessimistic. Life does ravel out toward the end. The study of hundreds of oldsters by Havighurst provided telling evidence of its progressive meaninglessness for most people.

This is one of the leading difficulties you ask your religion to help you settle. What you want is a way of relieving distress which becomes more operative as the troubles of later life become more serious. What you want is to reverse the play's bad construction, turning it into a production of mounting action rising steadily to a powerful finale. You don't want a murky failure; you want a smash hit.

To answer the question of pain by urging just suffering through, to suspend any real resolution until some hypothetical future, is almost worse than no answer at all. This justice theory does not meet the issue; it seems only to avoid it.

A third doctrine is that pain is creative. It does something that nothing else can do; the religious aspirant must expect to experience it; in a sense he must actually welcome it. "The idea of good appears last of all," reports Plato tersely in the *Republic*, "and is seen only with an effort." This is an application of the familiar view that life is a training school. It is as though God wants you to attend his college, but sets the entrance requirement as graduation from a prep school devoted almost exclusively to flogging.

The Oriental ascetic has been accused often enough of mistaking this symptom of religious striving for the cause of its inestimable result. The Christian, too, at various times, has been preoccupied with the efficaciousness of suffering, frequently adding unnatural austerities to those which daily life provided. The self-scourgings of St. John of the Cross are well remembered. Aldous Huxley's biography *Grey Eminence* gives a frightening picture of the scalp burns with which the priestly hero of the story, although the second or third most powerful man in France during much of the Thirty Years' War, continued to afflict himself almost daily. "When thou art ill of ease and troubled," says *The Imitation of Christ*, "then is the time when thou art nearest unto blessing. If thou wilt not suffer thou refusest to be crowned."

Some of the practices of Zen Buddhism seem to point to a certain intrinsic value in tribulation. The raising of frustration to intolerable heights through use of a cryptic meditation device known as a koan is said to bring results. In his book reviewing the findings of the famed Dr. Suzuki and other students of Zen, Alan Watts says that working with a koan brings the disciple to a frantic and inescapable impasse where, moreover, he is urged to redouble his efforts. "The Koan exercise is so devised as to concentrate the mind and stimulate the will to the highest degree. When the final dilemma is faced the disciple will meet it with his entire strength." Supposedly this brings an intuitive understanding of the larger truth behind the puzzle. The conflict has somehow caused the aspirant to leap the appearance and land on the side of the reality.

But that it is the suffering which does the good is anything but certain. Pain, like other strong emotions, tends to emphasize the sense of ego, which it should be the purpose of religious practice to transcend. It seems unlikely that suffering itself is the real remedy.

In fact, that suffering should possess any productive effect at all seems more than uncertain from its very definition. Psychological pain is the result of psychological conflict. Pain is not the producer of anything. Quite the contrary, it is pain itself that is produced, the certain result of incompatible motives.

Perhaps here is to be found a suggestion for a last and more rewarding viewpoint toward suffering. You suffer as long as you have conflict, and you have conflict as long as you have incompatible motives. To theories which try to explain or justify the suffering of the conscientious aspirant on the basis that it is illusory, or fair, or creative, this standpoint makes no attempt to justify pain at all. It claims simply that pain is a phenomenon of conflict and when you get rid of the conflict you get rid of the pain.

One of the interesting similarities between Hindu psychology and psychiatry is in their views of human dynamics. Both affirm two opposite and antagonistic instincts or drives: the life instinct (which the Vedantist sees as leading toward bondage) and a motive which the Freudian terms the death wish, viewed by the Vedantist as the will to liberation. As Behanan says in his attempt to make a scientific appraisal of yoga psychology, "While yoga would agree with psychoanalysis that pleasure is the guiding principle of the unconscious, it makes a slight exception in favor of those strivings which, although feeble, do exist to remind the individual of the utter futility of an endless pleasure-chase. This muffled voice, diametrically opposed to the dominant trend of the unconscious, speaks a different language and shows the way out for those who, like the yogins, are willing to subdue the clamor for experience in the interest of emancipation."

A man living in response mostly to the first of these drives will have conflict and pain no doubt. His frustration will result from the disparity either between the promptings of his wish for enjoyment and its inadequate satisfactions if these are few, or else from the boredom following them if they are ample.

Should it then come as any surprise that his sufferings should intensify when a man begins to obey his will to liberation? For now, in addition to the conflicts from a fading but still present first sector, he has taken on those of an entire new dimension.

It is said that the life instinct can be overcome, but the will to liberation can never be subdued. Instead, once aroused, it grows and strengthens. Should it therefore be so astonishing that as the call of this wish grows more insistent, and the earnestness to make good its promise keener, that every default will hurt the more? Falterings on the old obstacles of ignorance or ego become increasingly distressing the less frequently they occur. And every failure to make a perfect showing on the new moral virtues of truthfulness or continence or noninjury or tranquility seems less forgivable the more rarely they appear. Perhaps too, a heightening sensitivity accounts for some of what you feel. It seems likely that as your standards go up, the subtlety with which you measure your own observance of them must intensify.

One way of looking at the spiritual struggle is to regard it as mainly an episode of intensified karma-burning. As the production of new karma slackens off, your exertions are directed more wholly toward destroying the stock still on hand. In a sense you volunteer to accept and dispose of the remaining pain-producing tendencies at a more than ordinarily rapid rate. These might be compared, say, to battle scenes distributed at some distance from each other throughout a long motion picture film. Commencement of the spiritual effort begins to speed up the projecting machine. What would have appeared as a no more than normally turbulent showing now becomes hectic. One fierce engagement after another rushes past, until the sole impression left is that of a continuous spectacle of bloodshed and rapine. Actually all the battles would have appeared eventually anyhow, but the speeding up of the projector has made them seem overwhelming. However, by tolerating a shorter period of greater uproar, the spectator finishes with the discomfort sooner.

Whether this notion has any authenticity or not, it at least has one advantage. In urging you to undertake and dispose of now what will come eventually anyway, it argues for vigor and stamina, two qualities which the candidate badly needs. It prompts you to accept what Meister Eckhart called the "strenuous life" of discipleship.

As the indicator needle on the gauge of your spiritual struggle, pain exposes the presence of conflict. It reveals the existence still of contrary wishes, of wanting two things at once. Until you want only the One, mind and body, brain and viscera, you cannot attain the inestimable result. Pain is an unattractive tormentor, but it is also a good friend. It urges you to make your outlook single, and it punishes you into doing it.

If you want to look up suffering in the complete works of Swami Vivekananda you will be disappointed. In the eighty-five-page index to his writings the heading Suffering does not once appear. Neither does Pain. To find out what this spiritual Titan thought about suffering you have to look under the title Strength. When you think about it, it seems right that it should be that way.

Vivekananda expressed it positively. The only thing to do about suffering is to exercise those techniques which are known to eliminate it: to pull up the incompatible motives root and branch, to seek the One, and by God's grace to find the One, to be the One. Urges Swamiji, you should say to yourself: "This misery that I am suffering is of my own doing, and that very thing proves that it will have to be undone by me alone. That which I have created, I can demolish." Then he goes on: "Therefore, stand up, be bold, be strong. All the strength and succour you want is within yourselves. The infinite future is before you, and you must always remember that each word, thought, and deed, lays up a store for you and that as the bad thoughts and bad works are ready to spring upon you like tigers, so also there is the inspiring hope that the good thoughts, and good deeds, are ready with the power of a hundred thousand angels to defend you always and forever."

One of the most saintly, most compassionate and sensitive of spiritual advisers waved away the devotee who had come to him for help in resolving some deep suffering she was experiencing. "Be like me," he said, without a touch of ego. "I have never suffered a moment in my life." A Vedantist can understand how that can be true, or can come to be true, not only for this special man, but for everyone. There is suffering, but there is an end of suffering. It is this solution to the problem that you are really trying for, and it is the promise of this solution that keeps you working toward it.

Divine Love

Swami Satprakashananda

LOVE OF GOD is the very essence of spiritual life; without it religious practices are nothing but sheer physical and mental exercises. The sanctimonious observance of rites and ceremonies, or the worship of God for temporal interests, no matter how solemn, does not constitute spirituality.

The one purpose of all religious disciplines is to develop love of God within the heart of the aspirant. It is for this that he says prayers, chants hymns, studies scriptures, listens to sermons, makes offerings, observes fasts and vigils, and practices meditation. This love of God is the one supreme ideal of life as taught by all the great teachers of the world.

Even so, though we may know that God is the most lovable of all, the one inexhaustible source of all blessedness, goodness, beauty, and love, yet we do not feel that longing to know Him. Even though we know that it is through love alone that we can be united with Him, and attain eternal life, light, and joy, so dominated are we by our deep-rooted sense desires, our tenacious clinging to ephemeral objects, that we feel no yearning for Him. To counteract these inveterate tendencies, to transform worldly attachment into spiritual urge, to create a Godward flow of thoughts and feelings, the spiritual aspirant must undergo certain disciplines, for it is only through the life of law that he can enter into the life of love.

Three distinct modes of worship constitute the practical methods for the cultivation of devotion to God, namely, physical, verbal, and mental. The physical, or external, mode of worship is performed by bowing down in reverence to God, by the observance of rites and ceremonies,

263

the offering of flowers, lights, incense, etc., the practice of austerities, and personal service to the temple and the teacher. Verbal worship is observed by the saying of prayers, the chanting of hymns, the study of scriptures, and the repetition of a sacred name or formula, while the mental worship consists in the constant remembrance of God, the renunciation of attachment, self-resignation, contemplation, and so forth. Any or all of these modes of worship may be practiced by the aspirant, according to his own tendency, capacity, and situation in life. The practice of even one of these forms of worship, if followed with steadfast devotion, will generate love for God.

The repeated utterance of a sacred word or formula is a very simple method, yet nonetheless, most efficacious. No accessory is needed for its practice, which can be made audibly, semiaudibly, or mentally. Of the three methods, the mental is the most effective. It purifies the aspirant's mind to its very depths and enables him to hold his thoughts on God. In a sense, this constant repetition is a concentrated form of prayer. During prayer we think of God by numerous words and phrases, but as our spiritual sense deepens, and our feelings become intensified, a single word or phrase will convey all that God means to us. It becomes the focal point of all our ideas and sentiments regarding Him. For example, to a Christian who has caught the inner spirit of Jesus Christ, the repetition of his name may do more to intensify his devotion to Christ than a whole scriptural text would.

Every word represents an idea, and, just as each thought has its own word symbol, so are there word symbols, or seed words, as they are called, to express mystical experiences. Through the constant repetition of a seed word spiritual awareness is germinated, and love of God grows within the heart of the devotee.

Thus, gradually, by the practice of these different methods of worship, the mind becomes purged of all dross and dirt, and its attachment to the transitory values of here and hereafter, and there grows a natural longing for God. The aspirant seeks God passionately for His own sake, until, like the needle of the compass which always points north, his mind centers upon God under all the varying conditions of life. He remembers God constantly. This constant God-recollectedness is called *bhakti,* devotion.

During the preparatory stages the aspirant's attitude toward God is very much stimulated by his thought, and by a feeling of awe and reverence rather than of love. He feels that God is the ruler of the universe; consequently, he is more conscious of His splendor and power than of His sweetness and beauty. He seeks God that he may be freed from all bondages, that in Him he may find real life, real light, real joy, knowing that none but He is worth seeking and loving as the supreme goal of life. But, as love grows, the aspirant no longer indulges in such calculations. The might and majesty of God no longer concern him. To him God is all love, and love of God becomes the one motivating power of all his thoughts, feelings, and actions. Out of love of Him his hand works, his mind thinks, his heart feels. In short, he lives for God alone. The attitude of the loving devotee toward God is reflected in this prayer: "May my speech be engaged in the telling of thy glory; may my ears be engaged in listening to thy praise; may my hands be engaged in the performance of thy service; may my eyes see only that which is holy; may my head be ever bowed in reverence to the universe, thy abode, and may my mind be ever engaged in the remembrance of thy blessed feet."

Love and reverence are two different mental attitudes. So long as the worshiper thinks of the divinity as the almighty creator, or the stern ruler, or the dispassionate onlooker of the world order, he may have fear and reverence for God, but not love. He may even have the tendency to bow down before Him, but only from a distance. He will not feel drawn toward Him; there will not be the urge to become united with Him, or to embrace Him as his own. But, with the growth of devotion there comes a sense of intimate relationship to God. The more intensely the votary contemplates God's love and grace, the deeper grows his devotion to Him. He looks upon God as his very own; he feels that "I am thine, thou art mine." This feeling gradually manifests itself in various devotional attitudes according to the aptitude and disposition of the aspirant.

The Hindu psychology of devotion classifies these attitudes under five principal headings. The first is *shanta,* the serene attitude, in which God is seen as the immutable Self, the calm witness of all mental and physical phenomena. The second is *dasya,* the attitude of service. This includes the attitudes of the protected toward the protector, the servant toward the master, and the child toward the parent. Third comes *sakhya,* friendship. In this attitude the devotee feels that he is a friend and companion of God, and His playmate. Next comes *vatsalya,* the attitude of parent. The devotee looks upon God as his own child. Lastly comes *madhura,* the sweet attitude of the lover and the beloved.

It will be seen that in each succeeding attitude there is an increasing intimacy between the devotee and God. In each there is the reciprocity of love. In whatever way the devotee loves God, so does God love His devotee. Yet, even though God may play the role of master, father, mother, friend, or lover toward His devotees, He is actually our all in all, through all eternity, only we do not recognize Him. There is no other father, or mother, or friend, or lover than He. All earthly relationships are temporary, and therefore unreal. So it is that the devotee prays: "Thou alone art my mother, thou alone art my father, thou alone art my wisdom and my treasure. Thou art my all in all, O God of gods."

The Hindu scriptures strongly advocate the association of the holy as an effective means to the cultivation of devotion to God. Love of God is not to be found in temples or churches or books, however sacred. Love of God exists within the heart of the devotee, and by associating with the lovers of God, by conversing with them, by serving them, and by observing their ways, one may imbibe their spirit of love. As a matter of fact, love of God is not kindled within us until we come in contact with those who carry that burning flame within them. The grace of God usually comes through the grace of those who have already received it. Holiness is contagious. Robert Ingersoll once made the remark to Swami Vivekananda, "Had I been God I would have made health contagious instead of disease." "Little do we realize," replied the Swami, "that health is as contagious as disease, virtue as contagious as vice, and cheerfulness as contagious as moroseness." Moral and spiritual precepts, however sublime, may stimulate our thoughts and inspire us with noble feelings, but, unless we see them actually exemplified in the lives of great personalities, they do not implant themselves within us as the ideals of life and living.

Every human being is a potential lover of God. All our lives we have loved nothing but God, but our love has been misdirected. Through all our seeking after wealth, position, pleasure, friendship, love, and power there has been the search for God. It is the urge for the infinite, the eternal, the perfect that impels our seeking, and that is why our mind refuses to be satisfied with that which is limited and imperfect. We have ever sought for the highest and the best. God alone is the highest and best. Your true being cannot respond to any other ideal than the attainment of the highest and best, and when you knowingly seek God as the goal of your life, when you are fully aware that you are living for something beyond which there is nothing more to gain, something which, once gained, you can never lose, something which removes all sufferings, weaknesses, and imperfections forever, then only can you exert all the energies of body and mind to that end. To nothing else can our whole being respond, because we know, in the heart of our hearts, that all achievements on the relative plane, no matter how glamorous, are short-lived and not dependable. As the yearning for God grows, all thoughts and all feelings combine into one single stream flowing toward Him. Thus, in the conscious search for God alone does the integration of personality become possible. No lesser object can integrate our entire being.

Just as each and every water course is constantly struggling to reach the ocean by straight or circuitous routes, even so each and every individual is wending his way Godward directly or indirectly, knowingly or unknowingly. It is the basic urge from which all his desires and strivings derive. In fact, it is the mainspring of his thoughts, feelings, and actions, though he is hardly aware of it. Impelled by this innate tendency to meet the highest and best, the saint worships, the philosopher contemplates, the patriot gives his life for his country, the mother rears the children, the miser amasses wealth, the robber steals. The manifestations of the same pure force of divine love differ in various individuals because of dissimilarities in their mental and physical constitution, in the same way as radiant light expresses itself variously through diverse mediums, or clear water acquires various colors and tastes according to the nature of the soil through which it flows. Worldly desires are but love of God misdirected. When a person seeks God consciously and in the right way then begins his spiritual life. So a great devotee of the Lord prays to Him: "May I ever remember thee with that undying love which the unwise have for temporal things." Fundamentally there is no difference between sense attachment and devotion to God. The grossest sense desire can be transmuted into genuine love of God by turning it Godward. This is evidenced by the life of many a saint.

There are two distinct trends of love in the human heart. The one is to love, the other is to be loved. On the one hand, from your childhood you have been seeking someone to whom you can give all your love, whom you can make your heart's own. You have tried this with your parents, brothers, sisters, husband or wife, sons, daughters, friends, and even your pets, yet you have found none on whom your affection can wholly rest. Each one slips away from your loving hold somehow or other. Nobody seems to understand you. On the other hand, you have been looking for someone who will love you for love's sake, who will make you the sole occupant of his heart, but in this quest also you have been sorely disappointed. You do not find anyone who loves you as you want to be loved. Even your most intimate friends and relations fall short of your expectation. Always there is a gap between two meeting hearts, however close. Rare indeed is the beloved, rare indeed is the lover. After many a long struggle man realizes at last that God alone is the supreme object of his love and God alone is his supreme lover, and that the two predominant tendencies of his heart can find their fulfillment only in Him, who is Love, Lover, and Beloved in one. When such a feeling grows in the devotee's heart he cries out: "In this world, O Lord! in search of wealth I have found thee the greatest treasure. In this world, O Lord! in search of someone to love I have found thee the most lovable One. At thy blessed feet is the culmination of all knowledge; at thy blessed feet is the fulfillment of all desires; at thy blessed feet is the consummation of all love. Therefore, O Lord! I surrender myself to thee. Thou art my sole refuge, my goal, my abode, my sanctuary."

Basically, there are two perpetual streams of love in this world. The one is man's love for God, and the other is God's love for man. Running into different channels, they make numerous currents of love. It is man's love for God that assumes such varied forms as parental, filial, and conjugal love, as fraternity, patriotism, religious fervor, and as hankering after wealth, beauty, power, knowledge, fame, and so forth. And it is God's love for man that manifests itself as deep compassion for humanity, especially as saving grace, in the hearts of God-men and men of God. The great spiritual leaders and lovers of God are the confluences of the two streams. They are the mighty rivers of love flowing incessantly into the infinite ocean of love. They also form the channels through which flow God's love to humanity. By uniting with them through faith and devotion man receives God's grace, and within his heart there springs up a stream of love which flows toward God, until, like the small creeks which are united with the larger rivers, they reach the ocean.

Love of God is bliss itself. Even a modicum of it serves as a source of constant delight which does not depend on anything external, and which endures under all the conditions of life. As the love of God grows within, the devotee's entire being becomes vibrant with divine life, light, and sweetness. Fascinated and intoxicated with the nectar of divine love he lives in a state of ecstasy. He finds within himself a perennial spring of joy welling up from that fountainhead of all blessedness. One particle of that bliss makes the universe blissful; one touch of that beauty endows the face of nature with beauty; one drop of that love fills all hearts with love. Thoroughly contented, he never looks back upon the transitory pleasures and treasures of the sense world. Man hankers after earthly or celestial glories and joys simply because he has no idea of the supreme bliss he can find within himself. Having once tasted the manna of divine love all thirst for enjoyments is quenched forever. He realizes once for all how trivial are the sense enjoyments of even the highest paradise, how futile and foolish it is to run after them instead of striving for the recovery of the eternity and blissfulness of the Self.

Love culminates in complete union with God. As it grows deeper, the devotee feels an ever-increasing longing for the realization of God. It becomes the sole concern of his life. His entire being centers upon this one idea. He feels God's presence nearer and nearer, until he comprehends Him as the supreme spirit shining within his heart as the very soul of his soul. While he still needs mental forms, attitudes, etc., to grasp the formless spirit, he no longer contemplates on God in the external objects of forms and symbols, etc. Within his own heart he meditates on that particular form or aspect of the Divinity which he has chosen as his ideal, until, through continued practice, his mind becomes absorbed in the object of his meditation, and, by the light of knowledge which removes all darkness, he sees God revealed as his chosen ideal.

Yet it is by God's grace and love alone that He can be seen. Sri Krishna says: "With their minds fixed on me, with their senses directed to me, enlightening one another and always speaking of me, they find satisfaction and delight in me. To them, ever devoted, and worshiping me with love, I give the spiritual sight by which they attain me. Out of mere compassion for them, I, abiding in their hearts, destroy darkness born of ignorance by the luminous lamp of knowledge."

As love intensifies, the devotee's individual self becomes so completely unified with God that he realizes the divine being as his very Self, and as the Self in all beings. He lives in the full consciousness of the one Self immanent in the universe. Such a devotee completely surrenders his will to God. In the *Bhagavatam* it is said: "He who sees the divine Self in all beings and all beings in the divine Self is the best devotee of God. He who bears love to God, friendship to His devotees, kindness to the ignorant, and indifference to his foes, is of the second best type, and he who faithfully worships God only in the image, and not in His devotees or others, is a novice."

Through devotion is also attained the knowledge of Brahman, the impersonal, absolute being. Sri Krishna declares: "By devotion he knows me in reality, what and who I am. Knowing me in reality he forthwith enters into me." Regarding this attainment of God-knowledge through devotion, Sri Ramakrishna says: "By constantly meditating on God the devotee loses his ego; he realizes that he is God and God is he."

Even so, the devotee may not lose his individuality. There are some who return after this highest attainment of *samadhi*, and, while enjoying the bliss of divine love, guide and teach humanity.

This state of transcendental devotion is reached by very few, but he who has attained it sees everything, within and without, permeated with divine consciousness and bliss.

The Dark Night of St. John of the Cross

Translated from the Spanish by
Iris Tree

In a dark night I rose
With tremulous love afire
And left my sleeping house.
O blessed wonder, that did so conspire
To lead me forth unseen to my desire.

I was led forth, O wonder!
While all my house lay sleeping,
Disguised, by ladders slender
Down secret pathways creeping
I gave myself into the dark night's keeping.

Into the joyful dark
All silent and unknown
Where there was neither sign nor spark
Save in my heart alone
The fiery flame that shone.

O, brighter than sun's burning
This fiery flame did dart
And pointed to him, ever turning
Toward the long-known of my heart
Who waited for me in a place apart.

O guiding night,
O deep night to discover
Within that darkness dazzling bright
The true beloved to his lover
So that the one became the other.

Upon my breast of flowering love
He lay in sleep; and all I have

I gave to him, while high above
The winds that through the cedars wave
Leaned down and their sweet odors gave.

Through his hair the high winds streaming
Wakened, and his hand grew tense
Upon my neck, O gentle seeming
Yet falling in its sharp sense
Like pain upon my fainting sense.

And so I lay, forgetting all—
Myself with the beloved linking,
I lost myself—and letting fall
My heavy sorrows all unthinking,
Oblivious among the lilies sinking.

The Problem of the Religious Novel

Christopher Isherwood

I SUPPOSE THAT MOST novelists have considered, at one time or another, the project of writing a religious novel. Every writer of dramatic fiction, irrespective of his individual beliefs or doubts, is eager to find characters who will exhibit the maximum variety of reactions to external events. The saint is pre-eminently such a character. Because his motives are not dictated by fear, vanity, or desire—because his every action is a genuine act of free will —you never can predict what he will do next. He accepts life more fully, more creatively, than any of his neighbors. And therefore he is the most interesting person to write about.

The most interesting and the most difficult. For, in attempting to present such a character to his audience of average men and women, the writer cannot rely at all on that factor of familiarity, of self-recognition, which assists him so powerfully when he is describing average people, recognizable social types. He cannot expect his audience to come half way to meet him, exclaiming, "Why, that's just like Mr. Jones!" The saint, considered as an end product, resembles Mr. Jones as little as he resembles a giraffe. And yet Mr. Jones and Mr. Smith and Mr. Brown are all potentially saints. This is what the author has somehow to prove to his audience.

It is a task which demands the utmost persuasiveness, deftness, and cunning. At every step, prejudices and preconceptions have to be overcome. The public has its preconceived notion of a saint—a figure with a lean face and an air of weary patience, who alternates between moods of forbidding austerity and heart-broken sweetness—a creature set apart from this bad world, a living reproach to

273

our human weakness, in whose presence we feel ill at ease, inferior, and embarrassed. In other words, the dreariest of bores.

If I ever write a religious novel, I shall begin by trying to prove that my saint-to-be really *is* Mr. Jones. Somerset Maugham, for example, does this quite successfully in *The Razor's Edge*. Larry, when we first meet him, is an entirely reassuring character, lively, natural, normal, a typical American boy. I think that Maugham's choice of such a character had a great deal to do with the immense popularity of his book.

So far, so good. But now a second and much greater problem arises. How am I going to show, in terms of dramatic fiction, that decisive moment at which my hero becomes aware of his vocation and decides to do something about it? Maugham is rather vague at this point: he merely suggests that Larry's change of heart is caused by his experiences in the first World War. Aldous Huxley's *Time Must Have a Stop* avoids the moment altogether—making a huge jump from Sebastian the precocious, cowardly, inhibited schoolboy to Sebastian the mature, meditative man, already far advanced in the practice of spiritual discrimination. One of the classic examples of a conversion scene is, of course, Dostoevski's account of the duel, in *The Brothers Karamazov*, which starts the process of turning a stupid young bully of a Russian officer into Father Zossima, the saint. How beautifully Dostoevski handles this moment of transformation—without the least sentimentality, in terms almost of farce, yet with such warmth, insight, and naturalness! We share the young man's exquisite relief when he finds himself suddenly able, by fearlessly asking his opponent's pardon, to break the bonds of a rigid military code which has hitherto conditioned his behavior, and to perform his first act of pure free will. This is the kind of scene I should like to have in my novel —something slightly comic and entirely natural. In history, we know that many conversions have occurred as the result of a vision. But visions, unless you are writing historical fiction, like *The Song of Bernadette*, seem to me to be undesirable in the early stages of a story, because they excuse the author from explaining what is happening in his hero's mind. Dramatically, they are a form of cheating.

It is all very well to use words like "conversion" in an article for a religious magazine. They belong to an accepted terminology. I know that my readers will understand what I mean. But this kind of shorthand is never permissible for the novelist, with his mixed and highly skeptical audience. He has to explain, as though they had never been explained before, his hero's motives and objectives; and this, in a religious novel, is particularly difficult. How am I to prove that X isn't merely insane when he turns his back on the whole scheme of pleasures, rewards, and satisfactions which are accepted by the Joneses, the Smiths, and the Browns, and goes in search of superconscious, extraphenomenal experience? The only way I can see how to do this is with the help of the Joneses themselves. I must show that the average men and women of this world are searching, however unconsciously, for that same fundamental reality of which X has already had a glimpse. Certainly, they look for it in the wrong places. Certainly, their methods are quite unpractical. Mr. Jones will find nothing at the bottom of the whisky bottle, except a headache. But the whisky bottle is not to be dismissed with a puritanical sneer; it is the crude symbol of Jones's dissatisfaction with surface consciousness, his need to look more deeply into the meaning of life. The Smiths conform obediently to the standards imposed by the advertisements they read in their newspapers. They drive the prescribed make of car, smoke the recommended brand of cigarettes, spend their leisure time in the ways and at the places which are guaranteed as educational and enjoyable—and yet, at the back of their minds, there is a germ of doubt. Is this really what we were born for? Is this the whole meaning of existence? That doubt may, one day, be their salvation. It is the measure of their kinship with X. For the evolving saint does not differ from his fellow humans in kind, but only in degree. That is why X can only be understood, artistically, when his story is related to that of the Joneses, the Smiths, and the Browns.

The greater part of my novel would deal, of course, with X's struggles toward sainthood, toward complete spiritual realization. I think that most writers have erred in making this phase of their story too somber and depressing. True, the path of the spiritual aspirant is hard. The mortification of the ego is tedious and painful. But I see no reason for the author to sentimentalize his hero's sufferings, or to allow him to indulge in self-pity. Sportswriters find no pathos in the hardships of a boxer's training. The would-be saint is the last person in the world we should feel sorry for. His sufferings are purely voluntary. If his will slackens, they automatically cease. *The Garden of Allah* is not really a tragedy, unless one regards it as a tragedy of weakness. If the runaway monk did not genuinely want to return to the monastery, and was only bowing to public opinion, then it was very weak and silly of him to do so. George Moore, in his two novels, *Evelyn Innes* and *Sister Teresa,* has traced the development of a famous opera singer into a Catholic nun. It is a wonderful and moving story, full of acute psychological observation, amounting almost to clairvoyance. Moore is at his best in describing that moment of spiritual vertigo and despair when Evelyn, listening to the trivial chatter of the other novices, thinks, "How can I possibly stay here?" and then, remembering the equally trivial chatter at the dinner parties she used to attend, asks herself, "But how could I possibly go back to the old life?" Nevertheless, I feel that Moore, like many of his inferiors, has made his protagonist's spiritual history too gloomy—perhaps simply because he does not carry it far enough. We say good-by to Evelyn before she has made any permanent adjustment to her new life, and at a time when she has just lost her marvelous voice. The novel ends on a note of sadness, against which I protest. Surely the mishaps and setbacks which beset the path of spiritual progress can be recounted with some of the humor which invests one's failures in cookery or falls in learning to ski? Maugham, I believe, would agree with me here. There is nothing gloomy about Larry's career. Unfortunately, however, his creator has gone to the other extreme, and one gets the impression that becoming a saint is just no trouble at all.

And so we come to the last phase of the story, the portrait of the perfected saint. Here, I am sure, I should give up in despair. Nothing short of genius could succeed in such a task. For the mystical experience itself can never be described. It can only be written around, hinted at, dimly reflected in word and deed. So far, the novelists have given us nothing but brilliant glimpses—the incident of the Bishop's candlesticks in *Les Miserables,* the few interviews with Father Zossima, Huxley's sketch of Bruno Rontini. These three men are only minor characters in long and crowded stories. Maugham is greatly to be admired for his more ambitious attempt—even if, as I have indicated above, it is not altogether successful.

Tolstoy, toward the end of his career, outlined what might have been a masterpiece. We cannot be sure. The life of *Father Serguis* is told in less than fifty pages. Perhaps even Tolstoy felt himself unequal to the undertaking. Perhaps the truly comprehensive religious novel could only be written by a saint—and saints, unfortunately, are not in the habit of writing novels.

Values of Life

Swami Akhilananda

MAN WORKS with various motives. His life is regulated, coordinated, and unified according to the objective he chooses as his life's goal. This objective is the basis of his progress through his individual expression as well as in his collective life. His whole existence is an expression of that objective.

When we observe different individuals and civilizations, we find that some take greatest pleasure on the sense plane as their primary objective. Hedonism, or the pleasure principle of Freudians, is the goal of the vast majority of the people in the West; and it has also been the ideal of most Western civilizations. Those who adopt the pleasure principle (sense pleasure), as the goal of life regulate their economic systems and social organizations for the attainment of the greatest amount of pleasure that can be reached through them. They organize their educational system in such a way that education will make them fit for realization of the greatest pleasure on the sense plane. The political structure is regulated so that both those engaged in it and society itself will gain the greatest amount of sense pleasure; the political ideal is wholly subordinated to this principle. Industrial, commercial, and banking institutions are governed by it. Ethics and psychology become subservient to this goal. It is reasonable to say that even religion is subordinated to it; and man uses the holy name of God for economic progress, physical welfare, and other forms of pleasure.

Other individuals take intellectual achievements as the primary objective of life. They find greatest satisfaction in intellectual flights through literature, poetry, philosophy, and science. Their lives are also regulated according to the standard of intellectual achievement. They are not interested so much in economic progress or political power as they are in the higher pursuits of intellectualism. Their educational system is organized according to that ideal. Their sense of morality and religion must satisfy their intellectual cravings. Morality and religion must be supported by rationalism; they must be consistent, congruous, and systematic. As anything nonrational jars the intellectual sensibility of such people and becomes repugnant to them, they cannot accept any religious attitude which does not satisfy their rationalistic tendencies.

Some take aesthetic culture as their goal of life. It operates not only in their individual life but it also becomes the center of their collective life. They develop art, music, poetry, and the like; and all other activities of life are subordinated to that goal. Human relationships are based on aesthetic principles. Any expression, way of life, and activity which is not in conformity with the aesthetic sense of such persons will be negated by them, being repulsive to their sense of being. In fact, their whole life— economic, ethical, religious, etc.—is subordinated to aesthetic culture.

There are others again whose primary objective of life is religion. Pleasure is wholly subordinated to that goal. Their system of education is planned so that the religious ideal is reached by individuals and society. Economic, industrial, and political organizations are completely subordinated to religious principles. It goes without saying that they understand psychology and ethics in terms of religious evolution. Their standard of evaluation of people is based on religious evolution. According to them, a good man is he who can conquer his empirical self and his inordinate tendencies so that he can reach the highest goal of religion. His total mind is controlled so that it can be directed to the fulfillment of that ideal.

It should be mentioned that real religious idealists would never minimize the existence of aspirations and search for pleasure. They do not deny the existence of human cravings for pleasure, friendship, comfort, and security. Nevertheless, they realize that these cravings cannot be satisfied without baneful effect if they are not subordinated to a higher ideal which will give opportunity for their proper satisfaction and at the same time lead to the realization of the goal of religion. From their understanding of the human mind they come to the conclusion that man's desires have to be regulated, controlled, and transformed in order to reach the real ideal of human life. This ideal is regarded as the supreme value or supreme objective. It has been found from experience of human nature that the moment the supreme value of life is withdrawn from society and the pleasure principle is encouraged out of proportion and restriction, the human mind is vitiated and demoralized, resulting in an egocentric attitude in life with its various expressions. Let there not be any false idea that religion is pessimistic or so-called "other-worldly." On the contrary, it makes life in this world more satisfactory by removing conflicts and frustration. It gives real bliss and everlasting joy.

As students of philosophy we should evaluate the various objectives of life. We have seen from the pages of history time and again that the people who follow the hedonistic philosophy of life, or the pleasure principle, however Freudians and others may glorify it, create certain basic difficulties in human society. When a man tries to get the greatest pleasure on the sense plane and regulates his political and economic institutions accordingly, he naturally clashes with other people and other groups who are inspired by the same ideal. The desire for political power and consequent domination of other individuals is originally based on the pleasure principle. As man continues to regulate economic, educational, and social systems on this basis, he enters a peculiar situation in which his desires for more sense objects, such as money and commodities of life, are stimulated. Then he seeks greater opportunities for obtaining them through new markets. The history of civilization proves to us that the nations which cherish pleasure and success on the sense plane invariably become extremely aggressive in their political, social, and economic relationships. In fact, the economic conflict of the post-Renaissance civilization of the West is the basis of most of the individual and collective warfare. Even family relationships, individual and collective, are very much tainted by the desire for power and egocentric and selfish gratification through sense objects. This egocentric attitude separates one from the other in the family, society, and nation. It is intrinsically one of exclusion as it inspires a man to have the greatest amount of pleasure for himself or his group, which is the cause of an extreme form of nationalism in certain contemporary groups. It also creates the demand for exclusive rights and privileges, causing trouble between the haves and have-nots, capital and labor, and conqueror and conquered. Then all human efforts and activities produce more and more misery and pain, as man increasingly becomes extremely selfish and self-seeking. So the hedonistic outlook basically creates cravings for more and more satisfaction through pleasure; and, as one proceeds on this basis, the craving creates more and more dissatisfaction, frustration, and internal and external conflict. Gradually the dissatisfaction, frustration, and conflict affect mental equilibrium resulting in psychological disintegration and even physical deterioration, as proved in psychosomatic diseases. The pleasure principle as the goal of life is bound to create economic conflict, racial discrimination, psychological disintegration, and moral and spiritual bankruptcy.

It is true that both Marxism and the humanism of Comte are attempts to eliminate the causes of class trouble. Unfortunately, we find that these principles, however noble they may appear to be, cannot ward off the evils of the intrinsic effect of the hedonistic outlook on life. Many noble attempts have been made at different times by different individuals, but they failed to unify society and to remove class conflict. Moreover, we find that the individuals who are inspired by this outlook are disintegrating psychologically, morally, and spiritually; they are becoming impoverished, to say the least. Even religion is being utilized for hedonism, as we have already mentioned.

The late Archbishop of Canterbury, William Temple, expressed the following sentiments in an interview with the religious editor of the *Providence Journal and Evening Bulletin*: "I think it should be accepted as a principle, however, that advanced nations in the future should have a definite say as to backward nations: otherwise equity is impossible." His book, *Mens Creatrix*, also indicates that he confused religious ideals with politics.

Both the people who take intellectual achievements as their goal of life and those who follow aestheticism, generally swing to the groups who advocate the greatest pleasure on the sense plane, with political adjustment according to that ideal. Most of the contemporary scientists, rationalistic thinkers, poets, writers, and others subscribe completely to this viewpoint. As a result, we find that the intellectual and aesthetic groups are almost entirely absorbed by that standard. On the other hand, it is also possible that if the religious ideal becomes predominant in a civilization, the intellectual and aesthetic groups are attracted to religious culture. It may seem unfair to say that these two groups swing back and forth from one side to the other, yet this understanding is supported by contemporary and past history. It may be fairer to say that when hedonism becomes predominant, they are often utilized by the seekers of pleasure. It seems that unless man has a strong religious background he cannot keep intellectual or aesthetic standards to their highest level. Contemporary history also proves that the people who try to establish equality in political, economic, and social spheres on the basis of ethics and humanism, whether they are Marxian or otherwise, lose sight of their original objective in the course of their activities. It will not be unjust to say that their ideals are considerably stretched and diluted.

It is quite reasonable to ask at this point what we mean by the religious ideal. Is it following a few doctrines and dogmas, merely accepting particular religious personalities, practicing certain rituals and ceremonies, or believing in the divine Being? No doubt these are various phases of religion; they may be regarded as its secondary elements, yet they are helpful for the realization of the primary objective of religion. Many persons take a very narrow and dogmatic attitude toward religion. They seem to think that it has nothing to do with reason. The Barthian neo-orthodox groups in Europe, the neo-orthodoxy of America under the leadership of Niebuhr, and other similar groups are advocates of such thinking; they even go so far as to declare that the desire to know God is sinful. However, they admit that man must love God. But we do not find any explanation for their love of God. How can a man love anyone without knowing anything about him? Knowledge of a person is the background of love. In our everyday life we know a person first and then we fall in love with him. It is psychologically impossible to love someone without knowing anything about him. If the desire to know God is sinful, then love is an impossibility. So this viewpoint logically destroys any basis for religion. It seems that these groups are persuading the people to revert to certain dogmatic ideas without giving any rational basis for them. Moreover, the proponents of neo-orthodoxy and others with such thought patterns will not be able to satisfy the cravings and aspirations of people who are intellectually awakened. These attitudes will only discourage scientific thinkers as well as rational critics. We do not believe that religion is antagonistic to rationalism. We are thoroughly convinced that although religion is based on higher spiritual experiences, it is supported by the principles of reasoning. Firsthand religion, as experienced and taught by the great spiritual leaders, belonging to the many great religions, is beyond reason; yet it is supported by reason. It is also verifiable by various types of minds. Spiritual experiences can be explained in terms of logical principles. They are consistent and harmonious. Such experiences integrate the mind and help people to develop strong personalities so that they can live harmonious and peaceful lives. In addition, life itself becomes blissful. Those who come in contact with such personalities also enjoy bliss and satisfaction.

Some who do not belong to the neo-orthodox group but go to the extreme left are more or less followers of Auguste Comte. To them religion is pure and undiluted "social gospel." They no doubt mean well when they say that service to man is the sole purpose of religion; yet they forget that the main objective of religion is direct awareness of the reality, or God. They follow the second but forget the first commandment of Jesus. So they miss the mark altogether in spite of their desire to serve people. It will not be unjust to say that these attitudes in religion do not even succeed in establishing brotherhood and equality, as they do not spring from the experience of God which is the basis of real brotherhood, equality, and love.

As Swami Vivekananda says, religion is the manifestation of divinity that is already in man. According to Jesus, religion is the attainment of perfection. In order to manifest divine nature and love God completely, we must conquer our lower passions of greed, anger, hatred, selfishness, and love of power. So long as man seeks his own pleasure, individually or collectively, he necessarily becomes selfish, egotistic, and domineering. These qualities exclude him from his neighbors. As such, he can neither love God nor his neighbors. Divinity cannot be manifested so long as one remains greedy, selfish, arrogant, and full of the love of power. The words of Jesus: "Be ye perfect even as the Father in heaven is perfect," cannot be followed so long as we seek pleasure on the sense plane. The unconquerable desire for more and more sense pleasure removes all possibilities for peaceful living. When there is no peaceful state of mind due to restless cravings, there is no possibility of attaining perfection. "But the self-controlled man," according to the *Bhagavad-Gita,* "moving among objects with senses under restraint, and free from attraction and aversion, attains to tranquility. . . . That man who lives devoid of longing . . . without the sense of 'I' or 'mine,' he attains to peace."

The religious philosophy of life is inclusive and universal. As such, it brings out the best in the individual and enables him to live with others in harmony and peace. When he tries to manifest his "divinity" and "perfection," man necessarily becomes unselfish and loving to others. Selfishness, which is the logical conclusion of the pleasure, is antagonistic to love, unifying influences, and the attainment of perfection. A society which is based on pleasure and consequent selfishness is bound to disintegrate, as there are inherent causes for limitation and consequent destruction in it. Hedonism creates the spirit of competition, jealousy, and hatred.

So we come to the conclusion that if we take a far-sighted view of life, as students of philosophy ought to do, religious values are the highest goals of human effort. When a man takes religion as the supreme goal of life and regulates his activities accordingly, he can easily eliminate economic conflict, racial struggle, political warfare, psychological disintegration, and ethical bankruptcy; because in the highest form of religion unselfishness, sympathy, and thoughtfulness will be manifested and the sense of beauty, good, and permanency will be evolved. It goes without saying that without this highest goal of life, love is an impossibility. In individual and collective life, love degenerates into selfish demand and sentimentality without religious values. It is the primary duty of all students of philosophy and religion to manifest spiritual qualities in life and action. As Jesus said: "By their fruits ye shall know them. . . . Not every one that saith unto me, Lord, Lord, shall enter into the kingdom of heaven; but he that doeth the will of my Father who is in heaven."

Philosophical discourses and intellectual interpretation of religious values alone will not become the dynamics of individual and collective life. When they are practiced, however, man understands the true significance of religious values. Practical demonstration is the only condition for the establishment of a society on the basis of religious ideals.

Nature Abhors a Vacuum

Sister Amiya

NATURE ABHORS A VACUUM, it has been said, and it is the urge to fill a vacuum which causes all the miseries in the world. Greed is one of the cardinal sins, and there are few who can claim to be entirely free of it. The desire to possess is inherent in every man to a lesser or greater extent, and when this desire dominates the individual it is called greed.

Our first real possessions are our parents, and from that first point of possession our sense of ownership widens out till it becomes like the ever-widening circles on a shoreless sea. It never can reach an end. To all intents and purposes this sense of possession is normal; but the question is, what is "normal"? By what norm do we judge? Is it by anything we find in nature? We see nothing, no relationship in nature that would lead us to suppose that it is so, and, if we are honest, we shall see that it is only in the human species that this particular sense of ownership has developed. Sheep and cows do not have it! Bees cannot hoard the honey they strive so hard to gather long enough to call it their own. How then did this particular sense develop in man?

Man, as man, is more highly developed than the brute, in that in him has evolved the ego, which, in the animal, remains involved. This ego gives man the sense of "I-ness," the sense of separateness, of individuality. Along with this there are also developed reason, intelligence, and discrimination, and these powers, if rightly used, can raise man far beyond the limitations of the animal.

As the ego of the child gradually evolves he begins to look upon his parents as his own, and everything they do or say affects him. If the mother pets him, he coos; if she

slaps him, he cries. And why? Because of his identification
with her. She is "his" and he is "hers," and they react upon
each other. Out of this identification are born all the pairs
of opposites, and as these dual experiences are repeated
they bring with them other emotions. For example, the
sense of pain brings anger or aversion—even hatred; while
pleasure brings love or attraction.

As the idea of possession gradually takes hold of the
mind, its attachment to things and objects grows, and the
desire for more and still more increases, until, in some
cases, a man will go to the length of stealing, even murdering, to gratify his greed. There is no end to desire.
Satiety in one field leads only to longing and hunger in
another, until at last man becomes a slave to his appetites. His very nature abhors a vacuum, and yet the vacuum persists; he cannot fill it.

And why? Deep down, within man's very core, this well-
spring of longing lies hidden. Within him there is a something that cries out for gratification, for recognition. Man
feels this longing, and, because of his outgoing tendencies,
in his ignorance, he seeks its gratification in sense objects
which always elude him and forever leave the heart "high
sorrowful and cloyed." But, sooner or later the time comes
when his own reason tells him that, if he has this longing
so persistently, there must be some means of satisfying it.
And thus he begins to discriminate. What is this longing?
What is this urge within me which nothing outside can
satisfy? With this reasoning begins his search for the answer, and this search, again, is the beginning of spiritual
life. He begins to turn around, as it were, and look within
himself for the answer. For logically it would seem that, if
the desire comes from within, its fulfillment also must
come from within. And so begins another kind of struggle;
for answers to mighty problems do not come in a day,
sometimes not even in a lifetime. But the search, once begun, goes on relentlessly.

The answers given by the illumined knowers of truth
may be convincing intellectually, but to the untutored
mind they appear at first to be alarmingly confusing. First
we are told that God is. God alone is real; everything else
is unreal. To such a bold statement as this the mind naturally reacts. How can this beautiful world, with all the
lovely birds and bees and flowers be unreal? Then it is explained that, well, the world is unreal in the sense that the
snake which we ignorantly superimpose on the rope is un-

real. We see a rope lying on the ground in the darkness and we mistake it for a snake. In reality it is still a rope. Very good! Our intelligence can grasp that much, even though at this stage we still have an instinctive feeling that the world does appear awfully real. I touch it; how solid and firm it is! But then, so would the snake have seemed had I touched it, so let me accept the explanation.

Then the next question comes. If all this that I sense and perceive is God, then why don't I see Him? Why do I see everything *but* Him? The answer is: we do not see God now, because of our ignorance—our superimposition of the phenomena upon the reality—; remove the ignorance and He can be seen. Just as there are many clay pots of different sizes and shapes and colors, yet made up of one and the same substance, clay, so is God the one substance out of which all things are made. So far, so good. The mind has been able to grasp and accept this explanation also.

Now comes the most important question. What is this ignorance? And the answer is, *there is no ignorance.* God is the one eternal, unchanging, reality. He is existence, knowledge, and bliss absolute; outside of Him there is nothing. And you are that God! How can that possibly be, one naturally asks. How can I *know* that I am God? Where *is* He? Where am *I*? How can I remove the ignorance that hides Him if the ignorance does not exist? This ignorance is merely an *ignore–ance* of our true nature. The senses were made outgoing, in order to bring experiences to the mind; they were intended as servants to the true nature of man, instead of which they went out and became the slaves of nature. They ignored the inner man in their enslavement to the outer, and this is what is called ignorance. Sri Ramakrishna used to give the illustration of the policeman who, in his day, used to go around at night with a bull's-eye lantern, seeing all, yet himself remaining unseen. In order to see the policeman it is necessary that he turn the light upon himself. And so it is with man. In order to discover his true nature, he has to turn his gaze within; he must look into the recesses of his own heart.

How may one set about achieving this new order of living? The scriptures tell us that first it is necessary to hear about this truth from an illumined teacher, one who has experienced the truth for himself. Then we must think about it. This means that we must use our own discrimination and ourselves become convinced of its truth. We must not merely accept the words of another, and do nothing about it. Then, convinced intellectually, we must meditate upon it. For a merely intellectual understanding will get us nowhere. We have to experience it for ourselves, and we are told that this experience is possible to all. It is man's spiritual birthright. Then it is that, having accepted the fact that God *is,* and can be known, we begin our real search for Him.

We have learned that He is existence-knowledge-bliss. What exactly is meant by that? If He is existence *itself* then He does not actually *exist*—not in the sense that we understand existence. But *I* exist! Then it must be that I exist in existence itself—God. Then I am in God and, logically, it must follow that He is in me also! "In him we live and move and have our being." Then we think, if I am in God and He is in me, why don't I know it? Why have I been going around in circles all this time? But then again, we reason, merely to understand this intellectually doesn't help me much, unless it is of course that I feel an increasing hunger for that illusive something which has been haunting me all these years! What is this hunger? What can I do to satisfy it? "Blessed are they which do hunger and thirst after righteousness, for they shall be filled." Does this mean then that the hunger and thirst of the heart should be increased? Is God then that something within me which is seeking for recognition of itself? We realize that it is and that only through this insatiable hunger and the effort to satisfy it can He be known.

If we study the scriptures—any of them—we shall find the same answer given in all. Having heard and thought about this truth we must meditate upon it, for only through the process of meditation can this knowledge of God be attained. Meditation has many different forms according to the nature of the seeker, but in all processes there is the one practice stressed—purification of the heart. All impurities of the mind and heart have to be wiped away, and the surest means of doing this is by yearning. The heart has to yearn for God above every other thing. Therefore, the duty of every spiritual aspirant is to rid his mind of all preconceived ideas and theories, and to free it completely from attachment to everything he has so covetously called his own. Nature may abhor a vacuum, but God demands one; for He is a jealous God. We cannot serve God and mammon at the same time.

"Thou shalt love the Lord thy God with all thy heart and with all thy soul and with all thy strength and with all thy mind, and him only shalt thou serve." Which means that if we really want to find God we must love Him with every part of us. First we have to love Him with the mind; we have to remember Him constantly until this unbroken remembrance brings pure love in the heart and the soul wells up with an everlasting joy. Then we shall find that every ounce of our strength is being poured out in service to Him alone.

What follows this attainment of purity? "Blessed are the pure in heart for they shall see God." Faith is lost in sight. Then, we are told, through this one-pointed devotion to God the aspirant is lifted up beyond the limitations of the conscious mind until the creature becomes one with the Creator. Transcending all the states of consciousness he becomes one with God. Then does he see the one reality. Through his enlightened vision he sees the many-splendored thing, the one substance behind the appearance of the many. He sees it is the one God who resides in the hearts of all beings, and it is that God he serves—none else. All attachments are broken. Never again is he deluded; no longer is he conscious of a bottomless vacuum. His hunger and thirst are satisfied forever.

Meditation According to the Upanishads

Swami Aseshananda

TRULY HAS THE poet said, "Our sincerest laughter with some pain is fraught." There is no abiding joy in all the multicolored experiences of life. In spite of our best efforts we cannot hold on to happiness. In the midst of enjoyment all of a sudden a crisis comes in the form of a painful disease or the death of a dear and near one. From the crest of a high wave we are thrown into the depths of a yawning chasm. We are mercilessly battered by the onslaught of restless waves. The last ray of hope disappears. The world seems to be dark and gloomy. Mortal fear wrings our heart dry. The tragic picture we draw in the lines of our faces can more easily be imagined than described. The words of Matthew Arnold sink deep into our consciousness and make us stubborn pessimists:

> ... for the world, which seems
> To lie before us like a land of dreams,
> So various, so beautiful, so new,
> Hath really neither joy, nor love, nor light,
> Nor certitude, nor peace, nor help from pain;
> And we are here as on a darkling plain
> Swept with confused alarms of struggle and flight,
> Where ignorant armies clash by night.

Misgivings sway our mind. Feelings of frustration steal into our heart. We become seriously doubtful of the existence of the benevolent Being whom the theologians designate as God. Where is the proof? Can it not be but a pious hope, a figment of the mind? On the other hand, direct experience proves that the boat of life is drifting on a shoreless ocean without a rudder, without a helmsman.

We are living in an enigmatic world. Everything is

shrouded in a haze of mystery. To attempt to penetrate this haze by intellect and discursive reasoning leads ultimately to atheism. The problem becomes more complicated when we view the dark episodes, the hell of suffering, which good and righteous people have had to experience in their checkered lives. We find that a saint, a *mahatma*, the very salt of the earth, is visited with pain and tribulations of a perplexing magnitude. A holy man whose whole life has been a poem of sacrifice and consecrated service has been assailed by troubles. Why should he, of all men, be the victim of insult and rebuff and infamy in a world which is governed according to law and justice by the ruler of human destiny, a comforter of heavy-laden souls?

The same thought crossed the mind of Swami Vivekananda when he wrote to one of his friends, a friend who had been thrown into a cataclysm of grief: "Often and often we see that even the very best of men are troubled and visited with tribulations in the world. It may be inexplicable but it is also the experience of my life that the heart and core of everything here is good, that whatever may be the surface waves deep down and underlying everything there is an infinite basis of goodness and love; and so long as we don't reach that basis we are troubled, but once that zone of calmness is reached, let winds howl and tempests rage, the house that is built on the rock of ages cannot be shaken. May the sufferings and blows of the world draw you closer and closer to the Being who does not fail His devotees in the hour of their peril."

Apparently the question remains insoluble, a puzzle which baffles the understanding of a mere scholar, an intellectual philosopher. The problem of the ultimate nature of the universe and of existence cannot be solved by reason. The answer to this fundamental problem comes from a realm beyond reason. According to Vedanta, mind is the storehouse of enormous energy. There are three faculties of the human mind which can be used for the apprehension of truth and the gathering in of knowledge. They are styled by the teachers of the *Upanishads* as instinct, reason, and intuition. Through instinct, by the urge of the subconscious, man performs his automatic and reflex actions. In instinctive deeds man is bereft of I-consciousness. Instinct develops into reason. Reason functions on the conscious plane. Our intellectual pursuits and rational activities are associated with I-consciousness. Reason finds its fulfillment and highest consummation in pure awareness or intuition. Intuition functions on the super-conscious plane. Instinct acts with precision and accuracy in a limited sphere. The province of intellect is better, but it cannot lay claim to infallible knowledge. In the deeper problems of life it is only the light of intuition that illumines the path and works as an unerring guide.

Sometime or other we ask these fundamental questions: Who am I? Where do I come from? What is my destiny? But answers to these perplexing riddles cannot be found as long as we remain clogged within the bounds of the plodding intellect. Doubtful conjectures and intellectual pastimes must be hushed into silence. Goethe rightly says: "Man's highest happiness as a thinker is to have fathomed what can be fathomed, and to bow down in reverence before the unfathomable." Problems of God, the immortality of the soul, and the origin of the universe, cannot be solved until we transcend the realm of the intellect. We must go to the other side of the prism in order to envisage the white light of unity which has not been disintegrated into parts and fragments. The Vedas speak in unfaltering tongue of the futility and utter inadequacy of the human mind in probing into the depths of the reality which is at the back of the universe:

> Formless is he though inhabiting form. In the midst of the fleeting he abides forever. All-pervading and supreme is the Self. The wise man, knowing him in his true nature, transcends all grief.
> The Self is not known through study of the scriptures nor through subtlety of the intellect, nor through much learning, but by him who longs for him is he known. Verily, unto him the Self reveals his true being.

Religion does not consist in subscribing to this creed or that creed, but in actual realization, in coming face to face with God. Paying allegiance to a particular dogma or doctrine has only a secondary value. The substance of religion is not blind faith in belief or in intellectual understanding but in being and becoming. What counts most in spiritual life is character and a way of life molded by inner experience. The divinity within must be brought to one's perception. The ultimate proof of God's existence is a unique spiritual experience. Our different senses and mind fail to apprehend Him because He is not an object. He is the eternal subject, the witness of the changing phenomena of the universe. Sri Ramakrishna has illustrated this in a homely way. He used to tell the parable of the salt doll which went to the sea to measure its depth. As soon as it touched the water it melted and was fully absorbed in it. How then could it measure the depth of the sea? Similarly all descriptions of God by the limited mind are vain attempts to express the inexpressible. Hence the *Upanishads* say: "He who knows the joy of Brahman, which words cannot express and the mind cannot reach, is free from fear. He is not distressed by the thought, 'Why did I not do what is right? Why did I do what is wrong?' He who knows the joy of Brahman, knowing both good and evil, transcends both." All definitions of God by the human mind must be anthropomorphic. Silence is the homage that is to be paid in order to be able to describe the ineffable beyond. The same truth was reiterated by Meister Eckhart when he said: "Why dost thou prate of God? Whatever thou sayest of Him is not true."

God is the essence of bliss, the fount of eternal joy. All beings irrespective of creed and color, have sprung from bliss. They are maintained by bliss, and in the end they enter into the heart of bliss. Who could live, who could breathe, if the indwelling Self were not rooted in untrammeled felicity? God is the repository of all blessed qualities. He is the immutable spirit residing in the cave of the heart, drawing all men together. Beauty of form is only a dull reflection of the indescribable beauty of the spirit. A physical body, however attractive it may appear, is dead insentient matter. The power of attraction does not belong to it. We must look for the pull of attraction elsewhere. If nature, which is a mere patchy reflection, a shadow, is so beautiful, how marvelously beautiful must be the source, the mighty spirit that pervades every atom of our being, every particle of the universe.

But how to attain the vision of God and realize one's divine destiny? The Vedas say, through yoga. The word yoga means yoke or union—union of the individual soul with the supreme soul, which Emerson calls the oversoul. Yoga has been erroneously interpreted as crystal-gazing, fortune-telling, fire-eating, and other types of miracle-mongering. Yoga has nothing to do with any kind of miracles or occult practices. Yoga is a rational method of self-discipline and purification of the heart. "Blessed are the pure in heart, for they shall see God," says Christ. The *Upanishads* preach that the best way of purifying the heart is through contemplation and meditation. Meditation has been defined as an unbroken stream of thought focused on an object, like oil which is poured from one vessel to another in a continuous flow. The purpose of meditation is to still the modifications of the mind. Mind may be compared to a lake. It is full of waves created by multifarious desires which are perpetually rising to the surface. On account of the agitated condition of the surface we do not perceive our inmost Self, which is pure and divine. By steady practice of meditation one can quell the waves and attain to perfect calmness, which nothing in the world can disturb.

The *Upanishads* speak of the heart, shaped like a lotus bud, as the most appropriate place for divine contemplation. It is also called *Brahmapura*, the abode of Brahman. As meditation deepens, the aspirant is blessed with subtle perceptions which make his mind tranquil like the unflickering flame of a lamp burning in a windless spot. At the final culmination, the seeker after truth reaches the highest peak of realization in nirvikalpa samadhi—an all-annihilating experience in which space melts away and time stands still. The phenomenal world is totally obliterated from the consciousness of the meditator and knowledge of Brahman saturates every fiber of his being. There is no more distinction of subject and object, and the seer is engulfed and absorbed in the bliss of Self-knowledge, transcending the bounds of sorrow and grief. Then all the fetters of the heart are broken, and all the doubts of the mind are resolved by the blasting light of knowledge. The value of meditation cannot be overemphasized. Every *Upanishad* has a special chapter dealing with the method and means of meditation as an important practical discipline. Meditation is the *sine qua non* to spiritual realization. Daily practice of meditation is an essential prerequisite for a student of Vedanta, who views life as a sacred trust to be used for the emancipation of the soul, and for the service of man as the symbol and expression of God. The *Swetasvatara Upanishad* exhorts all spiritual aspirants and encourages them with the assurance that their labors will not be in vain. As you practice meditation, you will see in vision forms resembling snow, crystal, wind, smoke, fire, lightning, fireflies, the sun, and the moon. These are signs that you are on your way to the revelation of Brahman. As you become absorbed in meditation, you will realize that the Self is separate from the body and for this reason will not be affected by disease, old age, or death. The first signs of progress in the path of yoga are health, a sense of physical lightness, clearness of complexion, a beautiful voice, an agreeable odor of the person, and freedom from craving. "As a soiled piece of metal, when it has been cleaned, shines brightly, so the dweller in the body, when he has realized the truth of the Self, is freed from sorrow and attains to bliss."

Visions and voices and the supersensuous perception may be milestones on the road to realization, but they are not the whole story. They may be met with on the way, but one must not be attracted by their fascinating power. It is a precious saying that power corrupts. This saying is true in spiritual matters as well as in secular matters. It is best to ignore the visions and voices and keep perpetual vigil until the goal is reached. The *Upanishads* constantly remind us that the path is sharp as a razor's edge and that slackening of effort due to inadvertence or self-complacency will mean disaster. One must practice meditation with unwavering zeal and inflexible determination till the veil is lifted and the face of truth shines effulgent, dowering the soul with peace and eternal blessedness. As the *Mundaka Upanishad* says: "Affix to the *Upanishad,* the bow incomparable, the sharp arrow of devotional worship; then, with mind absorbed and heart melted in love, draw the arrow and hit the mark—the imperishable Brahman. Om is the bow, the arrow is the individual being, and Brahman is the target. With a tranquil heart, take aim. Lose thyself in him, even as the arrow is lost in the target."

How long does it take to hit the mark and arrive at the goal? This cannot be answered categorically. Realization of the highest good and attainment of freedom is not a question of time. Emancipation refers to an experience that implies timelessness. It cannot be attained at any given moment. No time limit can be set. Everything depends upon *shraddha,* which means sincerity, intense longing, and an affirmative attitude toward life. Negative thoughts are more deadly than a deadly poison. God is the searcher of our heart. He knows all our inner motives. We can draw His sympathy only through self-surrender and humility of spirit. We cannot move Him by eloquence or fine words. To the proud and the arrogant He is an all-exacting master. But to the meek and the gentle He is the ever-forgiving Father, kind and generous beyond human understanding. One who approaches Him with bended knee and perfect resignation will surely be uplifted and brought within the orbit of His grace.

The Ideal of Renunciation

Swami Prabhavananda

THERE EXIST IN THE world today two extreme schools of thought regarding both the spiritual life and the worldly life. On the one hand, there are those who totally deny the reality of the world; they say, "Brahman alone is real; everything else is unreal." And, because of their failure to understand the truth of this dictum, they try to run away from the world and its activities, and will resort to any means, even to the extreme measure of self-torture, in their attempt to overcome the passions of the flesh. On the other hand, there are those who deny the existence of anything more real than this world as they know it, and their own relationship to it. To such people this life is the be-all and end-all of existence, and all the passions and desires of the flesh are for their pleasure and enjoyment. It is probable that this extreme view arose as a reaction to the former view—but both views are wrong. Each has missed the truth.

Before attempting to explain the true ideal of renunciation, which, sooner or later, every one of us must practice, it may be interesting to learn what the great teachers of every religion have taught regarding this subject. As we turn to the teachings of Christ we shall find that he was one of the greatest exponents of renunciation. "He that loveth his life shall lose it; and he that hateth his life in this world shall keep it unto life eternal." "Lay not up for yourself treasures upon earth, where moth and rust doth corrupt, and where thieves break through and steal: But lay up for yourselves treasures in heaven. . . . For where your treasure is, there will your heart be also." And did he not tell the rich young ruler who came to him asking what he should do to gain eternal life: "If thou wilt be

297

perfect, go and sell that thou hast, and give to the poor, and thou shalt have treasure in heaven"? In these, and in many other sayings of Jesus, we find the highest ideal of renunciation expressed in no uncertain terms.

In the teachings of Buddha we find the same ideal based upon the Four Noble Truths, which are: In the world there is suffering; there is a cause for this suffering; there is a way out of suffering; and there is a peace which follows freedom from suffering. If we would tread the path that Buddha pointed out, we must first renounce the world. Again, in the *Upanishads* we read: "Not by wealth, nor by progeny, nor by much learning, but by renunciation alone can man attain immortal bliss."

In every great scripture we find this same emphasis. The Vedanta tells us that the first requisites for spiritual life are discrimination between the real and the unreal, between the eternal and the noneternal; the understanding of the truth that God alone is real; and the giving up of all desires and cravings except the one desire to realize God.

Viewed superficially it would seem that these teachings tend to agree with that school of thought which seeks to run away from the world and its activities. But it is not so. Such extreme views have arisen out of a misunderstanding of the ideal. One is reminded of the man with the gnat on his nose. To rid himself of the gnat he shoots at it with a gun, and in so doing shoots himself also.

And yet the dilemma exists. We are ushered into this world; we are given life, and with it the desire to enjoy its attendant pleasures. For a while we are happy, but gradually there creeps in a feeling of dissatisfaction. The pleasures we once enjoyed lose their savor; they turn to ashes. And yet the hunger remains. For, deep within the recesses of man's heart, there is a hunger for eternal life and abiding happiness—a longing for a joy that knows no end. We are taught to "love not the world, neither the things that are in the world," and yet this world is all we know. Then what shall we do in such a dilemma? To run away and hide in a cave or a monastery does not solve the problem. For too often we see that while such people may become indifferent to the world, they become extremely self-centered, and love only themselves. The solution therefore lies, not in compromising the ideal, but in understanding its true meaning. Once, when Rama was a little boy he told his father that he wished to renounce the world. His father, being a king, had other plans for his son, but instead of arguing with the boy he sent for a renowned scholar named Vashistha to come and instruct him. When Vashistha asked Rama why he wanted to renounce the world he said: "I want to find God." "But," asked the sage, "can you tell me where God is not? Is He apart from the world that you wish to renounce it?"

In this simple illustration we find the whole truth. Unless we can find the reality behind the appearance of this world we live in vain; our life and living have no purpose. Today you may think your goal in life is to attain this or that thing, and you may attain it, but still you have not attained the goal. Sri Ramakrishna expressed the truth of this when he said: "By adding many zeros together you gain nothing, they have no value. But place the unit one before the zeros and they immediately have value." Of itself the world has no value, no meaning. It is a shadow, and by clinging to the shadow we miss the substance. Behind this apparent life there is a deeper life; behind this seeming world there is a deeper reality; and life takes on new meaning, the world becomes more real for us, when we find the Reality behind the appearance—that Reality which is God.

At one time Sri Ramakrishna was accused of turning the heads of the young men who came to him, by teaching them the ideals of renunciation and thus making them unfit to take their place in the world. When Sri Ramakrishna heard about this he said: "By teaching them the true meaning and purpose of life I am preparing them to take their place in the world. But first let them develop devotion to God, let them gain self-control, and then let them go and live in the world. It is better that the boat should float on the water than that the water should get into the boat!" In other words, we must understand the ideal and purpose of life, for without this understanding none can truly live. If we wish to attain anything in life we have to set a definite goal, and if we analyze life we shall see that there is but one goal for all mankind—the realization of the truth of God. For in God alone is to be found the fulfillment of life.

What is it then that stands in the way of our realization of the goal? Is it something outside of ourselves? As we analyze life further we discover that the obstruction lies within ourselves. It is not the world, neither the things of the world; it is our own ignorance. Within us is the Atman, the very presence of God; He is the abiding happiness, the infinite wisdom and the eternal life we are all seeking. He is within and He is without, but instead of seeing that abiding reality we see something else—we see the shadows. "I am the Atman, but I do not know that I am the Atman. I consider myself an individual being." This attitude arises from what is known philosophically as *ego*—the sense of individuality, of separateness from God. And out of this sense of separateness there arise two main desires—the desire to attach ourselves to the world and things which give us pleasure, and the desire to avoid those things which give us pain. Thus we see that first there is ignorance, then that out of ignorance comes ego, which is the root cause of all attachments, aversions, and the clinging to life. When we can fully understand this truth we shall realize that the ideal is not renunciation of the world, but renunciation of the ego. As Sri Ramakrishna used to say: "When the ego dies, all troubles cease to exist."

There are two principal ways by which the ego may be renounced. One way is the path of analysis, or knowledge, and the other way is the path of love or devotion. He who chooses the path of knowledge must maintain a consciousness of his identity with the Atman. By analysis he must know: "I am not the body, nor the mind, nor the ego—I am beyond all these. I am the Atman—one with Brahman." Such a man, by constantly living in this consciousness, soon frees himself of all bodily desires. The activities of his body and mind will continue, but through them all he remains completely detached and unaffected. This path is, however, extremely difficult to follow, for as long as even the pangs of hunger and thirst affect him who attempts to follow it, he has not yet overcome the body-consciousness, and is therefore not yet ready to follow such a path. To illustrate his difficulties, Sri Ramakrishna used to say: "Suppose a man desires to reach the roof of his house, but instead of gradually ascending the staircase, permits himself to be thrown up bodily. What happens? He reaches the roof no doubt, but his method of reaching it may cause him serious or even permanent injury."

For the average man the easiest path to follow is the path of devotion. We all have ego, and as long as we live on the plane of the senses we cannot free ourselves from it. Therefore we should try to merge the ego in the will of the Lord—the Atman within. We should surrender it completely to the Lord and let Him use it as an instrument, but in order to do this it is first necessary to learn to practice constant recollectedness of God. We are told that we must love God, but how is it possible to love someone whom we have not seen and do not know? This question arises in the mind of every aspirant, and the same answer is given by all the seers and lovers of God. They say: you do not know God now, but if you will think of Him, if you will fill your mind with the constant remembrance of Him, you will come to know He is Love; then that love will grow in your own heart, until your very ego will become merged in it, and you will cry out, "Not I! Not I! but thou, O Lord!"

Then what follows? Out of this loving devotion to God there will come a normal and natural control of all the passions. For the more you advance toward God the less will be the strength of your cravings and desires for the objects of the world. The lower passions lose their power in the presence of something that is higher and greater. Thus we see that, no matter which path we may follow, we need not run away from the world and its activities. But one point the aspirant must always keep in mind: he must maintain constant remembrance of God.

Now again, as there are two main paths to follow in order to free ourselves from ego, so are there two distinct ways of life in which to practice the ideal of renunciation. They are the way of monasticism and the way of the householder. The difference between these two paths is that the monk, owning nothing, being completely devoid of all worldly possessions, practices renunciation both inwardly and outwardly, whereas the householder practices only the inner renunciation. The householder may have great possessions—he may have wealth, a wife, children, and friends; but he remains unattached to them. Having overcome the ego of attachment, he has no sense of possession; he sees God in all things and all things as belonging to God. Nothing he owns belongs to him. His mind remains free and completely detached.

In this connection there arises the very fundamental question of sex and chastity. This is one of the most misunderstood problems of modern life. On the one hand, the church still preaches that sex is sin and iniquity, and on the other hand, modern psychology tells us that repression is bad and that expression is natural and therefore good. Repression is not control. Both attitudes are extreme and wrong, because neither understands the ideal. Every religion teaches us that sex must be controlled and ultimately overcome. Psychologically the sex energy has to be transmuted into spiritual energy. In the Sanskrit language there is the word *ojas*. There is no English equivalent for this, but it means that energy which accumulates in the brain of one who has completely conquered the sex impulse.

In the scriptures of ancient India we read of the ideal life of the householders. Their life was divided into four stages. The first stage was the student period, when the child was sent to an illumined teacher and remained under his supervision for several years. In this holy association he was educated in the scriptures and in secular knowledge, and, most important of all, he was thoroughly trained in self-mastery and self-control. At the end of this student period he was free to choose which way of life he wished to follow, the way of monasticism or the way of the householder. If he chose to enter into married life, he did so with the understanding that marriage was not an institution for sexual license and selfishness but an institution in which he would find ample opportunity to practice self-control and unselfishness. Having passed through this second stage, he entered into a life of retirement from the world, and then, lastly, into the monastic life of complete renunciation.

But, no matter what stage we may have reached or what path we may be following, we must have that one positive ideal—the ideal of God. We must make Him the ideal, the way, and the end. As my master used to tell us, we must first hold on to the pillar, then we can spin around and around without fear. And so with life in the world. If we will but hold on to the pillar of God, there will be no mistakes in our lives, or, if there are mistakes, they will be corrected.

Brahmacharya

Sister Amiya

"I HAVE RECEIVED sanction from the president and trustees of the Belur Math to initiate three of you into brahmacharya. Other swamis will come for the ceremony, and you will be given your vows at the convent at Santa Barbara on September 22."

Hearing these words from Swami Prabhavananda I thought: "Well! So I am to become a nun of the Ramakrishna Order! How wonderful!" And I felt pleased.

But it did not end there. Indeed, that was the beginning, for the mind began to ask questions. "What is brahmacharya?" Generally speaking, in the West brahmacharya is known as the student period between the novitiate years and the final initiation into sannyas, and associated only with the young monks of India. It seems so far removed from the West—from America!

And the mind continued to question. "What are the vows? What does one give up?" And gradually one began to realize that this was no idle step to be taken lightly. A deepening sense of responsibility began to develop, so that, by the time the day of initiation dawned, speculation had long since yielded to awe. After all, it was not for nothing that these six holy men were willing to travel thousands of miles across the country in order to be present on this occasion. They, too, had long ago taken those same vows, and they knew their significance.

That September morning in 1947 dawned bright and fair. Many devotees had gathered early for the special worship preceding the initiation, and a feeling of excitement began to grow as the hour for the ceremony grew nearer. The shrine room was filled with flowers, and the worshipers overflowed into the eucalyptus grove outside the shrine room, where they listened in silence to the resonant chanting of the Vedic hymns by the swamis. Their words they could not understand, but the spirit behind them filled their hearts with quietness and peace.

The worship ended, and the seven swamis in their *gerrua* robes passed in single file to the room which had been prepared for the ceremony. There, in the presence of their own guru and the swamis Akhilananda, Satprakashananda, Vividishananda, Vishwananda, and Devatmananda, the initiates repeated their vows after Swami Yatiswarananda.

What those vows were, only those who took them could know, as only those who experienced it could ever know the tremendous spiritual power which pervaded that holy occasion. All thought, all memory of the outside world was forgotten. Nothing remained but pure spirit, and as one left that room one felt that all past mistakes, all past tendencies and impressions were left behind. Only the present remained; the present and the future with its tremendous responsibilities.

It may be said that within those vows were contained all the necessary requisites for the attainment of perfection, and which, if followed, could lead but to that end. But how? How can a modern person possibly conform to the rules of ethical conduct and high spiritual endeavor laid down by the sages of ancient India? Superficially, it seems almost absurd, and entirely out of keeping with the modern West; but, as one looks deeper, one can readily see that neither ethics, nor morality, nor truth has any boundary within time and place. Social customs may vary according to climate, creed, and race, but the basic rules of ethical conduct are the same everywhere. The truth taught by the sages of old is not different from the truth that Jesus taught. Just as the moral and ethical laws of Moses still serve as the norm of human behavior today, so do the principles of truth and righteousness of all religions still stand, no matter how much man may distort them and try to mold them nearer to his own limited conceptions. Truth is timeless and changeless, and it is to the unfoldment and knowledge of this truth, and the attainment of the freedom such knowledge brings, that the initiate into brahmacharya pledges his or her life, heart, and soul.

God Is Shy

Gerald Heard

WORSHIP IS SOMETHING which the West finds hard in its modern mood to justify. God does not need to be praised, we say, and certainly we find it hard to understand Pope Pius X's special commendation of the Hebrew 150 Psalms on the ground that these are peculiarly pleasing to Him because He wrote them Himself to show us how He wished to be praised.

But worship is not so hard to understand if we see that it is in fact an act of criticism. "Your Worship" addressed to a mayor—"The Worshipful Company of Cutlers"—such titles do not mean that the chief citizen is adorable or that the incorporated masters of a trade were hoping for divine honors. Both addresses declare only that these men are "worthies." They have been adjudged and found worthy of respect.

So worship, even when offered to the Supreme, is an estimate. We then have to ask, Worth how much? Worth for what? A good boat is called seaworthy. It will stand up to the tests of its element. It is not landworthy. So with all special works. But with man, because he is the supreme generalized creature, when we say he is worthy, we mean that he is worth while anywhere, always. We use as a synonym of his worth that he is "sterling." Sterling, in origin, means a currency which because of its purity is everywhere valid.

Man's worthiness is then the criterion whereby we rate and quote all other more partial worths. Christ made that clear with his question: What shall a man be given in exchange for his soul? Economically his price (his wage) may fluctuate and often hovers on the elimination line. He fails to make himself worth his keep. Morally too he can

305

become a drug on the market. But if a man has an eternal soul, then he can be the one constant standard of worth throughout time. If he sustains his spiritual integrity, then the world in the end must not only tolerate him but demand him.

The goldsmiths were the first bankers. That seemed natural. They had the stuff. But they themselves lacked worth. They had sterling but weren't. They were always going bankrupt under dubious conditions. Men were at a loss to find someone who wouldn't lose their money. A queer little sect had arisen then. They used to feel God's presence so vibrantly that when they sat together silently thinking of Him they quaked. So keen a sense of His presence had naturally a lag. When the next day they did their business they still felt that He was there. Why then swear and vow, seal, and bind? Your word given in that presence, made all other guaranty otiose. Business so done prospered. Growing business can take capital. Men invested with the Quakers. In consequence four of the great banking houses of London, when that city led the financial market, had Quaker origins. This is not a success story. Indeed it may well be a failure tale. Holiness, wholeness, is power—at its very lowest it will make you money. But the Quakers have held out for higher recognition. They studied their scriptures and saw that their avatar had said that a child of God may be recognized because he is a peacemaker. The Quakers made themselves more widely recognized and deeply trusted as peacemakers than as bankers.

So glancing at the story of this one small and far from occult sect we have discovered two things about the worth of man's soul. When it is upright it can make more money than all the crooks. When it is devoted it can make more peace than any army. In short, the nearer it comes to God the more powerful it is. Isn't this then, after all, going to end as a success story? Find God and men will find you everything else. If you want money, then cool clean millions. If you want fame (and the average man wants that generally more than cash), then you can have steady high-grade admiration, worth–ship.

The spirit of man is the candle of the Lord. From watching the spirit of man can we understand, estimate, "worth" the spirit of God? Yes, in a way, but mostly No. There is a principle now recognized in psychology called by its definer, Dr. Baudouin, the Law of Reversed Effort:

the more you try the less you can repeat your first spontaneous achievement. There would seem to be a similar law in theology, a law of increasing ignorance, we might call it. Even in the success religions we can see it. The first wonderful "hits"—of prophecy, psychotherapy, healing, or what have you—are not sustained. Men thought they knew God and His number. "He means me to be happy—to be healthy—to be a success—to help others —for our side to win—for us to know His intentions." And for a little while they seem to show they are right and then it is clear they weren't.

That brings us to the odd title borrowed for these lines. The term was coined by a devout Jesuit who for years with great success, but apparently with equally humble "misgivingness," counseled seekers. It would seem that what he was trying to startle his hearers into understanding was, simultaneously, their need for and their ignorance of God. Here was a knife-edge, up onto which he would try and make them mount with the prod of this koan. For either they would mumble a lot of unworthy—or utterly unestimating—praise-phrases about His highness, or else they would fall off the other side into a sentimental or "cupboard-love" false intimacy.

"God is shy," startles us—and a moment after it rouses our curiosity. We need that. In the West religious and irreligious share a fatal ignorance. They both feel that God is found: found and used (domesticated) by the believer: found out by the atheists. The conception of God as *Fascinans et Tremendans Mysterium* is alien to all our present-day thought. William James set the style in his patronizing remark, "God is a very useful ally for my social conscience." True we have lately seen a reaction. Neo-orthodoxy does now speak quite a lot of God as *Tremendans*, but not of His Fascination. Hence the scorn with which American theology generally speaks of all mysticism, and its contemptuous ignorance of Asiatic religion and all contemplation.

But theology means the science of God, and if that phrase is not to be blasphemously impertinent, then theology must adopt the humbling, guiding rule of all the sciences which would ever really know (and not be content with the feeling that they are knowing). Beware when you find what you are looking for. The pure in heart alone see God for they see pure of all "knowingness." They seek God not because they know but because they know they must know and know that they don't. They realize that all their present type of knowledge is really but part of an ignorance that covers the whole life of the senses.

This perception of their ignorance is, as Socrates saw, the first essential step to real knowledge. The second is the intuitional discovery that another quality of knowledge is obtainable—what Professor Radhakrishnan has called *integral knowledge*. Man cannot remember the saving knowledge he once had, but he can remember that he once knew what he has now forgotten. He is therefore driven to seek for he cannot say what. To his rational mind this need is inexplicable but for his entire nature it is peremptory.

How better, then, may he express the object of his desire than by his strange word "shy"—an object both alluring and elusive, fascinating and awesome: as powerfully, intensely attractive as are those dark ultramassive stars, and (as are they) as imperceptible, as unknowable save by their supreme power of attraction.

The Secret of Inner Poise

Swami Yatiswarananda

AS CHILDREN WE greatly admired a small metal inkpot which the gypsies used to sell, having a heavy weight on the bottom so that it could never tip over and spill the ink. This was a marvel that we could not understand until we learned later that the inkwell had its center of gravity always secure within, so it could not be displaced and permit the ink to spill. Here was an instance of perfect equilibrium in relation to outside forces such as the law of gravitation.

With reference to the emotions, this is like maintaining inner serenity in the midst of the disturbing events of life. This is poise. How can a human being acquire serenity and poise?

As young men we looked for poise in vain among the elders of our families, and also among our university professors. We discovered it at last in the disciples of Sri Ramakrishna. The greatest among those at whose feet we had the privilege of sitting was Swami Brahmananda, who possessed serenity to such an extent that he could even impart it to others.

Once two young monks in our monastery had quarreled and created a disturbance even among the others. Swami Premananda, who was in charge, went to Swami Brahmananda, head of the Order. "We older brother disciples have lived together in peace and harmony for many years," he said. "What shall we do with these boys? Ought we not to expel them?"

Swami Brahmananda replied quietly, "Brother, it is true that they have been making trouble; but remember that they have come to seek the Lord. Surely we can do something to bring love to their hearts."

Swami Premananda replied, "Brother, it is you who must bless them and transform them."

At the request of Swami Brahmananda all the monks —seniors and novices alike—gathered together. Swami Brahmananda entered in an exalted mood and as each monk came into his presence and bowed at his feet, he just touched his head in benediction. One who was present said, "That touch was like a cooling spring to a fevered body." And in the monastery again there was peace.

In our modern age we are suffering tensions and distresses. Hospitals are full of mental cases, and there are never enough accommodations for the psychologically disturbed. I am reminded of a story. Samuel Johnson, the English lexicographer, was courting a lady whom he later married. One time he said, "Mrs. Porter, I am of mean extraction, I am poor, and one of my ancestors was hanged." To this the lady replied: "I too am poor and of mean extraction, and if none of my ancestors was hanged I am sure there were fifty who ought to have been!" So it is with emotional instability. If none of us has as yet been sent to a hospital for the mentally unbalanced, it is probably not because some of us could not use such help.

Emotional stability is a wonderful thing to have, but in our age we see very little of it. But it must not be forgotten that the conflicts that appear in the outside world are only a manifestation of what is to be found within our own minds. These troubles may be reduced only if we can take greater care of our own minds and use them judiciously. It is a fact that just as our bodies are affected by poisons and disease germs, so also our minds suffer as a result of harmful emotions. We are in constant conflict with our environment, but our greatest struggle goes on within ourselves. We are our own greatest problem.

According to present-day Western psychologists, our inner conflicts are due to some such cause as "primitive egocentric drives" coupled with "forbidding consciences." Of course some persons, it is said, do not possess much of a conscience. Of such it has been remarked that if their consciences were removed it would be but a minor operation! Fortunately or unfortunately, however, most of us are not like that. We are eternally in conflict with ourselves. Such instincts as self-assertion, mating, acquisition, and flight awaken in us the emotions of egotism, pride, lust, jealousy, anger, fear, and others.

Nowadays we hear a great deal about complexes, instincts, and emotions. What are they? How are they related?

Psychologists tell us that instincts and emotions conflicting with each other produce complexes, and that complexes are emotional webs of ideas closely bound together by emotional bonds. According to some, our instincts and emotions can be grouped according to three main complexes: the ego complex, the sex complex, and the herd complex. The ego complex includes the instincts of self-preservation, acquisition, pugnacity, curiosity, repulsion, and flight; the corresponding emotions are a sense of superiority, pride, possessiveness, anger, disgust, and fear. The sex complex includes sex and parental instincts; the corresponding emotions are love, lust, jealousy, coyness, and tenderness. The herd complex includes the gregarious instincts, suggestion, and appeal; the corresponding emotions are loneliness, sympathy, distress, attachment, helpfulness, and trust.

Complexes are common to all human beings. They may be good or bad as they are used for good or bad purposes. They are good if used for constructive purposes and bad if they lead to destruction or cramping of the personality. Instincts of self-assertion, for example, may be turned to be used to control one's passions, using the energy so saved for higher evolution and thus for the good of one's fellow beings.

Psychologists are continually revealing to us how emotions play tricks on us and may bring about physical and mental illness. On the other hand, a proper direction and control of our emotions contributes to health and stability. Dr. Flanders Dunbar in her book *Mind and Body* tells of a psychiatrist who had a woman patient suffering from pains which suggested appendicitis; there were also some indications that the disorder might be psychological. While trying to find out the cause through psychoanalysis the doctor remembered a similar case of a colleague whose patient had died of a ruptured appendix. He therefore rushed his own patient to the hospital and had her operated on, and as it turned out, just in time.

Now the doctor himself became disturbed. The incident took place during the Christmas season and was still fresh in his mind when he was bidden to a family party to which he had no inclination to go. He developed a severe abdominal pain. A doctor friend examined him and recommended an immediate operation. But now the psychiatrist hesitated. As a mental healer he began to face the cause of his pain and soon came to the conclusion that the worry over the narrow escape of his patient had given him the idea of appendicitis. Then too he had had a recent talk with his mother, who had described how his father had died of appendicitis. All this strengthened the perception that his pain was psychological, that perhaps unwillingness to join the party had brought an unconscious desire to spend Christmas Day in the hospital. As soon as the man discovered its cause the pain left him. He went to the party and enjoyed it.

When such a thing can happen to a trained psychoanalyst there is no wonder that many of us select comfortable illnesses to suffer from, and sometimes even enjoy them. I know people who create worries if they have none and even magnify them, who periodically get themselves emotionally involved with others and create troubles for themselves and for those associated with them. They seem to thrive on tension. If we keep a steady watch over the wanderings of our minds we can in many cases detect our emotional troubles, end our self-created illnesses, and enjoy health and poise.

What is personality? The unconscious part of us and the conscious together make up what is called the personality, which reaches out to its environment and in turn is affected by it. Besides the continuous struggle with the outer world there is also a never-ending conflict in the inner world. So life becomes an incessant adjustment within ourselves and also with the outer world. Lack of poise is due to failure in this adjustment.

The eminent psychiatrist Menninger in his *You and Psychiatry* observes: "Our failures are expressed in one of two types of reaction: flight or attack. Both these reactions indicate instability. Sometimes we want to run away from everything that troubles; self-induced sickness and drunkenness are such expressions of flight. If they are not cured, personality degenerates. The *attack* reaction, if properly directed, may bring readjustment resulting in more or less complete poise. Through the right kind of fighting spirit, learning to fight the enemies within, we may attain a measure of poise and peace."

From the spiritual point of view, however, psychological stability is not enough. Egocentric poise on the psychological level may break down if put to a severe test. Most psychologists would have us believe that the basic conflicts within ourselves can never be completely resolved. At most some form of compromise may be hoped for. This is felt to be true also of the moral and spiritual conflicts we pass through in life. In the case of extraordinary souls who have attained spiritual illumination, however, the victory and poise attained are more complete than anything psychology can produce.

According to the spiritual view, man is a spiritual being. His personality is made up of body and mind, and also of soul. Behind the individual soul which holds together the mind and senses and the body is the supreme spirit, the nirvana of Buddhism, the Brahman of Vedanta, the God of all religions. Being established in this highest spiritual consciousness, our Buddhas, Christs, or Ramakrishnas could laugh at temptation and even death to them was the passage to immortality. This attitude is not possible for the psychologically conditioned individual or for an ordinary, half-heartedly religious human being. But the stability which even partially illumined souls attain is much higher than that which psychology can promise. Psychology can render very valuable service. It has its own value as a technique; but religion goes much farther and achieves results far beyond the scope of psychology.

Think of St. Augustine. Disgusted with himself, he was engaged in a hard struggle of flesh against spirit. He cried with tears in his eyes: "O Lord, how long? How long? Tomorrow and tomorrow! Why not today and why not now?" He was thus crying for illumination when he heard a voice: "Take up and read. Take up and read." Augustine opened the book of the Acts of the Apostles and read: "Not in rioting and drunkenness, not in chambering and wantonness, not in strife and envying, but put ye on the Lord Jesus Christ and make not provision for the flesh to fulfill the lusts thereof." All at once a great change came over him. His carnal cravings fell away. Augustine the roisterer was on his way to transformation. He had a glimpse of divine wisdom by which all things are made. "Have been" ceases to be real; there is only "to be," a being that is eternal. From the inner core of his soul Augustine prayed: "O Lord, help me to perceive thee. Help me to perceive myself, for by knowing thee I can know myself." Later a spiritual force which the mind itself was unable to grasp enabled this early Christian to look beyond the "vortex of his ego." This was a genuinely divine experience which made of Augustine a mystic and a saint with an inner poise born of spiritual consciousness. The secret of inner poise is the shifting of the inner life to consciousness of the divine.

We see something of this in the life of Ramakrishna's great disciple, Vivekananda. After his father's sudden death, the young Narendra had been passing through a very difficult time, for his family was in real distress and it was necessary to go in search of a job. He went from office to office without success. Those who had once called themselves his friends turned a cold shoulder. The world suddenly seemed to be totally evil. Some days there were not even provisions for the family, and when Narendra's purse was empty he would tell his mother that he had been invited out to dine and so remained practically without food. In the midst of these trials doubts came to him. "Does God really exist?" he wondered, "and if so, does He really hear the fervent prayers of a man in misery?"

One evening while returning home to Calcutta with tired limbs and a jaded mind, Narendra was overpowered with exhaustion and sank down on the outer porch of a house by the road. Suddenly as if by some divine power the coverings of his soul were revealed one after another. All doubts regarding the co-existence of divine justice and the presence of misery were resolved. By a deep introspection he found the meaning in it all. Bodily fatigue left him and his mind was refreshed with a wonderful strength and peace.

Later Vivekananda attained many spiritual experiences and became a rare illumined soul. Once in the western United States he was visiting a cattle town. Hearing him speak of philosophy, a number of university men who had become cowboys took him at his word. When he said that one who has realized the light is able to keep his equanimity under all conditions, they decided to put the visitor to the test. They invited Swamiji to lecture to them and placed a wooden tub bottom up on the ground to serve as a platform. When Vivekananda had commenced his address and was lost in his subject, there was suddenly a terrific racket of pistol shots, and bullets whizzed around his head. Undisturbed, Swamiji continued to lecture as though nothing unusual were happening.

This is spiritual poise, where the center of gravity has come to rest, not in the physical personality but in the divine consciousness, the soul of one's soul. Such illumination brings an entirely new outlook to a man or woman.

Sufism is the mystical aspect of Islam. Rabiah was a woman Sufi saint who used to remain absorbed in divine consciousness. When once asked, "Rabiah, dost thou love the Lord?" the saint replied, "Truly I love Him." "And dost thou regard the Evil One as an enemy?" With a smile Rabiah replied, "I love the Lord so much that I do not trouble about the Evil One."

Once Rabiah was sick and two holy men came to visit her. They looked upon illness as a punishment of the Lord. Quoting from the Sufi scriptures, they argued: "One whose prayer is pure, will God's chastisement endure . . ." and "He who loves his master's voice, will in chastisement rejoice."

Rabiah listened to the wise men and then replied in kind: "Ye men of grace, he who sees his master's face, will not in prayer recall that he is chastised at all." Rabiah was indeed a lover of God whose prayer had been: "O my Lord, if I worship thee from fear of hell, burn me in hell. If I worship thee from hope of paradise, exclude me from paradise. But if I worship thee for thine own sake, then withhold not from me thine eternal beauty."

A noted psychologist remarks this about a patient whose inner conflicts have been resolved through analysis, who has attained a measure of psychological poise: "His center of gravity which has been centered in others comes to rest within himself." It is true that in the right kind of psychological treatment the center of gravity may be brought to rest deep within an integrated personality, but the highest and surest poise can be attained, in the case of the average mortal, only by passing stage after stage through systematic moral and spiritual practice. We must learn to discriminate between the seer and the seen: my emotions are different from me.

We can learn to disentangle ourselves from our emotions: as we learn to look upon them as something different from our true selves, we come to acquire a strong upper hand over them. This in turn gives us the ability to face the realities of life boldly, to control our mind and its activity.

Swami Brahmananda used to warn against brooding over the past or magnifying our troubles in the present. Never weaken the mind through anything like self-pity or useless regret! If we can face our worst emotions and desires and still remain poised, we can make a new start, do something creative, and proceed with energy. Brooding over the past is a disease which every spiritual seeker must heal within himself as soon as its symptoms appear. We must disentangle ourselves from untrue or impure thoughts and emotions before we can even begin to apply our minds to meditation.

Anger, hatred, untruthfulness, greed, unchastity, or helpless dependence upon others—these shift the center of gravity away from our essential integrity and create conflict and discord, while purity and self-control soon make us masters of ourselves and generate harmony and peace. This is the first stage in the attainment of inner poise.

Listen to the exact words of our master, Brahmananda, as quoted in Swami Prabhavananda's *The Eternal Companion:*

> The easiest way to purify and steady the mind is to retire into solitude, control all cravings, and engage yourself in contemplation and meditation. The more you occupy the mind with holy thoughts, the greater will be your spiritual unfoldment. Just as a cow yields much milk when it is well fed, so when the mind is fed spiritual food, it will yield greater tranquility. Spiritual food consists of meditation, prayer, contemplation and japam.

Another means of steadying the rebellious mind is to let it wander but to keep watch over its wanderings. By maintaining this awareness we can gradually get hold of our thoughts and focus them:

> Another way to steady the mind is to let it wander, but to keep a steady watch over its wanderings. After a while the mind itself becomes tired and comes back to find peace in God. If you watch your mind, your mind will in turn watch over you.

Next we can pray and practice japam leading to meditation. This is not to indulge in parrotlike repetition of the deity's name, but there must be constant awareness of the meaning of the holy words filling the mind. Prayer and japam methodically create a new harmony which integrates our thinking, feeling, and willing—a great step toward inner poise.

But this sort of egocentric meditation is not sufficient.

As we meditate on the Supreme Spirit, we must also wholeheartedly surrender ourselves to God. Continuous practice of meditation reveals an introspective, intuitive power, by which the soul recognizes its contact with the Oversoul, in which it remains absorbed. The divine ecstasy which results transforms the soul completely.

When the God-man comes down from the heights of divine realization he brings with him a new vision and sees the Supreme Spirit in himself and in all things. Then is the mind at peace, unshaken by misery or success. Free from fear, attachment, or anger, the heart remains filled with love and compassion for all beings. Now is realized a new peace based on the unfailing foundation of divine consciousness, and in this state nothing in the world can touch one. One longs to share this peace and the bliss of it with others.

Traveller

Anne Hamilton

Rejecting agonies that hold
brain's convolutions fold to fold,
I pass my clouded body by,
thick with darkness let it lie,
and melt through walls without a door,
unlocked from the flesh my spirit wore.

I catch a curve of flowing wind
that carries me where dust is thinned
to particles so far apart
I almost see Conclusion's heart.
Almost I intimately seize
in my two hands the Mysteries;
Almost I hear from outer sky
the soundless Footsteps thunder by.

But Time and I come curving back,
down the wind's descending track
through the walls without a door
back to the place I was before,
to thin the density of pain,
to thin the tissues, thin the brain,
until my thickened flesh shall be
compelled to new translucency. . . .

Guides to the Spiritual Life

Gerald Heard

THERE IS A GROWING demand today for books on the spiritual life. But it is one that it is easier to make than to supply. Religious books are still being printed by the thousand. Yet it is hard to draw up even a small list which would meet the present inquirer's need. Why? Partly because most religious books are written by professionals in the language and to support the cause of their specific sect. True, they do wish to bring comfort and self-understanding to the reader, but they have also the obligation to prove that their religion is true and often that it alone is true.

This was always a grave handicap for those religions—till lately the only ones known in the West—which were and still mainly are exclusive. A large number of those people who today are wishing to inquire about the spiritual life actually left the religion in which they were brought up—or their parents did—because that religion seemed grossly careless about the truth of many of the statements which it made and even more grossly uncharitable to those who dared raise this grave question of truthfulness. Hence to offer them spiritual information in the terms of such theology is not merely not to attract them but to repel them. It is very hard for ministers and clergy to realize that "the return to religion" is not a return to orthodoxy, that it is a return to an interest in the spiritual, not because the interpretation of certain historic events has become any more credible.

The contrary is true. The reason why today so many people want to hear from experts about spirituality is simply because the economic revolution has failed and is over: the psychological revolution has begun. Not through creeds or rites but through anthropology, psychology, and

319

psychical research, free minds today are exploring a new empire of the mind. These are the people who are asking the real practitioners—not the purveyors—of religion to give them, not dogmas or closed systems, but data. What the world today needs, and an increasing number of pioneers are seeking out, is the psychologist who has gone beyond the limited findings of the psychophysicist, the restricted techniques of the psychoanalyst, who can also arrange the data of psychical research and finally—and this is the real proof of the adequacy of the process—bring about a co-ordination of his life which can henceforward interpret and embrace, explain and include all experience. That is the reason why Protestants today tend increasingly to read such masters of spirituality as François de Sales and Fénelon. These writers are felt at once to be experts. They speak very little of dogma and much of method.

When we go to a doctor we do not ask of him eloquence or the gift of a pretty way with words. We want neither rhetoric nor poetry; we want a diagnosis and a prescription. Poetry (and often not of the best—in other words, hymns), rhetoric (not seldom as weak as the rhymes—the weekly sermon)—these have been the two standard methods of Protestant instruction and edification. The great Catholic directors owe their popularity both inside and outside their communion to the fact that they are always precise, always great diagnostic psychologists and, even when their letters are found for centuries to be applicable to thousands of souls, they seem like all great physicians actually prescribing for a specific, individual case.

Instruction is in fact of very little use unless it is a reply to a question, and indeed its use is in ratio to the intensity with which the questioner puts his problem. Though the Western masters of spirituality are unfailing aids to those who would survey the problem of their own souls, still we need keenly something more. With this they would agree —they would say without sacraments and the graces of God that come through the church, decay may be arrested but progress can really not be made. A man may be "returned to normalcy" and may come to accept society and society to accept him and may even come to accept the universe with a resignation that may pass for peace. But he may never attain to that understanding of himself, of his fellows, and of nature, without which this world and this life remain an enigma only to be sustained with courage. It is at that point that the student who has benefited from the instructions of the Western directors has to ask himself: Should I not, must I not join their communion, if I am to attain to any kind of completeness? This problem, this issue—Shall I for the sake of profound psychological knowledge join a communion which excommunicates all others, which claims the right to persecute because it alone, it believes, has the truth?—tortured sixth-century Westerners. "Madman or Slave, must man be one?" cried Matthew Arnold. On the one hand was a materialistic rationalism which managed the outer world so as to obtain increasing power and was helpless to produce rational conduct from human beings. On the other hand was a church having great psychological insight and able to transform certain characters but apparently as indifferent to historic truth or scientific demonstration as it was disregardful of the rights of man.

That dilemma has now ended, and it may be that historians looking back on our age will take this change to be more momentous to human society than the discovery of atomic energy or the fixation of chlorophyll. For now we see with our growing knowledge of Vedanta not only that we may have all that Catholicism could give of method in spiritual training, and may have it without yielding one iota of truth, yes further may have it and keep the widest charity toward all other religions and systems, but that we may hope to have a far deeper and wider psychological knowledge than Western spirituality has so far attained. Two brief illustrations may be given of this. First, consider the attitude of the Occidental masters of spirituality toward psychic phenomena. Lacking the vast cosmology and subtle psychology of Vedanta, visions and all manner of psychic powers have either been thought to authenticate the dogmas of the Church—and so give those who experienced them a certain height of spiritual rank and authority—or if they did not support the church's theories—then they were diabolic. True, a great master such as John of the Cross allows there is a third source, the unknown parts of the human mind itself. But even he has only the vaguest notion of the vastness of this subject, of its importance as a correlate in the development of spirituality and the expert care that is therefore needed in guiding all who would advance any distance in the life of prayer. The second illustration is akin to the above. Owing to the West's ignorance of psychophysiology, the methods of training the mind-body were very crude and indeed dangerous. When we reflect on the "discipline"—the whip is still regularly used in all "enclosed" orders—when we study physical mortification as understood in Catholicism and when we compare the dangerous crudity of such methods with the subtlety, thoroughness, and variety of methods used by Vedanta and Mahayana—and indeed by Hinayana—we see the incomparable superiority of the methods of the East. Indeed as we have looked on Asia as a huge fringe area into which our physical science is only now penetrating, so now we must look upon our West as a penumbral belt into which the true psychology and psychophysiology of the East is infiltrating at last.

Finally the frame of reference of Vedanta—and its children Mahayana and Hinayana—is so much vaster and at the same time more rational than that narrow and hasty picture which Catholicism took from the backward sect of the Jews and never had the moral courage to reconstruct and enlarge. The doctrine of eternal punishment —a grotesque amalgam made from Hebrew emotionalism alloyed with Hellenic speculation—has always haunted and hindered the minds of the spiritual in the West. With its great metaphysics Vedanta has been able to preserve justice and ally it with mercy. On this count alone—and it is a big one—the eternal gospel as interpreted by the Orient is a surer guide to ultimate understanding than anything the West has till the present provided. Yet most people when they pick up some Oriental text—such for example as *The Crest-Jewel of Discrimination* of Shankara or the sutras of Patanjali—are daunted by the subtlety and gnomic elaboration of the system. That is why they should start with works written by modern masters of Indian spirituality. Swami Prabhavananda's *Eternal Companion,* the actual conversations of a great spiritual trainer, is such a book. A new volume of aphorisms on the spiritual life, *Toward the Goal Supreme* by Swami Virajananda, will prove to many readers as a sequel to the *Eternal Companion.* The volume can be started almost anywhere, and there is hardly a phase of the spiritual life that is not touched upon and illuminated. Practically any question that might arise in the mind of a seeker is raised and discussed.

Indeed it is hard to think of two books which could prove better helps to any inquirer who wished to see whether the thought of India could not help him toward an understanding of his own life and a mastery of his own nature. They should prove the kind of standard religious reading which for so long we have only been able to obtain from such authors as de Sales, Fénelon, Grou, and Chapman.

Indian Philosophy of Peace

Aldous Huxley

THERE ARE NO panaceas and no shortcuts. Man is an amphibious being who lives simultaneously or successively in several universes—in the world of matter, the world of mind, the world of spirit; in the individual world and in the social world; in the homemade universe of his own artifacts, institutions, and imaginings, and in the given, the God-made universe of nature and grace. In the very nature of things none of the major problems confronting such a being can possibly be a simple problem. Those who seek simple solutions for complex problems may have the best of intentions; but unfortunately there is an original sin of the intellect as well as of the will. This original sin of the intellect is our habit of arbitrary oversimplification. Those who act without taking precautions against this vice of their intellectual nature doom themselves and their fellows to perpetual disappointment.

Let us consider a concrete example. How is mass violence to be avoided? How is peace to be preserved, extended, and intensified? These problems are posed and must therefore be solved on all the levels of man's multiple existence. They are posed, and must be solved, on the political level; on the demographic level; on the levels of soil fertility and the production of food and raw materials; on the levels of industry and of distribution; on the ideological and religious levels; on the level of individual constitution, temperament, and character. To attack the enemy on only a single front may be, like the charge of the Light Brigade, magnificent; but it is quite certain to be unsuccessful.

The principal elements of our complex problem are these: First, some persons (the extreme somatotonics, in
324

Sheldon's phraseology) are organically tough, aggressive, ruthless, and power-loving. Second, the effective, although not yet the nominal, religion of the twentieth century is nationalistic idolatry. Monotheism, which never enjoyed more than a precarious existence, has everywhere been replaced by the worship of homemade local deities. Thus, Judaism has now been reduced from the status of a universal religion to that of a purely tribal cult; Greek Orthodox Christianity has become (along with communism) the instrument of Slavic imperialism; and attempts are presently being made to use Roman Catholic and Protestant Christianity in the service of the Western nationalities. In a world whose religion is nationalistic idolatry and whose politics are based on sovereign separatism, congenitally aggressive individuals are exposed to the maximum of temptation. Insane ideas and a bad system give them golden opportunities for being unrestrainedly themselves. Conversely, unrestrained somatotonia in high places results in a worsening of the political system and the propagation of a yet more lunatic religion.

The third major element in our problem is the fact that the population of our planet is increasing much faster than presently available supplies of food and raw materials. Hunger is a principal cause of political revolution and, in a nationalistic context, of war. The political consequences of this pressure of population upon resources are aggravated by inefficient production and inequitable distribution; and the fact of these inefficiencies and inequities constitutes the fourth element in our problem. If we want peace, we must find means for attacking all these causes of mass violence simultaneously. The task, it is only too clear, is extremely difficult.

In a very interesting essay by this title, Dr. Amiya Chakravarty discusses the Indian philosophy of peace. The great merit of this philosophy consists in the fact that it goes back to first principles. Peace, it insists, is more than a mere matter of political and economic arrangements. Because man stands on the borderline between the animal and the divine, the temporal and the eternal, peace on earth possesses a cosmic significance. "Tat Twam asi," Thou art That; consequently every violent extinction of a human life has a transcendent and eternal significance. Moreover the mind of the universe is, among other things, the peace that passes understanding. Man's final end is the realization that, in his essence, he is one with the universal mind. But if he would realize his identity with the peace that passes understanding, he must begin by living in the peace that does not pass understanding—peace between nations and groups, peace in personal relationships, peace within the divided and multiple personality. There are many excellent utilitarian reasons for refraining from violence; but the ultimate and completely cogent reason is metaphysical in its nature.

This does not mean, of course, that an exclusive insistence on metaphysics will solve our problems. To have a good philosophy is indispensable. But so are many other things. A good philosophy must be accompanied by good political institutions, good control of population, good agriculture, good soil conservation, good technology, good distribution of wealth, good occupational therapy for extreme somatotonics. In most parts of the world we find neither the physical nor the metaphysical conditions indispensable for peace.

Even in India, where at least the metaphysical conditions used to exist, the traditional philosophy of peace is rapidly giving place to a philosophy of war. Nationalistic idolatry, with its practical corollaries—tanks, troops, planes, and an enormous military budget—is now taking its place as the effective religion of the subcontinent. In the issue of *Mother India* of September 17, 1949, one may read an article on "The Grim Facts of the Kashmir Situation." After setting forth these facts, the author asks: "What are we to do?" His answer to this question is as follows:

All that can be said is most aptly summed up in the words of Sardar Baldev Singh on August 28. After declaring that India meant ill to none and wanted an amicable settlement, he uttered a note of warning. "I have heard it said by leaders of Pakistan that Kashmir is essential for the existence of Pakistan. There are some people in that country who even talk of settling the issue by force of arms. But if anyone feels one can gain anything by bluff or by threat of force, he is highly mistaken. . . . Our brave soldiers have fought under most difficult conditions and by their acts of bravery they have proved their mettle and saved the beautiful valley of Kashmir from destruction. I have not the least doubt that brave men and officers of our armed forces will add another glorious chapter to their brilliant record whenever they are called upon to do so."

Alas, one seems to have heard this sort of thing before, and not from the lips of Buddha or Mahatma Gandhi. Significantly enough, the latter's body was borne to the pyre on a weapon carrier; soldiers lined the route of the funeral procession and fighter planes circled overhead. The last of the great exponents of India's traditional philosophy of peace was cremated with full military honors.

"Give Us This Day Our Daily Bread"

Aldous Huxley

"GIVE US THIS day our daily bread." The phrase refers to the material food upon which the life of the body depends, and at the same time to that bread of grace and inspiration upon which depends the life of the spirit. In the world as we find it today both kinds of bread are woefully lacking. Most of the inhabitants of our planet do not have enough to eat, and most of them are the idolatrous worshipers of false gods—the state, the party, the boss, the locally prevailing political dogma. Being worshipers of false gods, they have rendered themselves more or less completely impervious to the grace, inspiration, and knowledge of the true God.

Idolatry and hunger, the adoration of the nation and the quest for markets, raw materials, and *Lebensraum*—these are the prime causes of war. If there is to be peace and harmonious collaboration among men, we must work toward the elimination of these two war-producing factors. In other words, we must work to provide all human beings with the bread that feeds the body and with that other bread of divine grace which feeds the soul. Everything that lies between the basic physiological need and the basic spiritual need is rather a source of division than of unity. All men agree on the value of food, shelter, and clothing, and all who are prepared to collaborate with grace are agreed on the value of spiritual experience. But all men do not agree, and have never agreed, on government, on economics, on art, on religion (in its dogmatic and ecclesiastical aspects).

This being so, the only sensible thing to do is to pay more attention to the things we can agree about, and less to those in regard to which no agreement is probable or
328

even possible. This means in practice that we should concern ourselves primarily, not as is the case today, with the problems of power and ideological orthodoxy, but with those of bread, material and spiritual. The problems of the first class are insoluble on their own level and, in the process of not being solved, lead to war. The problems of the second class are soluble and, in the process of being solved, contribute to the solution of the problems of power and orthodoxy and so make for peace. In the war-tormented world of today the most useful people are those whose concern is with daily bread—those who produce and conserve food for the bodies of men, and those who permit themselves, and who teach others to permit themselves, to be fed by the bread of grace that gives life to the spirit.

Swami Prabhavananda belongs to the second category of useful people, and one of the ways in which he makes himself most widely useful is the way of translation and interpretation. In collaboration with Christopher Isherwood he has given us an admirable rendering of the *Gita,* and more recently, in collaboration with Frederick Manchester, he has given us an equally readable version of the principal *Upanishads.*

"He who sees all beings in the Self, and the Self in all beings, hates none." The man who brings this constantly forgotten message out of the past, and who can show others how to see all beings in the Self, and the Self in all beings, is performing an important service to society. Those, on the contrary, who set themselves up as the servants of society—the politicians and the ideologists—see all beings as elements in the superego of the national state and the superego of the state in all beings; consequently they hate practically everybody and preach the necessity of this hatred to their fellows. These self-styled servants of society are actually society's worst enemies. Whereas the despised "escapists," whose concern is with that which lies beyond politics, on the spiritual level (together with the food producers, whose concern is with matters on the physiological level) are in reality society's best friends and the inspirers of the only reasonable policy.

A Hindu View of Christian Theology [1]

Swami Siddheswarananda

TO USE THE term "yoga" in connection with Christian mystics is to risk being misunderstood. It evokes in the mind the Indian tradition of spiritual life. Is it proper to speak of yoga in the theological treatises of St. John of the Cross without increasing the confusion already inherent in any mixture of traditions?

If in using the term "yoga" we do not imply Indian theological ideas, if the term is restricted to convey only its etymological meaning—union with God, the ultimate principle—then we are quite correct in speaking of yoga in connection with the life and achievements of any mystic in the world.

The cultural background of the spiritual experiences of saints varies in different countries. Faiths and dogmas have multiple expressions. Yet it cannot be denied that in the transformation of human life brought about by spiritual experience there are common points. It is the theological sources of faith that may be different from one another.

Yet let me make it clear from the very beginning that this study is not to contradict the Christian view of a single revelation. In this study I am making certain reflections arising from a confrontation of Christian theology with Indian thought and culture. I do not hope to reconcile irreconcilables. Still we cannot deny the possibility of finding in the spirituality of St. John of the Cross some affinities with Indian mysticism.

In all saints, saintliness is translated in their social relations as love. In this realization of love, the psychologi-

[1]Adapted from a lecture given at the Sorbonne in a series on the "Yoga of St. John of the Cross."

cal changes that men and women undergo who experience it—no matter in what culture they appear—have resemblances which cannot be ignored. When diverse cultural food assimilates itself into identical manifestations of love, a similarity arises which must be recognized.

To understand the yoga of St. John of the Cross, we must go beyond literal matters of *faith*. Yet we must not be unappreciative of the doctrines of the Christian revelation. The Indian attitude to every theology is one of respect. St. John gave some very fine commentaries on Christian theological notions in his famous works: *Ascent of Mount Carmel, Dark Night of the Soul, Living Flame of Love,* and *Spiritual Canticle*. St. John's theology and ethics are marvels of precise thinking, psychological acumen, and spiritual beauty. From the standpoint of Christianity we can have nothing but admiration for the saint's doctrinal exposition.

But as this is a comparative study, we must go beyond St. John's mere theology. We shall often look at him from our own Hindu viewpoint. It is believed that through such a shift of focus from time to time we shall be able to understand St. John all the better.

The source of all spiritual transformation is faith. To a Christian his faith is in the Bible revelation. To a Hindu it is in the Vedas. The notions of God, soul, and salvation given in the two traditions are different, and any attempt to establish forced identities cannot be fruitful. Revelation is sacred knowledge revealed from above to minds that cannot penetrate into the region of the supernatural. To judge the nature of revelation by intellectual standards is an act that militates against faith. The act of revelation is divine and it speaks of things beyond the possibility of the human mind to explore and grasp. Shankara says that with regard to the comprehension of facts that cannot be verified—such as the nature of our existence before birth and after birth—scriptures provide the only valid authority.

Consequently, if the Hindu accepts the possibility of revelations other than his own, he must find a way to reconcile his faith in his Vedas with that of another revelation whose truths are in contradiction to his. The Hindu approach is to take for the moment the vision of the other and see as the other would see, holding in abeyance his own belief in his own doctrines. It is this technique of taking different outlooks that enables the Hindu to arrive at his vast synthesis. His is no sterile syncretism or cheap eclecticism composed of borrowed elements that happen to complement each other. A civilization and culture that is not habituated to this spirit of enormous toleration has difficulty in appreciating it.

The synthesis that we speak of is the synthesis of all dharmas, of all ways of righteousness. But this term becomes an empty verbalism unless one refers it directly to the visions and realizations of the rishis, the ancient seers of truth. Here is demanded of us faith in the great ones. Until we develop their vision ourselves, all that we see and know are only partial aspects of truth. To have a global view with depth and profundity, one has to gain a new focus of adjusting the different perspectives. As in a stereoscopic view where two images appertaining to the two eyes are brought to a focal point that gives depth—a third dimension—in the vision of the rishis there is an integration of multiple perspectives; one who has realized Brahman has become Brahman.

Brahman, according to the *Bhagavad-Gita,* is that having infinite phases. Something beyond a totalization on a numerical basis is indicated; reality surpasses the entire notion of numbers. What appears as a part to the ignorant, the wise man sees as a whole. Different religions furnish different scales of observation and perspective. The level of truth from which the whole is seen is extrareligious, beyond all opinions. The expression of a realization of this level is something more than religious truth. It is metaphysical truth. To one who has realized it there will be no opposition between different theologies and the faiths based upon them, and the harmonization of all faiths on the basis of a vision of totality. According to Vedanta, to remain under the shadow of only one religious perspective which excludes others does not allow one that vision that is extrareligious. Indeed, to insist on the possibility of extrareligious truth, to those who give adherence only to religious truths, is to do violence to their faith. The admission of extrareligious truth is blasphemy in their eyes.

So when we study a faith like the one to which St. John of the Cross gave adherence, we have to hold in abeyance that total vision from whose summit all religions appear as multiple paths coming to the same goal. In the Christian faith the intrusion of any perspective other than that strictly allowed by revelation is considered error leading to heresy. In studying St. John we have to remain in the axis of his perspective. One of the great difficulties that prevents more understanding between a Christian and a Hindu is with regard to the content of the word "truth." When the Christian insists that he has the truth, he refers to the term in the religious sense. When a Hindu uses the same word he is thinking of its extrareligious meaning.

To St. John of the Cross, Jesus Christ is the only savior. Any union with God is impossible if this position is not accepted. As an article of faith the Christian accepts the theology of the Old Testament, its view of creation of the world, the picture it paints of sin, and its promise of a savior whose sacrifice on the cross is to bring a unique answer to the problem of salvation. Accepting this major premise, we can understand St. John following a line of faith that is not the Hindu's, by proclaiming Jesus as the only son of God.

The prophets of the Old Testament communed and conversed with God. Through this dialogue between man and God certain truths were revealed. St. John speaks of this in his *Ascent of Mount Carmel:* "In olden times it was necessary to ask God things relating to faith, and they were revealed according to his supplication. With Jesus Christ who is WORD in its complete form God has given us everything. He has nothing more to give us." "With the coming of Christ God has as it were become dumb and has no more to say, since that which He spoke afore time in part to the prophets, He has now spoken altogether in HIM, giving us ALL which is His Son." "That which God spake of old in the prophets to our fathers in sundry ways and divers manners, He has now, at least, in these days, spoken to us once and for all in the SON." "In this Son of God are hidden all the treasures of wisdom and knowledge of God." "He is all my vision and all my revelations."

The Indian mind is accustomed to welcome and venerate many incarnations. Such a notion has no place in Christian theology. As if anticipating the position of those who believe in different incarnations, St. John writes, making as it were God speak: "But now, any one who would inquire of me after that manner and desire to speak to him or reveal aught to him would be in a sense asking me for Christ again; and therefore he would be committing a great offence against my beloved Son, for not only would he be lacking in faith, but he would be obliging Him again first of all to become incarnate and pass through life and death."

In the Christian view, the coming of Christ was for a definite purpose, to redeem man from sin. Mankind suffers from the original sin; human nature was polluted at a historic moment when the behest of God was not obeyed by Adam and Eve. This sin has vitiated the blood of humanity and no human agency can save it. There is the promise of the scriptures that God, incarnated as man, by his sacrifice on the cross alone can save humanity. Jesus Christ as the son of God fulfilled this promise, and the way for establishing a new alliance between man and God thus was shown. The efficacy of the sacrifice made once for all time is the foundation of the faith for successive generations of mankind seeking to be liberated from sin. Wishing again for another incarnation is to doubt the validity of the sacrifice already made by Jesus. Jesus came to fulfill the promise of the scriptures. Every detail of his life runs on a pre-established plan, and he himself refers to the prophecy of the Old Testament as he enters into each new phase of his life. The cross is the way of salvation. To doubt the sacrifice that Jesus made is to wish another incarnation to go through all the suffering he underwent already. If he comes for a second time he has to pass through and repeat all the trials of his life once more. When this position of the Old Testament regarding sin and remission of sin through the blood of the son of God is not respected, the foundation of Christian theology is doubted. That means lack of faith.

When a Hindu argues with a Christian on the possibility of many incarnations, he is probably unaware of the importance to the Christian of original sin. To insist that a Christian should forsake that theological view of the fall of man is to show lack of respect for his beliefs. We must remember here that St. John, as a true Christian, reflects in his faith the whole position of the Old Testament. The notion of time in Judaic theology is static. Time was created and time must have a stop. It will end. Within this stasis the processes of history are dynamic. There is only one chance for man to fulfill his destiny. Man is born in sin and he who gives him redemption from sin is the son of God, Jesus Christ.

I am thankful to the great Russian theologian, the late Professor Nicolas Berdyaev, who explained this to me and enabled me to understand how the notion of time as conceived in Judaic theology is the key to the differences in the Christian and Hindu outlook. Time in Indian philosophy is not static but dynamic.

Taking in view the Indian attitude toward time, the Christian may be able to understand why the Hindu admits of multiple incarnations. The Christian should hold in abeyance the Judaic position and try to see the problem within the background of Indian philosophy and theology. Time is maya. Maya is not illusion. It is the kinetic aspect of reality. Sri Krishna says in the *Gita*, "I am time." There is neither creation of time nor end of time, as reality never ceases to exist. Reality is existence. As time is one with reality, there is manifestation of time and nonmanifestation of time. Time is shakti or power. It is cosmic energy having multiple forms of expression.

In maya, with which it is identified, time functions in infinite fields of consciousness. On the human plane, when consciousness incarnated in a body ceases to function with death, human personality does not terminate its history on earth. It takes innumerable embodied existences, in reincarnated forms, until all the karmas are worked out. As there is this upward movement of consciousness expressing itself through varied forms from that of a worm to that of the highly developed man, there is in nature, in maya, a downward movement, of the divine taking human form without the shackles of karma, having power to liberate beings enchained by karma. This descent of God on earth is the advent of an incarnation. As time, with which the Lord is identified, is dynamic, having multiple expressions, so there is no prohibition of the divine to reveal Himself in different periods of history.

The purpose of the divine incarnation is not, as in Christian theology, to wipe away an original sin contracted on a historic occasion. The Indian notion of sin is different. The word "sin" appears in the *Gita* and in other Hindu scriptures in many places. But there is nowhere in Indian theology any reference to the effect that sin entered into man as an external force on a certain day when man disobeyed God. The notion that God comes in human form to take away sin is common to both the traditions. In Hinduism sin is a deviation from the path of righteousness on the plane of conduct and morality. Disobedience is a moral error. But error is an obtuse interpretation of truth. There is no static quantity of the nature of error. It is relative to man's awareness of different levels of consciousness. The nature of sin is related to human consciousness as the blurring of the luster of one degree of truth, from a particular point of observation taken from another level of consciousness. There are grades of truth in empirical life. The experience of absolute truth comes only when man renounces his ego. That truth is inexpressible. At that level truth and reality become interchangeable terms. Truth becomes an intuition. It is the fourth kind of consciousness—the eternal *is*.

To the Christian, redemption from sin is the way toward liberation. To the Hindu, freedom from ignorance is the objective of the spiritual quest. If in the Christian terminology the word "sin" is continually repeated, so in the Indian language the term ignorance is repeatedly pointed out as the barrier separating man from his immortal heritage, knowledge of Atman. In the Christian theology there is only one way for man to be redeemed from sin. In Indian thought there are many ways to liquidate ignorance. The way given by the advent of a particular incarnation is only *one* of the paths. There are, in fact, systems of thought like the advaita Vedanta, in which the spiritual aspirant need not accept the mediation of any materialized form of God at all.

It is not so much disobedience to spiritual authority, but rather ignorance of it, which is the cause of deviation from the path of righteousness. The promise of the Indian scriptures is that the divine will take human form to reestablish the scale of spiritual values. The divine works this mission, not centering on one single event in his life—like the passion of Jesus or the resurrection—but by infusing into a decadent world a mass of spiritual power that radiates to all who are blessed to receive it; in individual lives the level of consciousness is heightened in varying degrees.

The incarnation is an ideal man; he sets the model for others to follow. This mission of the incarnation commences from the very beginning of this earthly career, unlike the life of Christ where his power to liberate man from sin comes only after he had fulfilled the promise of the scriptures, when the cross has become the effective way of salvation. From Bethlehem to Calvary, in the Christian view, was only preparation. The disciples and followers of Jesus were prepared by him from the moment he began his mission to believe in the forthcoming supreme event of his life, his sacrifice on the cross. The son of God became the savior of humanity in the moment of his crucifixion. It is faith in this that saves. St. Paul says: "If any angel from heaven preach any other gospel unto you than that which we men preached unto you let him be cursed and excommunicated." After quoting these lines, St. John of the Cross adds further: "Wherefore since it is true that we must ever be guided by that which Christ taught us, and that all things else are as nothing, and are not to be believed unless they are in conformity with it."

Thus what the Hindu considers to be a failure of tolera-tion appears for the Christian as the very cornerstone of his faith! If an orthodox Christian begins to believe in many incarnations, he takes Christ out of his historical setting and builds a new theology.

To the Hindu who incorporates Jesus Christ within his notion of many incarnations, there will not be any violence to his tradition. He will not be mixing up traditions. It is well known that Sri Ramakrishna had an experience of Christ; but the Hindu does not say that he had a Christian experience. To have a Christian experience, according to the tradition of the Church, one must accept as an article of faith the dogmas and the credo of the Church. Expia-tion of sin, by participating in the passion of Christ, results in union with God; man broke his promise and the possi-bility of the new alliance was established by Jesus Christ. No one can commune with God except through Christ, who alone has the power to reintroduce man to God. St. John the Evangelist is formal on that point. The notion of that God is the Biblical idea of Him. Sri Ramakrishna had the Vedic experience of divinity, totally different from the Judiac one. He did not seek union with the Judaic view of God: *he had already experienced* God as Indian mystics have from time immemorial.

According to St. John of the Cross the highest state that man can aspire to and realize on earth is the state of union, known in mystic language as spiritual marriage. This is the state St. Paul attained when he said, "I live, yet not I, but Christ liveth in me." In the words of St. John of the Cross: "According to this likeness of trans-formation, we can say that his life and the life of Christ were one through union of love which in heaven will be perfectly accomplished in the divine life of all those who shall merit being in God." This spiritual marriage may come to pass in this life as in the case of St. Paul, but, in the words of St. John, *"not, however, in a complete and perfect way.* The spiritual marriage is the highest

estate that can be attained in this life for everything can
be called an outline of love by comparison with the perfect image of transformation in glory." In the *Ascent of
Mount Carmel* this idea is still more clearly indicated:
"We shall see, we have not, we cannot have, permanent
union in the faculties in this life. We can have only a
transitory union." Complete union is possible only in
heaven, in the spiritual, glorified body.

This corresponds to one of the several ways of liberation of the Indian, the notion of *videhamukti*—liberation
that comes after the death of the body. So long as the
body lives, a human being, according to Christian theology, is not exempt from the possibility of sinning. No
great soul, however saintly he may have become, is canonized while alive. According to the Indian way, perfect
liberation from all impurities that come from the inner
carnal impulses can be gained even while here on earth.
Perfect union with God, which in the view of the Christian
is possible only in heaven, is possible for the Indian while
on earth. For the Indian—since he does not believe in
original sin—is not compelled to regard the material body
as being irrevocably polluted and therefore perpetually
in danger of becoming a prey of Satan, even when its
owner is purified.

An experience of Christ came to Ramakrishna later
after he had realized God. In Christendom devotees take
refuge in Jesus Christ in order to attain union with God.

Ramakrishna had an experience of Christ, and in the
rich background of his civilization and culture there is
scope for the acceptance of many incarnations. Ramakrishna did not subscribe to the Christian theory that there
can be only one incarnation. In accepting Jesus as an incarnation, Ramakrishna had no theological obligation to
admit the scheme of salvation announced in the Christian
scriptures, for he had already tasted God-consciousness
before the experience of Christ came to him. The incarnation, to the Indian, is God Himself; not merely the son of
God.

The fact of multiple incarnations is intimately related to
the other fact of the possibility of a soul working out its
karma through successive lives. The incarnation takes
upon himself the karma of the devotees who take refuge
in him. There is no dogma to the effect that the incarnation must suffer for this redemption he gives to suffering
souls. Yet the notion of vicarious atonement is not foreign

to Indian thought. In the case of Ramakrishna he suffered
because of the *transfer* he accepted of the sins of his
disciples. Swami Vivekananda once made an observation
to the effect that it was odd that the Master should suffer if
he was an incarnation. Hearing this remark, Ramakrishna
prayed to the Divine Mother and he had the following
vision. He saw before him another Ramakrishna envel-
oped in celestial light, full of vigor and health. A long
cortege of disciples were there. One by one he touched
them all as they came and prostrated before him. One by
one he saw them freed from their sins, attaining perfect
illumination. At the same time on his body appeared in
subtle form ulcers—a transfer of the karmas of the disciples. These irruptions then shifted to his throat and expressed themselves as the actual cancer he was suffering
from. Thus he knew that his illness was not due to personal karma, but had come as the result of accepting the
karmas of his disciples.

Sri Krishna died as a result of an arrow wound. But
that death is not the central event of his life, for the
Hindu's theory of salvation is not built around the way an
incarnation dies. To understand the Indian concept of the
incarnation, we have also to bear in mind one of the
fundamental principles of the Indian outlook in philosophy
which is totally different from the Christian view. In the
Christian view, man is the center of the created universe.
That view is anthropocentric. The Indian view is cosmocentric. The incarnation solves the problem of the personal and also the impersonal attitude toward life. The
incarnation lives in the borderland between the absolute
and the relative. He is eternal and yet relative at the same
time. In the *Gita* Sri Krishna instructs Arjuna to meditate
on his cosmic aspect. In the *Srimad Bhagavat,* a description is given as to how to identify the form of Krishna
with this cosmic symbolism, where different parts of the
body are identified with the different quarters of the
cosmos. The incarnation is the Vedantic infinite, one with
Ishwara, Hiranyagarbha, and Virat; God as the primordial
cause of the universe, God as cosmic consciousness, and
God as the cosmic concrete universe.

The impersonal is not a negation of the personal. It is to
see in the personal, the divine, and to know that everything is the Lord; it is the attainment of this vision that is
the experience of the mystics. This experience can come
as seeing the Lord as the chosen ideal in everything, as

the gopis saw Him; or as seeing in Him the whole of the universe, as did Yashoda when she saw in the mouth of the infant Krishna, a cosmic manifestation; or as seeing Him as Arjuna did, as an all-pervading spirit of the cosmos. When the boundaries of the personal individual view are crossed, the presentation of reality takes the aspect of reality as it is.

That reality as it is sensed and experienced by the mystic can be with form or without form. The experience of the impersonal does not restrict itself to the realization of the formless. Yet the same reality is also experienced by the mystics as formless. The impersonal as formless is realized in the experience of union with cosmic consciousness. In Christian theology the experience of the formless in the life of the mystics is considered as an experience of the transcendental aspect of reality. In the dualistic traditions of India there are parallels to the Christian notion of transcendence and immanence. In advaita Vedanta and the spiritual experience associated with it, transcendence does not appertain to reality. Reality does not undergo any modification. Nothing can be predicated of reality. Any definition of reality is to bring it within limitations. If it is said that reality is sat, chit, and ananda (existence, knowledge, and bliss)—or in other words, being, light, and love —the Vedantic implication is that it is not nonexistence, it is not absence of light, and it is not devoid of bliss. Shankara has repeatedly said that the aim of the *Upanishads* is to instruct us that any conceptualization of Brahman leads to error. To say that the supreme reality is transcendent is in a way to limit it. Reality remains self-revealed when ignorance goes. If the word "transcendence" has to be applied in any sense, it can be an application only to the level of vision colored by the ignorance of the aspirant after truth. It is this vision that changes, and reality remains ever as it *is*.

According to the Indian outlook we have to note two perspectives. One is the vision of the universe by the Lord. This is expressed in a concise form in the tenth chapter of the *Gita*. The other is the vision of the devotee. Among the various ways of experiencing the reality by the spiritual aspirant we can note three principal modes. These are expressed in the words of Hanuman: "When I have the consciousness of my body, O Lord, I am your servant. When I feel I am a creature with a thinking mind, I am a part of you. When I realize that I am Atman, there is no difference between you and me."

The Hindu who reads the Bible may readily see these same three approaches in the Christian scriptures. Christ's praying to his Father in heaven is an example of dualism. In Jesus' words, "I am the true vine and my Father is the husbandman," can be seen the viewpoint of qualified nondualism. The statement, "I and my Father are one," is a description of complete nondualism.

Although in India we accept many incarnations, we consider nevertheless the personality of all incarnations as *one unique person*. The *Gita* makes this point very clear in the fourth chapter. Sri Krishna says that he remembers all his past incarnations. In our ordinary human life that which gives unity to our character, building it around a solid psychic center, is memory. If there is loss of memory, or disturbed effects of it, there is no connecting link between the past and the present. On the contrary, if the threads of memory are not broken there is continuity of personality. Sri Ramakrishna, as an incarnation, had this continuity of memory identifying himself with past incarnations. Ramakrishna had the same continuity when he identified himself with Rama and Krishna. Through the unifying force of memory the identity of the incarnation as *one unique person* is established. He is not the only son of God to the Hindu; he is the *only person*, the person of God, that takes human form. The etymological sense of personality derives from the word "persona" or mask. The Lord puts on different masks, as Krishna, Rama, Christ, Ramakrishna, and others. He is conscious of the identity of the different personalities within his cosmic individuality. The word "individuality" (coming from the Latin word that expresses negation plus the word meaning to divide) has the significance of indivisibility. He is as the *Gita* says, indivisible, but appears as if he is divided.

Whatever view that devotee takes, be it anthropocentric or cosmocentric, it is the faith he has in his theology that is important. So long as faith works and transforms character, and particularly when that faith is traditional, depending on revelation, we have no right to question its validity. Let us take an illustration. Taking either view, the heliocentric or the geocentric—the sun-centered or the earth-centered—an eclipse can be predicted with exact precision. An identical result can be obtained through use of modes of calculation diametrically opposed to each other in their conception of the universe. In the same manner, whatever may be the difference in theology, when faith works, the result is the same—a transformation of character!

Scriptures are the words of God. Theology comes in to make their meaning more intelligible to us, not to amputate them nor to suit them to human convenience. Each scripture has an integral internal unity; each is a harmonious whole. If this is true with regard to Christian theology, it is equally true with regard to Indian theologies. Shankara, Ramanuja, and Madhwa strained their best to make the Indian scriptures systems of thought where there can be no discrepancies. They did not permit a certain section of the scriptures to be considered as true and others as having less validity. As revelations, the assigning of degrees of value to the scriptures is not warranted by orthodoxy. Swami Vivekananda accepted this position, considering the scriptures as various harmonious records of spiritual experiences.

Each position is *integral*. The question of *values* establishes *relations* between two or more positions having degrees of importance. Each view takes the problem out of its setting vital to the individual. Each plane of reference has to be accounted for separately within the particular angle of the individual's mode of outlook. The contents of one food may be richer; but so long as I am not eating it, its existence is of no value to me and the fact of accepting another's food—though richer in value—will be inappropriate.

So it is with regard to spiritual discipline and the theology inspiring that discipline. Sri Ramakrishna's spiritual experiences confirm that view. When he followed the Islamic way he could not for the time being accept modes of spiritual practice that conformed to the Hindu outlook. But the question of superiority or inferiority did not arise in his consciousness. Spiritual disciplines are for the transformation of character, to reach levels of consciousness different from those available in our mundane existence.

Theologies are not for hair-splitting intellectual manipulation. They form instead a substantial background of faith. Dedication for spiritual life comes out of love for the ideal. When love is transformed into faith, that faith becomes operative. We start doing a thing out of love for doing it. When there is no love, work becomes tasteless. The more we do a thing with our heart in it, the more confidence we get in what we do; for an act done with love is creative, and in the dynamism of creative work, our faith in what we do increases.

In spiritual life the end we seek to gain is love of God, which is infinite. Acts of adoration through love leave in us more and more hunger for the infinite which can never be expressed through words that are finite. This produces a wringing of the heart that pants for the infinite, in the way Sri Ramakrishna suffered when he cried out, "O Mother, another day is gone and thou hast not revealed thyself to thy child." The spiritual aspirant, not having yet tasted the integral experience, who still continues his acts of adoration, gains the *certitude of that state* through faith born of love for the ideal. Faith thus becomes the guiding star in his life and love toward the dedicated ideal —but not love as a sentimental outburst of a momentary feeling, and satisfaction in that feeling, which are grave dangers in the spiritual path according to St. John of the Cross—is expressed through acts that the scriptures ask us to conform to. Thus Sri Krishna says in the last verse of the sixteenth chapter of the *Gita:* "Therefore, let the scriptures be your authority in determining what ought to be done." Again in the second verse of the seventeenth chapter the Lord says, "Man consists of his faith, he verily is what his faith is."

This faith is divine; it is blind because it does not operate through the mind; mind, according to St. John, works through *discursive meditation.* According to the saint, when faith becomes ardent, man is blessed with *infused contemplation.* The spirit of the Lord infuses itself into the human soul, and the soul has nothing more to do. He has only to remain, in the words of Brother Lawrence, like a mass of marble allowing the chisel of the Lord to fashion him.

This dynamism of faith breathes into life and makes good music of the soul. Only a dedicated person can allow himself, like a lute, to be played upon by the Lord at his will. All real mystics brought out celestial music, the melodies that wrought a magic effect, first on themselves and then on those who heard them. The melody is the eternal refrain of *love.* But just as the music of West and East— each magnificent in its own way—is incomparable, so we should expect differences in the mystics' songs. The music produced in the lives of the Christian saints like St. John of the Cross and St. Teresa of Avila is as sweet as that of any Hindu saints. The notes are different, those of the latter, for example, containing the cosmic view, the theory of reincarnation, the affirmation that man is really born in bliss along with the whole of creation, and not in sin. In the music of Christian theology the dogmas and the credo are the essential notes of faith. In the same way, when we consider a particular theology we should not allow shadows of another theology to fall on it. Composite images may be good to find out a particular norm, but applied to the science of spirituality they produce discordant notes.

In the word of God, which is revelation, is transmitted the seed of faith. If love becomes dynamic through faith, a proper faith—of the sort described in the epistle of St. James—cannot but produce love of God. Love and faith in fact become interchangeable terms. They have identity in their inner significance, and the distinction in the use of the terms is one without difference. The light that illumines man is the light from God. Man, bound in sin according to the Christian thought, can get liberation from it only through the grace of God. The questions of free will and predestination, of individual exertion and the gratuitous gift of grace which are matters of such awful import to Christians, particularly Calvinists, do not disturb the Indian. The fact of man having successive lives on earth through the fact of the balancing power of karma, in the construction of an equilibrium between the negative and positive forces operating in life, reveals itself in the soul of man through the growth of a higher intelligence. This higher intelligence has its seat in God, and when ignorance goes, man will discover that all dualistic notions are illusions. With the destruction of the structure of this illusion, the particular dualism between free will and predestination, between human effort and grace, will also disappear.

The absence of the notion of karma and successive lives in the Christian outlook gives it an accelerated tempo. Human destiny has to find its fulfillment in this very life. The Christian has no time to lose, and what has to be done has to be done here and now, the only passage on earth. The notion of many lives makes the Hindu take his time more easily, breeding often lack of earnestness; he is not in a hurry as he has infinite time before him to work out his salvation!

One of the articles of the Christian faith is the second coming of Christ. That event can happen only when the whole world is evangelized in the name of Jesus Christ. The conversion of the pagans is a preparation for the second coming of Christ. Let us examine how the modern Hindu reacts to this so that he too can preserve his faith. If the missionary zeal is born of faith, the Indian reaction toward it is an awakening in the Indian masses of a consciousness of awareness of the essentials of spiritual glory; in short, it would make Hinduism dynamic. The word "aggressive" Hinduism has to be replaced by the term "dynamic" Hinduism, for the word "aggression" smells of violence and enmity to the opposing school of thought. As the Indian respects all faiths, the Christian is allowed all freedom in India to exercise his mission. But the Hindu would be *lacking in faith* if he allows the way of salvation of his race-soul to be violated by outside forces, permitting it to die in the menace of another faith.

A powerful movement is slowly coming into existence to try to reintegrate people who have strayed away from the Hindu fold. To apply the word "reconversion," however, is an anomaly, for the ignorant masses have never been really converted to anything else. An external conversion to Islam or to Christianity is no conversion. Psychologically it is as impossible for a Hindu to believe that Adam and Eve are his ancestors as it is impossible for a Pondichery schoolboy who learns by heart from a textbook published for French children that the Gauls, our ancestors, had blue eyes, to believe that his Indian forbears had blue eyes! Manu, Prajapati, and others are—according to his traditions—his ancestors. Real Christian theology can become a part of the Hindu's faith only if the subconscious mind accepts the first lessons in the catechism of the fall of man and original sin. Psychologically this is not possible.

In the experience of Christ of Sri Ramakrishna and through the Christian ardor of Mahatma Gandhi, the common man in India is alive at this critical point in history to the necessity of readapting the course of history in the same way India did long ago in assimilating the Buddhists back into the Hindu fold. This is done, not through a fiat from some reformer, but as a result of an awakening from within. It is not a mechanical adaptation. It is an organic growth.

In the different niches and sanctuaries where Indian gods and goddesses are worshiped, in the temples, images of Jesus Christ will receive the homage of India's millions. If the word "pagan" is used for those who have not faith in the Christian dogmas, to indicate his adhesion to his revelations and mythologies the Hindu is proud to re-clothe that much abused word with an Indian significance and to call himself pagan, attributing to that word its original etymological significance. That will in some measure be making reparation for the insults that have come down to him for so many centuries by allowing that word to be used against him in a disparaging sense. While the missionaries attempt to *Christianize* him, the Indian has begun the process of *paganizing* Christ. He is adapting Christ within the background of his own cultural traditions, offering him worship in ritualistic forms that are familiar to him in the adoration of Kali and Krishna. Full freedom is given to the Christian to exercise his apostolate. For in the rich soil of the synthetic spirit of the Hindu, no violence is done by venerating Christ in the way he is accustomed to honor his gods and goddesses. This is the exercise of the Hindu faith. If this is not warranted by historical facts, nothing is affected in the Hindu mind. He does not search historical evidences for the spiritual facts that are not of this world.

The process of fulfillment in time, and an absolute value given to history—essential to the Christian because of the Judaic notion of the static quality of time—are not articles of faith in India. When Ramakrishna was told of the doubts of the modern educated mind as to the historicity of Krishna, he replied that the fact that Lord Krishna expresses himself in the lives of mystics and devotees is incontrovertible evidence of his existence! The existence of a birth certificate for a spiritual hero does not give him any greater efficacy than that which mythology has awarded.

The cosmic mind projects values in ways that human minds are unable to fathom. The Hindu lives what the Westerner calls his mythologies. Kali, Ganesha, and Shiva are not historical personalities. Nor are they symbols, as apologetic Indians sometimes try to maintain. To keep a historical event within the historical framework does not satisfy the Indian mind. A spiritual reality grows, according to definite spiritual laws, and that reality becomes living in the experience of mystics. Thus the *faith* the Indian has in these realities is sustained. If a historical Krishna born in northern India has not come historically to the south, still evidence is produced by devotees who have not only had his vision but have found evidential marks of his objective presence in various places in the south of India! Nor are these to be confounded with illusions and hallucinations. It is through his legends that a spiritual reality lives. This *processing* of a spiritual truth, this making of a legend is something no hand of man can stay!

In the European languages, two lives of Ramakrishna have attracted the attention of the reading public. One is by Romain Rolland, who gives a careful historical version of the life of the Master. The other is by Dhan Gopal Mukerji, called *The Face of Silence*, where very few facts tally with history. Whenever I have met devotees of Ramakrishna in Europe I find it is the latter book they prefer, for Ramakrishna through this legendary version is more alive than through the research reporting of Romain Rolland. Yet we cannot accuse Dhan Gopal of having falsified the account of Ramakrishna. He made a legendary version of the life, and a legend breathes a breath of life which the dialectics of a Shankara or Ramanuja can never achieve. Dhan Gopal is an artist and the world owes more to the literary artists than to bare biographers; Balzac when he fell ill wanted to be treated, not by a flesh-and-blood physician, but by the doctor he had created in his novels!

Spiritual personalities like Rama and Krishna get out of the framework of history and really treat the soul that is sick and regenerate it into spiritual glory. They remain as the very salt of the earth. Mahatma Gandhi prayed to Rama and through repeating the name of Rama he got the power to awaken the masses of India. So we believe that in India the power of Ramakrishna will operate a renaissance in giving the Indian soul that alliance with its cultural past.

As I have said, the basis of love in spiritual life is faith. The expression of love is all-important—not theories of love. This has been eloquently brought out in the second chapter of the epistle of St. James: "If ye fulfill the royal law according to the scripture, Thou shalt love thy neighbor as thyself, ye do well: But if ye have respect to persons, ye commit sin, and are convinced of the law as transgressors. For whosoever shall keep the whole law, and yet offend in *one point, he is guilty of all. For he that said, Do not commit adultery, said also, Do not kill.* Now if thou commit no adultery, yet if thou kill, thou art become a transgressor of the law. So speak ye, and so do, as they that shall be judged by the law of liberty. For he shall have judgment without mercy, that hath showed no mercy; and mercy rejoiceth against judgment. What doth it profit, my brethren, though a man say he hath faith, and have not works? can faith save him? If a brother or sister be naked, and destitute of daily food, And one of you say unto them, Depart in peace, be ye warmed and filled; notwithstanding ye give them not those things which are needful to the body; what doth it profit? Even so faith, if it hath not works, is dead, being alone. Yea, a man may say, Thou hast faith, and I have works: shew me thy faith without thy works, and I will shew thee my faith by my works. Thou believest that there is one God; thou doest well: the devils also believe, and tremble. But wilt thou know, O vain man, that *faith without works is dead?*" (Italics ours.)

Our works are the reflection of our faith; faith is supernatural. Adhesion to the Christian or Islamic credo is faith. Brahman cannot be known through the mind and its faculties. No spiritual life is thinkable without faith in the supernatural.

Dr. Suzuki has shown in his essays on Zen that in Mahayana Buddhism, where there is not the least notion of a spirituality tinged with deistic ideas, there is still a basic need for faith. It may surprise us that in the realization of the "void," or Buddhata, the state of Buddhahood, one can attach much importance to faith. Words become surplus baggage in depicting a state that cannot be expressed in words. It can be got only by an inner vision, the figurative opening of a third eye. To quote Dr. Suzuki: "Metaphysically speaking we can say that this constant appeal to the spirit of investigation is based on *faith* solidly established in the functioning of and the activity of the Buddhata in each individual. It is in fact this Buddhata itself that conducts us to find out where the *one* sojourns."

In another place Dr. Suzuki explains that faith, and the spirit of investigation that induces the aspirant to perform spiritual disciplines, are not contradictory. Faith in the final end of religious practice "prepares the mind in such a manner that all other superficial activities of the mind are suspended. The very depths of consciousness is awakened and a power greater than the empirical ego illumines the whole of Reality."

This faith in the promise of enlightenment is given in an

exaggerated form in the discourse of the Zen master Lintsi: "O you disciples of Truth, if you want to obtain an orthodox comprehension of *truth,* do not allow yourself to be induced into error. Internally and externally if you meet with obstacles, mow that down. If you meet with Buddha kill him; if you meet with the Patriarch kill him; if you come across an Arhat, kill him; do the same with your parents and ancestors without any hesitation, for that is the unique way for liberation." The necessity to kill every dualistic conception, particularly the one that represents the chosen ideal, has been described by Ramakrishna in narrating his own experiences in achieving the advaita illumination. "As soon as the form of the Divine Mother presented itself before me I employed the sword of discrimination to cut her to pieces."

If the reign of faith is fundamental in spiritual practices where there is no place for dualistic conceptions, how much more should we respect the importance given to faith in dualistic religions. If in the advaita approach one must have such a faith as to cut to pieces his chosen ideal—a procedure abhorrent in the eyes of a bhakta—and if only on that faith all the tabernacles of thought and form can be negated to arrive at the ultimate affirmation, as Hindus we need not hesitate to give primacy to any form of faith, however dualistic, illogical, or irrational the content of the faith may appear to be. Negation means equally the negation of negation which is affirmation. Every faith is the language that God speaks in different countries and different epochs. It is lack of understanding of that language that creates want of comprehension.

Some years back I met a person in Geneva who was mocking at the Catholic ritual. Unable to suppress my indignation at this irreverence and knowing that no argument would be effective, I just stopped him and began to speak to him in my own language, Malayalam. Then I asked him in his language what effect my words had produced on him. He said that he had had a mind to laugh. "Why?" I asked him. Because, he said, he could not understand me.

To understand we must know the language of the other person. We must be able to understand the foundations of faith of another who does not belong to our religion, and then only we can arrive at a vast synthesis, which is the harmony of faiths taught by Sri Ramakrishna. Sri

Ramakrishna did not trouble himself to understand the various theological differences in faith. He exemplified the truth of faith by his various explorations into the spiritual realities of religion by making religion a matter of realization.

Faith in the supernatural, which is the integral element in all the orthodox religions of the world, demands of us renunciation of our ego and our will. This renunciation of will is the ideal of becoming *poor*. In the language of Meister Eckhart, "So long as you have a will to fulfill the will of God and you have any particular desire, even the one that lances you towards the Eternal, you are not really poor. Only, one is poor who will have *nothing*."

It is to this highest peak that the yoga of faith conducts us. The yoga of faith is the truly integral yoga. In the yoga of faith are contained all the other yogas. St. John of the Cross set such a supreme value on the realization of that poverty of which Meister Eckhart speaks. The word *"nada"* in Spanish means "nothing." How to arrive at this nudity of the senses and the mind is what St. John expounds in his theory of the dark night of the soul. Understanding, will, and memory are kept in abeyance by rigorous ascetic discipline. From discursive meditation the soul is led to the region of infused contemplation. The soul realizes its union with God through faith, hope, and charity.

Emerson and the East

Guido Ferrando

OF ALL GREAT American writers, Emerson was the one most influenced by Eastern thought, especially by Indian religious philosophy. It is not easy, however, to trace this influence through his writings, though they abound with quotations from Oriental books, mainly because Emerson was not a systematic thinker, but essentially a poet, even if he rarely displays the "faculty divine" which transforms the poetical vision into musical verse. He followed his intuitions and trusted the impulses of his own nature, the experiences of his own soul, rather than the knowledge and wisdom one can find in other men's writings. These he used only as a stimulus, not as guidance. "I value them," he said jocularly, "to make my top spin." Books are for nothing but to inspire. They are "the best of things, well used; abused, among the worst." "The only thing in the world of value is the active soul, which every man contains within him, although in almost all men obstructed and as yet unborn. The soul active sees absolute truth and utters truth or creates." But afterwards "the sacredness which attaches to the act of creation, the act of thought, is transferred to the record. The poet, chanting, was felt to be a divine man, henceforth the chant is divine also. The writer was a just and wise spirit, henceforward it is settled, the book is perfect. Instantly the book becomes obnoxious; the guide is a tyrant. Colleges are built on it; books are written on it by thinkers, not by Man Thinking; by men of talent, who start wrong, who set out from accepted dogmas, not from their sight of principles."

Emerson did not start wrong; he was still a young boy when he decided that he would live wholly from within, and follow the law of his own nature. Later on, after

351

he had been consecrated a minister of the Unitarian church in Boston, he saw that he could not attach any real value to the sacredness of traditions, that he could not, for instance, administer the sacrament of the Lord's Supper, since he did not believe in it, and refusing any compromise, preferred to resign his office and retire to the quiet and solitude of the little village of Concord where he spent the rest of his life meditating, writing, and lecturing.

Emerson read practically all the sacred books of the East that had been translated at his time, and was greatly interested in them; but it would be vain to try and determine the influence they had on him, by referring to his many quotations from them, or by picking up some of his ideas and some of his striking, vivid sentences which might seem to derive from, or to be inspired by, Oriental thought. While he read extensively, he remained intensely original, and whenever he quoted or took an idea from other writers, it was only as an illustration of a truth that had already blossomed in his own heart and mind. The philosophy and religion of the great Indian teachers influenced him in this sense, that they confirmed and even strengthened his fundamental intuitions, and revealed to him his deep affinity with the Indian approach to life. "It is not instruction," Emerson tells us, "but provocation, that I can receive from another soul. What he announces, I must find true in me, or reject; and on his word, be he who he may, I can accept nothing." When we read a book and think that some new truth is revealed to us, it is we who are creating it; there is a creative reading, as well as a creative writing. "When the mind is braced by labor and invention," Emerson says, "the page of whatever book we read becomes luminous with manifold allusion." We all know how true this is; how we may find in a book much more than the author ever dreamed of. But, Emerson warns us, "books are for the scholar's idle times. When he can read God directly, the hour is too precious to be wasted away in other men's transcripts of their readings. But when the intervals of darkness come, as come they must—when the sun is hid and the stars withdraw their shining—we repair to the lamps which were kindled by their rays, to guide our steps to the East again, where the dawn is."

Emerson, who in his long day had many hours in which he was able to read God directly, as He reveals Himself in nature and in the soul of man, during moments of darkness turned often to the East for inspiration. The light of Asia came to him through his love for the infinite, the absolute. "Philosophically considered," he says, "the universe is composed of Nature and the Soul. . . . Two cardinal facts lie forever at the base: unity or identity, and variety; oneness and otherness. It is impossible to think and to speak without embracing both. The mind is urged to ask for one cause of many effects; then for the cause of that; and again the cause, diving still into the profound; self-assured that it shall arrive at an absolute and sufficient one, a one that shall be all." "In the midst of the sun is light; in the midst of light is truth, and in the midst of truth is the imperishable Being," say the Vedas. Urged by an opposite necessity, the mind returns from the one, to that which is not one, but other or many; from cause to effect; and affirms the necessary existence of both, as each involved in the other. "The problem of thought is to separate and to reconcile these strictly blended elements, whose existence is mutually contradictory and exclusive. Now in all nations, in all times there are minds which incline to dwell in the conception of the fundamental unity. This tendency finds its highest expression in the religious writings of the East, and chiefly in the Indian scriptures." These writings contain little else than this idea, and they rise to pure and sublime strains in celebrating it. The same, the same; friend and foe are of one stuff; the ploughman, the plough, and the furrow are of one stuff; and the stuff is such and so much that the variations of form are unimportant." You are fit," says the supreme Krishna to a sage, "to apprehend that you are not distinct from me. That which I am, thou art, and that also is this world, with its gods, and heroes and mankind. Men contemplate distinctions because they are stupefied with ignorance." "The words I and mine constitute ignorance. What is the great end of all, thou shalt now learn from me. It is soul—one in all bodies, pervading, uniform, perfect, pre-eminent over nature, exempt from birth, growth and decay, omnipresent, made up of true knowledge, independent, unconnected with unrealities, with name, species and the rest, in time past, present and to come. The knowledge that this Spirit, which is essentially one, is in one's own and in all other bodies, is the wisdom of one who knows the unity of things. As one diffusive air, passing through perforations of a flute, is distinguished as the notes of a scale, so the nature of the Great Spirit is single, though its forms be manifold, arising from the consequences of acts. When the difference of the investing form, as that of god and the rest, is destroyed, there is no distinction."

Such is, then, the essence of Eastern thought, as Emerson understands it: there is only one Self, one universal soul or creative spirit, the Atman, and the goal of man's life is to become aware of the identity between his individual soul and the universal one, or, if he is of a devotional nature, to lose himself in Brahman, the absolute, and so realize the complete unity of creation. In striking contrast with this tendency to unity, as Emerson points out, is the other tendency to diversity, which finds its typical expression in European thought. The genius of Europe is active and creative; while pure, abstract speculation tends to unity, action tends directly backwards to variety in the manifested world. The speculation of the East is religious; the speculation of the West is intellectual and scientific. One loves infinity, the other delights in boundaries; one affirms the unity of spirit, the other the manifold power of nature. These two principles interpenetrate all thought: the one and the many. "Each student," Emerson tells us, "adheres by temperament and by habit, to the first or to the second of these gods of the mind. By religion, he tends to unity; by intellect, or by the senses, to the many."

There is no question about the tendency that Emerson follows; by temperament, by education, one might say by heredity—he was the son and grandson of a clergyman—he belongs to the class of those who believe in the universality of the spirit; he is a religious man. Here lies his profound affinity with Indian thought. Even before he had come in touch with the wisdom of the East, while still a young man, he formulated his philosophy of life in his first book *Nature*, in which are contained most of the ideas he expounded later in his *Essays* and *Lectures*. His philosophy is not a system; it is more a vision, an expression of a faith which consists for him in accepting the affirmations and revelations of the soul. It is not easy to give a clear and satisfactory exposition of this vision; but it is quite easy to get at the central, basic idea of it, because Emerson repeats it over and over again, in different words, in different forms, according to the different angles from which he looks at life. It is expressed in a compound word of his own creation, the oversoul; the universal soul of which everything living is a part. "The overpowering reality," Emerson says, "is that unity, that oversoul within which every man's particular being is contained and made one with all other. . . . Within man is the soul of the whole; the wise silence; the universal beauty, to which every part and particle is equally related; the Eternal One. And this deep power in which we exist, and whose beatitude is all accessible to us, is not only self-sufficing and perfect in every hour, but the act of seeing and the thing seen, the seer and the spectacle, the subject and the object, are one. We see the world piece by piece, as the sun, the moon, the animal, the tree; but the whole, of which these are the shining parts, is the soul." The correspondence of this beautiful statement with the teachings of the sacred books of the East, especially with the words that Krishna speaks to Arjuna, is so great, that it needs no comment.

But how are we to become aware of this supreme truth; how can we realize our divinity, our ineffable union with God? We live in succession, in division, in parts, in particles; in a world of illusions, of conflicting thoughts and emotions; how can we attain unity? It is useless, Emerson warns us, to look for help from outside, and it is foolish to believe that one can learn the truth by reading a book or by listening to a teacher. This truth cannot be received at second hand: it is an intuition; we ourselves must be our own book and our own teacher. Trust thyself, is Emerson's advice; in self-trust all virtues are comprehended, and one becomes free and brave; free from the illusions of our mind, our senses, our emotions that build a wall around us, and brave through wisdom, because fear always springs from ignorance. The justification for this self-trust lies deeper than can be fathomed; it is based on the fact that man is one. But how can we have a complete self-reliance, as long as we look upon ourselves as separate beings; how can we get rid of this illusory feeling of separation, of opposition to the world, and liberate ourselves from the slavery of thoughts, since every thought is a prison?

The first step to take, Emerson says, is to get in touch with nature, to learn to see nature, not only through our eyes, but through our hearts, so as to feel in harmony with it and to realize that we are a part of it. Naturally this requires solitude, without which one cannot have any real meditation and contemplation; and solitude is not to be found simply by retiring from the outward world and by closing ourselves in a room. We are not solitary, though nobody is with us, if we read, or write, or allow fleeting thoughts and remembrances to pass through our mind. "If man would be alone, let him look at the stars. The rays that come from those heavenly worlds will separate between him and what he touches." Or let him walk in silence through the woods. "In the woods is perpetual youth . . . in the woods we return to reason and faith. There I feel that nothing can befall me in life, which nature cannot repair. Standing on the bare ground, my head bathed by the blithe air and uplifted into infinite space, all mean egotism vanishes. I become a transparent eyeball; I am nothing; I see all; the currents of the universal Being circulate through me; I am part or parcel of God."

Sister Lalita

Frederick Manchester

I saw her as I came and went,
I saw her queenly, meek, and mild,
As innocent as any child,
A flower among her flowers content.

I come again, and in her place
Are silence and a vacant room,
And in my heart a sudden gloom
That I no more shall see her face.

There was a word I would have said,
Though what it was I hardly know;
I let the days glide by, and lo,
I now must say it to the dead.

And Sudden Sight

Anne Hamilton

A sound is heard where there is none to speak;
Legions of light tremble on waves of fire:
And sudden sight shows *this is Time!*, the peak,
The ebb, the flux in waves that never tire.
The matter-shapes are there, familiar, strange,
Beautiful and horror-filled and clear;
In delicate substance, gnat to snowy range
Are born, disintegrate, and disappear.
All forms of earth and thought arise and fall
In cyclic surge of Time, a fiery clock
Upon the nether life; the crests rise tall,
Flatten and whirl and die. On the bright Rock,
Bliss waits above the waves, above the shoal,
Though Time is death to all things but the soul.

Origins and Consequences of Some Contemporary Thought Patterns

Aldous Huxley

UNLIKE ART, science is genuinely progressive. Achievement in the field of research and technology is cumulative; each generation begins at the point where its predecessor left off. Furthermore, the results of disinterested research were applied in such a way that the upper and upper-middle classes of all industrialized societies found themselves becoming richer and richer. It was, therefore, only to be expected that the West's professional thinkers, who all sprang from these classes, and whose education had made them familiar with the methods and achievements of science, should have extrapolated the progressive tendencies of technology, basing upon them a general theory of human life. The world, they affirmed, was becoming materially, intellectually, and morally better and better, and this amelioration was in some way inevitable and inherent in the very nature of things. The theory of progress—a theory which became a dogma; almost, indeed, an axiom of popular thought—was novel and, from the orthodox Christian standpoint, heretical. For orthodoxy, man was a fallen being and humanity, if not actively deteriorating, was statically bad, with a badness which only grace in cooperation with each individual's free will could mitigate.

The belief in all-round progress is based upon the wishful dream that one can get something for nothing. Its underlying assumption is that gains in one field do not have to be paid for by losses in other fields. For the ancient Greeks, *hubris*, or overweening insolence, whether directed toward the gods, or one's fellow men, or nature, was sure to be followed, sooner or later, in one way or another, by avenging *nemesis*. The dogmatists of progress imagine that

they can be insolent with impunity. And their faith is so
strong that it has been able to survive two world wars,
and several revolutions of almost unprecedented savagery,
and remains flourishing in spite of totalitarianism, the revival of slavery, concentration camps, saturation bombing,
and atomic missiles.

Belief in progress has affected contemporary political
life by reviving and popularizing, in an up-to-date, pseudo-
scientific form, the old Jewish and Christian apocalypti-
cism. A glorious destiny awaits mankind, a coming golden
age, in which improved gadgets, more grandiose economic
plans, more elaborate social institutions will somehow have
created a race of more virtuous and more intelligent
human beings. Man's final end is not (as all the masters of
spirituality have always affirmed) in the timeless eternal
now, but in the not too distant, Utopian future. In order
to realize this temporal final end, the masses ought to
accept, and their rulers need feel no qualms in imposing,
any amount of suffering and moral evil in the present. It
is a highly significant fact that all modern dictators,
whether of the right or of the left, talk incessantly about
the golden future, and justify the most atrocious actions
here and now on the ground that such actions are means
to that glorious end. We see, then, that scientific and
technological progress has produced a boundless faith in
the future, as something necessarily better than the past
or present. But the one thing we all know about the
future is that we are profoundly ignorant of what is going
to happen, and that what in fact does happen is generally
very different from what we anticipated. Consequently any
faith based upon what is supposed to be going to happen a
long time hence must always be hopelessly unrealistic. But
to act upon unrealistic beliefs is generally fatal. In practice, faith in humanity's progress toward a future assumed
to be bigger and better than the present is one of the
most potent enemies to liberty, peace, morality, and common decency; for, as recent history has clearly shown,
rulers feel themselves justified by what they fondly imagine
they know about the future in imposing the most monstrous tyrannies and waging the most destructive wars for
the sake of the entirely hypothetical fruits which those
tyrannies and wars are expected (goodness only knows
why) to bear some time, let us say, in the twenty-first or
twenty-second century.

The dogma of progress is by no means the only intellectual consequence of scientific and technological advance. As theory, pure science is the reduction of diversity to identity. As a praxis, scientific research proceeds by simplification. These habits of scientific thought and action have, to a certain extent, been carried over into the theory and practice of contemporary politics. Where a centralized authority undertakes to make plans for an entire society, it is compelled by the bewildering complexity of the given facts to follow the example of the laboratory worker, who arbitrarily simplifies his problem in order to make it manageable. Scientifically, this is a sound and entirely justifiable procedure. But, when applied to the problems of human society, the process of simplification is a process, inevitably, of restraint and regimentation, of curtailment of liberty and denial of individual rights. This reduction of human diversity to a quasi-military identity is achieved by propaganda, by legal enactments and, if necessary, by brute force. Philosophically, this ironing out of individual idiosyncrasies is held to be respectable, because it is analogous to what is done by scientists, when they arbitrarily simplify an impossibly complex reality, so as to make nature comprehensible in terms of a few general laws. A highly organized and regimented society, whose members exhibit a minimum of personal peculiarities, and whose behavior is governed by a single master plan imposed from above, is felt by the planners and even (such is the power of propaganda) by the plannees to be more "scientific" and therefore better than a society of independent, freely co-operating and self-governing individuals.

The first step in the simplification of reality, without which (since human minds are finite and nature is infinite) scientific thought and action would be impossible, is a process of abstraction. Confronted by the data of experience, men of science begin by leaving out of account all those aspects of the facts which do not lend themselves to explanation in terms of antecedent causes rather than of purpose, intention, and values. Pragmatically they are justified in acting in this odd and extremely arbitrary way; for by concentrating on the measurable aspects of such elements of experience as can be explained in terms of a causal system, they have been able to achieve a great and ever-increasing control of the energies of nature. But power is not the same thing as insight, and as a representation of reality the scientific picture of the world is inadequate, for the simple reason that science does not even profess to deal with experience as a whole, but only with certain aspects of it in certain contexts. All this is quite clearly understood by the more philosophically-minded men of science. But unfortunately some men of science and many technicians have lacked the time and inclination to study the philosophical basis and background of their special subject. Consequently they tend to accept the world picture implicit in the theories of science as a complete and exhaustive account of reality; they tend to regard those aspects of experience, which scientists leave out of account because they are incompetent to deal with them, as being somehow less real than aspects which scientists have arbitrarily chosen to abstract from out of the infinitely rich totality of the given facts. Because of the prestige of science as a source of power, and because of the general neglect of philosophy, the popular *Weltanschauung* of our time contains a large element of what may be called "nothing-but" thinking. Human beings, it is more or less tacitly assumed, are nothing but bodies, animals, even machines; the only real elements in reality are matter and energy in their measurable aspects; values are nothing but illusions, which have somehow got mixed up with our experience of the world; mental happenings are nothing but epiphenomena, produced by and wholly dependent upon physiology; spirituality is nothing but wish fulfillment and misdirected sex; and so on. The political consequences of this "nothing-but" philosophy are clearly apparent in the widespread indifference to the values of human personality and human life, which are so characteristic of the present time. Within the last thirty years this indifference has expressed itself in a number of dangerous and disquieting ways. We have witnessed, first of all, the wholesale revival of slavery in its worst and most inhuman forms—slavery imposed upon political heretics living under the various dictatorships, slavery imposed upon whole classes of conquered populations, slavery imposed upon prisoners of war. Next we note the increasing indiscriminateness of slaughter during wartime. Area bombing, saturation bombing, rocket bombing, bombing by atomic missiles—the indiscriminateness has steadily increased throughout the second World War, until now no nation even makes a pretense of observing the traditional distinction between civilians and combatants, but all devote themselves systematically to general massacre and a destruction of cities so complete that the survivors are doomed to suffer distress and hardship for years to come. Finally there are the phenomena of deliberate starvation of whole populations, concentration camps, torture, human vivisection, and forced migration; or the removal, at the point of the bayonet, of millions of human beings from their homes to other places, where their presence will be more convenient to the rulers who happen for the moment to be in power. When "nothing-but" thinking is combined with the other intellectual products of applied science—faith in progress and desire for "scientific" uniformity and simplicity—the results, as anyone can see who takes the trouble to look at the world around him, are truly horrifying.

Active and Contemplative Life

Swami Prabhavananda

BEFORE WE CAN understand the kind of a life we must live, we must know the end, the goal, and the purpose of life and living. In regard to the end or the goal of life, all religions are in complete agreement. Jesus says: "Be ye perfect even as the Father in Heaven is perfect." St. Paul explains this goal by saying: "Ye are complete in Godhead." The *Upanishads* declare: "Blessed is he who realizes God in this life, if not, he has lived in vain." "There is no happiness in the finite, in the Infinite alone is happiness." Shankara says: "A man is born not to desire life in the world of the senses, but to realize the bliss of a free soul in union with God."

To attain perfection in union with Godhead and thereby enjoy the bliss of a free soul is the one goal of human life. Your life and achievement on earth will determine your life after death. The degree to which you have unfolded the divine qualities in this life will determine the degree to which you will enjoy union with God after death. There is an erroneous idea prevalent in the mass mind that heavenly felicity is to be attained only after death. But the many scriptures of many religions and the illumined seers of God in every age and in every country point out very definitely that the heaven is within ourselves and that it has to be attained here and now. "Ye shall know the truth and the truth shall make you free." "Marvel not that I said unto thee, Ye must be born again." And this birth in spirit is to be had here and now. The *Upanishads* emphasize, "Attain liberation *here* and *now*, *not after the fall of the body*."

There is a proverbial saying amongst the Hindus, "When the husking machine dies and goes to heaven, what will it

364

do there but husk!" If we have not been able to overcome hatred, jealousy, passions in this life, we shall not be able to overcome them after death; for we carry the same quality of the mind to the other world. What we have to earn we must earn here on earth. We must reach the unitive knowledge of Godhead and enjoy the bliss of heaven even in this life.

According to the Hindu theory of evolution, nothing is superadded in the course of evolution, but what is only potentially existing becomes unfolded. The whole of the tree potentially exists in the seed. Now if we study the process of evolution in the universe we find in one extreme what we may call dull, dead, inert matter, and in the other extreme a Christ, a Buddha, a Ramakrishna, children of light, light themselves. These have become one with God. God, whom we see unfolded in these children of light, is therefore existing potentially in the minutest atom. Swami Vivekananda rightly defined religion as the manifestation of divinity already in man. To unfold this divinity already existing within is the end of evolution and the goal of life.

Through the process of evolution God, Sat-chit-ananda, existence, consciousness, bliss absolute, God who dwells everywhere, becomes unfolded. Shankara by his subtle logic proves that existence, consciousness, and bliss absolute are not attributes of God, but identical with God, nor are they different from one another. God is existence *itself,* and that which is existence is also consciousness and is bliss *itself* as well. We shall not enter into that subtlety of his reasoning. But let us simply state the fact that God who is existence, consciousness, and bliss absolute, *is everywhere.* "The light shineth in darkness but the darkness comprehended it not." Though He shines everywhere, He is not comprehended by all because of darkness.

Take the mineral kingdom, for instance. There is God there; there is life, and there is consciousness. But this life and consciousness remain covered by the darkness of matter. In the vegetable kingdom we find, though darkness of matter predominates, that there is a certain release of life and consciousness. Within the past forty years, a Hindu scientist, J. C. Bose, conclusively demonstrated that the plant can breathe, has life and consciousness, and does act and react. In the lower animal kingdom we find consciousness predominates, but there is not evolved self-consciousness. In man the self-consciousness is unfolded but man again is a slave to matter. In the illumined seer, in a Christ or a Buddha or a Ramakrishna, we see that infinite consciousness infinitely released. They have become one with God. Self-consciousness or the sense of ego is not yet evolved in the lower animal. In man is evolved self-consciousness. A God-man again transcends the sense of ego, the ego which limits the infinite consciousness or God in man. Sri Ramakrishna used to say, "When the ego dies, all troubles cease."

To transcend this ego and unfold the infinite consciousness is what Christ would call "the birth in spirit," and Buddha would call "the awakening." The *Mandukya Upanishad* speaks of it as "Turiya, the fourth, the transcendental consciousness."

The condition for the birth in spirit, for the inner awakening, is in the words of the Bible: "Love God with all thy heart, with all thy soul, and with all thy mind." In other words, we must devote ourselves completely and wholeheartedly to loving contemplation of God. Our consciousness becomes matter-bound or released to infinity according to the object of consciousness, the object of our love. If we devote our mind to worldly objects, our mind remains clouded by the darkness of matter, and if we devote ourselves to the inner light, the covering of darkness is removed, and the light shines forth.

The natural tendency of the mind, however, is to run outward toward the objects of sense. Senses are drawn naturally to objects and the mind is attached to the senses because of ignorance of the inner light.

Why does the mind become attached to the senses and the objects of the senses? It is because through ignorance it accepts the shadow of life, the appearance of a world as real.

There is the infinite God, the inner light, within each one of us. There is also the covering of darkness. The mind receives the reflection of the inner light, gets the fragrance, as it were, of God—existence, consciousness, and bliss absolute; does not know wherefrom the fragrance comes; seeks to find fulfillment in the objective world by running after the shadows of life. Thus the mind becomes externalized.

In the *Yoga Sutras* of Patanjali, the causes of our bondage to life are said to be first, *avidya*, the universal ignorance which covers the face of reality. From this ignorance, or forgetfulness of the presence of the divine reality within, there arises next the sense of ego. Then there come in man *attachment* to pleasing things of the world, *aversion* to unpleasant things, and lastly, *thirst for life*.

Swami Vivekananda used to say, if the room is dark, you cannot remove the darkness by crying aloud "It is dark! It is dark!" But bring the light and the darkness will vanish. Our mind is darkened by ignorance. To remove the ignorance, we must look to the inner light that shines in spite of the covering of darkness. In short, contemplation of God is the direct means to reach the Inner Light of God.

This does not mean, however, that we must give up activity, or that we should neglect our duties. On the other hand, duties must be performed in order that we may practice detachment through action and rise above the sense of ego, the obstacle to the uncovering of the inner light. In the words of Sri Krishna in the *Gita*:

> Let him who would climb
> In meditation
> To heights of the highest
> Union with Brahman
> Take for his path
> The Yoga of action.

Work in the spirit of egolessness is a means to contemplative life.

In this connection, let me emphasize once more that in regard to the end, all religions are in complete agreement. That end is the life in union with God. Contemplative life is a stage in our progress that we arrive at through selfless action. Action is not the end, but only a means. But unfortunately the modern man, if he makes any concession to contemplative life, will regard it only as a means to greater urge to action and achievement in the external world. The modern man, through his progress in the knowledge of science and his outward achievements in the external word, has come to believe in a sort of millennium; he thinks that with a greater progress of machines, man will also have greater moral and spiritual progress. Instead of making the attempt to reach the unitive knowledge of Godhead, instead of trying to live a life of inner check and a life in union with God, he is busy in achieving progress in the external world by trying to bring more cash and comfort to mankind.

History, however, has proved again and again that Utopia can never be reached in the external world; that it is like a dog's curly tail. Straighten it out; it will curl up again. To quote the words of the great American poet-philosopher Ralph Waldo Emerson:

> There are two laws discrete
> Not reconciled,—
> Law for man, and law for thing;
> The last builds town and fleet,
> But it runs wild,
> And doth the man unking.

Unfortunately again, the professed Christians also have begun to believe that by bringing progress in the outward world through action they can bring down heaven on earth, and that God needs the help of man to achieve this millennium. I was once told by a professor of theology that God has not yet reached His fullness and infinitude and that we as human beings must help God to achieve His fullness! What an egocentric theology it is, I thought to myself! Just the very opposite of what Jesus had taught! No, on the contrary, *we need God*. We need to forget ourselves, and wipe out all sense of ego, in love for God and in His contemplation.

The ideal, the end of life, is the unitive knowledge of Godhead—this must never be forgotten. The modern man in the name of practicality often regards a man with the spiritual ideal as a queer creature, a dreamer. Suppose you see a man walking with a heavy burden on his shoulders. You ask him, "What is this burden you are carrying?" He answers, "I don't know." "Where are you going?" "I don't know." If such are the answers you receive from the man to your queries, what would you think of him? Would you consider him a practical man? Yet, such is the irony of this age that he who tries to find an answer to such questions is considered a dreamer.

True it is that everyone tries to form some ideal, some end he may strive to achieve. But until a man learns the spiritual ideal, he cannot find the exact purpose of life and living, and in the words of the *Gita,* "his will wanders in all directions, after innumerable aims."

We must understand the spiritual ideal and our will

then in the words of the *Gita* "must be directed singly toward one ideal." No compromise must be made with this ideal and then it is possible to "develop that concentration of the will which leads a man to absorption in God."

Contemplative life, absorption in God, is a stage in our development. To achieve that we must be active. Work is a means and not the end. To quote the words of the *Gita* which teaches absorption in God: "Nobody can become perfect by merely ceasing to act. A man who renounces certain physical actions but still lets his mind dwell on the objects of his sensual desire, is deceiving himself. He can only be called a hypocrite. The truly admirable man controls his senses by the power of his will. All his actions are disinterested. All are directed along the path to union with Brahman. The world is imprisoned in its own activity, except when actions are performed as worship of God. Therefore you must perform every action sacramentally and be free from all attachment to results."

What is the secret of worshiping God through actions? Try to understand that behind our surface life and our outward consciousness there is the deeper life, the inner consciousness which is identical with God. The appearance of a world cannot exist without some Ground behind it. That Ground is Brahman—God—reality. Learn therefore to see God within yourself and in the universe. Then act with your senses and let your work be the worship of God. To quote the words of the *Gita* again:

> If a man sees Brahman
> In every action,
> He will find Brahman.

Religion and the World Crisis

S. Radhakrishnan

MODERN CIVILIZATION, with its scientific temper and secular humanism, is uprooting the world over the customs of long centuries and creating a ferment of restlessness. The world has found itself as one body, but physical unity and economic interdependence are not by themselves sufficient to create a sense of universal human community. In spite of the external unity, the world mind is anarchical and unruly. More than ever before we are divided and afflicted by formidable evils of fear, of suspicion, and of misunderstanding. To remove these evils, which are the originating causes of wars, to give a soul to the growing world unity, is the task assigned to our generation. In this great work of creating a new pattern of living, a new social mind, some of the fundamental insights of Indian culture may perhaps be found useful.

After the two wars which this generation has passed through, we are impressed by the utter inadequacy of a secular view of life and the urgent need for a renewal of faith, a renaissance of spiritual values. The war which ended with the wiping out of two cities by the atom bomb has disclosed the strength as well as the weakness of our civilization. It has given evidence of our intellectual penetration and marvelous endurance. It has also revealed our greedy and grasping nature, our fundamental insufficiency, our essential lack of self-control. What we suffer from is not intellectual error or even moral ignorance, but it is spiritual blindness. No amount of science and art, commerce and industry, obedience and discipline, can maintain whole an edifice whose foundations are unsound. The kingdom of man belongs not to the most intellectual or even the most disciplined, but to the most virtuous, the

370

spiritually wise. The leaders of thought and science who enfranchise the mind, the poets and artists who persuade the heart, the moral heroes who serve humanity, have all their place, but the first place belongs to the seers, the convinced and inspired souls, the creative men of affirmation, who tell us that man is not simply body and mind, that our personal insufficiencies and social maladjustments are directly traceable to the neglect of the spiritual and the divine, and absorption in the pursuits of the physical and the animal, the instinctive and the intellectual.

From the beginning of her history India has looked upon religion not so much as a revelation to be attained by faith but as an effort to unveil the deepest layers of our being and get into enduring contact with them. Religion is spiritual life, which is different from a vague religiosity or conventional piety. Religion is not a solemn routine or a superstitious faith. It is not submission to authority or subscription to a formula. Properly understood, religion is a summons to spiritual adventure, to individual regeneration, to a change of consciousness, from the ordinary ignorant state, when we are cut off from our true Self, to a greater consciousness in which we find our true being. It is to rise from *vijnana* to *ananda,* from the order of thought to the order of charity, to use Pascal's words. To uncover the inner springs of regeneration we must turn inward, deepen our awareness, grow into completeness, develop a more meaningful attitude toward life, an attitude which will free us from bondage to the external forms and hardening of the spirit. Religion, if authentic, means an illumined mind, a changed heart, and a transformed will.

Such an intensification of religious consciousness will naturally be accompanied by an intensification of social consciousness. The great Indian thinker Shankara tells us that one has first a consciousness of the Divine in oneself and next the consciousness of the Divine in all. We first grasp the kingdom that is within us all, and then it becomes manifest in our relations with the world. "When we realize the one Lord in whom we all dwell, how can there be any talk of friend and foe?" Oneness with our fellow men becomes then the leading principle of our life, not merely a policy for economic co-operation and political unification. It becomes a principle of deeper brotherhood, an inner realization that only in the life of our fellow men is our own life complete. Such a feeling, which is not only an idea but the truth of our being, is the only secure base for human unity.

Science has put at our disposal potencies of universal force, but the human individuals who use them are little communal egos with nothing universal in the light of their knowledge or the life of their affections. The nationals of a country are prepared for the worship of their nations, for the immolation of the innocent by the affliction of subtle propaganda, blinding their vision and splitting their ears. Attempts to unite the peoples of the world, the Christians of the world, the workers of the world, the capitalists of the world, have failed because of the armed and irrational exaltation of the nation state. In pursuits of the mind and spirit there was hitherto an element of international collaboration. But today even the scientific workers are conscripted into the service of the state. Science and scholarship, whose essential purpose is to foster universal values, are being betrayed by their votaries, who are compelled to conform to the policy of the state and give to a group what is meant for mankind. We are bruised and bewildered, our deepest emotions are stirred, by the incredible forms of savagery in which even intelligent and sensitive men are required to acquiesce. If we believe in humanity, we must throw off our national disguises and develop a new social discipline.

The war has contributed to a coming together of the peoples and the mingling of races and cultures. No nation can keep itself in isolation. All will have to depend on all. The Eastern and Western worlds, which used to live more or less separately, have been brought into close contact. Civilization is ceasing to be European or Asiatic and is becoming of the world. Whenever East and West met in the past, a cultural renaissance was the result. The development of a world wisdom worthy of our time and place is in process today. The search for world peace—there can be no other peace—is not a mere moral aspiration but an urgent political necessity. The time is so short. The need is so desperate. If we are to live as members of a world community, a unity, if not identity, of spiritual outlook and aspiration is essential and we must do our best to develop it.

In the different religions themselves there are movements for the reunion of the sects within them. This attempt at reunion requires to be extended to the great living faiths of mankind. In the sphere of religion, also, there is room for diversity and no need for discord. If the sects of a particular religion can get together, giving up their claims for the exclusive possession of the truth of that religion, it is not too much to hope that the religions themselves may modify their claims to the exclusive possession of spiritual truth. Belief in such exclusive claims and monopolies of religious truth has been a frequent source of strife and a formidable obstacle to co-operation in the world of spirit. The creeds are guides to the religious goal, bidding us to pass from words to the vision, which is the work of each individual soul. When they claim for themselves eternal and complete truth, they must in the name of love and reason seek to convert others who, according to them, are in error. Fierce fanaticisms, which fought and killed, tortured and imprisoned, burnt and persecuted in every way imaginable for the sake of dogmas and rites which did duty for spirituality have marred the fair name of religion. If we reflect on the matter deeply, we will perceive the unity of spiritual aspiration and endeavor underlying the varied upward paths indicated in the different faiths. The diversity in the historical formulations of the fundamental spiritual truths tends to diminish as we rise in the scale of spiritual perfection. All paths of ascent lead to the hilltop. It is immaterial what approach we take. "As the birds fly in the air, as the fish swim in the sea, leaving no trace behind, even so is the pathway traversed by the seeker of spirit." This convergent tendency and the remarkable degree of agreement in the witness of those who reach the hilltop are the strongest proof of the truth of religion. To neglect this unity of spirit, to underline the diversity of religions, is philosophically unsound, morally unjust, and socially dangerous. Religion for the Indian mind is life in God, love of man, and charity for all.

If religion becomes unique and universal, a flame which cleanses mankind and so cleanses the world, then will the cry of St. Joan in Bernard Shaw's epilogue to that play be fulfilled: "O God, that madest this beautiful earth, when will it be ready to receive Thy saints?" Then will come a time when the world will be inhabited by a race of men with no flaw of flesh, no error of mind, freed from the yoke not only of disease and privation, but of lying words and of love turned into hate.

How to Remold the Personality

Swami Gnaneswarananda

THE SAMKHYA SYSTEM of Hindu philosophy establishes the dualistic theory of creation, which holds that evolution is caused by the combination of *purusha* and *prakriti*. Purusha, figuratively the "father principle," is the "efficient cause," and prakriti, the "mother principle," is the "material cause"; out of this combination everything in this universe has been projected. For example, when a potter fashions a pot he uses several materials, of which the lump of clay is the principal one; these he manipulates by his intelligence in order to bring the desired result, namely, the pot. Here the potter's intelligence is the efficient cause, and the ingredients form the material cause. In the evolution of the entire creation, purusha, the intelligent cosmic principle, is the efficient cause; and prakriti, or primordial matter and energy, is the material cause.

Let us analyze the nature, qualities, and also the mode of expression of prakriti. There are certain fundamental qualities or gunas inherent in her for which she is called *sa-guna*, or "with qualities," whereas purusha is *nir-guna*, or "without qualities." Every manifestation in nature is expressed from the inherent qualities of prakriti. Purusha does not contribute variety of any kind because he does not have any in himself. Although many, he is just the same in quality as in quantity in every manifestation. If in nature anything is large or small, beautiful or ugly, round, flat or cubic, attractive or repulsive, high or low, good or bad, advanced or undeveloped, these distinctions are caused by the difference in the proportion of the qualities of prakriti.

Essentially, prakriti has three gunas inherent in her which may remain in two different states; namely *avyakta* or potential, and *vyakta* or kinetic. When the gunas remain potential they do not find any expression whatsoever, and there cannot be any evolution or manifestation of prakriti. This state is called *pralaya*, or the state of calm and peaceful sleep of cosmic nature. Then, after a period, the gunas begin to stir, their balance and poise are lost, giving prevalence to one guna over the other two. As soon as this loss of balance takes place, evolution or manifestation begins, which is called the vyakta or kinetic state of prakriti. Thus, manifestation is always caused by the unequal distribution of the gunas.

In every manifestation in nature there is preponderance of one guna over the other two, which is the root cause of that special manifestation. When we find something in nature very beautiful, peaceful, calm, poised, and pure, we must understand that in that entity there is a predominance of the quality of sattwa, or the guna of equilibrium and poise. Where there is restlessness, activity, ambition, or competition in a particular entity, there is the prevalence of rajas. If in another entity we find inertia, laziness, indolence, or any other expression of a morbid, dull, ugly, or repulsive nature, tamas is unmistakably predominant.

These three gunas of prakriti can be compared very aptly to the three phases of energy spoken of by modern physics. Energy can be in three different states; *equilibrium and poise, attraction and repulsion,* and *inertia or potentiality.* These three gunas of prakriti are like three layers of a glass dome that encircle the ever-effulgent divine perfection of the purusha within. Sattwa is clear and transparent, rajas is many-colored and ornamented with intricate designs, and tamas is dark and coarse. Therefore, the predominance of sattwa means that the inner divinity is shining undisturbed in its intrinsic qualities of poise, equilibrium, peace, and restfulness, in the entity in which it is thus perfected. In other words, when prakriti is in a state of repose and harmony she gives more opportunity to purusha, or the cosmic intelligence within, to manifest his pristine excellence.

Only in a sattwic agent can the manifestation of the perfection of purusha be very distinct and unobstructed. In a rajasic one, owing to the predominance of attraction and repulsion, the surface or the phenomenal expressions always remain in a state of disturbance. Consequently, the inner perfection of purusha cannot manifest itself as clearly as it does in the previous case.

Suppose that the surface of a lake is in a state of rest and calmness. The reflection of anything upon it will be very clearly and distinctly visible; whereas, if the lake changes to a state of disturbance and turmoil, all reflections on the surface will appear very disturbed and distorted. Similarly, when the prakriti of any entity remains in a state of peace and poise, the perfection of purusha finds more opportunity for manifestation; whereas, if she becomes disturbed, the inner divinity of purusha can only express itself indistinctly, or in a distorted, disfigured, and disproportionate way.

In a tamasic agent, who is constantly overpowered by the influence of inertia and laziness, the perfection of purusha cannot shine through at all. The brilliance, intelligence, strength, and divinity of purusha, although present equally in the tamasic agent as in the sattwic, does not get an opportunity to express itself, owing to the coarseness and opaqueness of the outer dome of prakriti.

In view of this theory, the special contribution of Hindu psychology has always been: Each soul is potentially divine. That absolute divine perfection is present equally in every atom, from the highest angels, gods, and demigods, down to the lowliest creatures. Any difference lies in the expression, not in the existence of that divinity. Consequently there is infinite possibility for every individual to advance toward divine perfection. No soul can ever be "lost"! Wherever the outer shell of prakriti is clean and pure, there the purusha or divinity finds more expression; but if it is disturbed or coarse, or in a dormant state, divinity does not get the opportunity of finding clear expression.

Essentially, there is no distinction between the high and the low in regard to the fundamental, basic principle, which is the same everywhere. It is absolutely wrong to say that only man has a soul, but that beasts, birds, trees, and insects do not have one. It is that purusha, in the language of Hindu psychology, which is called the soul. It is the expression of that divine principle of purusha behind every manifestation of prakriti. Although infinite and absolutely perfect in its nature, the soul being caught in the net of the three gunas appears limited. As soon as his reflection on prakriti is stopped, Purusha attains to his pristine state of perfection and divinity, which is called *moksha*, or the attainment of the final illumination.

Everything in nature is an expression of the three gunas. The correct method of knowing any particular individual, or of analyzing his state of being and possibilities, consists in comprehending the state of his gunas. If we want to understand any person, or want to educate, or help him, the first thing necessary is to diagnose precisely the condition of his gunas, and appeal to, approach, or handle him accordingly. It is a pity that many commit damaging mistakes in their human relationships only because they do not know how to handle and treat every individual differently. Suppose a student has to be cared for and educated by a teacher. The first thing necessary would be a diagnosis of the gunas or condition of the student. The teacher must know what type—sattwic, rajasic, or tamasic—that student represents. If he is a sattwic agent, the mode of education must be quite different from what it would be if he were of another type. Herein comes the very logical and scientific theory of *adhikara-vada,* or the principle of imparting education in consideration of the capacity, taste, general demeanor, and unfoldment of the student. A method, standard, or ideal very beneficial for the sattwic student, might not be at all good for a rajasic or tamasic type. For that reason, any attempt to standardize education or religion—religion according to Hindu psychology is but a system of education—is absolutely wrong, unscientific, and harmful. Of course, in a general way, there can be three broad principles or modes of education: sattwic, rajasic, and tamasic. But even these modes should not be applied too generally because the teaching must be modified and individualized according to the capacity of each individual student. In matters of spiritual discipline and teaching, these three gunas receive very deep consideration, and so the Hindu teachers developed a special science of studying them.

Not only in the case of spiritual education, but also in our ordinary daily life, we can realize how much more conveniently we can contact and sustain our relations to various individuals according to their stage of development, if we know what psychological station they occupy. For instance, friendship with a sattwic person would require one kind of expression, or no external expression at all; whereas, friendship with a rajasic type would necessitate quite a different expression and demonstration. On the other hand, a tamasic friend—if true friendship is at all possible with him—will demand still another mode of demonstration. This is true, more or less, in every human relationship. I may even apply this principle to business life. If we clearly know what type of person we are dealing with, and knowing that, if we can regulate our mode of dealing, our method of expression, and our system of appeal, according to the particular guna of that person, we can gain our end without any difficulty.

But let it be understood that in every entity all three gunas are present. When we designate a type by the name sattwic, rajasic, or tamasic, we do not mean that there is only the one guna present in that person. It is in view of the predominant guna that the type is named. When there is a predominance of sattwa, with the other two present but overpowered, we call that type sattwic, and so on with the other two types. The overthrow and control of the two lower gunas are demanded for the advancement of man. Culture of any kind involves control of the unnecessary gunas by the one which is necessary. In some kinds of acquisition there can be a need, at least for the time being, of the predominance of rajas. Under such circumstances an advanced person must be able, according to the demand of the situation, to suppress his sattwa and tamas, by means of the rajas. Thus absolute control must be gained over all three gunas to attain the result that one wanted from a particular action. Under certain other circumstances there might be the need, even, of gaining the predominance of tamas over the two other. Suppose one wants to sleep, rest, or relax. At that time if one's rajasic element is predominant, one cannot get rid of the restlessness of one's mind. Although the physical body may be at rest, the mind remains terribly active. In other words, it is the quality of rajas which is controlling the person at that time. For that reason he cannot sleep. Many people suffer from insomnia because their minds remain so occupied with the thoughts of their business or other affairs, that even when they want to retire they cannot do so because of the prevalence of rajas. Under these circumstances tamas is of great value. Therefore, one must have absolute control over these three so that, according to the demand of the occasion, he may summon the required guna.

However, as a general principle of discipline, an inferior guna has to be controlled and subdued by the culture of a superior one. Tamas must be overpowered and suppressed by rajas; and rajas, by sattwa. We have to bear in mind that there is no provision for a double promotion in this school of Dame Nature. A person occupying the state of tamas cannot jump into that of sattwa without going through the intermediate one of rajas. Many confuse tamas with sattwa, because, superficially, from external signs and expressions, sattwa appears very much like tamas, and vice versa. A person enjoying a genuine calm and peaceful state of sattwa appears very much the same as a person who is extremely lazy and inactive. It happens very often that a lazy person interprets his lethargy in terms of peace and poise, and a coward his cowardice in terms of forgiveness and universal love. The fact remains that the coward does not retaliate because he is afraid, he does not dare to protest, but deceives himself and tries to deceive others by saying that he does not act because he believes that forgiveness is the greatest virtue. One can deceive the world, but the inner divine Being who sees everything, knows everything, and hears everything cannot be deceived.

The way, then, is to cultivate and promote these gunas in their natural succession. Rajas should be controlled by sattwa, just as tamas should be controlled by rajas. When the predominance of sattwa is gained, one enjoys wonderful peace and calm. But even that is not the final stage. Sattwa, like the other two, belongs to prakriti. The goal is to transcend prakriti and attain the full consciousness and realization of purusha. It does not require so much endeavor and struggle to transcend sattwa as it does to control tamas or rajas. Sattwa is like a calm and steady fire; as soon as the last log is burnt no desire remains to put more on, and naturally the fire will go out. Sattwa exhausts itself by working out of its own power, and eventually leads the soul toward that transcendental stage which is beyond the influence of prakriti.

By their food preferences, general characteristics and manners, dress, and religion and ethics, these three types are recognized and distinguished one from the other. By controlling and diverting these external tendencies, one can promote and purify the inner gunas. One food naturally appeals to a tamasic person, another to a rajasic, and still another to a sattwic. If gradually a tamasic type tries to create a taste for rajasic food, it will be found within a short time that the person has become rajasic by nature. The same is true about dress and general characteristics.

There have been numerous illustrations of this law in the lives of great men. In order to accomplish their mission, some great spiritual masters had to adopt certain rajasic methods, but such is the influence of the gunas that even they were caught in the trap. For a long time it was very difficult for them, saintly though they were, to come out of that net. There is the story of a great master who for the good of humanity had to accept the office of a king. At first he thought that as long as he knew the truth, what difference could it make if externally he lived like a king or a beggar? Living in the palace, the royal environment, food, dress, and living, gradually influenced him and degraded his guna. He became an out-and-out rajasic and forgot his higher spiritual qualities. His disciples, realizing the truth, wanted to rescue their teacher from that stage of bondage; therefore, one of them approached the king and pointed out to him how he was entangled. But such is the influence of rajas that even the *saint* could not see that he was bewildered. The king scornfully dismissed his disciple without accepting any of his advice. However, the disciples did not give up, but held a conference to find the proper remedy. One experienced student suggested, "He has been constantly eating rajasic food; if you can manage somehow to keep him on a pure sattwic diet for a while, it will awaken in him his lost sattwic qualities." Whereupon one of the disciples disguised himself as a dealer in food and told the chef of the palace that he would supply the king with special delicacies of rare variety, should he care to try them. The chef examined the food and found that it was all right, and served it to the king. The king seemed to like the food and gradually began to crave it. When that was accomplished, the disciple stopped the supply. The king missed his favorite dish and wanted to know why it was not served. The chef told him how the strange food dealer had appeared, and disappeared again, and that no one else knew where to get that food. The king insisted on seeing the person who had brought the food. To his utmost surprise one of his own disciples appeared as the food dealer. The king this time realized his own condition fully as soon as he was told by the disciple; and immediately throwing off the power of rajas, he walked out of the palace, the holy man again.

Illustrations of this kind are plentiful in Hindu literature. It is for this reason that particular attention is paid by the Hindu to the question of his food. If he is fastidious and sometimes fanatical about his food, there is a deep meaning behind it. It is a pity indeed, that very often the spirit becomes lost and that people adhere foolishly to mere forms! However, by changing the choice, liking, and taste in dress, food, enjoyment, pastimes, and things of that nature, one can gradually improve one's spiritual personality.

I shall formulate some of the characteristics of these different gunas in regard to the most prominent features of human life:

Religion and ethics. The ethical and religious ideal and expression of a sattwic is universal, tolerant, peaceful, spontaneous, and unostentatious; that of a rajasic is self-righteous, aggressive, tumultuous, superficial, and ostentatious; while that of a tamasic is narrow, superstitious, full of fear, enforced by compulsion, cruel, and queer.

Manners and conduct. The general expression, characteristics, and manners of these three types are different. A sattwic agent in his general manners is deep, sure, calm, compromising, enduring, steady, and true; a rajasic is over-enthusiastic, boisterous, fickle, changeable, domineering, unsteady, and impatient; whereas a tamasic is callous, indifferent, careless, inaccurate, clumsy, and cold.

Food. In the choice of food, the natural taste of a sattwic is for fresh, natural, mild, wholesome, pure, clean, moderate, and soothing food, as well as for that obtained by not causing pain or injury to any being in this world. The food of a rajasic agent is concocted, unnatural, exciting, alluring, pungent, and obtained by causing pain, injury, and harm to others. Tamasic food is characterized as stale, putrid, unclean, impure, repulsive, and immoderate.

Dress. A sattwic agent likes the dress that is appropriate, clean, neat, proportionate, aesthetic, unpretentious, and modest. The rajasic taste is superfluous, brilliant, gaudy, colorful, exciting, ostentatious, and immodest. Tamasic taste is characterized by slovenliness, carelessness, lack of proportion, uncleanliness, queerness, and lack of all aesthetic sense whatsoever.

By controlling these standards and by accepting as a matter of discipline a higher set of expressions, one can promote the desired guna. If a tamasic person wants to advance, he will do very well by choosing the food, dress and other expressions of rajas whereby he will gradually unfold its inner qualities. In the next step, let him change it for sattwa, by choosing again corresponding food, dress, and manners. It is a well-known psychological fact that by imitating some of the modes, manners, and customs of a higher order, one gradually develops inwardly those higher qualities.

The story is told of a fowler who used to hunt the birds and beasts of the forest. Nearby was a lake in which many aquatic birds like ducks and swans flocked together. The hunter tried to shoot them, but so alert were the birds that before he could come within range with his arrows, they would sense his approach and fly away. Never could he shoot a single bird in that lake. One day he noticed a holy man coming to bathe in that lake; but the birds did not take to flight; instead, they flocked around him, some sitting on his body with him patting them. Seeing that, the hunter thought that he also would dress as a holy man, go to the lake, and catch the birds. He approached the water with grain in his hand and called the birds. Seeing that the birds came and were very friendly to him, he did not feel the desire to hurt them. He thought he would catch them later. Doing the same thing day after day, he absolutely forgot his idea of killing them. One day the thought occurred to him that if by mimicking a holy man he could gain the confidence and friendship of all the dumb animals, how much more wonderful it would be if he could actually become holy. He worked hard to become sattwic—and never did he forsake the holy robe.

Begin by imitating the great in their mode of life. Gradually you will become confirmed and fixed in strength, purity, peace, and poise. Finally the stage will come when you will transcend all the gunas and enjoy transcendental rest, peace, and bliss of divine perfection in samadhi.

Three Key Answers to Three Key Questions

Gerald Heard

I

THERE IS NO more striking way in which the teaching of the saints reaches our hearts than in their sudden answers to really searching questions. Three of such answers are given in the following lines. It should be possible to make a collection of such pointers as might be of great value to souls who happen to have reached some turning point in their lives. The three authorities here quoted are very different, yet their replies all give the sense of authenticity and applicability—they are wide and at the same time instant.

The first to be quoted is Thomas Aquinas. He is thought of as the supreme schoolman—the strange medieval brain that could best play that odd form of verbal chess whereby you mated each other with syllogisms and gave much display of allowing your opponent to be answered, but in matter of fact never yielded him the slightest concession on any of the issues debated. The whole thing was a foregone conclusion. But Thomas was, in spite of his occupation—which included that of a diplomat—a saint—one who was always breathless spiritually because he never could breathe in deeply enough of the atmosphere of the soul for lack of which we are always suffocating and most of us in coma. Thomas at the end of the mass in St. Nicholas Church in Naples on St. Nicholas' Day, as he celebrated, saw; and after a silence of days was at last willing to say why he had ceased to write his *Summa*: "Because what I have seen makes all that I have written mere chaff." And when he had said that he was silent again and after a few weeks he was released. The veil, the membrane of the mind-body through which the soul can at best but breathe with pain, was at last removed.

We are told that once he was asked, "How can I love God?" He replied, "Will to love Him." The answer is as searching as it is simple. The problem of loving God is very real. The soul knows that it must do so, if ever it is to escape its deadly captivity to the self. But the love of God is different from any other love. The two loves we know are of persons and things. Things we love by interest —which means by so penetrating their nature that we understand them. We cannot take that kind of interest in God for we can never hope to understand Him. There is the intellectual love of God but that has nothing to do with the analytic method that has yielded such remarkable results in our handling of inanimate nature and such ludicrous results in theology—the sad pretense at a science, which produces only greater confusion of the mind and enmity in the heart. We cannot then love God as we love things.

Our only other method of human love is our love for persons. Again we love very largely because we think we understand our friend. Most affection is little lasting because we find that our knowledge was inaccurate. But we have, if we are patient and have a real need for affection—and not merely wish to have someone listen to us—quite extensive opportunities of understanding one another. We are very much the same—much more than our egotism lets us allow. And being gregarious creatures we have to depend largely on one another. Though then affection is always snapping it is always being spun again— we are like spiders in that respect. And of course in all human affection there is some wish for return. Mother love which used to be thought so selfless has now won the title of smother love.

Of course, because the above are our only two ways of human loving we cannot begin by loving God except from motives in which these two urges are paramount—we hope to gain a return; we hope to understand. Yet everyone realizes the hard truth in Spinoza's famous saying: "He who would love God must not expect God to love him."

There is, however, a third faculty in man beside the two others of interest and affection; there is the will. True, you cannot ever wholly separate the three basic faculties. But it is possible to recognize that one or the other does take the lead in any enterprise of behavior. As we may be first touched by a person and then become interested in him, and contrariwise we may be interested in a thing—an art or science and then become devoted to it —so the will may be the starter. True, the will very seldom is the initiator in anything that has to do with our life in this world; it comes in afterwards to give us persistence. We start because, as we say, our interest was caught or we were touched. In fact, we were passive at the beginning; only after, and to keep us going, did the will take over.

But as God is not to be understood—as our minds can understand—or to be loved in the possessive way that our hearts naturally like to love—there is then only one way to love Him truly and that is as Thomas says, through the will, by willing it. That is of course not an irrational act. As the Christian church has held, the existence of God can be deduced. By the balance of probabilities—which is the basis of all our rational acts—it is more likely than not that the supreme Being does exist. But it is hard to love a deduction or indeed to have any devotion toward a plus balance of probability. But that again does not mean that one ought not. One may experience rightly some guilt because of one's inability to feel either affection or vivid interest in the Being Who, though He be incomprehensible and is not for our convenience, can nevertheless be argued to be worthy of adoration. We may know we ought to love Bach's *B-Minor Mass*, but because our musical taste is very poor we may only feel boredom, yet not ashamedly. Therefore, after we have discovered first about God, that His existence can be deduced, and next about ourselves that we cannot love in any human way a deduction, we find out thirdly, that we have a faculty that just fits our very awkward need—*we have the will.*

We don't like using the will for two reasons: in the first place, it is tiring; and in the second, when we use it we don't seem—at least for a long while—to get any results— either outward or inward. The will is, always, for us in the future tense. Inwardly when we use the will we don't get that warm sensation that rises from the movement of the feelings. We have little or no sensation when the will works and often when we do have a sensation it is far from pleasant—we feel we are committed, that we have foolishly trapped ourselves. Nevertheless, we know that acts of the will are our supreme human endowment—the one way we ever get control over ourselves or our environment. In a piece of doggerel which shows better than worthy verse a great Victorian poet's real conviction and probably acute regret, Tennyson wrote:

> O well for him whose will is strong
> He will not have to suffer long.

The way to enlightenment and liberation is through acts of the will—there is no other. We find ourselves a mass of fantasy and wishful thinking—and so we shall end in the anecdotage of senescence unless we have painfully compacted that mush, by acts of will, into a firm one-pointed consciousness by the time we are old. For whether there is a God or not, or whether we can love Him or not, there is no escaping the fact that this world is so made that we can will and out of our will a consistent consciousness can be made. But if we try to get our wish we shall end at best disillusioned—at worst in complete fantasy.

The human will is then the specific faculty whereby man gets into touch with the supreme Being. "Thy will be done," as Eckhart says, is the one complete and all-powerful prayer. "But I can't go on saying that," is the usual answer and a fair one. If we think that we are simply saying encore to the infinite, our part becomes a little otiose. He does not need our aid, still less our applause to encourage Him to do what He is always intending and can never be turned from.

It is here that faith comes in—the naked faith of which the masters of prayer so often speak. We make an act of faith that when we exercise our will and intend that we shall will only what God wills then something actually does happen. We will and thereafter don't feel or speak or behave a whit the better. "Nothing has happened," says the ordinary consciousness. "Had anything taken place I should have felt the effect." Yet we know that when the high nonsensuous consciousness works, our everyday consciousness is utterly unaware of it. While you are actually doing it you will have no feeling of any sort to guide you when you have "hit" right and when you have missed. We know that God is regarding us and that we can regard Him. When then we bring ourselves into an act of relationship with Him by willing that His will be ours we are like a patient who puts himself into the focus of an X ray. He will feel nothing or see nothing while the operation is on. And not for some days will he experience any improvement. He might say, even when the improvement comes, "As I saw nothing to account for it when being given the so-called treatment, what beneficial effect I now experience may just as likely be due to some natural improvement and have nothing to do with this theory of invisible radiation."

But this illustration makes the relationship easier than it actually is. We know that God is confronting us; we know by deduction that as He exists we do come into relationship with Him whenever we make an act of the will to do so. But that is all. As to how He will act, when and where, we are of course always in the dark—the dark of blind faith. T. H. Huxley used to speak of life being played by each of us being confronted by a "veiled antagonist" on the other side of the board. The simile is a telling one—one anyone with the slightest experience of prayer knows to be descriptive of much of the time spent in prayer. In chess the greater the master with which one is confronted the more certain one may be that his moves will leave one in the dark. One may be sure only of two things—that every time I move, without exception a move of reply will be made, and secondly, every one of those moves is directed to take away all my freedom to move. Yet even here the analogy is far too feeble. For the best chess master has a finite mind and must play a game confined within the simple rules of the game, a game which is to end with one of the antagonists unable to move. The game the soul plays with its Maker is not only played with an infinite opponent, whose resources are inexhaustible, but also the aim of His "play" is not to take away the soul's freedom but to restore that freedom to it and to keep on so doing until at length the soul has won the power to retain it. Even if we were allowed to view the "board" entire—instead of through the slit aperture of what we call the present moment—how could we hope to understand at each move, or a whole lifetime of moves, the strategy of the Master?

We are therefore confined to the one exercise which is germane to our attempt—our intention to love God if we only knew how. We can and must keep on making these blind acts of the will, knowing that to each of these openings of the soul by the soul God responds by a reply of infinite inscrutable aptitude. Of course it is not easy—perhaps it is the hardest thing in the whole of our lives. For it means that we must never complain—which is with us even a stronger passion than our appetite to enjoy. It means in the end we shall know that there is no chance or accident because we can now practice the constant presence of God. And that end is far off, not because it is not rationally obvious, but because the nearer we get to really willing to do God's will the purer the opportunities He can and will give us of so doing. At the beginning He mixes the satisfaction of our desires with the performance of His intention. So people feel we are something of a success—of course a very nice one, but we *are* lucky and religion is something that the ordinary man might well invest in—it pays. Then that goes and we fall back on a less obvious aim; we have to comfort ourselves that at least we are resigned and are growing in virtue through the way we accept our failure. Then that goes, too. Like Job, the soul has to yield its last desperate cry, "I will not let mine integrity go from me," and can only mutter, "Yea, though he slay me, yet will I trust in him." For at the worst in the deepest darkness, the polar facts remain. God is and nothing that can happen to my fortunes alters the facts which show deductively that the supreme Being exists.

And the other fact is that I have a will. Though that will may produce no results, I can keep on making acts with it. My holding on to my intention or my surrender of my intention—those two facts have really no more to do with whether I succeed in carrying out my will than has the existence of God to do with whether He comes to my aid at the time and in the way that would soothe my feelings. It seems clear then that Thomas Aquinas' saying is true and apt. It is hard but it is the precise answer to the pressing question, the most pressing question in the whole of life: How shall I love God?

II

The second of the three key questions asked of masters of spirituality is: How shall I find God when I have lost Him?

We have been told that we love by wishing it, by the will. This advice when it is followed leads inevitably to our "getting results." We find that something has begun to happen. It may be what we hoped and wished. It may not be. But it will be something that intensely interests us. We may be able to describe it by the terms others have used. We may not be able to describe it at all.

One thing, however, is so probable that it may be said to be almost certain. We shall begin to think that what we have found, however dim and odd it is and however hard to tell anyone else of, is something that we have gained for good. We may say that we are converted for life, that we "have a new heart"; or we may say we have found the autotherapy that suits us at last, that we do know ourselves and have penetrated down to self-knowledge and interior peace. One thing we are sure of is that we shall never lose this state and go back to what we were before, any more than we shall once again become an adolescent. Indeed one of the surest symptoms of this state is that we feel very mature, really grown up, rather solemn, quietly assuredly rational, patient with others who seem to be curiously unsure. In short, we are in a state of self-contained discreet self-satisfaction.

Then it goes. We may do something that accounts for this. We may have done nothing in particular. Just being comfortable in the way described above seems enough— and certainly it should be—to lose us our modest complacency. Then the discomfort may well be intense. We had become used to a certain experience and that experience not only freed us from a lot of rather silly and some harmful ways we had of killing time and soothing our sense of futility, before we found this other way. That experience made us able to entertain ourselves and not be frightened or disgusted at ourselves, as we had never been able to do and to be before. If religion is, as Dr. Whitehead used to say, "What a man does with his solitude," this new exercise of using the will to make acts of comprehensive interior attention certainly made loneliness more interesting than most company. But now we have to own that we are in a terrible muddle because, having thought we have found God for good, we now have to own that we have lost Him.

If we have been having feelings—however quiet and refined—the glow has gone out of them. If we have been enjoying thoughts that seemed to clinch matters—we find that the neat bindings have become loose. Eckhart gave the answer to the question: What am I to do when I find that I have lost God? as follows: Go back to where you last had Him. Eckhart does not seem to have blamed the person who asked. He seems to have taken for granted that this losing was part of the process of learning—as the lung has to empty to take a new breath, as the mind when learning a language seems to have phases of forgetting before going on to a new and wider grasp of remembering. The author of the *Imitation of Christ* certainly thought these fluctuations were unavoidable, and the author of the *Cloud of Unknowing* in one of his shorter works likens them to the tidal and wave conditions that a voyager on the sea must be prepared to find and in which he must learn to handle his ship.

The Desert Fathers held strongly that the short prayer pierces heaven. As sustained pressure of unwavering attention is impossible to most of us, we must and can by a series of blows, or lance thrusts as the *Cloud of Unknowing* calls the process, pierce for moments into that upper atmosphere. And, though we cannot stay there we can bring back something that makes us more resolved to continue striving, to cause what has still to be only an instant, to become eternal.

Certainly the time when anyone never loses hold on God would seem to be equated with the time when they have attained constant practice of the presence, and surely that must be very close to the unitive state. Father Baker notes, with that curiously pleasant diagnostic detail he employs, that the soul was bound in the twenty-four hours to go through a series of such dislocations, interruptions of its current from its source. He thought that for twenty minutes after a meal it was not possible to retain the awareness of the presence of God and that sleep generally "de-ordinated" the attention. Perhaps some people would deny that—but he certainly had much experience and the state that he was referring to was probably a very distinct and clear condition of recollectedness or to use a favorite word of his, "abstraction."

Here it seems interesting to note that man would appear to be a creature whose consciousness is an "alternating current" rather than a continuous one. We are tidal creatures. There seem to be in the daily cycle three such rhythms and each one of them may—maybe should—strain or even detach our hold on the unseen eternal. There is the tide of sleep-waking, the wave of the diet-nutritional rhythm, and the ripple of the breath. Perhaps behind that again is the heartbeat. Each of these sway and swing the frame of mind and angle of thought and base of feeling out of its position and throw it into another. May it not be that this is a necessary part of our training in achieving constancy of consciousness? Even if we let go we are free to catch hold again before we have been swept too far from our moorings. And if we do not let go, the strain, like the gentle pull on the thread when it is being spun, gives us tensile strength. Consciousness has continually to be reminded that it must keep conscious or it ceases to be so. Of course, at the beginning we all know how slow we are to wake up to the fact that we have fallen asleep. That is the great value of following a rule of life. For then when we have fallen to sleep round comes a duty, an "office," a call to prayer and, though we feel as uninclined to it as we feel uninclined to get up out of a warm bed at two o'clock in the morning, we have to do it whether we like or no. However badly we do is better than letting the whole thing slide because "one does not feel in the mood." Of course one does not; the mood has gone and it is for us to make the next one.

The spiritual life is then for all beginners and perhaps for all the middling lot which the Western mystics call "proficients" and we might term "professionals," a constant and ever more rapid recollection. We are continually pulling ourselves together because we have in the stream and fluctuation of time and under the wash of events, begun to fall to pieces and to become completely unraveled. Progress in the spiritual life, one supposes, might be gauged by the speed with which one catches up with the unraveling before too many stitches have been dropped and unknitted. Most people find that they are getting a little handier at the task as the years go by, if they really think the matter is important. Of course, if one lets oneself become badly "de-ordinated," engrossed in some addiction of the body, some anxiety of possessions, some desire for social approval, then that is as though one's knitting had been caught in the paws of an extremely agile and ill-willed monkey. Before the remnants can be recovered little may be left of long periods of patient work. François de Sales himself said he might easily lose what had taken him many years to work—in a quarter of an hour: one outburst of hastiness or of what the world would call righteous anger might prove fatal to the endeavor of a large part of a lifetime. It appears that our knitting is always done by chain stitch and not lock stitch.

But however far we have become unraveled there is

always this advice to help us back. We have lost God, but once we had Him, not of course in actuality or we would never have lost Him, but in potentiality; we were on the way, on the trail. All we have to do is to trace back to that moment and there start again. Of course, though the advice is clear, it is hard. Discouragement keeps on tempting us to cheat and advises us to try and start where we are. That will not do. Recollection is, in one of its meanings, remembering. We have, like senile people in their talking, wandered, and we must go back to the last time we were coherent. We must trace back to where the deviation and the dissipation began.

But as we continue, we do find that we do not have to go quite so far back, each time we slip, as we had to do earlier. That does not mean that the task gets easier. For the goal is constant recollectedness. We have to work up the whole series of approaches that lead to perfect instantaneity. When we are past being swept away by passions, then we have to learn to correct the tidal displacement of mood and consciousness made by the tide of sleep. Some Sufis say that it takes several years before the sleep-mind will accept the attitude of the waking-mind. And even when it does, most of us know that it is still very capricious. Sometimes in sleep we can control the dream, sometimes we can detach ourselves from it, knowing that both dream and earthly waking are dreams. But most of the time we are its object and not it ours. Then there is becoming aware of the optimum psychophysical lucidity which appears somewhere in the alimentary cycle. Swami Brahmananda thought that the best condition for meditation was when the stomach was partly filled. Sir John Woodroffe quotes a Tantric authority saying that the stomach should not be wholly empty because this produces a slight but definitely distracting tension in the mind. And of course about the care of the breath so that the lucidity that opens between each inhalation and exhalation may be caught: about this Sanskrit authorities have told us much.

Every one of these "dips" after a "crest" will tend to "ebb us out" until we lose touch with the shore we should hold to. But Eckhart seems to teach, and experience would seem to confirm, that if we would have the courage to trace back the moment we discovered our loss, we should be able to find the spot where it began and once there we could start anew.

Again, of course, the temptation to discouragement appears. We feel we cannot go on this hindsight search time and again. We fear we are making no progress if we spend nearly all our time going back. But this may be a complete misapprehension of our process and progress. For each of these returns is really far more like a zigzag ascent in which, it is true, after going right we then turn left, but always the traverse whether to right or left goes up and each drive is on a higher level than the one before. By this going back we are learning two essential things; self-knowledge—the structure of the human mind and the kind of things that throw it off its rational attentions; and further, we are learning true humility. This humility is the real stuff, for it leads to true discrimination so that at last we can make the distinction between ourselves and the thing that is always straying. When we reach that stage it would appear that we discover that the straying part of ourselves loses its power to wander. We begin to make the final recollection, we at last "come to ourselves"; we remember who we are. And once we do that the journey is over. For the whole notion that we were far away from our source and goal was the illusion and the distance we were from God was never more than the depth of our illusory self-love.

III

The first of the three basic questions which we have been asking is the question of a devotionalist. And the answer is given by a devotionalist. For, in spite of all his scholastic rationalism Aquinas was a spiritual lover, devoted to his Christ Jesus. Beside this first question the second is psychological. For Eckhart was perhaps the most jnana of all the Western mystics of whom we have adequate record. The first question tells us how to love God —when we have made up our mind that it is this that we would rather do than anything else. The second tells us what we may do when we find that in spite of our intention to "adhere," we have lost contact with the eternal Being who is our life.

The third question is practical. It is then, as should be, answered by a man who was the most practically successful of all the saints canonized by the church of Rome.

By founding the Jesuits, Ignatius Loyola gave back to the Roman church half the territory and all the intellectual prestige that Rome had lost to Protestantism. The non-Christian world was reassaulted with a vigor that none of the other founders of the orders had been able to mobilize. Indeed, the missionary attack compared with that which the Church had not been able to summon since it made peace through Constantine with the imperial power. After Ignatius' work took shape, to be a scholar and a devout Christian became no longer a paradox but something of a commonplace. Jesuits made a new architecture for Europe—tired of medieval gothic and Renaissance pedantry—captured the teaching profession and, in a little while, were makers of astronomic instruments for the Emperor of China—who was therefore not unimpressed with their metaphysics—and founders of a communist paradise for the preagriculturists of the Paraná, who were captivated by their teachers' wonderful skill in music.

Ignatius knew what he had done and what was growing from the plan he had laid down. Working up from his psychological instrument, the *Exercises;* by the selection of lieutenants who could supplement his genius; by adopting the techniques of militarism to the needs of ecclesiasticism, he had already made a company whose head he named the general—and whose headship he accepted for himself—a generalship commanding such complete obedience over men of outstanding ability that the Jesuit general was soon called the Black Pope.

The actual Pope, however, was as capable as Ignatius of perceiving what a mixed blessing such an offer of service could prove to be. Ignatius himself was far too capably complex a character not to have many enemies. One of them was elected Pope when the Society was yet young, yet had shown its mettle. When Ignatius heard of the election, he said (and it is obvious he was no more a rhetorician than a coward) his "bones became like water." The self-control of this man had become so complete that his closest associates bore witness that when he was merry they never knew whether he felt cheerful, when he showed black anger if he was inwardly the slightest disturbed, when he was peaceful that there might not be despair or bitter pain in his heart. This self-statement of his condition is therefore valuable and need not be doubted. The destruction of the Order was probably the one thing that could really affect this utterly mortified nature.

Yet when someone with more psychological curiosity than consideration asked, "What will you do if the Pope dissolves the Order?" he replied, "One quarter of an hour in orison and it would then be all the same." Again, it does not seem possible to doubt his word. And when we examine the reply we see there is about it a realism and definitude which makes it not only convincing—carrying its own authenticity in the very style of it—but also arresting and informative. For in the first place it is an answer to a question so general and so grim—and yet so specifically aimed at those who have tried to be of service —that nearly everyone has heard it asked yet hardly dared face it. Even the good too often take refuge in the plea (so little substantiated by history) "God could not let His work (which of course I have been doing) come to naught!" What would you do, what could you do, if your lifework—in which you had sublimated your passions, sunk your possessions, and exchanged your pretensions— should be put to death and you, poor pointless thing, left to live on? Every man of energy must know how helpless he is should his work, the meaning of his social, economic, and physical being, be taken utterly from him and he become an unwanted failure. And in the second place the answer is an exact, diagnostic reply. Ignatius knows what is at stake, what the failure of the Society will mean for him, because of what it will mean to his loyalist friends and for the Church which he adored and which was still fighting an undecided counterattack. Ignatius was not a contemplative. His vocation was action, his call to save his communion.

Ignatius does not, then, play the stoic or any of the roles of the superior person. He does not dismiss the painfully apt curiosity telling the inquirer not to be inquisitive and so wrap up his wound in the mantle of offended dignity. Nor does he make light of it all. He might have carried conviction, if he had laughed it off. He had proved his toughness, yes, and his capacity for humor, so that he might have felt it wise to say that it would really make no difference. Or he might have said, "God will never let it happen." Again he had shown that his belief that he was doing God's will was rigid enough to have made such a statement credible. He does not use any of the great clichés. He gives a timetable. And that is characteristic of him. For like all moderns he was interested in time in a way that the medieval was not. His *Exercises* show that— so many weeks to have acquired this attitude toward hell, so many to gain that toward heaven.

So when he says "one quarter of an hour" there can be little doubt he means exactly what he says. Ignatius prayed by the clock. He was making a careful estimate and calculation between two things and the distance between them. He knew he loved his work and the extent and weight of the hopes he had for its success. He knew it was his life as far as he, an individual, had any reason for living. But he also knew how he was involved, engrossed. This was a certain degree of real discrimination—the power to see the two things—the work and the person who worked—Ignatius Loyola. And the being that looked on and saw both the Society of Jesus and its founder, with an equal detachment—that being it was who could see what to do with Ignatius, what must be done with the busy passionate Spaniard, if that creature's reason for living was suddenly taken from it.

The central being Ignatius never quite lost touch with; though he evidently by his own words did not always keep in close contact with Him. In fact, the distance that Ignatius found was separating the two sides of himself at the crisis in his life was precisely fifteen minutes. He was out from the shore, away from his base a quarter of an hour. Give him that time and he would know what to do with it. In that little space he would be able—he had evidently done so before—to pay in the slack of the line that kept him and the Atman apart. Then, once that contact was really made, once the eternal life had absorbed the temporal, the fluctuations in the waves of circumstance would make no more difference to him than billows of mist, sweeping past a walker, can make him sway. "Orison" was for Ignatius what we should probably call induced contemplation, that total awareness of reality which many who have practiced meditation can after some time summon by an act of the will. In Ignatius' case it was not an instantaneous act. We may venture to think that in Ruysbroeck—to mention another Westerner—it would have been if not instantaneous at least a matter of seconds. Ignatius lived too busy a life to be in immediate contact, but—and in this he differs from many of our busy churchmen of today—he did not neglect to keep in mind the time it would take him to recover the essential contact. And, of course, he was aware that each day, by his contemplative prayer—which we are told he never neglected—he brought himself back to that distance. Had he found that his distance was increasing then there is little doubt he would have put himself into "retreat." Ignatius had no intention of gaining the whole world and losing his own soul. The quarter of an hour was as much "free play" or "slack line" as he allowed himself.

Ignatius' reply is then very germane for those—the vast majority—who feel that they must live active lives but find, in Father Baker's phrase, that that life does "de-ordinate" them. Does not the answer to this very common state we have all experienced lie in Ignatius' advice? Know how far you are out; take care never to be beyond where you can recollect yourself. Day by day—three times a day—make at least an honest checkup, and if you find the distance between you and your anchorage is increasing, take more time till you are once more within sufficient distance to make yourself fast and secure should the wind come down and the sea rise. This checkup Ignatius calls the "examin." It does not take long—one honest glance will show how much one has drifted in the three or four hours one has been attending to surface things. Of course, the necessary rehauling may take considerable time and exertion.

A similar illustration of this practical power in an "active" is given at the beginning of a Japanese monk's account of his penetration into Tibet, when that country was closed to outsiders. A Tibetan abbot, whose big monastery lay near the frontier, had permitted a foreign pilgrim to enter. The Lhasa government, learning this, not only degraded the abbot—which meant that he lost a powerful and dignified position—but condemned him to be drowned in the almost freezing waters of the source stream of the Brahmaputra River. He was taken in his criminal garb to be drowned. When they arrived where he was to be bound and sunk in the stream he made the Ignatian statement, "Permit me to read over slowly to myself three times the *Diamond Sutra* and then it will be all right." The time was permitted him. He then with complete composure let himself be lowered with a heavy stone round him, into the stream. After some time the body was raised. He came to life again. He quietly submitted to be once more immersed. A second time he was raised, only to be found once more alive. Only at the third time was his release completed.

So many people today talk of Brother Lawrence and the continual practice of the presence of God, and when they do so they often disparage any regular times of prayer and meditation. They say to spend all one's time with exercises, or even a good part of it, is both pretentious and unnecessary. And yet we know that when many such good social workers meet disaster their conduct does not differ—for it cannot—very much from that of the most casual liver. They are still desiring the fruit of their works and have not achieved karma yoga. But they may be right that they cannot give their lives to trying to achieve a constant contemplative state. They must also realize, if they read Brother Lawrence with the slightest real care, that the state he reached was very advanced and had taken a life of austerity, which they would consider unhealthy.

May not the middle step between that Carmelite perfection and the way that most of us feel compelled to live, lie in the Ignatian advice, "Know how far you are out; never let it be more than a quarter of an hour; and see daily that you keep that distance—see that it is not growing!" Then when ruin and death come to complete our detachment, they will serve this, their intended purpose, and we too shall be able to add to the authentic record of essential advice, "Fifteen minutes in prayer and it will be all the same. The one remains, the many change and pass."

Notes on Zen

Aldous Huxley

WE ARE ACCUSTOMED in religious literature to a certain large solemnity of utterance. God is sublime; therefore the words we use about God should also be sublime. So runs the unexpressed argument in favor of the grand style. In practice, however, it happens not infrequently that sublimity of utterance is carried to self-stultifying lengths. For example, at the time of the great Irish potato famine of a century ago, a special prayer was composed for recitation in all the churches of the Anglican communion. The purpose of this prayer was to entreat the Almighty to check the ravages of the blight which was destroying the Irish potato crop. But from the outset the word "potato" presented a difficulty. Quite obviously, in the eyes of early Victorian divines, it was too low, common, and proletarian to be pronounced in a sacred place. The horribly vulgar fact of potatoes had to be concealed in the decent obscurities of periphrasis, and consequently God was requested to do something about an abstraction, sonorously called the succulent tuber. The sublime had soared up into the empyrean of the ludicrous.

In similar circumstances, we may guess, a Zen master would also have avoided the word "potato," not because it was too low for use in a religious context, but because it was too conventional and respectable. Not succulent tuber, but plain, monosyllabic "spud" would have been his idea of a suitable alternative.

Sokei-an, the Zen master who taught in New York from 1928 to the time of his death in 1945, conformed to the literary traditions of his school. When he issued a religious journal, the title he chose for it was *Cat's Yawn*. This studiedly absurd and antipompous name is a reminder

399

to all who may be concerned that words are radically different from the things they stand for; that hunger can be stayed only by real potatoes and not by even the loftiest verbiage about the succulent tuber; that mind, by whatever name we choose to call it, is always itself and cannot be known except through a kind of direct action, for which words are only a preparation and an incitement.

In itself the world is a continuum; but when we think about it in terms of words, we are compelled, by the very nature of our vocabulary and syntax, to conceive of it as a something composed of separate things and distinct classes. Working upon the immediate data of reality, our consciousness fabricates the universe we actually live in. In the Hinayana scriptures craving and aversion are named as the factors making for the pluralization of Suchness, the illusion of discreteness, egoity, and the autonomy of the individual. To these world-distorting vices of the will the Mahayana philosophers add the intellectual vice of verbalized thinking. The universe inhabited by ordinary, unregenerate people is largely homemade—a product of our desires, our hatreds, and our language. By self-denial a man can learn to see the world, not through the refracting medium of craving and aversion, but as it is in itself. ("Blessed are the pure in heart, for they shall see God.") By meditation he can bypass language—bypass it at last so completely that his individual consciousness, deverbalized, becomes one with the unitary consciousness of Suchness.

In meditation according to the methods of Zen, deverbalization of consciousness is achieved through the curious device of the koan. The koan is a paradoxical, even a nonsensical, proposition or question, upon which the mind is concentrated until, utterly thwarted by the impossibility of making sense out of a paralogism, it breaks through into a sudden realization that, beyond verbalized thinking, there exists another kind of awareness of another kind of reality. An example of the Zen method is supplied by Sokei-an in his brief essay, "Tathagata":

A Chinese Zen master was giving a tea party one freezing night. . . . Kaizenji said to his disciples: "There is a certain thing. It is as black as lacquer. It supports heaven and earth. It always appears in activity, but no one can grasp it in activity. My disciples, how can you grasp it?"
He was indicating the nature of *Tatha*, metaphorically of course, just as Christian ministers explain the attributes of God. . . .

The disciples of Kaizenji did not know how to reply. Then finally one of them, Tai Shuso by name, answered: "You fail to grasp it because you try to grasp it in motion."

He was indicating that, when he meditated in silence, Tathagata appeared within himself.

Kaizenji dismissed the tea party before it had really begun. He was displeased with the answer. If you had been his disciple, what answer would you have made so that the Master could have continued the tea party?

My own guess is that the tea party might have been prolonged, at least for a few minutes, if Tai Shuso had answered in some such way as this: "If I cannot grasp tatha in activity, then obviously I must cease to be *I*, so that tatha may be able to grasp this ex-me and make it one with itself, not merely in the immobility and silence of meditation (as happens to the arhats), but also in activity (as happens to the bodhisattvas, for whom samsara and nirvana are identical)." These, of course, are mere words; but the state described, or rather faintly hinted at, by these words would, if experienced, constitute enlightenment. And meditation upon the logically unanswerable question contained in the koan may suddenly take the mind beyond words to the condition of egolessness, in which tatha, or Suchness, is realized in an act of unitive knowledge.

The wind of the spirit bloweth where it listeth, and that which happens when free will collaborates with grace to achieve knowledge of Suchness cannot be theoretically foreknown, cannot be prejudged in terms of any system of theology or philosophy, cannot be expected to conform to any verbal formula. Experience is determined only by experience. In Zen literature this truth is expressed by calculatedly outrageous anecdotes about enlightened persons who make bonfires of the scriptures and even go so far as to deny that what Buddha taught deserves the name of Buddhism—for Buddhism is the unteachable, immediate experience of Suchness. A story illustrating another of the dangers of verbalization, namely, its tendency to force the mind into grooves of habit, is cited in *Cat's Yawn*, together with a commentary by Sokei-an.

One day when the monks were gathered in the Master's room, En Zenji asked Kaku this question: "Shaka and Miroku (i.e. Gotama Buddha and Maitreya, the future Buddha) are the slaves of another. Who is this other?"

Kaku answered: *"Ko Sho san, Koku Ri shi."* (Which means, "the third sons of the Ko and Sho families, and the fourth sons of the Koku and Ri families," a piece of nonsense signifying that the capacity to become identified with Suchness exists in every human being and that Gotama and Maitreya are what they are in virtue of being perfectly "the slaves" of that immanent and transcendent Buddha-Nature.)

The Master accepted his answer.

At that time Engo was the head of the monks of the temple. The Master related to him this incident. Engo said: "Pretty good, pretty good! But perhaps he hasn't yet grasped the real point. You shouldn't have given him your acknowledgment. Examine him again by a direct question."

When Kaku came into En Zenji's room the next day, the Zenji asked him the same question. Kaku replied: "I gave the answer yesterday."

The Master said: "What was your answer?"

"Ko Sho san, Koku Ri shi," said Kaku.

"No, no!" the Master cried.

"Yesterday you said 'Yes.' Why do you say 'No' today?"

"It was 'Yes' yesterday; but it is 'No' today," replied the Master.

On hearing these words Kaku was suddenly enlightened.

The moral of this story is that, in Sokei-an's words, "His answer fell into a pattern, a mold; he was caught by his own concept." And, having been caught, he was no longer free to become one with the freely blowing wind of Suchness. Any verbal formula—even a formula which correctly expresses the facts—can become, for the mind that takes it too seriously and idolatrously worships it as though it were the reality symbolized by the words, an obstacle in the way of immediate experience. To a Zen Buddhist the idea that a man can be saved by giving assent to the propositions contained in a creed would seem the wildest, the most unrealistic and dangerous of fancies.

Hardly less fantastic, in his eyes, would seem the idea that high feelings can lead to enlightenment, that emotional experiences, however strong and vivid, are the same as, or even remotely analogous to, the experience of Suchness. Zen, says Sokei-an, "is a religion of tranquility. It is not a religion which arouses emotion, causing tears to well from our eyes or stirring us to shout aloud the name of God. When the soul and the mind meet in a perpendicular line, so to speak, in that moment complete unity between the universe and the self will be realized." Strong emotions, however lofty, tend to emphasize and strengthen the fatal illusion of the ego, which it is the whole aim and purpose of religion to transcend. "Buddha taught that there is no ego either in man or in dharma. The term 'dharma' in this case denotes Nature and all the manifestations of nature. There is no ego in anything. Thus what is known as 'the two kinds of non-ego' means that there is no ego in man and no ego in things." From metaphysics Sokei-an passes to ethics. "According to his faith of non-ego," he asks, "how can we act in daily life? This is one of the great questions. The flower has no ego. In the spring it blooms, in the autumn it dies. The stream has no ego within it. The wind blows and waves appear. The river bed drops abruptly and there is a waterfall. We ourselves must really feel these things within ourselves. . . . We must realize by our own experience how this nonego functions within us. It functions without any hindrance, without any artificiality."

This cosmic nonego is the same as what the Chinese call Tao, or what the Christians call the indwelling spirit, with which we must collaborate and by which we must permit ourselves moment by moment to be inspired, making ourselves docile to Suchness in an unremitting act of self-abandonment to the order of things, to everything that happens except sin, which is simply the manifestation of egoity and must therefore be resisted and rejected. Tao, or nonego, or the divine immanence manifests itself on every level from the material to the spiritual. Deprived of that physiological intelligence which governs the vegetative functions of the body and through whose agency the conscious will is translated into action, lacking the aid of what may be termed "animal grace," we could not live at all. Moreover it is a matter of experience that the more the ego's superficial consciousness interferes with the workings of this animal grace, the sicker we become and the worse we perform all acts requiring a high degree of psychophysical co-ordination. The emotions connected with craving and aversion impair the normal functioning of the organs and lead, in the long run, to disease. Similar emotions and the strain which arises from the desire for success prevent us from achieving the highest proficiency not only in such complex activities as dancing, making music, playing games, doing any kind of highly skilled work, but also in such natural psychophysical activities as seeing and hearing. Empirically it has been found that malfunctioning of the organs can be corrected, and proficiency in acts of skill increased, by inhibition of strain and negative emotions. If the conscious mind can be trained to inhibit its own self-regarding activities, if it can be persuaded to let go and give up its straining for success, the cosmic nonego, the Tao that is immanent in all of us, can be relied upon to do what has to be done with something like infallibility. On the level of politics and economics the most satisfactory organizations are those which are achieved through "planning for unplanning." Analogously, on the psychophysical levels, health and maximum proficiency are achieved by using the conscious mind to plan its collaboration and its subordination to that immanent order of things which is beyond the scope of our personal planning and with whose workings our busy little ego can only interfere.

Animal grace precedes self-consciousness and is something which man shares with all other living beings. Spiritual grace lies beyond self-consciousness, and only rational beings are capable of co-operating with it. Self-consciousness is the indispensable means to enlightenment; at the same time it is the greatest obstacle in the way, not only of the spiritual grace which brings enlightenment, but also of the animal grace, without which our bodies cannot function efficiently or even retain their life. The order of things is such that no one has ever got anything for nothing. All progress has to be paid for. Precisely because he has advanced beyond the animal level to the point where, through self-consciousness, he can achieve enlightenment, man is also capable, through that same self-consciousness, of achieving physical degeneration and spiritual perdition.

One Element [1]

John van Druten

THERE IS NOTHING, perhaps, in the whole narrative of my personal history which would have seemed more improbable, had it been foretold to me twenty years ago, than the fact of my being where I am this morning: In a Vedanta temple in Southern California, about to deliver an address on the subject of religion. In those days, religion meant nothing to me; my attitude toward the world, my personal philosophy, if any, was what Aldous Huxley has called "the philosophy of meaninglessness." This was a philosophy based upon the concept that there was neither meaning nor purpose to human life, and that the world operated as a kind of accidental machine. There was neither plan nor principle to it, and the answer to the riddle of the universe was that there was no answer. That was the prevailing, I might almost say the fashionable philosophy of what may be called the younger artistic, intellectual, or pseudointellectual sets of the twenties; and Huxley himself, in his earlier writings, when that was his own philosophy as well, was very much our prophet. We would probably have named him as our "favorite author" in a confession album. It is interesting that so many of us should have followed him in his later development and his expounding of what he has called the perennial philosophy, the least hint of which, then, would have aroused in us either boredom or contempt.

There was another author whose influence in those days on the younger people of our kind was very great. It was no philosophy of meaninglessness that he preached; indeed, such a philosophy was wholly alien to his ideas, al-

[1] Given originally as an address.

though I am sure that few of us realized that fact. The quality in his work that attracted us was a ruthless, brisk iconoclasm; but in the noise of falling idols—which is always the pleasantest of sounds to adolescent ears—I think that we believed we were hearing the same message. It amazes me to reread Bernard Shaw today; to realize how much we missed, and how distressingly true it is that we get from books only what we want to find in them. There are whole passages over which the mind, if not the eye, of those days seems to have passed without even noticing that they were there. I can well remember the first appearance of a work called *The Adventures of the Black Girl in Her Search for God,* and my own dismissal of it as of small interest or importance because the subject matter held no interest for me then. Yet, in this book, Shaw himself comments on the disregard for the subject of metaphysics as an infallible symptom of a foolish and meretricious mind, damning all persons who, no matter what their worldly achievements may be, have never paused to ask themselves the basic question of what the world and the whole problem of living was really all about.

Leaving aside any question of religious belief on my own part, how could I (and I think I can speak for others of my generation as well) have read that passage from the pen of the great master, and continued happily with the younger Huxley? Huxley, himself, has partly answered this question in reference to the same period in his own development. In his book *Ends and Means* he refers to the question of whether or not the world possesses a meaning, and if so, of what is the nature of that meaning; and he says:

> This is a question which, a few years ago, I should not even have posed. For, like so many of my contemporaries, I took it for granted that there was no meaning. This was partly due to the fact that I . . . had motives for not wanting the world to have a meaning: consequently assumed that it had none, and was able without any difficulty to find satisfying reasons for this assumption. Most ignorance is vincible ignorance. We don't know because we don't want to know.

The motives to which he is referring were, of course, mainly selfish ones: promptings of the ego seeking to justify its cravings and attachments. Acquisitiveness and the desire for sexual liberty were strong motives, and so, too, for the artist, were vanity and self-importance. By and large, we all of us had motives, and to spare.

Since we believed in meaninglessness, then, because we desired it, what caused us to relinquish that desire? What first made us start accepting even the possibility that there might be more to it all than we had previously allowed ourselves to believe: that the world might be "about" something, after all: that there might be, not only for the world as a whole, but even, just conceivably, for each one of us as well, something that could be described as the Divine Will by which we are made and moved? That phrase, too, or its import, I could have found in the works of Bernard Shaw, in *Androcles and the Lion*, a play which, at that time, I regarded largely as an intellectual farce, and certainly never saw as containing any signposts toward a religious faith which any of us could share.

In that play, the young woman Christian martyr is being asked to save herself from the arena by sacrificing to the Pagan gods, being urged to realize that the name cannot matter if the offering in her own mind is being made to the true God. She cannot do this. She knows religion to be a great and uniting thing, no matter what its creed, but she knows, too, that the Romans have no religion and are asking her to bow before an iron statue that is the symbol of their own cruelty and hatred, and she would die rather than do it. This is the play that I regarded as a gay and frivolous entertainment only.

Now the play of *Androcles* was written in 1912, and its printed preface on "The Prospects of Christianity" is dated 1915. Those are significant dates; just before, and just after the beginning of the first World War. Was that, conceivably, what Shaw was talking about, and could the iron statue have been the iron god from the substance of whose body all the armaments, the weapons of death and destruction, were even then being fashioned? There was a time, not very much later, when it seemed so, when the threat of war appeared again. That time was in the thirties, and it was that threat, I think, which was largely responsible for, I will not call it the conversion, but at least the willing suspension of disbelief, that I have spoken of above. We suddenly found ourselves possessed by a new belief: a belief in pacifism: and, with it, by a need to find some justification, deeper than reason, for our holding that belief. The only justification, ultimately, seemed to be a religious one: at any rate, the only justification which was finally unarguable: the justification of a religious conviction.

It was obvious that the religion could not be of the kind that had been preached by the bishops and the lesser clergy in support of the last war, and would presumably be preached again in support of the next one. Just as the last war had caused a number of men and women to lose their faith in a God who was supposed to approve of it, so the threat of the next one caused a number to start searching for a God in whose name they could denounce it.

If all of this sounds deliberate, a form of rationalization which deliberately adopts a creed or a philosophy to bolster a belief of which the basic cause may have been only a personal sense of fear, we must remember that the philosophy of meaninglessness and our adherence to it had also sprung from the fact that it suited our books, providing a justification for our living as we wanted to live—selfishly, irresponsibly, identified with our own egos, their vanities, their material desires and cravings, in a world where all men were separate and individual. Under the threat of war, we were no longer able to live so. Perhaps that was what was wrong: survival, even if only a physical survival, was more important than pleasure: if the survival of *one* was to be assured, so must the survival of all. Perhaps, then, separativeness was not, after all, the rule of the universe: perhaps it was true that in some sense we were all brothers, sons of the same father.

It was in that moment, I think—the moment we were ready to assume that hypothesis, and to make no matter how timid an act of faith by proclaiming it—that we took the first plunge, or made the first slide, from the dry land of pure materialism into the water of the spiritual. And, just as it is rare that anyone who has ever learned to swim even a few strokes will be content to remain on dry land for the rest of his life, so it is rare, once the first intimations of the spirit have been accepted as being even possibly true, for the novitiate to return contentedly and permanently to his old world of materiality. He must venture forth again, even if only occasionally at first, into this new element in which he has so miraculously found that it is possible at least to move and keep afloat. Everything that swimmers have told him in the past, to which he has not listened, is suddenly proved to be true, or possibly true. Whether he will ever become a champion must depend on a great many factors, including—and indeed mainly—the strength of his desire, and the degree of his application; but from now on he can swim, and *must* swim. That, I think, is true of the religious life, with the saint or the mystic in the role of the champion; and the analogy suggests another, bearing the authority of Sir Thomas Browne who, I recently discovered, spoke of man as being "the great amphibium," implying, it was suggested in the essay in which I found the quotation, that man is, or should be capable of being, equally at home in both elements: land and water: body and spirit: time and eternity.

But as we go on with our swimming lessons we may well make a new discovery, depending on who was our swimming teacher: a discovery which, if we accept it, breaks down the analogy completely. The author of the essay to which I have just referred was Evelyn Underhill, the English woman writer on mysticism and the life of the spirit. Her creed was that of Anglo-Catholicism, and the distinction between the two elements, and the need for somehow reconciling them, would seem to be the basic tenet and problem of that creed, as indeed they are of most brands of Christianity. But many of us who had seen Christianity, at any rate in its more orthodox forms, invoked in support of war, had begun to suspect, or to learn, that it was just the conception upon which that analogy was based that had been responsible for most human ills and troubles—and for war, especially. The discovery to which I referred is the fact that both elements are ultimately the same, and that that fact is the meaning of life, and the purpose of life its realization. Not two elements, but one: not body *and* spirit, but spirit only. Not man praying to an external God, but man recognizing, or seeking to recognize, God as the ground or nature of his own being.

It would seem a long way from the philosophy of meaninglessness to this conclusion, and there are many roads by which it can be traveled, but the adherents to that philosophy have, I think, one advantage when they find themselves forsaking it for the perennial philosophy. They, at least, have no image (or no more than a vestigial and already rejected one) of an anthropomorphic God—an external God of attributes—to dislodge from their imaginations. To one raised as an orthodox Christian, God is very hard to conceive purely as spirit. The little one-letter word "a" sticks somehow in the memory. "God is a spirit," he has learned. That means a spirit, not a man:

not even with the form or appearance of a man: not even, perhaps, with any form at all—it is not too hard to go that far—but still a spirit *of* something; a spirit with qualities, such as goodness, love, mercy, and the like. But that is not what is meant by spirit, Brahman, principle, infinite mind, the infinite invisible, or the divine reality of the perennial philosophy. To one accustomed to such phrases as "the goodness of God," it is hard to make the transition to the conception which renders such phrases as apparently meaningless as "the appleness of an apple."

Yet is that last phrase wholly meaningless? Is it not even pregnantly significant, suggesting a quality in the apple that is in some way eternal, divorced from any values that it may have for the beholder, any question of its edibility, its place in a color scheme of decoration, its relation to anything but itself? In mediocre paintings of still life, the apples not infrequently evoke comments such as: "Really, they look good enough to eat," or "Can't you just feel how crisp they would be if you got your teeth into them?" But is there not another quality, for which the best name *might* be "appleness," with which the greatest painters have endowed the apples that they reproduced on canvas? Does one not, even, very occasionally, in a swift, sudden flash of revelation, catch it oneself in the apples of real life? It is an experience which everyone must have had in some form or other at some time, and I think that one is never quite sure just what it is that it betokens, but accepts it gratefully as having value of itself, and with the slightly bewildered sense of having stepped for an instant outside time into eternity.

Such an experience occurred to me about three years ago, and I tried the same morning to record it in a diary, hastily, with no attempt at good writing but in a form that was hardly more than a series of rough notes by which I would be able to recall it as it had seemed to me at the time of its happening, uncolored by any possible later memories of it as a memory. Here are the notes, just as I wrote them then:

It was in a drugstore in Beverly Hills, and I had just sat down to breakfast at the counter. Beside me sat a very large and very healthy man in work-clothes—a man in his forties, I would say—eating a very large and healthy breakfast of fried eggs, hot cakes, and potatoes. They looked good: *he* looked good, exuding an unconscious physical strength and well-being. The food looked good in the way that painted food in advertisements looks good.

Suddenly, I saw everything around me like that. A colored woman brought in a tray of raw hamburgers—round, pinky-gold pats—that looked inordinately appetizing. I looked at all the food, and it all had the same quality. The waitress, small and dumpy, was smiling and friendly; having served her customers, she looked around and asked, "Well, is everyone happy here?"

Everyone seemed to be. Each person, like the food, seemed *right* and meaningful. The fat, high-capped chef, tying on an apron that compressed him with its string like a bundle of laundry: all the customers: there was not one ugly person there. I don't mean that they were all good-looking—but that there was not one bad, or even stupid or irritating face among them. The whole scene looked as though it had been painted by a great and loving painter, who had given it its own and timeless values.

From there on, my notes go into an attempt to analyze the meaning of the experience which lasted, I would guess, about fifteen minutes in all. I had had others that resembled it, though none, I think, of quite the same quality or intensity. There have been days at my home in the desert —days of an intense stillness—when the whole place seemed as though it were imprisoned in a crystal globe, bright with sunshine, murmurous with life: as though there were an invisible presence standing on the threshold of one's consciousness, or of the garden—one was never quite sure which—so that one wanted to say, in a breath no louder than a whisper: "Oh, come in." I could remember a moment of convalescence after sickness when to sit in sunshine in the garden of a hospital in Mexico, to look at the gold and rose-colored trumpets of hibiscus, and the pale blue starry flowers of the plumbago, to watch a lizard run along a wall, seemed an experience of such intensity as to be almost unbearable. But this was something different. Never before had the presence, or the spirit, seemed to infuse such simple things as coffee cups and spoons, and plates of scrambled eggs, and the physical presences of people breakfasting at a counter.

Nor had the experience, I realized, any connection with my own circumstances. It was not the sense of euphoria that accompanies a really good meal eaten in physically beautiful surroundings with the right companion. This had no relation to me, personally. It was the realization of the fact, I think, which gave me the first clue as to what might be its significance. I remembered a passage in a book called *A Life of One's Own*, by Joanna Field, a book which is a voyage of exploration by the authoress into her own psychology: a passage in which she sets out to describe a technique she had evolved for achieving something akin to this experience of mine. It is a technique involving a distinction between what she calls "narrow" and "wide" attention. She writes:

> I would find myself breathing deeply, in the calm impersonality of shapes or colors, or even in a sudden glimpse of someone's character seen from a view-point that had stepped clear of the distortions of my personal interests. And once, when I was lying, weary and bored with myself, on a cliff looking over the Mediterranean, I had said "I want nothing," and immediately the landscape dropped its picture-postcard garishness and shone with a gleam from the first day of creation, even the dusty weeds by the roadside. Then again, when ill in bed, so fretting with unfulfilled purposes that I could not at all enjoy the luxury of enforced idleness, I had found myself staring vacantly at a faded cyclamen, and I happened to remember to say to myself "I want nothing." Immediately I was so flooded with the crimson of the petals that I thought I had never known before what color was.
>
> At that time it seemed odd that my mind should respond so quickly to a phrase, to what seemed mere words, spoken casually, when it could be so mulish about my carefully willed intentions.

Yes, but *I* had spoken no such words, had uttered no such "Open sesame": I had made no effort to achieve this sharpened vision: it had happened to me, gratuitously, unsought for, by the grace of God—or *as* the grace of God. Delving once more into its nature, it seemed to me (and I am quoting from my own diary again) that "everything had become detached from personal associations into a timeless essence of its own." Timeless, and impersonal: those would seem to be the key words, and to be the qualities, too, which differentiated the experience from the purely euphoric one in which my own personal happiness, my sense of myself as a participant in the experience, of its being *my* experience, were the essential ingredients. I have no recollection of myself in this incident, or of my state of mind. I do not remember whether I was eating breakfast, or merely having a cup of coffee, but I know that the eggs and the hamburgers did not look good to me because I was hungry: the people looked good in the same way, and there was nothing that I wanted from *them*. I did not want to make friends with them, and there was not one of them whom I found physically desirable. But I was keenly and intensely happy that they existed, not for anything that I personally could derive from the fact of their existence, but simply in the absolute, for some ultimate meaning or significance that was good for nothing but itself: that was, in fact, not "good" at all, but was sheer good-*ness*. A recognition, then, of goodness; or, rather, of what the German mystic, Eckhart, called "is-ness," which is surely the better phrase, since goodness imports values, moral or ethical, and may even presuppose its opposite; whereas "is-ness" implies no more than the sheer essence of being, than which, indeed, there can be no more.

If such experiences as this could be sustained, so that the whole of life presented itself as though it were a work of art, charged with an essential, yet never an explicit, meaning, would not that be as near a realization as can be hoped for on the material plane—this side of samadhi, so to speak—of the allness of spirit, of God, not omnipresent, but *as* omnipresence?

Is there any way in which those moments *can* be sustained, or their recurrence induced or rendered more frequent? Joanna Field's suggestion is a clue, but needs reinforcement I think, by an awareness of a deeper implication. To say "I want nothing" is good: it removes, if sincerely voiced and meant, the intrusion of a personal desire: but there remains in it the suggestion of a deliberate achievement by oneself. It seems to me that one thing more is needed: a realization that of oneself one can do nothing: that all that is hindering or standing in the way of these moments being perpetual, is the sense that there is a separate self at all, even a self which can say "I want nothing." It is when the self can know that it has no separate existence, no "life of its own," but is already a part of what it wishes to behold, the very thing that it is trying to induce—when, in short, it can say: "That which I am seeking, I am"—it is then that it becomes aware of the eternal Self which is its own self, and the self of all the people in the drugstore and in the whole world; which *includes* the whole world, and in fact *is* the whole world.

That is when the self knows God as its own being, and can say with full understanding: "I and the Father are one." And it is then that such moments can become eternal, and the world is charged with such meaning that it would seem as though the mere realization of that fact —the fact that it *has* meaning—were meaning enough. To decipher that meaning further would be to decipher God, and to do that one would have to *be* God. And then there would be no need for deciphering, nothing to decipher. But if the purpose of life is the realization of oneself as spirit, or of spirit as oneself, and if God *is* spirit . . . then . . . ? This is the recurring decimal of all thought, where the human intellect returns again and again upon itself until it concedes the ultimate paradox of its own nonexistence in the light of infinity, which is the point where decimals cease to recur. And the philosophy of meaninglessness is a dream in the mind of a nonexistent dreamer who, since in the light of infinity he has never existed, cannot now even say: "That was once *my* philosophy." It was only what the self that he thought he was, thought that it thought. And now thought has ceased to be thought, but has become knowledge. And that is life eternal.

The Inner Voice

Gerald Heard

A MAN WENT OUT to a shrine to pray. Three demons saw him approaching and decided to waylay him. They were of different ages and of course, as all devils are liars, the youngest looked the oldest and the oldest the youngest. Thus, the oldest one had then the right of precedence. And certainly, because of his disguise, he looked the more presentable.

"Where are you going?" he remarked to the man as he met him in the path.

"Oh," said the man, just a little discomposed by meeting a stranger and being asked a personal question, "Oh, I thought I'd just stroll out and have a look at a little shrine that's out in this direction. It's a pretty little place, I believe, and I felt I needed a quiet walk in the country. Good for one's peace of mind, you know!"

"You look all right," said the demon. "I shouldn't have thought with your looks you needed rest, retirement. If you're feeling gloomy, it isn't solitude that will set you up. It's company you need. Why, I can see at a glance you're the type of man who pines when left alone and is the life and soul of good company. Someone has been putting inferiority feelings into your mind—telling you you're a failure, that people don't like you and all that. Just jealousy. Don't let it sway you, a fine, handsome, obviously popular person like you. Forgive the personality, but to tell the truth I not only took to you the moment I saw you but I got the feeling that you'd been hipped over something. Solitude's all right for mopes but not for he-men. Look, I'm just going along to a party—it's going to be fun. There's only one thing that isn't quite right. There are a

415

lot of first-rate girls coming but we're short on men. Won't you help us out?"

The man wavered. Perhaps, after all, a party would prove more helpful than prayer, if he was really the sort of man who was a party success. But he couldn't help doubting that; in spite of the kind words and generous offer of this nice, well-set-up stranger. "You see," he said, "though no doubt I look all right, maybe quite passable, the truth is I'm far from strong. My doctor has told me that late nights are quite wrong for me. Indeed, it was he who told me that I ought to take this quiet walk every now and then. Thank you so much, but I must be getting on."

"Oh, I'm so sorry." The handsome devil's face registered the most courteous consideration. "Of course I should have noticed. Forgive my selfishness. I was so keen on getting a few good-lookers together for our little dance. Of course, good looks like yours so often deceive—the typical T.B. appearance. Of course you are right to take care. But are you sure a damp wood is the right place for you, and a long walk? Exertion is the consumptive's most insidious enemy. Rest is your ally. Come along with me. I know of a wonderful physician who's had amazing successes with cases such as yours. He's told me he's saved innumerable lives with just one simple motto regularly applied: Avoid Any Effort. Come along." The demon took the man's arm. "You lean on me. I'm a close personal friend of this great specialist. I know if I turn up with you, though he's extremely busy, he'll make time to see you."

But the man somehow didn't like the touch of this new friend. "Excuse me, perhaps later, but just now I think I'll think over your kind offer," he said and disengaged himself.

"All right," said the demon but his voice certainly didn't sound so. "All right, you croaking old hypochondriac, no wonder you're taking to God. Who else would want your company?"

The man turned his back and the demon vanished into the bushes. As he was the senior the others kept silent and only in silence the second obeyed when the failure remarked to him, "You next."

The man therefore found himself again confronted. "I didn't know this lonely road was so popular," he remarked to himself as the second passer-by came up to him. This second man wasn't, surely, as handsome as the first but he was if anything even more reassuring. He looked so sound —a sensible, shrewd person whose advice would always be valuable. And he seemed inclined to offer it. At least he was inclined to be of service.

"Have you heard the news?" the second devil asked straight away. "I thought not," he added as the man looked blank, "or, of course, you wouldn't be sauntering out into the country on a day like this."

"A day like this?" the man queried.

"Why of course, after all this depression and slump, the market's at last got up like a man after a long and refreshing sleep. It's kicking off its bed covers and boy! who'd be anywhere today but down in the business quarter. There's nothing underhand or get-in-first-and-leave-you-out today. Why, it's all brotherhood, all of us together. This is the common man's day. Business wants him with his patient savings. Capital is zooming. Put your money in now and by next year, why you'll be able to be a social benefactor, build a church or what have you, and never feel the pinch of giving. That's what prosperity used to be and that's what it's going to be again if people, people like you and me, aren't escapists but come right in and all pull together."

"But," said the man, trying to avoid saying where he was going, "but I don't think I want to make more money. I haven't much but it's enough. You see, I like a quiet life and—my interests really aren't economic; they're rather psychological."

The other didn't seem put off. On the contrary his interest seemed to grow. He actually looked concerned. "You've only got a little?"

The man became a little more defensive. "Well, as I've said, I have enough but I'm not of course a rich man with money to throw away."

The other said nothing for a moment but sighed, then adding, with a gentle smile, "Yes, I can see your interests are psychological. But did you never think that you are able to have your psychological interests because of your economic security? Would you, could you care—if I may be forgiven a very crude and inaccurate term—could you care for the state of your soul if the cupboard was bare?" He paused and then went on, so quietly, consultively, patiently, "And we, whom no doubt you dismiss as crude dollar-diggers, ignorant of the rich deposits of the human spirit, I wonder if it ever crosses your mind how often we spend long, wakeful nights thinking not merely of the public welfare as a whole and how trade may be stimulated and enterprise rewarded, but just of the thing you've mentioned, psychology! Do you ever think how mysterious money is, how, if again I may use a strong phrase, how sacramental, how mystical money really is? Why, credit is just the faith that moves mountains. And credit like faith is dead if it hasn't works to back it. You must show that you believe, prove it. It's just because you little people, playing for security and thinking you have it, turn your backs on your responsibilities that you wake up one fine morning to find that you've let the day of opportunity pass and the very basis of your life has gone. Then you may whistle for your peace of mind and it will be cold comfort to know that your silliness and indifference have allowed scamps to beat the market and get away with your pennies. No, my dear sir, do your duty today, and tomorrow, once again secure by your act of faith in your fellow men and your co-operation with their effort—an effort needing constant repetition—tomorrow be free to take your quiet walk in the country and enjoy your psychological inquiries."

"Well," said the man, "thank you so much for the tip. I'll get along tomorrow and see my broker. Just today I have an engagement I really oughtn't to break."

"All right." The second demon echoed his leader's tone. "All right, and only have yourself, and no one else, to blame when you wake up some fine day broke!"

He strode off and the man once again set his face toward the shrine, only, at the next turn of the path, to find a third wayfarer. This third devil seemed in more of a hurry than the other two and almost passed the man before, suddenly wheeling in his tracks, he asked him, "Excuse me; have you just come from the city?" To the man's "Yes" the stranger then added another question, "I wonder whether you mightn't help me. There's an election on, municipal; most people don't pay attention. It's one of the hardest tasks of a good citizen to get men interested in their home politics. Naturally it is a difficult game, and then people think they can wash their hands of it when they've said that it's dusty and when things get damp, of course a bit muddy. But you've had to have first the dirt track before you had the cement pavement, haven't you? And what's that got to do with you? Why it's simple as pecking at pie. People are so bored with our hard work they just won't attend on real points. They vote, believe me, I know, just by faces. Now you've got just the face we want. You remind people a bit of Washington and then in another light of Lincoln with just a dash every now and then of Teddy Roosevelt or a gleam of Jefferson. Come along, we can put you up. We'll do all the work for you. All you have to do is to be photographed enough times and televised. We'll write the scripts for you and you'll have nothing to say but the round good stuff."

"But I don't want to touch politics. I don't think people are altered that way. . . ."

"And so you're just going to stand back, sweep your robe aside, and all the dirt of politics will vanish. Because you refuse to approve, you refuse to co-operate; the horrid thing will lose face, flush, and hide itself, and we'll all carry on in philosophic anarchy without anything so crude as a machine or any apparatus of getting consent from the people and keeping them content at least below revolution's bursting point!"

"Well," the man tried to put in but was swept aside.

"And because you are too pure and high to go in, therefore, of course, politics being under the ban of your disapproval, no one else will dare take the place you have put under your interdict. The lowest type will shun what your moral anathema has declared impermissible. A vacuum of complete purity will descend on all statesmanship, on all administration! No, you're not such a hypocrite to tell yourself such a story as that! You know, because you won't take the offered place, won't let yourself be used (and use the opportunity to do the little good that so comes your way), then scamps will come in. You are not preventing evil by refusing to use mixed means—on the contrary, you are leaving the door open to those who will certainly spend all their time making a mess of things to their own advantage, and, my fine Pharisaic friend, will make it hot for superfine secessionists like you as soon as they catch sight of you, mark my words! You're nothing but a conscienceless, dishonest escapist!"

The man was shaken by the storm of moral denunciation. "But I don't feel fit to rule."

"Well then you show yourself fit to be kicked around. It isn't democratic to desert your social duties. This is just moral treason and you'll deserve the capital punishment that it demands."

Again the man was shaken by the moral fervor of his challenger. "I'm awfully sorry," he said. "I do see your point. It hurts me a great deal. I don't honestly see my way. I haven't a clear answer to what you say and yet I can't see it's really right to do evil that good may come or even to act without knowing what the real consequences will be. You see, when you met me I was going to ask advice on these points. . . ."

"Of whom? Haven't I answered your question?"

"Well, I was going to ask someone else; I was as it happens, if you must know, going to pray!"

The face of the moral reformer went purple with passion. "Hell!" he exclaimed with really intense conviction and darted off down the path.

The man felt quite giddy and a little sick. These three people, how very odd, how very apt, how very challenging. None of them had said anything that the man himself did not in part agree with and what they had said, he found he had no clear, clinching, convincing answers to. They had been so sensible, so cogent; he so weak and always protesting, excusing, ill thought out. He had started out to pray just because he was a bit uncertain and now he was twice as uncertain. He had thought he knew what he wanted to ask and now he didn't know even that; he didn't even feel sure that he ought to be asking anything, whether he oughtn't to be getting back and doing something, either having his psychophysical health looked into, or his financial situation, or the state of the city politics. Wasn't he escaping out here, repressing the real problems? Oh what a mess he was in! He couldn't even pray now; he couldn't do anything. He stopped, exhausted, feeling at the end of his tether—the path, too, had become overgrown—he was lost.

Then a voice said out of the thicket, "My child, though you didn't know the answer you knew those who came to you to prevent your coming to me did not know it. Though when you started out you thought you knew what to ask, now you know your ignorance. Now you may stay still and I will speak to you, for at last you are really silent, really listening."

Notes in Regard to a Technique of Timeless Realization

Hubert Benoit

Translated by Aldous Huxley

TRANSLATOR'S NOTE:

Dr. Benoit is the author of *Métaphysique et Psychanalyse,* which was published last year in Paris. Himself a psychiatrist, he has attempted in this very interesting, but rather difficult book, to relate the findings of Freud to the philosophy of Vedanta and Zen Buddhism. And since theoretical psychology and abstract metaphysics are never enough, he has gone on, in the following notes, to discuss a technique of realization.

Of particular importance, it seems to me, is what Dr. Benoit says of the imagination as being simultaneously the screen which separates us from objective reality, spiritual and material, and the compensatory mechanism which alone makes tolerable the life of unregenerate humanity. If we lacked our compensatory fancies, we should be so completely overcome by the misery of our condition that we should either go mad or put an end to our existence. And yet it is because of these compensatory and life-saving fancies that we are incapable of seeing into reality as it is. What is ultimately our worst enemy is proximately our best friend.

It is interesting, in this context, to compare what Dr. Benoit says with some of the recorded statements of the Zen masters of China and Japan. "Allow a flash of imagination to cross your mind, and you will put yourself in bondage for ten thousand kalpas." And this applies even to the imagination of ultimate reality. For the imagination of Suchness, or Emptiness, or Brahman, is just as much of a homemade impediment to the actual experience of that reality as is the most mundane fancy. By exercising oneself in the imagined tranquility and perfection of the Void one may produce a kind of quietistic samadhi; but, for the bodhisattva, such a samadhi will be no better than hell, since it guarantees the enjoyer of it against the actual experience of Suchness in the Ten Thousand Things, of eternity within time.

And here is an anecdote which I quote from Dr. Suzuki's most recently translated volume, *The Zen Doctrine of No-Mind*.

A Vinaya master called Yuan came to Tai-chu Hui-hai and asked: "When disciplining oneself in the Tao, is there any special way of doing it?"

Hui-hai: "Yes, there is."

Yuan: "What is that?"

Hui-hai: "When hungry one eats, when tired one sleeps."

Yuan: "That is what other people do; is their way the same as yours?"

Hui-hai: "Not the same."

Yuan: "Why not?"

Hui-hai: "When they eat, they do not just eat, they conjure up all kinds of imagination; when they sleep, they do not just sleep, they are given up to varieties of idle thoughts. That is why their way is not my way."

In a word, the realization of eternity in time, of Suchness in the world of appearances, is possible only when we put away our all too human gift of compensatory fancy and learn to see reality as it is. In order to enter the kingdom of heaven we must become not merely like children, but in a sense like animals—reproducing the immediacy and spontaneity of instinct upon a higher level.   A. H.

The average sensual man is without the consciousness of the self as a self-sufficient totality. He is unceasingly aware that something is lacking. He comes into the world bearing with him a negation of self-consciousness, or a negative consciousness of self (original sin). Consequently all his pleasures are of a negative character; they are but the impressions, on the physiological or imaginative plane, of a partial and momentary appeasement of his sense of original lack, of congenital defect. If we study human sensibility from the point of view of the realization of being, we shall find that it is pointless to concern ourselves with pleasure; for all that we experience is only the increase or decrease of a fundamental pain. Suffering is not an act of self-consciousness, but rather an act of the absence of self-consciousness.

But the absence of self-consciousness is illusory. Man possesses everything needed for the existence of self-consciousness; but these prerequisites for self-consciousness are not in the right state. It is like ice and water; ice possesses the nature of water, but possesses it in a state in which the properties of water are not apparent. Man is of the nature of God, but in a state in which this is not apparent. Apparently he is not divine, and because of these deceptive appearances, his present consciousness is limited to a knowledge of appearances; he is not aware of his divinity, he is not self-conscious. We can put the matter differently and say that he possesses self-consciousness, but does not know it or have the enjoyment of it.

We see then that, inasmuch as it produces in man the illusion that he lacks self-consciousness, suffering is illusory and deceptive; it misleads man and is the explanation of his illusory servitude.

But here an important distinction must be drawn between physical suffering and moral suffering. Physical suffering works on the gross plane of manifestation, a plane divided by the barriers of space and time. Here a part of the not-I affects a part of the "I." This partial negation by a partial object is not illusory, since it does not negate anything real. (From the standpoint of "being" there is no "reality" except in wholeness.) From the standpoint of "being" such a negation is not illusory, but merely null. Of itself and directly, it does not constitute an impediment to the realization of self-awareness.

"Moral" suffering, on the other hand, works on the subtle plane of manifestation—the plane of images, unlimited by space or time. There the image of the totality of the not-I (a totality which is merely represented, symbolically, by some concrete object) affects the image of the totality of the "I." Such suffering is illusory and deceptive; for it causes a man to believe in the nonreality of the total-self, divine, infinite, sufficient, nondiscriminated. Hence it is that only "moral" suffering constitutes an impediment to the realization of self-awareness.

"Moral" suffering working on the image plane is closely bound up with the play of the *imagination*. It is in the failure to master the imagination that human servitude resides.

The play of imagination is a necessary corollary of "original sin." Man is born with the potentiality of self-awareness, but without the immediate possibility of enjoying it. (He is ice and not yet water.) He is also born with the need for this enjoyment—the need to become "water," the thirst for the absolute. Man cannot achieve realization (the melting of the ice) except by the most penetrating comprehension. The years which precede the full development of the intellect are a period, during which man must accept his situation as a nonrealized being. But man would refuse to go on living, would do away with himself, if this inability to enjoy self-awareness were not compensated by something else—by some *ersatz* enjoyment which imposes on him and so makes him bear his lot with patience. Man, one can say, is born head downwards, and he would fall into the horizontal position (which is incompatible with his true nature and therefore fatal to him), if it were not that a kind of gyroscope came into play. This gyroscope is the imagination. To use another metaphor, imagination is a kind of inner cinema film which creates an appearance of wholeness. This appearance gives man the consoling illusion of possessing true "being." Its only and irremediable defect is that it lacks a dimension and that, consequently, the totality of the self and the totality of the not-I remain unreconciled.

Imagination does not bring realization, but only the fallacious hope of realization. (In imagination, man conceives of realization as the victory of the total-I over the total-not-I.) It is this fallacious hope that gives man the patience to bear his lot and protects him from suicide. In this way man finds himself moving in a vicious circle. Imagination assuages the craving for the absolute, but through the "moral" suffering which flows from it, imagination constitutes the chief impediment to realization. It is like the case of one who scratches himself because his skin itches, and whose skin itches because he scratches himself. Imagination is not the primary cause of man's failure to realize self-awareness. But inasmuch as it is the necessary compensation for nonrealization, it acts, when the possibility of realization presents itself, as the bolt that bars the door. It helps a man to await the possibility of realization; but when this possibility comes, its automatisms hinder him from achieving self-awareness.

The automatisms of man's physiological life are not a bar to realization. The impediment is created by the automatisms on the image plane. This being so, the work of liberation must consist in an unremitting struggle against these automatisms on the image plane.

This work must be carried out as a practical exercise undertaken at times when the subject can withdraw from the immediate excitations of the outer world.

The exercise. Alone, in a quiet place, muscularly relaxed (lying down or comfortably seated), I watch the emergence within myself of mental images, permitting my imagination to produce *whatever it likes*. It is as though I were to say to my image-making mind, "Do what you please; but I am going to watch you doing it."

As long as one maintains this attitude—or, more exactly, this relaxation of any kind of attitude—the imagination produces nothing and its screen remains blank, free of all images. I am then in a state of pure voluntary attention, without any image to capture it. I am not paying attention to anything in particular; I am paying attention to paying attention to anything which might turn up, but which in fact does not turn up. As soon as there is a weakening of my voluntary effort of pure attention, thoughts (images) make their appearance. I do not notice the fact immediately, for my attention is momentarily asleep; but after a certain time I perceive what has happened. I discover that I have started to think of this and that. The moment I make this discovery, I say to my imagination, "So you want to talk to me about that. Go ahead; I'm listening." Immediately everything stops again, and I become conscious of the stoppage. At first the moments of pure attention are short. (Little by little, however, they tend to become longer.) But, though brief, they are not mere infinitesimal instants; they possess a certain duration and continuity.

Persevering practice of the exercise gradually builds up a mental automatism which acts as a curb on the natural automatisms of the imagination. This curb is created consciously and voluntarily; but to the extent that the habit has been built up, it acts automatically.

The principle of the liberative method is now clear. Man triumphs over his imaginative automatisms, not by pitting himself against them, but by *consciously* allowing them free play; his attitude toward them is one of *active neutrality*. His final triumph is the end product of a struggle in which his voluntary attention does not itself have to take part. (Such participation, it may be added, is incompatible with its pure, impartial nature.) Man rules by dividing; refusing to take sides with any of his mental forces, he permits them to neutralize one another. It is not the business of man's divine reason to lay hold of its oppressors and overcome them, but rather to escape from them, leaving the two camps face to face, neutralized and reconciled. It is not for divine reason to overthrow nature, but to place itself above nature; and when it succeeds in taking this exalted position, nature will joyously submit. (It should be noted that the curb which is imposed by the exercise of the automatisms of the imagination is not imposed by the opposition of divine reason to automatic nature, but by the opposition of one pole of our dualistic nature to the other pole.)

During the exercise the subject, in so far as he practices it successfully, feels himself relieved from his fundamental distress. After the exercise he falls back into this distress, which may be momentarily greater than usual. The reason for this is that he has fallen back into his ordinary state of inner passivity, so that there is nothing to neutralize his distress; at the same time his imagination, curbed for a moment, does not at once recover its compensatory power. On the whole, however, the longer the exercises are repeated, the more the subject finds himself relieved of his basic distress.

The aim of the exercises is to deliver men from their ordinary condition of wretchedness; but they do not achieve this directly. Directly they achieve the progressive development of a curb on the automatisms of the imagination. Liberation will come—and will come abruptly—only when the construction of the curb is complete and is as strong as the automatisms of the imagination. At that time we may expect the ultimate neutralization which will reconcile man's inner dualism.

In this context it is interesting to study the state which, according to the Zen masters, precedes *satori* (enlightenment). At this moment the curb on the imagination has become so strong that it holds in check all the affective reactions to the stimuli of the external world. All the illusory significances which the subject used to attribute to things (significances which depended on his affective reactions) now disappear, and the subject is permanently divided into actor and spectator—but the actor has become unapparent. "It is like two flawless mirrors reflecting one another." No longer is there any distress (*angoisse*), and the subject experiences a kind of pure and total alleviation—which is not, however, the state of positive blessedness. There is now a condition of unstable equilibrium between the forces that delude and stupefy and the forces that tend to awake us to reality. The subject no longer has the old, false consciousness; but he does not yet possess the new consciousness. (In Zen, this state is called *tai-i*, literally "great doubt.") Hence the subject who is in this state says of himself that he is "like an idiot." The screen separating him from objective reality has worn thin and lost its opacity. Finally, in response to some sensory stimulus, *satori* breaks through. In the past, stimuli from the outside world reached the subject through this screen and had the effect of stupefying him; now that they reach him directly they awaken and enlighten. The screen is imagination, is associative and discursive thinking. And it is this screen that separated the subject from objective reality and prevented him from realizing the absolute identity of the "I" and the not-I. ("The eye with which I see God is the same," says Eckhart, "as the eye with which God sees me.")

The work of liberation cannot be carried out by one who is in immediate contact with external stimuli. It is not that I am incapable of achieving a state of pure attention in the course of everyday living; but I cannot maintain such a state under the continuous assault of my affective reactions to external stimuli. My efforts cannot achieve more than instantaneous flashes of pure attention. These infinitely brief instants fail to neutralize our basic distress. Indeed, my efforts may increase this distress by hindering the compensatory action of the imagination. Pure attention is a two-edged sword; if I succeed in achieving pure attention, I am working for my future liberation; but if I strive for it without success, I merely intensify my bondage. It is therefore essential that we should work upon ourselves only when we know clearly what we are doing, and only under conditions in which the work can be carried through successfully.

Between the exercises, as my training in them goes forward, I notice in the course of everyday life a certain spontaneous working of the curb which the exercises have built up. This manifests itself by the appearance within me of a certain "active neutrality," which runs parallel to my normal and natural attitude of passive partiality. This does no harm because it comes gradually, in proportion to my capacity for tolerating a weaning from compensatory imagination. It is in this "normal" way that the exercise must penetrate little by little into the heart of life. We must refrain from making deliberate efforts to jerk ourselves into a state of pure attention during the course of everyday life. Such efforts must be reserved for the times when we retire from life into our exercise.

What a man can and ought to do in his everyday life,

between his periods of exercise, is to undertake a persevering labor of theoretical understanding by means of
his discursive reason. It is impossible for a man to understand that the exercise is well founded, impossible for
him, above all, to refrain from making a direct effort at
realization in the course of everyday life, if he has not
uprooted from his mind, by patient intellectual work, all
the erroneous ideas which have been inevitably implanted
during the first part of his life—ideas of affective "morality," of a God and a Devil whom one loves or fears as
persons, of "spiritual" ambition, of a belief in the useful-
ness of direct struggle against one's instincts, and so on.

This uprooting of erroneous ideas should also have made
it possible for a man to establish in his life the most
positive of possible compensations, involving the least possible distress, and poising him in the best equilibrium of
which his constitution is capable. This equilibrium will be
achieved, of course, in the head-downwards posture which
is congenital to man; but it is necessary, nonetheless, for
the work of liberation. The man who is badly compensated and imperfectly balanced, is fascinated by concrete existence and is unable to absent himself from life,
even momentarily, in order to perform the exercise. The
intelligent man will therefore accept the necessity of finding his equilibrium head downwards; but he will recognize
that this is not an end, but only a means. The Gospel tells
us that we must be reconciled with our brother before we
pray; the balancing of our being in the conditions of
everyday life represents this reconciliation. This means
that a man may have to work long and laboriously on his
ordinary nature before undertaking the work of transcending it. It is in this sense, and only in this sense, that it may
be necessary for a given individual to give up certain
temporal satisfactions, if the procurement of these satisfactions must ineluctably be paid for by an increase of his
basic distress. Asceticism has in itself no efficacy—at any
rate where timeless realization is concerned. Nevertheless a
certain asceticism may be necessary for the achievement
of the inner state of maximum calm, without which the
exercise cannot be properly carried out.

Grace and Self-Effort

Swami Prabhavananda

THE MOST IMPORTANT thing necessary to a spiritual aspirant is the longing for God and the desire to seek and find Him. There are many religions in the world, innumerable sects with their varied theories, beliefs, and doctrines, but these are helpful to us only in so far as they help to create in us the desire to realize God and show us the means and ways to reach Him. They are of no avail if we simply believe in them and give an intellectual assent to their philosophical or theological doctrines. Creeds and theories and beliefs alone do not and cannot transform the character; hence they cannot give us the stability of inner peace.

Sri Ramakrishna tells the following parable: A pundit hired a ferryboat to take him across the river. He was the only passenger, so he began to talk to the ferryman. "Do you know the Samkhya or Patanjali philosophy?" he asked the man. "No sir, I don't," he replied. "Do you know Nyaya, Vaiseshika, or Vedanta, or any of the systems of thought?" "No sir, I don't! I am just a poor man who earns his living by ferrying this boat. I know nothing of all these things of which you speak." The pundit felt sorry for the man's ignorance, and in a somewhat superior manner he began to teach him some of the various doctrines. He was very proud of his learning, and was glad of the opportunity to air it. Suddenly, however, a storm arose, and the small boat became unmanageable; the waters became more and more turbulent, until finally the boatman asked his passenger: "Sir, can you swim?" "No, I cannot," the pundit said in alarm. "Well then, good-by, sir! I am afraid your learning and knowledge of the

429

scriptures will avail you little now in your hour of need if you cannot swim!"

In the same way, when we are battered by the storm and stress of life, our learning and knowledge of theological doctrines are of no avail if we have not fortified ourselves by learning how to enter the kingdom of heaven, the haven of peace where God dwells. According to the *Chandogya Upanishad:*

The Self within the heart is like a boundary which divides the world from That. Day and night cross not that boundary, nor old age, nor death; neither grief nor pleasure, neither good nor evil deeds. All evil shuns That. For That is free from impurity: by impurity can it never be touched. Wherefore he who has crossed that boundary, and has realized the Self, if he is blind, ceases to be blind; if he is wounded, ceases to be wounded; if he is afflicted, ceases to be afflicted. When that boundary is crossed, night becomes day; for the world of Brahman is light itself.

Therefore, the only struggle must be to reach the light, the world of Brahman. Our sufferings and tribulations are direct and immediate experiences, and it is only the direct and immediate experience of the kingdom of God that can overcome the tribulations of the world.

"Erudition, well-articulated speech, and wealth of words, and skill in expounding the scriptures—these things give pleasure to the learned, but they do not bring liberation," says Shankara. "A buried treasure is not uncovered by merely uttering the words 'come forth.' You must follow the right directions. You must dig and work hard to remove the stones and earth covering it, then only can you make it your own. In the same way, the pure truth of the Atman, buried under maya and the effects of maya, can be reached by meditation, contemplation, and other spiritual disciplines such as a knower of Brahman may prescribe—but never by subtle arguments."

Longing for God, longing for liberation from the tribulations of life, is the important thing for the spiritual aspirant. Of course everyone wants to be free from suffering and misery; but, like some lower animals, our vision does not range beyond a few feet, so that we see only our immediate troubles and sufferings, and struggle to free ourselves from them only. Our vision is limited so that we do not try to get at the root, the source, of all our tribulations. The root cause of all suffering is ignorance, and to free ourselves completely from all suffering is knowledge—knowledge of God, the one reality.

Sri Krishna says in the *Bhagavad-Gita:*

> Among those who are purified by their good deeds, there are four kinds of men who worship me: the world-weary, the seeker for knowledge, the seeker for happiness, and the man of spiritual discrimination. The man of discrimination is the highest of these. He devotes himself to me always, and to no other. For I am very dear to that man, and he is dear to me.

It does not matter how the longing for God first arises, for Sri Krishna also says, "Certainly all these are noble." The important thing is that, with whatever motive you begin your spiritual life, or for whatever reason you seek God, if your only purpose and goal is God, if you devote yourself solely to God, you will find that all other thirsts and cravings leave you, and gradually, as your heart becomes purified, intense longing arises; that one desire, the desire for God, becomes the one paramount thing in your life. That is the one and perhaps the only condition needed to become a true spiritual aspirant.

Now the problem is: How is our longing satisfied? How do we find God?

Those who have realized Him declare in no uncertain terms that it is only by His grace that God becomes known. I have known a few such blessed souls, the illumined ones, and they all unequivocally have asserted that it is through His grace and His grace alone that they realized God. Christ also tells us: "Ye have not chosen me but I have chosen you"; and the *Upanishads* say: "Whom the Self chooses, by him is he attained."

Yet again, these very great souls urge us to exert ourselves. They do not teach us to sit quietly and wait for grace. They insist that we ourselves strive strenuously to find God. Sri Krishna says, "What is man's will, and how shall he use it? Let him put forth its power to uncover the Atman, not hide the Atman: man's will is the only friend of the Atman: his will is also the Atman's enemy."

This seeming contradiction is resolved in one of the sayings of Sri Ramakrishna: "The breeze of God's grace is always blowing; set your sails to catch this breeze." This is further explained by the following saying: "A man may have the grace of his guru, he may have the grace of God and his devotees, but if he has not the grace of his own mind the others avail him nothing." The grace of your own mind is needed to set the sail to catch the breeze of grace. God is not partial; neither is His grace conditional. He is like the magnet which draws the needle: when the needle is covered with dirt, it does not feel the attraction of the magnet. But wash away the dirt, and at once the needle feels the drawing power and becomes united with the magnet. One of the names of God in Sanskrit is Hari, which means "one who steals the heart." God is the one attraction in the universe, but in our ignorance, and because of the impurities of our heart, we do not feel this attraction. Sri Ramakrishna used to say: "Weep! Weep for the Lord and let your tears wash away the impurities in your heart."

But again, this yearning of the heart for God, this longing for Him, does not come suddenly; that is why we need to practice spiritual disciplines and exert ourselves. Those who practice spiritual disciplines and regularly pray and meditate will come directly to the experience of divine grace. It is a psychological experience, almost exactly like the magnet drawing the needle. For example, you are trying to concentrate your mind on God with great regularity, yet the mind still remains restless. Through regular practice there grows yearning in your heart to see Him, yet still you seem to be striking your mind against a stone wall. You see nothing but darkness. Then suddenly from somewhere within, or from somewhere without—you are not sure whence—you feel another power drawing your mind inward, and you find yourself diving deeper and deeper within, in spite of yourself. You seem to be in another domain, the world of light, where no darkness enters. Following this, many spiritual visions come; ecstasies are experienced; you come face to face with God. But whenever these experiences come, whenever you are lifted up into this higher consciousness, it is your experience that it is God Himself who, by His grace, is lifting you up, attracting you unto Himself and giving you the ineffable joy and vision.

This, then, is a direct experience of God's grace, which comes only when your heart has become purified through the practice of spiritual disciplines.

Vyasa, the commentator on yoga aphorisms, compared the mind to a river flowing in opposite directions. One current of the mind flows toward the world, and the other flows toward God, toward the attainment of liberation from the bondages of the world. First there must arise a struggle in man's life, through the awakening of spiritual discrimination, to dam the flow of the downward current, the current that flows toward the world and worldly enjoyments. It is when one has been victorious in this struggle that he gets completely drawn into the Godward current, and experiences the grace of God. And when he at last realizes this grace, he enters forever into that kingdom which no storm or strife can ever reach.

Is Old Age Worth While?

Gerald Heard

OLD AGE is a favorite one for Occidental moralists and literary men. The Romans, when they wished to be cultured, turned to it as a convenient theme to practice on, as essayists. It had the double advantage that it proposed to the elderly that senescence after all might not be so bad, and dictated to the young a proper respect for those who, though become infirm, yet continued to cumber the scene. But Cicero and Seneca are not very convincing, while when we reach Marcus Aurelius we find suicide proposed as a solution for the awkwardly advanced physiological conditions.

In short, the "consolations" of old age are not those we find really efficacious when employed on ourselves, but rather those euphemisms, uttering which, we find it always possible to endure the sorrows of others and to extract from their miseries seemly moralizings. Nor, as "progress" has swept our Western culture onward, do we seem to be getting any wiser about old age or resigned to its processes. The romantics of course made no bones about it. Youth would not endure but it was the only time worth having: old age is the very mischief. The attitude is neatly epigrammatized in Leigh Hunt's touching effort to draw bravely his post-mature balance:

> Say I'm weary, say I'm sad,
> Say that health and wealth have missed me,
> Say I'm growing old, but add,
> Jenny kissed me.

Jenny being the vivacious Jane Welch, herself so rapidly to ripen into the formidably acidulated Mrs. Carlyle. John

Milton had written—when a young man—that it was possible to live,

> Till old experience doth attain
> To something like prophetic strain,

but when he was old himself the strain that was felt by his daughters was one of exasperation, not of inspiration.

It is hard then to see that the West has shown, as Albert Schweitzer has maintained, an attitude of life-acceptance. As a matter of fact, the further we advance in power over our environment, the more we seem to be determined to take only the hors d'oeuvres from life's menu, and to turn with disgust from the rest of the table d'hôte. We have monkeyed about with monkey glands and other Tithonus tricks. They have proved—as the Greek myth-makers knew—far from happy, and lifting faces hasn't lifted hearts.

Of course such an attitude is not even good naturalism. We are refusing to face up to the physiological facts. For, as Dr. Julian Huxley has pointed out in his *Uniqueness of Man,* we are the animal which is marked specifically by the strange characteristic, the unique feature, that only when our reproductive acme is over do we enter into our particular, outstanding way of life. Man qua man is the not-young, yes and further he is the post-mature. Ever since he became man he had to decide what to do with this extension of living when impulse was over and reflection had to begin. To define middle age, then, as merely "the feeling that tomorrow you'll feel better" is of course to refer to the standards of sensation, an experience which should be judged by the standards of evaluation. Middle age is when man becomes specifically man and he is man then because he has learned to disregard euphoria and to focus his attention on understanding.

So much, we see, anyone must achieve who will not show himself or herself to be too old at fifty and unfit for maturity. But lately we have added another story to the castle of life. As human beings we achieve a middle age hardly ever known to any animal in the wild state and the advance of our society depends on the fact that we can and do enter onto this plateau of reflection. But further this power of research and reflection has made possible an even newer thing—healthy old age, at least physiologically healthy, provided the reducing rules, the diet of involution is observed. Alas, however, little as most people like leaving body-identified youth for mentally-interested middle age, fewer, far fewer, relish the prospect of leaving the moderate and chiefly rational pursuits and activities of mid-life for the quiet acceptances, deeper insights, and death-spanning vision of a non-adhesive old age. We have, in short, been granted by our status as human beings a new upper-level apartment of middle age and have done little to fill it with adequate psychological furnishing. Then by our status as physiological researchers we have placed on the top of this second story still a third—and this, which we should have filled with the observatory equipment for studying the heavens—we have shrunk from, trying to skulk in the basement of life's building, though the inevitable elevator of time has our skirts caught in its gate and is dragging us remorselessly toward the roof.

We may then say that the chief problem that confronts us, not merely individually but socially, is the problem of life's new offer, a third term. And we may add that as youth is not youth without hope; and middle age is not middle age without reflection; so old age cannot be old age, but simply an inability to die, unless it has achieved vision.

That, however, men today nearly all agree in this hemisphere, is easier said than done. Indeed instead of finding space for middle age's capacity to review experience, we hustle the oldsters off their feet and out of their minds. Nor have we done any better as to the right of youth. We have certainly not given them much reason to indulge in the exercise of hope. That being so both for the first and second stories and terms, no wonder old age lacks vision.

Yet all of us who have had the opportunity of learning from the East's tradition know that in that system there is contained precisely that triple psychology which we need to furnish out and make purposive sense of our present physiological series. Youth which should be inspired by hope can generate that hope because under the brahmacharya vow the young live for a future which now they are earning. There can be no hope without denial—a fact the West has objected to recognizing. Then follows the life of the householder who, by self-control, has learned to enjoy that balanced situation of authority and responsibility which is the sober joy of those who understand this middle, transitional world. When this second state has fulfilled the first it in turn becomes the way to the third. The Sanskrit view of life turns around and points rightly forward the sequence of life, which we have gotten the wrong way round, and so must live not in hope, but in continual repining. For old age is seen, in the traditional way of life, not as a decline and frustration but as an explication. We unfold from us and put aside those gloves and swathes with which we have had to handle this world and with a freer touch and wider reach we stretch out already through our thinning integument, able to handle the unseen and immortal.

It will certainly require a revolution—in the literal sense of the word—a revolution in our whole outlook, if we are to get this matter of old age straight. But if we don't, not only shall we have an increasing number of elderlies on our hands, creatures alive but, like Saul on Gilboa, repenting that their life is still whole in them, a pest and bore to themselves and to all around them, but we shall have a society gravely handicapped by this sagging load at its upper end. We shall have a generation of senescents costly to keep, useless for production and, final frustration, utterly unlovely and unlovable. The outlook is grave enough to startle us—it is grave enough already to have startled all those who view human population and its age groups as a problem in worthy living. Further, when we examine it we see that the problem of old age is only that extreme point—like gangrene in the foot—where the sick state of the whole age groups of man—the three generations of youth, middle age, and old age—becomes first evident. Middle age and youth are just as wrong to-day and we have the problem of old age because youth was not taught how to wait and middle age how to act without possessiveness toward action. Peace of mind, acceptance, and their consequent vision cannot be extemporized. These which should be the third state of man when he is ready to be free of incarnation, are the results of the first two parts of life being lived well and with understanding.

There is however no need to despair. Because the collapse of the body does not end the casual "field," but only leaves it free once more to involve itself with such an envelope-instrument, everyone, however old, may set himself at once to re-educate himself. He may not in the time that remains be able to root up the basic wish to repeat pleasure rather than go on to fresh understanding, but the mixture of desire and knowledge that is the nature of all men who are in this middle world, may, before the next shift of costume and scene, be altered a little, perhaps quite a great deal, in favor of knowledge and against craving. As for the younger groups, of course their outlook is more hopeful, but at the same time the drag of desire is more strong. Sometimes it would seem as though, for most men, there lies a stretch of comparatively open water and good breezes between the storms of passionate youth and the ice pack of old age's exhaustion. It may be, as hygiene and the discipline of diet gain on us, we may recover the extensive period of healthy old age that seems to belong to people who have lived according to the tradition. If that is so we may yet see, if we will only make our spiritual knowledge equal to our physiological, a recovered old age when many may go far toward freedom for themselves and to becoming real inspirations to the age groups below them.

About the Ramakrishna Order

SRI RAMAKRISHNA is already generally acknowledged to have been one of the greatest spiritual leaders India has ever produced. He was born in a Bengal village in the year 1836, and spent nearly all of his adult life in the grounds of a temple at Dakshineswar, near Calcutta, meditating and instructing his disciples. His teachings are recorded in *The Gospel of Sri Ramakrishna* by M. (Mahendranath Gupta), translated by Swami Nikhilananda, and published by the Ramakrishna-Vivekananda Center of New York. There is also an official *Life*, published by the Advaita Ashrama of India. And there are biographical studies by Romain Rolland and Max Müller (the latter presently out of print).

After Sri Ramakrishna's death in 1886, his two leading disciples, Swamis Vivekananda and Brahmananda, founded the Ramakrishna Order of Monks. This Order was at first very small, consisting only of Sri Ramakrishna's direct disciples. Among these were Swamis Saradananda, Shivananda, and Turiyananda, whose names appear among the contributors to this book.

Brahmananda remained in India, became head of the Ramakrishna Order in 1901 and held that office until his death, in 1922. (His life and teachings are recorded in *The Eternal Companion*, by Swami Prabhavananda, published by Vedanta Press.) Vivekananda, on the other hand, was chiefly active in bringing Ramakrishna's message to the West. In 1893, he visited the United States to attend the Parliament of Religions which was being held at the World Columbian Exposition in Chicago. His speeches there and on subsequent occasions aroused extraordinary enthusiasm, and he followed up this success by founding

439

the first American Vedanta society in New York City. In
1899, he paid a second visit to America and also traveled
in England and on the continent of Europe. He died in
1902. There is an eight-volume edition of his *Works*,
including lectures, essays, and correspondence, and a *Life*;
both published by the Advaita Ashrama. Four small vol-
umes of selections from the *Works* are also published by
the Ramakrishna-Vivekananda Center of New York.

Later, four direct disciples of Sri Ramakrishna came
from India to carry on the work which Vivekananda had
begun; and from that time onward the Order has had to
meet an increasing demand for teachers. Each Swami who
has come to this country has done so upon the invitation
of some group of Americans who wished to learn more
about Vedanta philosophy; in no instance has he been an
invading "missionary," imposing his presence upon an
apathetic or unwilling public. Although the Vedanta societies in America are officially under the authority of the
Ramakrishna Order of India—whose headquarters are at
Belur, Calcutta—each American center is, in fact, an independent unit. Nearly all of them have their own boards
of trustees, made up of American citizens. The Swami in
charge gives lectures and holds classes for the study of
Vedanta philosophy and literature, including the *Upanishads*, the *Bhagavad-Gita*, the works of Shankara, and
Patanjali's *Yoga Aphorisms*. In some centers there are
resident students; two have monasteries and convents attached to them. At the present time there are twelve
centers in the United States (New York (2), Providence,
Boston, St. Louis, Chicago, Los Angeles, Santa Barbara,
San Francisco, Berkeley, Portland, and Seattle), one in
England, one in France, and one in the Argentine.

Side by side with the Ramakrishna Order, Vivekananda
established the Ramakrishna Mission, an institution which
has grown steadily throughout the five decades of this
century. There are now a hundred-odd centers in different
parts of India, devoted either to the contemplative life, or
to social service and educational work, or a combination
of both. The Mission has its own hospitals, dispensaries,
high schools, industrial and agricultural schools, colleges,
libraries, and publishing houses. It has been consistently
active in relieving the victims of earthquakes, floods,
famines, and epidemics.

The magazine from which the contents of this volume
have been selected was started in January, 1938, under

the auspices of Swami Ashokananda of the San Francisco center and Swami Prabhavananda of the center in Los Angeles. During its first three years, it was called *The Voice of India;* after that its title was changed to *Vedanta and the West.* Its publication was discontinued in January 1971.

A previous volume of selections from the magazine, called *Vedanta for the Western World,* is published by Vedanta Press.

The Contributors

Akhilananda, Swami: head of the Vedanta centers of Boston and Providence.

Amiya, Sister: formerly a nun of the Sarada Convent at Santa Barbara.

Apurvananda, Swami: member of the Ramakrishna Order in India.

Aseshananda, Swami: head of the Vedanta Society of Portland, Oregon.

Atulananda, Swami: of Dutch parentage, was associated with the Vedanta Society of Northern California before moving permanently to India in 1923.

Benoit, Hubert: French psychiatrist and author of *Métaphysique et Psychanalyse*.

Christine, Sister: American disciple of Swami Vivekananda, later associated with educational work of the Ramakrishna Order in India.

Dispeker, Franz: translator into German of several works on Vedanta; died 1955.

Ferrando, Guido: professor of Italian literature and authority on Dante.

Frazer, Mimi: a devotee.

Gnaneswarananda, Swami: until his death in 1938, was head of the Vedanta center in Chicago.

Hamilton, Anne: Los Angeles poet and literary specialist.

Heard, Gerald: writer and lecturer.

Huxley, Aldous: novelist and essayist on the perennial philosophy.

Isherwood, Christopher: writer and co-translator of Vedantic classics.

Mahadevan, T. M. P.: Professor of Philosophy, University of Madras.

Manchester, Frederick: professor of English literature, formerly at the University of Wisconsin.

Nehru, Jawaharlal: Prime Minister of India.

Nikhilananda, Swami: head of the Ramakrishna-Vivekananda Center of New York.

Omkareswarananda, Swami: member of the Ramakrishna Order in India.

Prabhavananda, Swami: head of the Vedanta Society of Southern California.

Pratt, James Bissett: late professor of philosophy at Williams College, Massachusetts.

Radhakrishnan, S.: first Vice President of India.

Saradananda, Swami: direct disciple of Sri Ramakrishna and longtime Secretary of the Ramakrishna Order.

Satprakashananda, Swami: head of the Vedanta society of St. Louis.

Shivananda, Swami: direct disciple of Sri Ramakrishna and second president of the Ramakrishna Order.

Siddheswarananda, Swami: head of the French Vedanta center at Gretz; died 1957.

Tagore, Rabindra Nath: late Indian poet and educator.

Tree, Iris: British dramatist, poetess, and actress.

Turiyananda, Swami: direct disciple of Sri Ramakrishna, appointed by Vivekananda as the first head of the Vedanta work in California.

van Druten, John: playwright and novelist; died 1957.

Vivekananda, Swami: leader with Swami Brahmananda of Sri Ramakrishna's direct disciples and first preacher of Vedanta in America.

Vividishananda, Swami: head of the Vedanta society of Seattle.

Watts, Alan W.: writer and lecturer on Zen Buddhism.

Yale, John: monastic member of Trabuco monastery.

Yatiswarananda, Swami: head of the Ramakrishna Ashrama of Bangalore in Southern India.

MENTOR Books of Related Interest

☐ **VARIETIES OF RELIGIOUS EXPERIENCE by William James.** A new edition of James' classic work on the psychology of religion and the religious impulse.
(#MY1025—$1.25)

☐ **THE NATURE OF THE NON-WESTERN WORLD by Vera Micheles Dean.** A noted expert on foreign affairs throws new light on the conflict between East and West as she probes the beliefs, traditions, and emotions that motivate the people of the non-Western nations.
(#MY1039—$1.25)

☐ **THE MEANING OF THE GLORIOUS KORAN: AN EXPLANATORY TRANSLATION by Mohammed Marmaduke Pickthall.** The complete sacred book of Mohammedanism.
(#MY914—$1.25)

☐ **THE TEACHINGS OF THE COMPASSIONATE BUDDHA edited with commentary by E. A. Burtt.** The best translations of the writings of the great Oriental religion of Buddhism.
(#MQ884—95¢)

☐ **THE WAY OF ZEN by Alan W. Watts.** The outstanding comprehensive explanation of Zen Buddhism, the unique Oriental philosophy which shows how to live with serenity and fulfillment in a frustrating and confusing world.
(#MQ829—95¢)

☐ **THE MEANING AND END OF RELIGION by Wilfred Cantwell Smith.** A unique study that concentrates on the individual's orientation to life as dictated by his religious beliefs.
(#MT575—75¢)

SIGNET and MENTOR Titles You Will Enjoy

☐ **THE STORY BIBLE: Volume I by Pearl S. Buck.** The winner of the Nobel and Pulitzer Prizes retells the Greatest Story Ever Told in the living language of our times. In VOLUME I, the immortal stories of the Old Testament are brought to life with a power and immediacy for the modern reader. (#Y5080—$1.25)

☐ **THE STORY BIBLE: VOLUME II by Pearl S. Buck.** This superlative rendering of the New Testament brings the crowning achievement of Pearl Buck's career, THE STORY BIBLE, to a triumphant conclusion. Here, adding relevance to its wisdom and freshness to its beauty, is the story of the birth, life, death and resurrection of Jesus. "Compelling, moving . . ."—*Library Journal* (#Y5079—$1.25)

☐ **THE SERMON ON THE MOUNT According to Vedanta by Swami Prabhavananda.** A fascinating and superbly enlightening Hindu reading of the central gospel of Christianity by the renowned author of books on Indian religious philosophy. (#MY1150—$1.25)

☐ **AMERICAN INDIAN MYTHOLOGY by Alice Marriott and Carol Rachlin.** A collection of myths, legends and contemporary folklore from some twenty North American tribes, this profusely illustrated volume is one of the most comprehensive studies of Indian lore in America. (#MY1145—$1.25)

☐ **GILGAMESH: A Verse Narrative translated by Herbert Mason.** "Like the Tolkien cycle, this poem will be read with profit and joy for generations to come."—William Alfred, Harvard University. One of the oldest and most universally known stories of mankind, the Gilgamesh epic tells of man's unsuccessful quest for immortality. (#MY1135—$1.25)

MENTOR Titles of Special Interest

☐ **THE ANCIENT MYTHS by Norma Loore Goodrich.** A vivid re-telling of the great myths of Greece, Egypt, India, Persia, Crete, Sumer, and Rome.   (#MQ1012—95¢)

☐ **MYTHS OF THE GREEKS AND ROMANS by Michael Grant.** The world's great myths and their impact on creative arts through the ages. Illustrated.
(#MW1112—$1.50)

☐ **GREAT DIALOGUES OF PLATO, translated by W. H. D. Rouse.** A new translation into direct, forceful English of **The Republic** and other dialogues of the great philosopher of ancient Greece.   (#MW1147—$1.50)

☐ **THE ANVIL OF CIVILIZATION by Leonard Cottrell.** This fascinating history of the ancient Mediterranean civilizations reveals the long-buried secrets of the early Egyptians, Hittites, Sumerians, Assyrians, Babylonians, Greeks and Hebrews, brought to light by archaeological discoveries.   (#MY951—$1.25)

☐ **THE SATYRICON by Petronius, translated by William Arrowsmith.** A classic recreation of Nero's pleasure-loving Rome by the cultural cynic, Petronius. In a brilliant new translation.   (#MQ1027—95¢)

THE NEW AMERICAN LIBRARY, INC.,
P.O. Box 999, Bergenfield, New Jersey 07621

Please send me the MENTOR BOOKS I have checked above. I am enclosing $_____(check or money order—no currency or C.O.D.'s). Please include the list price plus 15¢ a copy to cover handling and mailing costs. (Prices and numbers are subject to change without notice.)

Name_____

Address_____

City_____State_____Zip Code_____
Allow at least 3 weeks for delivery

Other MENTOR Books About Ancient Greece and Rome

☐ **THE GREEK STONES SPEAK** by Paul MacKendrick. The glory that was Greece brought back to life through a detailed and authoritative study of archaeological finds. More than 175 photographs and drawings.
(#MW1078—$1.50)

☐ **MYTHOLOGY** by Edith Hamilton. A widely-read retelling of the Greek, Roman and Norse legends of love and adventure. "Classical mythology has long needed such a popular exposition and Miss Edith Hamilton has given us one in this volume, which is at once a reference book and a book which may be read for stimulation and pleasure."—The New York Times. Illustrated. Charts. Index.
(#MY1196—$1.25)

☐ **THE ILIAD OF HOMER** translated by W. H. D. Rouse. A brilliant prose translation of Homer's great epic of the Trojan War, by the late distinguished scholar.
(#MT650—75¢)

☐ **THE ODYSSEY OF HOMER** translated by W. H. D. Rouse. A modern prose translation of the world's greatest adventure story, the travels of Ulysses. (#MT677—75¢)

☐ **THE PHILOSOPHY OF ARISTOTLE.** A new translation by A. E. Wardman and J. L. Creed of the basic writings of Aristotle. With Introduction and Commentary by Renford Bambrough.
(#MY804—$1.25)
